Reimagining Europe

SUNY series in Contemporary French Thought

David Pettigrew and François Raffoul, editors

Reimagining Europe

Thinking in Crisis

Edited by

Georgios Tsagdis, Rozemund Uljée,
and Bart Zantvoort

SUNY
PRESS

Published by State University of New York Press, Albany

For information, contact State University of New York Press, Albany, NY
www.sunypress.edu

Library of Congress Cataloging-in-Publication Data

Names: Tsagdis, Georgios, editor. | Uljée, Rozemund, editor. | Zantvoort, Bart, editor.
Title: Reimagining Europe : thinking in crisis / edited by Georgios Tsagdis, Rozemund Uljée and Bart Zantvoort.
Description: Albany : State University of New York Press, [2024] | Includes bibliographical references and index.
Identifiers: LCCN 2024009183 | ISBN 9781438499796 (hardcover : alk. paper) | ISBN 9781438499819 (ebook) | ISBN 9781438499802 (pbk. : alk. paper)
Subjects: LCSH: Europe—Civilization—Philosophy. | Europe—History—Philosophy. | Europe—Emigration and immigration—Social aspects.
Classification: LCC CB203 .R384 2024 | DDC 304.8094—dc23/eng/20240923
LC record available at https://lccn.loc.gov/2024009183

Contents

Part III: After the End

Introduction

Imaginaries of a Perpetual Crisis and the Future of Europe: On the Project of Reimagining Europe

GEORGIOS TSAGDIS, ROZEMUND ULJÉE, BART ZANTVOORT

Europe is in crisis; indeed, Europe finds itself amidst a perpetual, over-laying manifold of thematized and unthematized crises. Some of these directly concern its territory and identity: the refugee exodus and the more recent invasion of Ukraine have brought Europe to, and arguably beyond, a breaking point. In parallel, "supplementary" discursive crises of nationalism, xenophobia, Islamophobia, revisionism, and diverse forms of insularity have both proceeded from and precipitated new forms of cultural-political desolation. Next to these geography-bound crises, Europe has shared in the anxieties wrought by the pandemic and the deeper agony of climate collapse and the sixth extinction. Despite bearing less of their brunt, due to geographic and economic parapets affording temporary shelter, Europe recognizes that all that was is no more.

As its global privilege erodes by ever greater waves of misery crushing upon its shores, Europe is swept up against the straits of its history, having to confront the closure of what, looking backwards, one may determine as the "European project." This project, notwithstanding its Greco-Roman, Christian Medieval, and other prehistories, ran roughly from the late Renaissance and the global spread of colonial domination, up until the ruins of the Second World War. Since then,[1] Europe has wallowed in a series of epilogues, weighed down by a past that cannot be overcome. Faltering at this historic threshold, in Europe one has

1

come to realize both from within and from without that the next step is without a "beyond," tangled up in the immanent, shared trouble of planetary politics.

Europe's own philosophical tradition is primed to understand this suspended step as a crisis of spirit, effecting a dissolution of Europe's self-understanding. In Derrida's words, this is the moment "when the movement of Spirit fails and European discourse and its decisions do *not* coincide with Spirit's return to itself in absolute knowledge."[2] At this juncture, the crisis of European spirit should constitute an awakening call, the sounding of an alarm. The crisis of spirit should—at last and at least—be a moment of *krinein*, a moment when the need for a judgment is understood; the moment, when, perhaps, a decision (if only perhaps provisional and incalculable, threatened and threatening) is reached. At present, however, the horizon of a decision appears to recede interminably. The crisis of spirit indicates, precisely, a crisis of crisis, a state in which the recuperation of the manifold crises has become impossible.

Indeed, the very notion of crisis and its constitutive temporality have undergone a transformation, thereby calling attention to the paradoxical nature of its meaning. Drawing on the intertwining of a medical and a religious paradigm, *krisis* has always designated an exceptional moment or phase, a moment of "decision." In the Hippocratic tradition, the word referred to that moment in the course of an illness, following or anticipating intervention, when it was decided whether the patient would succumb or revive. In the Christian tradition, the word invoked the Last Judgment, the moment upon which the eternal fate of souls was to be decided and, by the same token, the course of secular time concluded and replaced by the eternity of heavenly glory. However, the moment of divine judgment was understood as a *revelation*, inasmuch as the fate of the souls was not so much imposed upon them, as it was made apparent. Not only in the Calvinist doctrine of predestination, but in all denominations, the moment of Revelation shows forth what the divine economy and the path of each soul has already made inescapable; similarly, in the case of illness, in the decisive moment, no decision is taken; rather, the fate of the patient and the thrust of the illness, as a whole, are revealed. Upon the moment of crisis, no one decides, yet all is decided. A rupture between a before and an after is effected.

Today, however, we inhabit a new temporality of crisis and a new mode of indecision. Instead of a passage, crisis designates at present an enduring state, a constant emergency and permanent uncertainty, indefinitely extended into the future. Thus, the paradox of crisis, by definition the evental disruption of normalcy, is normalized in all domains of social life, becoming the *Leitbegriff* of modern politics. At this point, judgment is divorced from the idea of resolution and repeatedly postponed; as a consequence, the prospect of a decision diminishes evermore, tangled in labyrinthine, principally bureaucratic processes of decisions that never conclude. Proceduralism, devolution, and inclusiveness allow everyone to decide, without anything being decided. From waste management to border control (sometimes indistinguishable from one another), the exercise of power is "algorithmized" even where digital algorithms are absent. The diffusion of sovereignty and the dominion of a cybernetic governmentality mean that in the ocean of crisis there is no *kybernētēs*, no helmsman, no decision. Europe is no longer a continent, but a tempestuous sea, a conglomerate of abiding eddies.

The naturalization of crisis announces itself as inevitability; in order to numb the truth that what was will no longer be, Europe proclaims about the permanent crisis: "It was always thus and always thus will be." In its inevitability, crisis has become an instrument of rule, serving to legitimize those governmental processes that dispossess citizens and deprive them even further of any possibility of decision—if the state has resolved not to decide, citizens should not take the possibility of a decision into their hands. Thus, responsibility is hollowed out, and meaning, or rather sense, is blunted.

Historical and linguistic sense are among the first senses to be distorted. One's very relation to history, historical consciousness, and historical conscience at once, as well as the capacity to utter and articulate what is politically significant become exceedingly difficult and therefore exceedingly necessary. As Fredric Jameson remarks, this process entails a weakening of history itself, resembling a schizophrenic position, in which the subject is essentially reduced to an experience of material signifiers, referring to nothing other than "pure and unrelated presents in time."[3] In this depthlessness of time, we are witnessing the tragedy of European history as a farcical rerun, the aporia of language confronting the aporia of history. We cannot speak; we must speak; we shall speak. The question "What is Europe?" must return to and measure up against the question of entelechy: "What was it to be?" If something of the potential to reimagine Europe is to be conjured up, it can only happen in dialogue with the imaginaries that have guided Europe to its abiding crisis. The questions of internal and external borders, of homogeneity and coherence, identity and equality, legitimacy and rights, democracy and representation can only be raised insofar as the question of Europe, its destiny and its destination, is raised as a whole, from its forever receding origin to its incalculable future.

We cannot evade or ignore these questions. Philosophy, in turn, cannot evade or ignore the old, profound, and intimate nexus that has tethered it to Europe's constitution and destiny. Throughout European philosophical history, Europe as project, idea, and ideal has been thought in tandem with the essential task of philosophy. In the works of Kant, Hegel, Husserl, Heidegger, and others, we find a conception of philosophy as a science of universality and Europe as the place where this universality is destined to unfold itself. In this manner, Europe has always served as the privileged domain of universal reason. Europe must now mobilize all of its resources to consider its *locality* in the face of not only the deterritorializing forces of global capital but also of the abiding and necessary effort of postcolonialism to break open the circumscribed space that for centuries constituted the center from which a material and intellectual domination of the expansive horizon of the colonized periphery was effected. Accordingly, the decolonization of philosophy is a task of liberation, incumbent on every non-European thinker, as much as it is a European vital duty.

The stakes of this duty are painfully palpable, as the European response to its different crises remains beholden to its history of exceptional universalism and the corresponding question of who is to be included within it. The motto of the EU, "unity in diversity," at best facile in its vagueness, becomes actively malicious when the self-understanding of the European community is premised unequivocally on its philosophical tradition, when universal reason is viewed as Europe's essence, and a foreigner is welcomed to the European community, only insofar as they conform or assimilate to this reason—a particularly European version of the "good immigrant." Francois Fillon, an erstwhile French presidential candidate, summed up this entrenched disposition when he stated that France is not a multicultural society and that foreigners must assimilate because "when you come to someone's house, by courtesy, you don't take over." Welcoming the other only insofar as they do not disrupt the European way of thought and life, and thus, by extension the European body politic, is premised on a weaponization of the universality of European reason, which keeps exploiting the "other" in ways that remain eerily similar to the colonial use of this very same reason. From the incapacity of decision making on the supranational level to the rise of nationalism within its states and its inhumane response to migration, Europe shows at one and the same time it is growing ever more monolithic and ever more disjointed. Unless the aforementioned vital duty of confronting its philosophical legacy is assumed, a duty that involves the realization that this legacy cannot lead to a singular Europe and does not demarcate a privileged interior and interiority, this contradiction will continue to deepen.

The aim of the present edited collection is to undertake a fraction of this task. All its contributions seek to reimagine Europe beyond essentialism. Some of its chapters do so by investigating what remains to be thought of in the works of Plato, Descartes, Hegel, Husserl, Heidegger, and Patočka, trying to identify the ways these thinkers can aid us in contesting Europe from *within*. Other chapters turn to postwar philosophers such as Derrida, Agamben, and Esposito, who seek to think Europe from a perspective of *limits, thresholds* or *margins*, in order to open a thought beyond the European closure and to explore the possibility of a community, established not under a transcendental signifier (God, man, the race), but rather guided by difference. We hope that you will find each contribution insightful both in itself and in its place in the overall project.

The Structure of the Present Volume

The contributions to this edited collection do not allow for a very strict thematic division. We have, however, decided to divide the book in three parts, each part emphasizing another aspect of the discourses on Europe within the philosophical literature. The chapters in the first part, titled "Idea, Memory, Method," engage, in different ways, with the question whether there is such a thing as an originary idea of Europe that could be discovered within its own tradition. In the first chapter, titled "The Divided Origin: Re-membering Plato's Europe," Georgios Tsagdis queries the foundations of the Greek *polis* and its significance for the Hellenic world, in order to prepare a ground on which its legacy can be placed and understood and from which its relevance for contemporary Europe becomes apparent. It does so by looking at the *polis* in *motion*, that is, at war, or rather, at a series of internal, external, and fictional wars, the way they are cast in the Platonic corpus and more specifically in the dialogues *Timeaus*, *Critias* and *Menexenus*, as the backdrop against which political life can be set into relief. Guided by the work of Nicole Loraux and Pierre Vidal-Naquet, this exploration enables, accordingly, an understanding of the ways in which the polis fabulates its glory and remembers its wounds, in order to constitute itself, to establish its origin and thus demarcate its political space and historic destiny. As Tsagdis argues, the legacy of these modes of originary remembrance continue to inform our European imaginaries.

The second chapter, written by Vera Bühlmann, is titled "*Entwurf* of the Method and Ethics of Its Discourse: Notes on Cartesian Rationalism, Reconsidered." Here, the question is asked whether we can think of Europe as a project, and if yes, of what sort—a utopian one? One of infinite critique? A pragmatic one of realpolitik? An exclusively European, a global, or even a universal one? This article characterizes the political form of Europe as an architectonic form, in Massimo Cacciari's sense of an *Entwurf*. Such architectonic *Entwurf* is more than a construction in terms of its applied logics (reasoning), in that it keeps "feeling the pull of its own throw." Can there be an aesthetics to such a "feeling-torn," in the sense that "feeling the pull of the throw" would not be entirely passive, but could also form an active ethics and logics? The essay explores how such an aesthetics can take shape through a relation to the Cartesian notion of *methodic doubt*. Engaging with Descartes's commonly overlooked *World* (1629–33), it examines the role of impersonal and geometric fabulation, with which Descartes proposes to accommodate one's own conduct of reason discursively and architectonically. Accordingly, the essay proposes to address geometric fabulation, its objective ideation, and its notion of an impersonal subject as the reference pole for an architectonics of political form. It relates the idea of an architectonic aesthetics (of how to feel the pull of the throw in an *Entwurf*) to the Cartesian notion of methodic doubt, foregrounding that such a method proceeds in discursive pursuit of an indefinite objective, rather than being guided by dogma or by formalism. The overall interest is to examine if and how we can find helpful direction today with respect to our contemporary impasses as to how political form is to be reasoned adequately—and how to think of Europe as a project worthwhile to continue imagining.

Frank Chouraqui's chapter, "Europe as the Crisis of Play," introduces a hypothesis about the essence of European modernity, namely, that it should be defined as the cultural invention of seriousness. The essay begins by examining one of the things that we take to be questioning the very essence of modern Europe, namely, the current refugee crisis and its effects on European societies and institutions, including reactionary populism. Chouraqui suggests that what this crisis indicates by contrast is that Europe is to be defined as a social, historical, and existential compound informed by the mismatch of care and action and proceeds to examine the relations between Europe so defined and the more traditional Nietzschean idea of Europe as nihilism. Proposing that the resulting notion of Europe is most consonant with a remark from Johan Huizinga's *Homo Ludens* (1938), where the latter seems to define European modernity as the dismantlement of play, Chouraqui shows how the examination of the refugee crisis and nihilism on the one hand and of play on the other can reflect fruitfully on each other.

Riccardo Villa's contribution, "Of Ships and Palaces: Inverted Images of Europe in Crisis," describes the image of Europe in terms of architectonics, in which history is not just a reconstruction, but a double movement of construction and deconstruction. Drawing on Carl Schmitt, Manfredo Tafuri, and Massimo Cacciari, Villa understands Europe as *project*: something that breaks away from established grounds of evaluation, while still feeling "the pull of the throw." Thus, Europe finds itself beyond historical, analytical, or geopolitical definitions, while nevertheless producing its future in an agonistic entwinement with such definitions.

The chapters in the second part of the book, "Europe's Other(s)," deal with the question of Europe in relation to its (self-)difference. Thomas Mercier's contribution is titled "Europe and Its Phantoms: Walter Mignolo's Decolonial Critique of Jacques Derrida's Deconstruction." Mercier asks how we can rethink "Europe" after postcolonial and decolonial critiques exposed the intimately colonial dimension of the European project—a project that has advanced in the world under the name "modernity." In this perspective, "reimagining Europe" would suggest breaking away from a certain image or self-image of Europe, one indexed on universalism, Eurocentrism, and colonialism, so as to imagine a "provincialized" Europe, at last. This would be a Europe from which former colonies would be "de-linked," as suggested by Walter Mignolo, in order for Europe to become what it has perhaps always been: just one culture among others, a regional space and a local history that merely imagined itself as global power and took over the phantasmatic role of forefather and civilizational leader.

In "Europe without Eurocentrism? An Essay in Critical-Colonial Studies," Chiara Bottici and Benoît Challand argue that the critical question of our time is not rejecting or supporting the European project but rather trying to understand the possibilities that such a process opens (or closes) for those who are *inside* as well as *outside* of it. The chapter adds therefore another, yet often underexplored, layer of criticism, namely, a critical-colonial approach. By showing how Europe was created in its colonial peripheries and still thrives there, Bottici and Challand propose to look at the project of European integration with a double lens. In particular, they reflect on the theories produced by those who are *in* or in the *margins* of, but not *from*, Europe, to rethink the European project in a global context marked by mass migration, challenges to established forms of citizenship, and the new forms of oppression.

Agnes Czajka's "A Europe of Refugees" asks what Europe does and should stand for and what it means to be European. Czajka asks furthermore to what (histories, ideas, and ideals) and to whom (to which "selves" and to which "others") Europe is responsible or indebted. She finds that although, at times, such "soul-searching" risks, and indeed comes dangerously close to, the narcissism and navel-gazing that typifies Eurocentrism, it is not devoid of critical potential. Focusing on the current "refugee crisis," the chapter explores the critical potential of bringing together and interrogating the work of Derrida (on Europe and crisis), Nietzsche (on the "good European"), and Agamben (on the refugee). In his gloss on Arendt's "We Refugees," Agamben explores the possibility of looking to Europe "not as an impossible 'Europe of nations' . . . but as an aterritorial or extraterritorial space in which all the residents of the European states . . . would be in a position of exodus or refuge, and the status of European would mean the citizen's being-in-exodus . . . like in a Leiden jar or in a Moebius strip, where exterior and interior are indeterminate."[4] Bringing Agamben's work into conversation with that of Derrida and Nietzsche, the chapter explores the critical potential of figuring Europe as a Europe of refugees.

The third and final part of the book is titled "After the End" and questions, from different angles, how to think Europe, and the idea it has of itself, in terms of its finitude, its decay, and its possible revival. In his contribution, "The End of Europe: Herder and Hegel on Progress and Decline," Bart Zantvoort remarks that the idea of Europe has long been thought from the perspective of its end, not just in the sense of the telos or goal of its trajectory of historical and philosophical development, but also in the sense of Europe's decline or demise. When conceptualizing the decline of Europe, thinkers such as Nietzsche, Spengler, Heidegger, and Horkheimer and Adorno will readily come to mind. However, as this chapter shows, the narrative of decline goes back much further: it is rooted in the historicism of Hegel and Herder and is bound up in a curious way with the progressive notions of historical development that both these thinkers share. This chapter will explore Herder and Hegel's ideas on Europe and cultural development and decline in order to shed light on three issues: first, the way in which the narrative of cultural decline and the decline of Europe are interwoven with the notion of historical development and progress in history; second, the organic model of the rise and decline of cultures developed by Herder and Hegel and its relation to the narrative of universal history; and third, the historical law by which, according to Herder and Hegel, cultures decline and what this can tell us about the decline of Europe.

Ovidiu Stanciu's essay, "The Ends of Europe: On Patočka's Concept of Post-Europe," lays out the main tenets of Patočka's discussion of the concept of "post-Europe" and "post-European humanity" as they emerge from his late works *Heretical Essays in the Philosophy of History*, *Plato and Europe*, and *Europe and Post-Europe*. Stanciu insists on the intimate link established between the political end of Europe and the intrinsic finitude of the European historical project. He reconstructs Patočka's philosophical genealogy of Europe and post-Europe and explain that his diagnosis of an "end of Europe" rests on a critical discussion of the teleological narrative of Europe advanced by Husserl in his *Crisis*. Finally, Stanciu attempts to make sense of Patočka's thesis that the demise of Europe does not foreclose the possibility of a renewal, that even after its historical collapse, there still remains a "specific future for Europe."

The third essay in this part is by Lorenzo Girardi. His chapter, "Patočka, the Second World War, and the European Project," provides an evaluation of the Second World War as a turning point in Europe's spiritual and political life, as envisaged by Patočka. Girardi argues that Patočka's concept of "solidarity of the shaken" needs to be actively given shape and institutionalized so as to make it a factor in history, as Patočka puts it. The way this has arguably taken place is discussed in a manner that might account for Patočka's pessimism, while also linking it to his so-far-underdiscussed indications of the importance of political institutions. Girardi links this to the use and abuse of reference to the Second World War and the Holocaust in contemporary discourse in and on Europe.

Thomas Telios's chapter, "Solidarity as Freedom: Jürgen Habermas, Jean-Luc Nancy and the Future(s) of the European Project" begins with the claim "We have never been European" in order to dismantle the Habermasian European project down to its elements and trace its limitations back to what Telios calls Habermas's "political solipsism." While, in toto, Habermas's ethics is pluralist qua its discursivity, its epistemology remains solipsistic qua its universal-pragmatist epistemological assumptions. This also has far-reaching consequences regarding which political model of identity should be furthered. Telios shows that Habermas's new concept of a *"legally constituted civic* solidarity" that came to replace his older moral understanding of solidarity cannot rectify these problems. Telios argues that, nevertheless, the concept of solidarity needs to be upheld. In the last section, he turns to Nancy's concept of freedom and interprets it as a model for European solidarity that results in the creation of a third space, where the differences of the various national states, while being respected, encounter each other and give rise to a shared and common *European form of life.*

Rozemund Uljée's essay, "The Promise of Europe," seeks to demonstrate, with reference to Derrida, that despite its troubled past, Europe still holds a promise for philosophy. The aims of this chapter are twofold: the historical aim is to trace the philosophical self-understanding of Europe with regards to universality throughout its history. The philosophical aim consists in showing how the notion of the promise reveals how Europe can no longer be thought in teleological terms. In other words: Europe does not work as a transcendental schema that regulates our historical experience of meaning. Instead, as Uljée argues, Derrida's account of the promise, and the temporal structure that belongs to it, shows that what Europe is and aspires to be must be invented anew each time.

Notes

1. Undoubtedly, every origin is preceded by another origin; the first always appears as second. Accordingly, the prologue of the epilogue is already written by modernist art and philosophy, as new modes of existence coalesce around the First World War.

2. Jacques Derrida, *The Other Heading: Reflections on Today's Europe,* trans. Anne-Pascale Brault and Michael Naas (Bloomington: Indiana University Press, 1992), 31.

3. F. Jameson, *Postmodernism, or, the Cultural Logic of Late Capitalism* (Durham: Duke University Press, 1991).

4. Giorgio Agamben, "We Refugees," *Symposium* 49, no. 2 (1995): 118.

Part I

Idea, Memory, Method

The Divided Origin

Re-membering Plato's Europe

GEORGIOS TSAGDIS

The following assembles a series of thoughts, which draw their significance from the enduring urgency with which they have determined, continue to determine, and will ineluctably persist in determining the fate of what, for lack perhaps of an overarching term, one might understand as occidental political thought *and* practice. In that sense, the gesture of this chapter redoubles what is being gestured: *in toto, the absence of origin*, or more precisely, the *desire* for origin, as it runs up against what precedes it, while being presupposed by it in order to sustain its originary function. Tracing Europe's most originary reflections on its origin in the earliest extant theoretical-political assertions of Hellenic philosophy, the chapter renders visible the magma of secondary quasi narratives, values, and concepts that support its never quite stable, never quite originary origin.

If this gesture appears to be animated by nothing other than the familiar, deconstructive logic of the supplement, it is perhaps only fitting that the chapter draws from the small family of thinkers who influenced the project of deconstruction in ways often unnoticed and unaccounted for, namely, the *avant la lettre* transdisciplinary "Paris School" and in particular two of its members, Pierre Vidal-Naquet and Nicole Loraux. Accordingly, the chapter examines the ways in which Athens conceives, narrates, and remembers its origin, as much as the ways in which it remembers its dismemberment, the fate of a civil war that its glorious origin could not account for or accommodate. Plato will remain throughout the horizon and measure of this examination. The origin of the *polis* will thus emerge not only as simply political, but at one and the same time as *historical*, where history in turn is understood as kinesis or motion, necessarily divided, articulated, *membered* and thus *re*-membered; but also always potentially arrested, in the *stasis* of a dis-membering civil war. If Europe has today a legacy, I consider it to be none other than the task of re-membrance: a memory and recovery of all its originary divisions, an attention to the magmatic cracks joining its theoretical-political tectonic plates.

The way that this chapter proceeds then is by looking at two constitutive myths of origin. The myth of Atlantis, expounded in the Platonic dialogues *Timaeus* and *Critias*, in which the empire of Atlantis wages war against Athens and the whole of Europe and the Athenian myth of autochthony to be found in both of the aforementioned dialogues but that receives a bolder ideologic formulation in the dialogue *Menexenus*. The closing section turns upon these myths of origin to examine the potential for dis-memberment that the division of origin entails and demonstrate the necessity to re-member this dis-memberment anew, in order to confront Europe's legacy and to create a new memory and a new origin, anew divided.

Before delving into the analysis on the origin of the *polis*, and in specific of Athens as the exemplary *polis*, the first *polis* to understand and represent itself as such,[1] a scheme of correspondence will help this analysis fall into place, insofar as the structural kinship of the world of ancient Greek cities to modern or contemporary Europe is far from immediately apparent. To make sense of this structural affinity, the notion of the limit, or in political terms, that of the border, and accordingly the questions of interiority and exteriority, as well as of singularity and plurality must be raised. One soon recognizes that the Greeks grappled explicitly and implicitly with the same questions that "we," or, in any case, those who call themselves Europeans, have long asked and continue to ask today: Is Europe one or many? Can it exist with the unity of a unit, or is it destined to remain a mere union? What are Europe's internal and external borders? Should these borders be suspended or entrenched?

The Greek cities, so unlike modern European states in most respects, share with them in the recognition of an interior and an exterior, the latter in turn organized, thematized, and operative as the interior of a higher, encompassing quasi unity of Hellenism. This unity was most commonly actualized in the anthropologically significant religious feasts and athletic events such as the Olympic games, but more importantly perhaps for the present examination, in the historico-political experience of the Persian Wars, as well as the Peloponnesian and Corinthian Wars that confronted the Greeks with their shared identity, precisely by tearing it apart, pitting one *polis* against another. As such, and while reiterating the need to remain wary of glossing over their profound dissimilarities, the experience of the Peloponnesian War carried with it a momentum that shook the Greek world the way that the Great War shook Europe, setting in motion nothing less than the demise of both. As for the Persian Wars, which had preceded it, although they seem to lack a direct counterpart, their photographic negative is, as will become apparent in the following, nothing other than the European history of colonial wars.

The Myth of Atlantis: Dis-covering the External Inside

As is already evident, the experience of war will be pivotal in the present exposition. *Polemos* fascinates not only Heraclitus, but all Greek thought, which is constitutively agonistic. Tellingly, in the eighteenth book of the *Iliad*, Hephaestus forges two cities on the shield of Achilles, one at peace, the city of anthropologists, the city of repetitive time, or in Loraux's terms of *aiōn*, the other, the city of historians, the city at war: both cities are called *beautiful*.[2] For Plato, the exemplary significance of war is almost technical at this juncture. The paradigmatic *polis* molded in Socrates's speech, which occupied in terms of dramatic time the previous day and which makes up the *Republic*,[3] is likened in today's discussion, which makes up the preamble to the *Timaeus*, to a painted or reposing animal.[4] Accordingly, war is understood as the motion of the *polis*, its *mobilization* or *kinesis*, its cinematics, which, as in the impetus that drove Muybridge's endeavors, makes visible what can never be seen at rest.[5]

Mobilizing the exemplary city is difficult; it requires an exemplary war. Critias, the interlocutor of Socrates and Timaeus, offers to undertake the task. The figure of Critias makes apparent the complex stratification of the Platonic text, compounded by the osmosis of the historic and the fictional. Critias, Plato's cousin, was the most famous and arguably most ruthless of the Thirty Tyrants who were imposed on Athens by the victorious Sparta at the close of the Peloponnesian War. At the close of the Athenian civil war that ensued and that will become significant in the second part of this chapter, Critias was to meet his own violent death. This paramount historic figure then, assumes the task of relating on the Platonic stage an exemplary war of Athens, which is explicitly undertaken by the well-trained fictional men of the *Republic*, but which is also explicitly historical, a war of *one and the same* Athens, even if this identification of the two *poleis* hinges on a bare name.[6] Plato addresses here the question of the identity of the *polis* with its *demos*, with a profound, oblique caesura: the *historic polis* of Athens, peopled by the *utopic demos* of the *Republic*, will be shown at war with *imaginary* Atlantis. In the face of this provocative elision of fact and fiction, Plato will go so far as to acclaim the speech of Critias as a *transition* from the *tale* or myth (*en mythō*) of the *Republic*, to the *truth of a fact* (*epi talēthes*).[7]

So it is that this "true" story, very much like the merely probable story (*eikos logos*) of the *Timaeus* that will precede it, is replete with lacunae, punctuated perhaps with more holes than words. Plato, the master of the *en abyme* narrative,[8] sets up the mirrors. First, there was Athens; and Atlantis. Then, nine thousand years before the first relation of the story,[9] Atlantis, which lay beyond the pillars of Hercules, set out to conquer Libya, Italy, and the whole of the Mediterranean. Athens stood alone against the threat from the West, as it would thousands of years later stand at Marathon to fight against Persia, the threat from the East, and emerging, in both cases, victorious.[10]

At this point of the story, a major lacuna seems to obstruct and obscure its transmission. For the story is related for the first time to the venerable Solon, another figure at the intersection of the historic and fictional planes. Historically, Solon is " 'the man of the middle,' the reconciler who [in archaic Athens] puts an end to the *stasis* between rich and poor, Aristotle's hero";[11] within the Platonic plot, Solon is the character who transmits the story told by an Egyptian priest of Neïth, a local goddess identified by Critias with Athena and by Plutarch with Isis.[12] In this osmosis of the historical and the fictional, Plato introduces Egypt as a surviving heterotopia able to bridge two bygone utopias even as he goes on to explain that Saïs, standing as a synecdoche for Egypt at large, was only founded a thousand years *after* the events of the war[13] and the subsequent earthquakes and floods that plunged Atlantis into the depths of the ocean and robbed Athens of all its warriors,[14] if not, presumably, its whole population. For a thousand years, then, between the end of the war and the subsequent natural disaster, the memory of Athens and Atlantis wandered from mouth to mouth, impervious and untainted, until the Egyptian priests could record it, saving from orality and thus from oblivion the story of the greatest of wars. It is these written records that account for the Egyptian wisdom, while orality consigns the Greeks to perennial infancy. "O Solon, Solon, you Greeks are always children: there is not such a thing as an old Greek,"[15] exclaims the Egyptian priest, taunting the great lawgiver on the tacit and paradoxical premise that those who have *only* speech, *don't even have that*, reduced as they are to infancy (*in* + *fari*, nonspeech). Accordingly, Athens, at once older and younger than Egypt, in its lack of institutionalized memory, can only know its own history through the mouth of an other culture, an other apparatus of religion and power, worshiping a goddess of a foreign name, whom Plato—closing anew the circle—identifies with Athena.

Recapping and resuming the transmission, the impossible has happened: the story of the war is preserved for a thousand years until the Egyptians can record it and relate it to Solon. Solon, upon his return to Athens, relays it to his friend and relative Dropides and he in turn to his son, Critias the Elder, the grandfather of the present, infamous Critias,[16] who calls upon divine memory, Mnēmosynē, to support his address to the company of Socrates, Timaeus, and Hermocrates.[17] And where is Plato? The question that haunts the whole Platonic corpus makes us realize that next to the five mouths recorded in the dialogue and the innumerable mouths and hands that carried it forth for nine thousand years, there are countless more mouths and hands, leading up to the hand of Plato and leading, inescapably, beyond it, as the story will be handed down in interminable iterations, from scribe to scribe and Platonist to anti-Platonist, furnishing in the process the depository of the European imaginary.

For the history of the story of Atlantis is the history of a fascinating errancy; like every errancy, it is guided by both internal and external forces. A pivotal external force identified by Vidal-Naquet is the desire of nations, such as sixteenth-century Spain, seventeenth-century Sweden, and twentieth-century Germany to utilize the myth of Atlantis in order to excise from their histories the biblical sanctioning of the elect status of Israel.[18] But if this history of mad, albeit politically motivated, conjectures could not be tampered by the rational interventions of a Montaigne or a Gianbattista Vico, if someone like Athanasius Kircher would go so far as to produce a *map* of Atlantis and Novalis would cast it as a place of ideal beauty,[19] it is because the tale of disappearance[20] that the Platonic text weaves has ensured that the historic and the imaginary are infinitely overlaid.

If as Vidal-Naquet imputes, one would have to wait until the year 1779 for Giuseppe Bartoli to demonstrate for the first time that Plato's project was not historiographic, but that the war between Athens and Atlantis was in fact "at once a 'Persian' war and a civil war,"[21] it is because, for this parallel to be established, the historic claims of the dialogue need to be at the same time underwritten and undercut. The import of this double gesture, which as is already clear animates the present reading, has for the most part escaped Platonic scholars, even as the tension that requires it rivets the Platonic text and generates incessantly centrifugal effects. Vidal-Naquet, who is among the most attentive to this interior constitutive tension of the Platonic text, considers the claim placed in Critias's mouth—namely that, if Solon could have devoted himself to poetry, the material of his account would have furnished the greatest poem of antiquity—as proof that the narrative operates in the domain of fiction.[22] However, Vidal-Naquet's remark is too quick in glossing over the historical valency of poetry in ancient Greece, exemplified in the Homeric epics and the Trojan cycle, which contrary to the myth of the Atlantis, a reverse kind of modern errancy insisted for centuries upon regarding as *mere* fiction.

So, what, in this infinitely refolding story that a Borges would have dreamed of composing, is still significant? Perhaps nothing less than the very significance of imagination in the construction of memory, first and foremost the memory of the origin. What the myth of the Atlantis repeats through its intra-, inter-, and extratextual folds is that memory is *at one and the same time* the memory of what cannot be changed and of what remains possible—the one because of the other. Memory is thus at one and the same time the memory of more than *one*. It is plural. Plato shows Atlantis as a utopia, while also presenting it *as* Persia and Athens—the one because of the other. And so it is that Europe is Greek and Roman as much as it is Judaic, Islamic, Slavic, Mongolic, Nordic: impossibly and fictionally plural, reiterating its future possibilities *as* memory of an origin infinitely receding into the past, as it simultaneously approaches from the future. In order to appreciate the stakes of this memory, it is worth carrying forth with the outcome of the Atlantic war.

Wishing to pursue the story of Atlantis, expectations—if one were so rash as to form any—are soon frustrated. One learns that Athens will eventually win the war, but the point that animated the dialogue, namely, the Socratic desire to behold the exemplary city in motion, is diverted. There won't be an account either of the war or of its outcome. One might be able to reconstruct a picture of the Atlantic imperial maritime might heading against the twenty thousand Athenian hoplites and see immediately how this Atlantis can be superimposed first on the Persian and later on the Athenian empire, the hoplites of which have become cowardly and complacent in the false security of sea warfare.[23] But this is all; there are no battles, no treaties, no conclusions. What Plato offers instead, first in the *Timaeus* and then in the *Critias*, aside of an errant promise, is the story of the foundation and ruling of the two cities: *Republic* reloaded.

It is perhaps then meaningful for the conclusion of this section to collate a few details on the two cities, juxtaposing their differences and similarities, in order to offer in turn a conjecture on their fates. Platonist scholarship commonly casts Athens and Atlantis as diametric opposites: this is far from the case. Both lands are chosen by Poseidon and Athena in accordance with the gods' natural domains (*kata tous topous*), not according to strife.[24] Being thus both allotted to their respective guardian gods with perfect harmony, they both give birth to autochthonous populations. The soil of both is indeed plentiful, laden with generous abundance.[25] Finally, although their languages differ, the one is translatable into the other, both being also translatable into Egyptian, down to or perhaps *beginning with*, the translatability of proper names. This overlooked Rosetta Stone at the heart of the Platonic text ensures a significant community of meaning while also insisting on the preservable identity, one might say, *interiority*, of a *mere* name, such as that of Athens.

But there are differences, precisely at the loci of similarities. Autochthony is accounted for differently in each case. Athena, at one and the same time *philopolemos and philosophos*, chooses Attica because its climate will make its soil most conducive to bringing forth men of *phronesis*. She and her brother Hephaestus[26] proceed then to implant (the word here is *empoiēsantas*) virtuous autochthonous men and set upon their minds civic order.[27] Thus, although Athenians are autochthonous, they have not grown wild, as pure nature, but are divinely implanted, indeed, cultivated.[28] Nothing of the sort is related about Atlantis, and one should attend to this silence. Euēnor and Leukippe are born of the Atlantic soil, being its first bloom and the first royal couple.[29] They have then an only child, Cleito, and it is only when they die that Poseidon comes into the fray, having fallen in love with the orphan girl, whom he determines to keep safe and prisoned liked a caged canary at the heart of the island of Atlantis.[30] Cleito soon gives birth to five sets of twins. The first of each pair is decreed by Poseidon to be the lord of a province of the land, while the first of the first pair, Atlas, is ordained king of the whole kingdom.[31] Atlantis can thus be seen as the fruit of a divine rape and fiat, of which Athens appears—at least at first—unsullied.[32]

Athens also appears to differ from Atlantis with regard to its wealth. Although the soil of both is naturally rich, and although Atlantis, like classical Athens, is a commercial behemoth, Atlantis is also the center of a much larger empire, which, like Persia, can draw on the resources of numerous dominions and is thus able to attain superlative splendor,[33] which Critias describes at length. The people of Atlantis are, however, unaffected by the din of precious metals and the allure of rare goods, until the divine blood of Poseidon in them starts to thin out, and greed begins to foment. Or at least, so it is with the rulers, since the Platonic text, which seems strained in this regard, nowhere instils divine blood into the common people of Atlantis, which are for the most part passed over in silence. Is it because the political eudemonia of Atlantis relies on the quasi-biological presence of divine blood, while that of Athens on the civic order impressed into the minds of the whole *demos*, that the one degenerates into greed, pride, and lawless ambition while the other does not? Whatever the reason, Zeus decides to punish Atlantis (*dikēn epitheinai*) and gathers the council of gods to announce his plan. Here, at the moment of greatest suspense and consequence, the narrative of Critias breaks off.

The frustration of having failed to see the city in motion is sealed. For centuries, it was commonly believed that the conclusion of the dialogue was lost. It is, however, plain that we are not dealing with a truncated manuscript, that the dialogue cannot be concluded, and that it was never intended to be. The full spectrum of possibilities that its caesura opens is rarely acknowledged. For, ultimately, *it is unclear* what Zeus is about to announce to the summoned gods. Is he going to punish Atlantis by inciting the desire of an expansive, colonial war which it is ultimately bound to lose? That is, is he going to induce hybris and direct Atē to compel the empire to reckless ruin? Or is he preparing a divine plague of earthquakes and floods that will submerge the empire? Or is it again, perhaps, a third unknown retribution? It is readily assumed that the justice invoked will take the form of a natural disaster. However, it then becomes rather impossible to explain the *periodic regularity* of these disasters, as related by the Egyptian priest, and perhaps more importantly, that at the very least, *this* catastrophe would have to have a blanket punitive effect of equal measure upon the virtuous Athenians, insofar as floods and other natural catastrophes in the Egyptian record appear to have universal reach.

Questions proliferate as divine wrath is suppressed in the truncated Platonic text. Indeed, it is unclear whether the vices of the people of Atlantis were so grave and whether, after all, they should be punished for being merely human, having lost the divine blood that Poseidon mixed into their race by raping Cleito. Perhaps ultimately the fault of Atlantis was simply that it lied beyond the Pillars of Hercules, beyond Europe, yonder from the frontier of the Same and far into "the boundless sea of diversity" to which the myth of the *Statesman* refers.[34] According to this myth, the age of Cronos is succeeded by the age of Zeus,[35] who reimposes control and order. It might be hard to see what kind of order the total annihilation of Atlantis achieves, but it is worth entertaining this thought: Atlantis is the non-European power that seeks to overtake Europe; it is the otherness that attempts to engulf identity; it must, as such be eliminated. Yet the long Platonic preamble, the hall of mirrors in which the identity of the Atlantis is refracted first into Persia and then into Athens, has prepared us to recognize that the punishment of the Atlantis stages a war *within*, a war taking place in an immemorial, mythical past and a historic future at once; perhaps one should say that this punishment stages the legacy of *crisis*. This is where the true otherness, the true danger and thus the true hope lies. The Atlantic lesson consists *in re-membering* the interiority of the exterior.

The Myth of Autochthony: Seeking the Interior Outside

A countergesture to this effort for re-membrance, animates, however, equally the Platonic corpus. Its strongest expression is found In the *Menexenus*, where Plato puts in the mouth of Socrates a funeral oration, that is, a public commemoration of the war dead,[36] both akin *and* antagonistic to the famous oration of Pericles, recorded by Thucydides—one of the most celebrated pieces of ancient rhetoric *and* history. The scant attention *Menexenus* has by and large received is thus surprising, being in truth as Loraux exclaims "a minor dialogue only for those who fail to see in the funeral oration its character as civic discourse."[37]

Part of the scholarly unease with *Menexenus* is rooted in the dialogue's peculiar character as a parody of a serious genre, a parody, however, not in the least comedic, even if there is, in Loraux's words, "not a single element that Plato does not borrow from Aristophanes: the exhaustible character of the speech-celebration, the pictures of the illusions of the grandeur that overcome the audience, the euphoric effect of eloquence, the imaginary voyage to the Islands of the Blessed,"[38] is all there. Aristophanes, Eupolis, and other comedians parody the funeral oration in order to neutralize it,[39] rob it of its pretensions, expose its lures and charms, its *goēteia*,[40] reminiscent of the insidious rhetoric of Gorgias. This charm is so strong as to keep each time Socrates under its spell "for more than three days,"[41] having him and his fellow Athenians believe to have already achieved, while still alive, the immortality of the glorious dead.[42]

And yet, there is no comedy here.[43] As a parody without comedy, the *Menexenus* seems to lack a genre.[44] In fact, its closing section is composed with a forceful beauty and gravity that would compel Athenians in the day of Cicero to keep reciting the Socratic oration at their annual public burial ceremonies.[45] If a parody could ever be taken so seriously, it is because the dialogue's nongenre opens up for Plato a space of freedom in which he can articulate *at one and the same time* the memory of the Persian Wars and of the noblest Athenian hours, when at Marathon, Salamis, and Plataea Athens, and Sparta stood united, along with the later memory of the Peloponnesian War when Athens, in its imperial conceit turned against Sparta, leading up finally to the more recent memory of the Corinthian War, where Athens allied with Persia against Sparta conducting the most shameful of wars, concluded in a most shameful peace, in order to regain a pitiful semblance of its erstwhile maritime power that led it to ruin.[46] By re-membering these integral members that constitute the historic body of Athens, Plato is able to express his loyalty, but also his heartbreak and fury,[47] at the degradation of Athenian democracy into a ruinous, imperialist populism,[48] initiated by Pericles and perpetuated by the ilk of his successors.[49]

This is the reason Plato adopts this nongenre to write a piece that is both occasional, written in all likelihood upon the conclusion of the Corinthian War in 386 BC, as well as evergreen, bringing its fruits forth to the present day. Plato chooses this nongenre in order to attack Pericles, albeit not directly and perhaps not personally, as the instigator of the Athenian decline, and more importantly perhaps, Thucydides, who turns imperialist ideology into history, by glorifying Pericles and intimating that if it weren't for the great man's untimely death, the project of the Athenian empire might have been successful.[50] Perhaps worst of all, Thucydides represents the first theoretician of what one has come to call *Realpolitik*. Loraux writes: "In developing his general theory of maritime power, Thucydides inevitably distances himself from a traditional form in which greatness belongs to the city by its very essence."[51] This is a significant development, and yet, no more than Thucydides does Plato wish to uncover an Athenian "essence"—the myth of the Atlantis makes this apparent in its recognition that Athens is nothing but a bare name, which in its nudity corresponds to a domain of memory and imagination. Plato knows that Athens, like Atlantis or Europe, is capable for the best and the worst, as it aspires respectively to virtue and power.

Yet Plato wishes to temper the maritime pride of Athens, to draw it closer to the humility of its humus, or soil. He employs thus here again, as he did in the *Timaeus* and the *Critias*, the myth of autochthony,[52] in order to flatter and win over the Athenian imaginary,[53] before driving home the gravity of the crime conducted among Hellenes and even among Athenians, one brother turning against another. In the words of Charles Kahn: "The proud racial boast of the average Athenian is thus invoked to blacken even further [the Athenians'] recent treaty with the Barbarian."[54] For even if other Greeks are *meixobarbaroi*, of mixed barbarian blood (245d), an unbreakable solidarity towards them and among them must be sustained. A forceful, perhaps, piece of classical rhetoric, but a perplexing, if not provocative, philosophical claim. If, however, this exhortation appears to confirm the ideology of Athenian racial supremacy—even if only by means of the lip-service it pays to it—its tacit operation is different.

Along with the re-membering of the glorious *and* the inglorious past of Athens, a re-membrance conducted here, as much as in the case of the myth of the Atlantis, along the vector of imagination, Plato *also* proposes an altogether other imaginary, one in accordance with the tradition of the funerary oration, in which "the city recognizes itself as it wishes to be."[55] By presenting this ideal as truth, Plato offers a performative vindication of the lifelong commitment of Socrates to make Athens this other, better place.[56] Plato is not content here, as he is in the *Gorgias*, to critique. He wants rather to imagine another potentiality.[57]

Athenians and all of their brothers, beginning with those of mixed blood, but ultimately including no less, those thoroughly "barbarian," can claim the proposed potentiality of virtue, insofar as they are willing to participate in the truth of this gesture.

For this is a gesture that neither lulls nor flatters. Its critique is articulated as an already actualized counterreality to which the Athenians have to measure up if they wish to be Athenians, if Athens is to amount to anything more than a mere name, but *also* if it wishes to remain committed to this mere name: a contradictory, if not absurd, commitment. The Platonic gesture becomes thus a call to a *universality without a universal*, sustained by a mere name.

In order to entertain this possibility, Plato must resist the pull of the funeral oration, which commonly slides from the praise of the dead to the praise of the living and the *polis*.[58] Thus, Plato gives the last word to the dead, who speak not for the glory of the living, but address the latter for the sake of the unborn. It is indeed beyond doubt that the dramatic time of the discussion of Socrates and Diotima is set years after they are both dead. We must thus appreciate with Vidal-Naquet that the dialogue, in its Platonic staging, takes place between ghosts.[59] Moreover, since these ghosts relay the words of the glorious dead, and Socrates exhorts his spectral audience to imagine his words as coming directly from their dead fathers (246c),[60] spectrality appears to multiply—as with the myth of the Atlantis—*en abyme*.[61]

What the glorious dead principally remind the living are the stakes in the tension that Thucydides invokes in his definition of the Athenian polity. For according to Thucydides, under the leadership of Pericles, Athens was a democracy in name (*logōi*) only, while, in actuality, in its works (*ergōi*) it was the "rule of the first man" (*hupo tou protou andros archē*).[62] In tandem, Plato has Socrates say: "One man calls it democracy, another what he pleases. But in truth it is aristocracy with the approval of the multitude" (238c). Accordingly, the Athenian polity is an aristocracy of merit (238d), on the basis of perceived (*dokein*) virtue and knowledge (239a)—*perceived*, not merely because even an exhortation shouldn't eliminate the potential for error, but because this potential is catalytic—it is at the level of this perception that the stakes of democracy hinge. The speaking specters know better than anyone the thinness, the transience of perceptions, the illusoriness and elusiveness of phenomena. They know that democracy is often saved only by the skin of its teeth from an abysmal slide into a tyranny of the one, the few, or the many, while at other times, it is not saved at all.

For Derrida, the ambiguity and ambivalence of the name of democracy in the *Menexenus* is what truly calls for thought, as it opens the question of the possibility on the one hand of an other democracy, even a democracy to come, and on the other hand, of an altogether irremediable democracy, marked by the legacy of autochthony, which nowhere escapes the *compulsion*, as the Platonic text has it,[63] to link the equality towards the law (*isonomy*) to the equality of birth (*isogony*).[64]

As we have seen, however, the Platonic text refolds in exacting ways. Autochthony in it is a provisional gesture, one that Derrida would certainly claim is structurally bound to remain forever provisional and therefore unshakeable. And yet, it is this labor that the Platonic text exacts, the labor to think of *isonomy* beyond *isogony*, at once through both re-membrance and imagination and to discover thus one's own polity as always other. The dead exhort: if you are to be yourselves, yourselves that you have always been, your true selves, you must be always and already other; other than you have been, other than you are, other than you are bound to be. This is the task that Plato exacts to make converge on the one hand an untenable, always deplorable, democratic legacy rooted in the privilege of birth, the privilege of origin, and on the other, a democracy to come, an other democracy, so truly other, that will perhaps barely bear the name of democracy.

Stasis: Dis-membering the *Polis*

Insofar as the promise of a democracy to come proceeds upon the originary division of the origin, it must incessantly remember that this promise can in turn be dismembered, that perhaps it has already been dismembered. For the *polis*, the "immobile prime mover" and "the irreducible kernel of meaning; opaque like everything appertaining to the origin, but the source of all value,"[65] always runs the danger of being torn apart, dis-membered by strife, consumed by profound violence. Indeed, every community has already at least once, and therefore more than once, experienced such strife. Dis-membering appears thus as a condition of re-membering, the latter designating not merely a return of memory and a re-collection of the shards of the origin, but a recuperation of the disaster.

The greatest disaster for the Greeks is nothing other than civil war, or stasis: a name that designates rest or arrest, but also stance, standing upright as a warrior and thus standing apart; taking up a position and thus finding oneself in opposition. From Solon to Aeschylus, stasis "is a deep wound in the body of the city."[66] Plato, in the first book of the *Laws* presents stasis as the harshest (*chalepōtaton*) war, the war against foreigners (*allophylous*) being much milder (*praoteros*) (629d). Tellingly, "stasis" utters the opposite of what it connotes; inasmuch as the Greeks understand war as motion, stasis is a *Gegensinn*. It has already been noted that the myth of the Atlantis is invoked by the desire to witness the utopic city of the *Republic* in *motion*, that is, to observe it at war. Even the Peloponnesian War, the war of the Greeks among each other, Thucydides qualifies as *megistē kinēsis*, the greatest motion.[67] However, the war within the city, factional and fratricidal, receives the name of stasis: a *nunc stans*, an arresting moment in which the city is brough to a halt.[68]

The disaster of *stasis*, Greek civic thought attempts to overcome by trying to "erase its political origin—for example, by assimilating it to an illness (*nosos*) malevolently fallen from the sky."[69] Civil war becomes thus a true dis-aster, a misalignment of the stars.[70] This however does not explain much; it blankets over the dis-memberment of the community and the bifurcations of causes and effects. Suddenly, the pragmatism of Thucydides appears salutary, in understanding *stasis* as a phenomenon coeval with political life.[71] In the words of Heraclitus: "Even the *kykeōn* [a brewed concoction] separates [*diistatai*], if it is not stirred."[72] Harmony, and this means no less political harmony, is only possible on the basis of a meticulous, unceasing intervention; a static community devolves quickly into *stasis*.

Perhaps this seemingly perennial danger of civil war has its own history. In Homer, the *polis* lacks an interior and is unperturbed by strife; war begins outside the city walls. By the time of Aeschylus, however, *stasis* has already become "coeval" with the *polis*.[73] Tracing this history, re-membering the origin of dis-memberment is an exceedingly difficult, if at all possible, task. Yet that much is important to conjecture: the political emerges from the *polis* as a pacified process of dis-memberment. It is the opposition of *logos* by *logos*, which results in the democratic vote, that for Gustave Glotz is capable to stave off civil war.[74] All the same, the language of war is not abolished. The peacetime vote signals in fact a division, a disagreement that runs deep, a difference (*diaphora*),[75] dominated by a combative vocabulary extolling and striving for wartime victory (*nikē*).[76] Every such victory is another thorn in the unity of the city, resulting in the dominion of one faction over an other that goes by the name of *kratos*. "This is why, already in the fifth century B.C., democrats avoided the word *dēmokratia*," which is used by the adversaries of the regime in a disparaging manner.[77] Not only does in a democracy the *dēmos* rule over the ancestral aristocracy and other institutional factions, but this *dēmos* comes into being as originally dis-membered.

Thus it is that the original dis-membering must be continuously re-membered. In Aeschylus's *Oresteia* it takes Athena's intercession with Erinyes (furies), on behalf of the city, and the promise of honors in perpetuity, for them to hold off *stasis*, to become Eumenides ("the benevolent ones").[78] However, no matter how much one devotes to the appeasement of the furies, the time of tearing will come. After it, what recent discourse has construed as the "healing" of division, must begin its work. Yet, how to heal? And quite when is the time of dis-membering over, exactly when should re-membering begin?

For the Athenians, a precise historic moment can be indicated; a catalytic instance that designates a new before and after. One recalls that one of the praises Socrates heaps upon the Athenians in the *Menexenus* hinges on the divine contestation between Poseidon and Athena over the guardianship of Athens. The image of quarrelsome gods, unacceptable for Plato, assumes a strategic place in a flattering funerary oration, which exploits the pride that Athenians took in being coveted by gods. Indeed, the divine contestation seems to have figured in numerous funerary orations and was enshrined on the Parthenon's west pediment, sculpted by no other than Phidias and Ictinus.[79] And then, in the last years of the fifth century BC, the second of the ancient month of Boedromion, the day upon which Poseidon and Athena were alleged to have contested, is struck out of the calendar, excised from recorded and recording time.[80] The remembrance of this mythical incident that informed Athenian identity and discourse is suddenly surgically removed.

Loreaux's *Divided City* summarizes the labor she devoted to making sense of this gesture. Its causes are perhaps not difficult to appraise: on the other side of the aftermath of the Peloponnesian War and the blood shed first among Greeks and then among Athenians, divine discord became an intolerable symbol, if not the accursed origin, of stasis. Thus, the Athenians decide to forget. Next to the excision of the day from the calendar, they dedicate an altar to Oblivion (Lēthē), the child of Strife (Eris) in Hesiod's *Theogony*, which according to Plutarch's *Table Talk* they erect in the Erechtheion, the sanctuary of the first, autochthonous, king of Athens, in order to reconcile the divine quarrel.[81]

But if the experience of the civil war is the apparent wound that demands the erasure of memory, or rather, the ban of re-membrance, and if it leads to an architectonic and a temporal intervention, the logic of the ban imposed and its implications are far opaquer. For certainly, a ban on memory does not amount to forgetting—neither in the short, nor in the long run. Is the city afraid that letting time instill its healing forgetting will not be enough?[82] Is this an attempt to accelerate politically the rhythm and thus the effect of social time?

The memory of harm the Greeks call *mnēsikakia*: "In Plato, this is said of the victorious party that retaliates with banishing and killing; in Aristotle as well as in judicial speeches in Athens after 403 B.C., it more specifically designates the act of initiating proceedings against acts of civil war."[83] In sum, then, what the Athenians attempt to institute with the injunction *mē mnēsikakein* is a model amnesty,[84] which presents itself as a *re-membering amnesia*, an amnesia that can bring the factions of the community together again. The common origin of amnesia and amnesty divides itself from the start in *amnēstia*. For as with *stasis*, we have in the paradox of the constant reminder to forget, a *Gegensinn*: amnesty is precisely not amnesia; one cannot forget as long as one is called to forgive.

At this stage, one might leave behind the minutiae of the warring Athenian factions,[85] and the political fate of Athens, the historical relevance of which seems to enter its own slow trajectory of oblivion, upon its noble resolve to forget the violence of stasis.[86] However, the *Gegensinn* of *amnēstia* will haunt the future not only of Europe, destined to centuries of war, but of every dis-membered community. As with the furies in *Oresteia*, in the face of the impossibility to undo civil wrath, a *polis* will have to neutralize, domesticate it.[87] In the institutional ban of memory, marked by a vacuum in their calendar, the Athenians will thus undertake, not the slow work of forgetting, but of domestication: in the place of the previous celebration of strife, they will now talk interminably about the ravages of strife;[88] they will attempt to live on by pledging to forget, that is, as long as memory survives, to re-member dis-memberment.

Coda: Remembering the Present

The above reflections trace the complex, infinitely layered story of Athens, its people, their glory and shame, hope and destiny. This story, in its Platonic mediation, shows itself to be plural, internally diverse, and animated by two countertendencies: the first, striving to discover a community's origin outside its history in the domain of pure possibility or imagination; the second, being surprised at recognizing all that is other, what the city could have never been, as part of its actual history. The origin of the community is thus interminably divided and demands to be interminably re-membered, coarticulated, member by member, to constitute a body politic.

Athens thus calls Europe to memory, insofar as the former's plural origin is included as one among the many origins of the latter. By showing what is external and other as always already within, the myth of the Atlantis in the *Timaeus* and the *Critias* calls "us," Europeans, to respond to the external within and thus to an infinite and infinitely critical responsibility towards ourselves. Its counterpoint, the myth of autochthony in the *Menexenus*, coming from the lips of the dead, reminds us, through hyperbolic parody, that in our memory and our imagination we are also always already other, that we must be, if we are to be the ones we have always been and hope to be. We thus find ourselves already inside and outside the walls of the *polis*, the walls of the fort Europe, the walls of our well-tempered souls.

If, however, the origin is always already divided, if walls have always already been there, new walls will be added. Every new dis-membering will require a new remembrance and will constitute a new, divided origin. The present always has the capacity to become origin. The task is to prevent this origin from cannibalizing all future nows, in order to allow the future to become origin, anew. Stasis is ultimately the arrest of the origin, the paralysis of the capacity to re-member.

Notes

1. This "first" functions, like every origin, *en abyme*: Athens is certainly not the first urban community to recognize itself as a polity. Within the European geographic and narrative space, however, it offers the earliest surviving testimony of a sustained reflection of a city on its character as a *polis*.

2. Loreaux, *The Divided City*, 16–18.

3. Plato, *Republic*, 529b.

4. Plato, *Timaeus*, 19b–c.

5. It is interesting in that regard that in his namesake dialogue Critias calls his own account, as well as that of Timeaus, a mimesis akin to painting or sculpting (Plato, *Critias*, 107b), thus immobilizing the cinematics anew.

6. Plato, *Timaeus*, 27a–b; Loreaux, *The Invention of Athens*, 296–97.

7. Plato, *Timaeus*, 26c–d.

8. Plato's dialogues often recede, dramatically, into a hard-to-identify vanishing point, involving narrations, reiterated by later narrations, creating the familiar Droste effect, with each layer inflecting, if not altering, what is reproduced. This becomes perfectly clear in the following, but the ubiquity of this Platonic narrative technique has a general significance. In the way of adducing another example, Plato composes the *Symposium*, c. 385 BC, setting the dramatic time of the narration at c. 400 BC, which recollects the actual taking place of the gathering at 416 BC. In this receding temporal framing, one hears Diotima's even older account on love, reiterated by Socrates, transmitted via Aristodemus, and related eventually by Apollodorus to Glaucon. Plato's own location, as composer of this picture, remains, as in the case of the *Timaeus*, elusive.

9. This sets the events at 9,500 BC.

10. Vidal-Naquet, *The Atlantis Story*, 19.

11. Loreaux, *The Divided City*, 102.

12. Herodotus. *The Persian Wars*, II.28.

13. Plato, *Timaeus*, 23e.

14. Plato, 25d.

15. Plato, 22b.

16. Plato, 20e.

17. Plato, *Critias*, 108d. The question remains open whether this evocation is meant to underwrite or undercut the historic reliability of the account. Critias insists that one must remember (*mnēsthōmen*) that, as it is being remembered or recorded (*emēnythē*), the war took place nine thousand years ago (108e).

18. Vidal-Naquet, *The Atlantis Story*, xvii.

19. Is it so surprising that Novalis does not see Atlantis as an "empire of evil"? Cf. Vidal-Naquet, 105.

20. Vidal-Naquet, 134.

21. Vidal-Naquet, 30.

22. Vidal-Naquet, 17.

23. Cf. Plato, *Laws*, 707a–e.

24. Plato, *Critias*, 109b. A strife that figures heavily in the Athenian lore into which the *Menexenus* taps.

25. The present abundance of Athens is only a glimmer of the horn of plenty her soil had been blessed with, later to be ravished by the flood (Plato, 110e).

26. Their brotherhood is of a paternal lineage, and this is significant for the otherwise maternally derived kinship.

27. Plato, 109c–d.

28. A similar claim is found, amplified, in *Menexenus*. Socrates commends Athens: "In the age when the whole earth was causing creatures of all kinds—wild animals and domestic livestock—to spring up and thrive, our land showed herself to be barren of savage beasts and pure. Out of all the animals she selected and brought forth the human, the one creature that towers over the others in understanding and alone acknowledges justice and the gods." Plato, *Menexenus*, 237d.

29. Plato, *Critias*, 113d.

30. Plato, 113d.

31. Plato, 113e–14d. It is unclear what having the pairing of king achieves; one hypothesis would be an oblique reference to Sparta. Another, more likely, to the significance of the even number in the Pythagorean tradition, examined below. Moreover, in this respect, the Platonic account of Atlantic autochthony resembles the Homeric account of Athenian autochtony, according to which Erechtheus the king of Athens is son of Gē and Hephaestus. See Homer, *Iliad*, book II, line 547.

32. At least within this narrative. *Menexenus* also stages the "quasi rape" of Athena by Hephaestus. The latter pursued Athena and ejaculates on her thigh; Athena wipes the semen away and lets it fall on the earth, whence Ereichthonius, the future king of Athens, is born. Contrary to the impression that the *Menexenus* affords, Ereichthonius is not the first kind of Athens, so that the myth of origin shows itself to be only an episode within a much deeper past.

33. Plato, *Critias*, 117e.

34. Plato, *Statesman*, 273d. Proclus links the myth of the Atlantis to that of the *Statesman*, bringing into the context the deep Pythagorean doctrine on Sameness and Otherness, or the Odd and the Even (Vidal-Naquet, *The Atlantis Story*, 49).

35. Plato, *Statesman*, 268d–74e.

36. *Leichenrede* in the German, a speech of corpses.

37. Loreaux, *The Invention of Athens*, 312.

38. Loreaux, 311. If the funeral oration is a means of bestowing glory to tragedy, "tragedy remains the principal target of ancient comedy." Loreaux, 306.

39. Loreaux, 307.

40. Loreaux, 265.

41. Plato, *Menexenus*, 235c.

42. Loreaux, 266.

43. Moreover, "parody never lacks ambiguity, and in ancient comedy the eulogy of Athens is not always a caricature. It is permissible to praise Athens provided that the reference is to the past." Loreaux, 308.

44. The dialogue possesses some of the characteristics of what Fredric Jameson calls "pastiche" (i.e., "blank parody, parody that has lost its sense of humour," Jameson, "Postmodernism and Consumer Society," 284), but it remains too political and pedagogic, as it draws on various genres without flattening them; moreover, its absence of humour is not a loss, but a deliberate, efficacious suppression.

45. Kahn, "Plato's Funeral Oration," 229.

46. The peace, known as the King's Peace, undid the most significant achievement of the Persian Wars, namely, the securing of Ionia's independence, by recognizing the sovereignty of the Persian king over all Asia Minor and prohibiting the Greek cities from forming alliances. Cf. Kahn, 224, 227.

47. Kahn, 229.

48. Kahn, 224.

49. Kahn, 232.

50. Monoson, "Remembering Pericles," 494–95. At the same time, Monoson suggests that Thucydides was aware and critical of the inherent problems with the Periclean project.

One of the ways Plato discredits Pericles is by having Socrates claim that he learned the oration from Aspasia, the *hetaira* of Pericles, who is also composing the speeches of the great man. However, the surface misogyny is complicated, not only by the fact that Socrates receives no less all that is significant in his speech from Aspasia but also by the recollection of the function of Diotima in the *Symposium*, and perhaps further by the resonances of a complex subtext of religious practices that run between the two dialogues. Moreover, "If silence [as Loraux says] is as necessary and natural to a woman as logos is to man, a woman cannot deliver a speech without profoundly disturbing the order of things." Loreaux, *The Invention of Athens*, 323. This is precisely what Plato wants, compounding the choice of a woman with her profession as an elite prostitute and a very significant public figure for Athens. The status of Aspasia as prostitute makes it further possible to read the whole dialogue under the sign of *eros* and *charis*. Cf. Monoson, "Remembering Pericles," 498–99.

51. Loreaux, *The Invention of Athens*, 292.

52. Thucydides, in contrast, tellingly avoids the myth without altogether rejecting it. Loreaux, 292.

53. The racial chauvinism of *Menexenus* is also echoed in the *Laws*. Similarly, Isocrates (*Panegyricus*, 48–50) credits the Athenians with an innate intellectual superiority over all other humans; Lysias (*Epitaphios* 43) says that in the Persian Wars the Athenians "showed their authentic and autochthonous virtue to the barbarians from Asia." Cf. Rosenstock, "Socrates as Revenant," 336.

54. Kahn, "Plato's Funeral Oration," 228.

55. Loreaux, *The Invention of Athens*, 312.

56. Rosenstock, "Socrates as Revenant," 341.

57. Kahn, "Plato's Funeral Oration," 224.

58. Loreaux, *The Invention of Athens*, 268.

59. Vidal-Naquet, *The Atlantis Story*, 15.

60. Cf. Monoson, "Remembering Pericles," 492; Rosenstock, "Socrates as Revenant," 338.

61. Rosenstock, "Socrates as Revenant," 331.

62. Thucydides, *The War of the Peloponnesians*, II.65.9–10.

63. *Anagkazein*. Cf. Plato, *Menexenus*, 238e–39a

64. Derrida, *Politics of Friendship*, 103–4.

65. Loreaux, *The Invention of Athens*, 329.

66. Loreaux, *The Divided City*, 24.

67. Thucydides, *The War of the Peloponnesians*, I.1.2.

68. The stand-off of the cold war can be thus read as an exemplary stasis, a war of reticence, tearing apart a humanity that was meant to have come together to heal the wound of the Second World War.

69. Loreaux, *The Divided City*, 25.

70. In a similar manner, Sartre and de Beauvoir, who among others read Camus's *Plague* as an account of the infectious spread of Nazism, critiqued it as a moot naturalization of a human evil that cannot be disavowed.

71. Palmer, "Stasis in the War Narrative," 409.

72. Heraclitus, Fragment B125.

73. Loreaux, *The Divided City*, 23.

74. Loreaux, 22, 25.

75. Loreaux, 101.

76. Loreaux, 21.

77. Loreaux, 70

78. Loreaux, 31.

79. Loreaux, 175.

80. Loreaux, 174.

81. Loreaux, 43, 173.

82. Loreaux, 145,151.

83. Loreaux, 149.

84. Loreaux, 29.

85. As Loreaux notes, this amnesty does not exchange a forgetting of victory in exchange for a forgetting of resentment—for the *dēmos*, being both the injured and the victorious party appears to be compromise inself twice over in its decision to forget. Loreaux, 251, 263.

86. Loreaux, 248.

87. Loreaux, 163.

88. Loreaux, 189.

Bibliography

Derrida, Jacques. *Politics of Friendship*. Translated by George Collins. London: Verso, 1997.

Heraclitus. "Heraclitus." In *The Texts of Early Greek Philosophy: The Complete Fragments and Testimonies of the Major Philosopers, Part I*. Translated and edited by Daniel W. Graham. Cambridge: Cambridge University Press, 2010.

Herodotus. *The Persian Wars, Volume I: Books 1–2*. Translated by A. D. Godley. Loeb Classical Library 117. Cambridge, MA: Harvard University Press, 1920.

Homer. *Iliad*. Translated by Robert Fagles. London: Penguin Books, 1998.

Isocrates. *To Demonicus. To Nicocles. Nicocles or the Cyprians. Panegyricus. To Philip. Archidamus*. Translated by George Norlin. Loeb Classical Library 209. Cambridge, MA: Harvard University Press, 1928.

Jameson, Fredric. "Postmodernism and Consumer Society." In *The Continental Aesthetics Reader*, edited by Clive Cazeaux, 282–94. London: Routledge, 2000.

Kahn, Charles H. "Plato's Funeral Oration: The Motive of the Menexenus." *Classical Philology* 58, no. 4 (1963): 220–34.

Loreaux, Nicole. *The Divided City: On Memory and Forgetting in Ancient Athens*. Translated by Corinne Pach with Jeff Port. New York: Zone Books, 2006.

Loreaux, Nicole. *The Invention of Athens: The Funeral Oration in the Classical City*. Translated by Alan Sheridan. New York: Zone Books, 2006.

Lysias. *Lysias*. Translated by W. R. M. Lamb. Loeb Classical Library 244. Cambridge, MA: Harvard University Press, 1930.

Monoson, Sara S. "Remembering Pericles: The Political and Theoretical Import of Plato's Menexenus." *Political Theory* 26, no. 4 (1998): 489–513.

Palmer, Michael. "Stasis in the War Narrative." In *The Oxford Handbook of Thucydides*, edited by Ryan K. Balot, Sara Forsdyke, and Edith Foster, 409–25. Oxford: Oxford University Press, 2017.

Plato. *Complete Works*. Edited by John M. Cooper. Cambridge: Hackett, 1997.

Rosenstock, Bruce. "Socrates as Revenant: A Reading of the Menexenus." *Phoenix* 48, no. 4 (1994): 331–47.

Thucydides. *The War of the Peloponnesians and the Athenians*. Translated by Jeremy Mynott. Cambridge: Cambridge University Press, 2013.

Vidal-Naquet. *The Atlantis Story: A Short History of Plato's Myth*. Translated by Janet Lloyd. Exeter: University of Exeter Press, 2005.

2

Entwurf of the Method and Ethics of Its Discourse

Notes on Cartesian Rationalism Reconsidered

VERA BÜHLMANN

New European Bauhaus

There is currently a process underway to build a New European Bauhaus—a place dedicated to concerting together in the invention of future ways of living. It is supposed to become a platform in the service of cultivating radical inclusion—inclusion with regard to arts, technologies, science disciplines, and differences in cultural and social identities. With this initiative, the European Union responds to the digital transformations. These transformations challenge us to invent adequate instruments that would be in support of circular and cyclic modes of process and qualitative transformations that follow a logic of mutual commerce and endowment, saturation rather than separation, disjunct synthesis, and cohabitation rather than demarcation and classification. Keywords are *data science* and the *algorithmic condition, machine learning, artificial intelligence, circular economy, green deal,* and *climate.* What makes this initiative perhaps especially timely is the question put center stage by the president of the European Commission and instigator of the idea of the New European Bauhaus, Ursula van der Leyen: How can this ecological and economical project also become a project of culture?[1]

Nothing has perhaps oriented modern architecture more than a keen interest in relating art and architecture with mathematics—the New

Bauhaus Initiative of the EU Parliament does not appear to continue the enthusiasm and trust of the moderns in the adequacy of this relation. Its emphasis is on discursive agendas and practices, and the analytical-logicist understanding of Cartesian rationalism plays almost an antagonistic role therein. This text proposes an unorthodox reconsideration of Cartesian rationalism in light of Descartes's own contextualization of his famous text on method, which actually was partly (but significantly) in relation to studying weather phenomena and their inherent nonlinear and circuitous nature, their metricity and scalarity. The interest of this text, hence, is to consider how Descartes could actually be a conspirator rather than an antagonist in figuring out how dealing with the current ecological and economical challenges "can also become a project of culture." There is a notion of *discourse* as *Entwurf* to be uncovered in Descartes, and complementary also a notion of *Entwurf* as *discourse*, whereby there comes to stand an irreducible role for ethics that belongs to Cartesian method, and that is to mediate the communication practices between mathematics and artistic cultural practices and their political agendas. Concretely, what would it mean to complement the modern interest in letting art be directed by mathematics with its inverse direction, whereby mathematics subjects to artistic direction in turn—as Michel Serres has recently emphasized it in *Musique* (2011)? This would mean paying attention to how the nothingness of the axial "origin" informs the axiality that gives orientation—like a cipher informs the codes that articulate it. This text attempts to think Descartes's proposed universal method without eclipsing the algebraic role of code in the analytical geometry employed by Descartes. It is the constitutive role of code within Descartes's universal method that promises a fruitful tuning between his and our historic constellations; it is also what legitimates such a counter-canon reconsideration in Cartesian rationalism. What we can learn from Descartes, in this light, is not only a form of circular writing, but also an idea of how architectonic contemplation differs from philosophical contemplation by departing from and returning to a primacy of commonsense intellection. Such a rationalism needs to respect metaphysics as a first philosophy (*prima philosophia*)—but, by a *via negativa*: an appreciation of metaphysical speculation alone will never run out of cause for doubt, with which the universal method in Cartesian rationalism needs to be endowed (doctrine of methodic doubt). Effectively, I will argue, repositories of metaphysical gestures become the wellspring of abstractly embodied gestures for thinking with which architecture ideates mathematically. There is an aesthetic side to such ideation that will be outlined by turning to Paul Valéry, who is admittedly a great admirer of Descartes and who gives us, with his *Introduction to the Method of Leonardo da Vinci*, as well as with "Eupalinos or the Architect," two precise texts that help to grasp how we might reconnect with an architectonic understanding of analytical thought.

Witness to the reformation wars, Descartes sought to constitute a scientific form of rationalism that would be capable of preserving a certain autonomy for science from both, religion/theology and politics—an autonomy in ethics, which he put into the authority of architectonics and which he made the principle of his geocentric philosophy. His geocentrism was essentially concerned with keeping a mediate relation between knowledge and the world. His famous text *Discourse on the Method of Rightly Conducting One's Reason and of Seeking Truth in the Sciences (Discours de le méthode pour bien conduire sa raison)* originated in the context of his book entitled *The World* or *Treatise on the Light (Traité du monde et de la lumière)*. It is about how to think and speak of a physical nature of light in proportion to the light of insight cast by human intellect. Inevitably, such a novel physics was bound to challenge the theological codifications of divine insight and intellection, and Descartes never dared to publish this book during his lifetime. Today, the famous text *Discourse on Method* is usually read as if it were a stand-alone piece, detached from this context. Reconnecting what has become the founding document of modern rationalism within its proper context of inception is enough to find oneself engaged in a reading of Cartesian rationalism deemed unorthodox today[2]—let's embark on the adventure!

In the light this text seeks to cast, we can find how in Cartesian rationalism, discourse is the subject of architectonic *Entwurf* that aims at hosting the cohabitation of politics with philosophy. Against the common reading, Cartesian method was not about identifying and determining the essence of what can be known in terms of objective description of things. Rather, it was an impredicative method that had, as I will argue, nothing in particular to teach. The process of clarification his rationalist method seeks to accomplish literally sets out to ideate the plenitude of any imaginable opinion at all. It is a subtractive and analytical method, but it cannot be reduced to a formalism. It is the special peculiarity of Cartesian rationalism that the method he proposes for the analytics of such procedure is itself subject to *Entwurf*—and this *in each particular case of proceeding by it*. Method itself is rendered topical and subject to architectonic constitution. To speak of *Entwurf* of the method, algebra-ically and hence together with its inverse sense (that method needs to be followed by proceeding analytically), this means that the analytical space is indeed one that exists in parallel to the real, the physical one. But this parallelism is the architectonic site of an active and vibrant analogy, according to which self-formation is set up in parallel to world formation. This is (very likely) why his book *The World* was written in the rhetorical form of a fable, and *Discourse on Method* in the poetic gesture of an autobiography. His *Meditations on First Philosophy*, where Descartes foregrounds the importance of methodical doubt, appear as an inversive form to that of philosophical contemplation—they appear as a form of architectonic contemplation.

The active analogy that edifies the architectonic site of this parallel-ism (between the domain of analysis and that of the real) is embodied in the instruments (and the abstract instrumentality) that relates knowledge and the world. This is also where a reconsideration of Cartesian ratio-nalism holds such great potential for our own situation today, for coming to terms with all those novel mentalities of data science, social media platforms, artificial intelligence, and machine learning. The Cartesian method had been already akin to a circular form of writing with which we seek to come to terms today—namely, a notion of method, in the singular because universal, but in the pluralist terms of algebraic coding.

Rationalist Instrumentation, Architectonic Contemplation

Before turning with more detail and closer reference to Descartes's universal method itself, I want to start by considering how we could think about the aesthetic implications for such a Neo-Cartesian ratio-nalism. For this, I want to turn to Paul Valéry, who never fell short in emphasizing his rejection of theories of the arts that rely upon irrational substances like genius or inspiration, and who also never fell short in acknowledging his great admiration for René Descartes. In a famous text entitled *Introduction to the Method of Leonardo da Vinci*, Valéry arguably probed the Cartesian method by inventing a kind of parallel transport of it such that he could self-instruct himself through it, by using it as a guide when seeking to get in touch with the extraordinary "*ésprit*" of Leonardo da Vinci—this great Renaissance polymath mind. He begins his text: "There remain of a man those things of which one is set dreaming by his name and by the works which make of his name a mark of admiration, of hate, or of indifference." He continues: "Remembering that he was a thinker, we are able to discover in his works ideas which really originate in ourselves: we can re-create his thought in the image of our own."[3] Thus Valéry prepares the reader's attention for what is to follow. Continuing, he elaborates on how he thinks about such strange parallelism; he begins by asking why it would be useful to have a means at work that allows one to recreate another person's thought in the image of one's own. He explains:

> An ordinary man we represent to ourselves with ease: we can reconstruct his elementary actions and reactions from our own simple experience. We find the same processes in the indifferent acts that constitute the exterior aspect of his life as in our own; we are the connecting link between our acts, as he was between his, and the radius of activity that his existence suggests to us does not extend farther than the radius of our own. But if we allow that this individual excels in some respect we shall have more difficulty in imagining to ourselves the works and the ways of his mind.[4]

The problem is well familiar. But what to do? Here, Valéry introduces a crucial component of such architectonic thought, namely, what he calls "imaginative perception." This means to open the gates to inventive fancy, as a constitutive part of such creatively self-instructive method. "In order not to be confused in our admiration we shall be forced to stretch our imaginative perception of the quality that dominates in him and of which we no doubt possess only the germ."[5] Here shines up the importance of a demiurgic universalism (literally the universalism of public work, of skilled work in the service of a public).[6] Like Plato's rationalism crystalizes in the cosmos's workings as set up in the *Timeaus*—an early *architectonic* model of the cosmos, because it speaks of the cosmos in terms of its workings and construction rather than, like Hesiod, in the terms of cosmogonic genealogies of myth. Its rationalism consists in setting up a possible model of correspondence between the intelligible and the sensible. Descartes's rationalism too starts out from fabulating how a correspondence between the sensible and the intelligible could possibly be established. In Descartes, this is the model of the world as a plenum with cracks that are always immediately being filled up with light[7]—a mechanical model whereby the question of the true nature of light is being bracketed out and that is the core of his book *The World or A Treatise on Light*.[8] We will come back to this later. First let's remind ourselves briefly here of the template of such fabulation, namely, Plato's *Timeaus*.

The Platonic demiurge famously engenders a universal soul by an act of what we could perhaps best call "metaphysical fabulation," or more precisely a fabulation of architectonic discreteness. Plato calls this speculative universal soul the "being of wholeness." It acts as the knowledge-facilitating medium in Plato's rationalism—the medium or substrate that is to establish a public domain for knowledge. This fabulous substrate, this rationalism imagines, needs to be distributed equally throughout the entire range of its scope. For this, the Platonic demiurge takes "the three elements of the same, the other, and the essence"[9] and mingles them in a cup. Out of it, he creates numericalness. This, he sets out to partition into measured blocks of pure ratios, working thereby along the principles of the Pythagorean theory of number through harmonics (circle of fifths). Plato tells us: "When he [the demiurge] had mingled them with the essence and out of three made one, he again divided this whole into as many portions as was fitting, each portion being a compound of the same, the other, and the essence."[10] He then took all the numbers thus produced, a partitioned and formed wholeness, which was now (after the preparations discussed) made up entirely of blocks of ratios, and he "stretched it and cut it into two," and "crossed, and bent [it] such that the ends meet with ends."[11] Like this, two intertwined circles are eventually created, an inner and an outer, and we are told that they revolve around the same axis. The motion of the outer circle is called the Same, and the motion of the inner circle that of the Diverse. To the outer circle belong the intelligible forms, and to the inner belong the sensible and corporeal bodies. But what both of these circles are made out of, namely the soul of the universe that had been engendered through speculative fabulation, is dispersed throughout all of it; this is the precondition for Plato's demiurgic rationalism to work—and it is what makes the demiurge's fabulation *architectonic*.

As we know well, everything that might be fabulated in the Platonic oeuvre stands in the service of the dialectic dialogue—and like the Cartesian method of self-instruction, it too is a manner of doing philosophy that aims, before all else, at an education and instruction of the self in the service of a truth—that is, in the service of knowledge that is not a good, knowledge as something for which there ought to be no intermediates, no merchants; whether it nevertheless is to be regarded as a kind of property—this is subject of dispute especially with respect of communist readings of Plato. But this is not our subject here.

Being informed about the basic strokes drawn in the background of every philosophical rationalism molded according to this template is important because it alone can convey the crucial importance of the Cartesian method as a *universal* method. His project was, arguably, to offer a universal method that would proceed with like qualitative subtlety as the dialectic method does in Platonism; but it was not to proceed primarily via words, but via mathematical ideation and geometric fabulation. Like this, the Cartesian method sought to proceed without the hierarchical master-pupil relation at work in classical dialectics (or the master-slave relation in modern dialectics). Instead, in the light in which this text suggests to look at it, Descartes sought to offer a method for self-instruction that works automatically, but with the subject capable of stepping-aside of itself—through the constitutive employment of instruments of mediacy—when proceeding according to this method.

The fabrication of such an instrument is at stake with Paul Valéry's interest in *The Method of Leonardo da Vinci*, when he maintains that one can effectively construct such an instrument out of the work of someone whom one admires and wishes to study—such as to "discover in his works ideas which really originate in ourselves: we can re-create his thought in the image of our own,"[12] as he put it. Let us return to it now.

If we admire the work of somebody else, Valéry maintains, we must at least possess the quality at work in it within ourselves—even if only undeveloped and as a germ. Something can only speak to us if we are already in principle possession of it. Thus far, this would appear to support a nonuniversalist setup, one that rather sought to keep likeness with likeness, according to a notion of order that is not open but conservatively closed. Valéry, however, continues:

> But if all the faculties of his mind are widely developed at the same time, or if the results of his activity seem to be considerable in all fields, his character becomes thereby more and more difficult to comprehend in its unity, tends to escape from our efforts to understand it. There are distances from one extremity to another of this intellectual area such as we have never covered. The continuity of the whole escapes our

perception as do formless scraps of space which are divided
from each other by objects that we know and which are for
us no more than chance intervals; as, at each instant, myriads of facts, over and above the small number established by
language, are lost.[13]

Instead of disregarding or dwelling on the subjectivist problem of unequally
developed intellectual dispositions, Valéry generalizes the problem into
one of the scale of nature: "At each instant, myriads of facts, over and
above the small number established by language, are lost."[14] We see
here his commitment to Cartesian physicalism, which—as we will elaborate later—sought to liberate imagination from psychological theories
of faculties purportedly natural specifically to the human soul. Such a
physicalism was essential to Descartes, insofar as his philosophy was not
to compete with theology; it was to complement it, within the clear
bounds of what regards the world, the domain of life. Valéry continues:

Nevertheless we must go slowly, take time before them and
conquer the difficulties that the conjunction of apparently
heterogeneous elements lays on our imagination. Every
intelligence here gives itself up to inventing a unique order,
a single activity, and desires to impose its own image on the
system which it imposes on itself—a clear-cut image. With a
violence which depends on its range and its lucidity, it fin-
ishes by reconquering its own unity, just as by the operation
of some mechanism a hypothesis becomes clear and proves
itself to be the thing which has made the whole, the central
revelation in which all has had to happen, the monstrous
intelligence or strange animal which has woven thousands of
pure connections between many forms, and of which those
puzzling and varied constructions were the creations—instinct
building its habitation.[15]

The mechanist paradigm he adapts, lets him speak of instincts generically
as one speaks of forces in physics. What appears like a striking hubris
of seeking to understand everything through scaling it to proportions
of one's own limited dispositions, is actually an inversion of direction:
acknowledging the greatness of the topic of one's object of admiration
is turned into a source for learning to rise up to its greatness, gradually

so, and step by step. What is more: the method that is at play hereby facilitates a public communication and sharing of what has been wrought through such knowledge-as-self-forming-labor—and this without claiming any ownership of the gained insight and understanding as a sole truth because it is established *by method*: "The production of the hypothesis is a phenomenon which admits of variations but not of chance. Its value is the value of the logical analysis of which it must be the object. It is the basis of the method with which we are going to occupy ourselves and which we are going to utilize."[16] Valéry will state decidedly that even though his text is about the method of Leonardo da Vinci, it is not about the man; rather, it is about a miniature model of inference drawn from having sought an intimate encounter with his mind through an engagement with his work and the pursuit for a method that can give unity to the difficulties that the conjunction of apparently heterogeneous elements present in his work.

> It remains to give a name to this creature of thought in order to set a limit to the elaboration of terms ordinarily too far apart and likely to escape from any attempt to associate them. No name seems to me more suitable than that of Leonardo da Vinci. Whoever imagines a tree to himself must also imagine a sky or a background against which to see it standing. That is logic of a kind that is almost self-evident and almost unrealized. The figure I imagine reduces himself to an inference of this nature. Little of what I say of him must be considered as applicable to the man who has made the name illustrious: I am not following up a coincidence that seems to me impossible to make clear. I am trying to express a point of view with regard to the detail of an intellectual life, to make one suggestion as to the methods which every discovery implies, one chosen amongst the multitude of things that may be imagined, a model, that may well be thought a rough one but in every way preferable to strings of doubtful anecdotes, to commentaries in the catalogues of art collections, to dates—erudition of that sort would only falsify the purely hypothetical aim of this essay.[17]

We will not delve into the model of Leonardo da Vinci's method as drawn up by Paul Valéry here. But we will attend some more to how the drawing up of such models is, for Valéry, the core skill of the architect—namely, the ability to build with timeless form through mathematical ideation. For this, we need to consider a closer look at the role of *Entwurf* in such ideation.

Massimo Cacciari, the Italian philosopher and former mayor of Venice, has foregrounded the particularly strange act of bracketing time—and keeping it in suspension—that is involved thereby. *Entwurf* is not properly a project, he maintains.[18] As its name suggests, it does not just cast itself ahead and into the future (as does the project)—rather, it casts itself off of something (as its German prefix *Ent-* indicates). It embodies a strange kind of gesturing in abstraction; *Entwurf* literally embodies the gesture of an act of thinking that *sets itself apart* while at the same time *recollecting itself anew*—informed by the character of a particular project (from which *Entwurf* is not separable). In the light of our context here, I suggest calling such gesturing at work in an act of abstraction, thought-in-act, *architectonic contemplation*. Architectonic contemplation is not entirely introverted, like philosophical contemplation tends to be. In *Entwurf*, what is at stake is indeed a strange acting-in-suspended-intermediacy: it is all about an introverted kind of exteriorization of ideas, through picturing not so much the ideas themselves, but an aesthetic reality in which they could have a certain lasting presence, a certain duration. *Entwurf* does not have a cause exterior to itself; but there is a metaphysical causality at work in it. It needs a milieu in which the gesturing subject does not dwell, is not at home. In short, *Entwurf* is in need of an ecstatic site where one is not properly oneself—it depends upon participating in an epiphany, the sudden and remarkable happening of a realization. It is involved with a strange sort of "liberating capture." Cacciari speaks of such a metaphysically challenged (and challenging) stance—namely, to be tensely suspended and kept in stasis, struggling to find and maintain a stance vis-a-vis eventuality—with the poignant formula of *feeling the pull of the project's throw*.[19] *Entwurf* is about bearing with the tenseness of going pregnant with an idea, a pact with oneself to delay the birth of this idea, with the intent to draw stimulation for mathematical ideation from such an act of bearing-with. It is about conceiving *how to work its delivery out*, as a world-fitting project. Paradoxically, this involves a certain conspiracy with impotence and death.

Here lies the similarity to Valéry's engagement with the spirit of Leonardo, through attending to his work—"every intelligence here gives itself up to inventing a unique order, a single activity"—by searching for a method one did not master before "giving oneself up to a system that imposes itself," but that can be found, nevertheless, entirely within one's own "desire to impose its own image on the system which it imposes on itself—a clear-cut image."[20]

Architectonic Form Originates in Death, or Eupalinos's Mathematical Ideation

With another one of Valéry's texts, *Eupalinos or Architecture*, we have a witty and brilliant document pondering just this idea. In order to explore architectonic ideation, Valéry draws up a plot that involves Socrates and Phaedrus, two figures well known from the Platonic dialogs. The setup is striking, as he has Socrates, master of the dialectic form of verbal dialog, talk with Phaedrus, known as the defender of the idea of the soul's immortality and proponent of a distinction between first and second nature. In Valéry's dramatic piece, they meet each other at a river in the land of the dead. Apparently, Phaedrus is deemed to have been right, in Valéry's reception. He has Socrates say: "This river is the river of Time. It casts only the souls upon this bank; but it carries away everything else without effort."[21] But Phaedrus's response strengthens the position Socrates is commonly associated with: "Every instant I imagine that I am going to discern some form, but what I think I have seen never succeeds in awakening the least image in my mind."[22] Hereby, Socrates appears to have been right as well. We are transported to the dramatic site of a contemplation that dwells in doubt, and indeed we will see shortly that what is at stake in this plot is the question of how a methodical doubt, namely, that of how analysis could possibly be linked up with a situation of standing beside oneself, with a stance in ecstasy.[23] Next we hear Socrates explaining to Phaedrus how he makes sense of the situation they happen to find themselves in:

> That is because you are witnessing the true flow of beings, motionless yourself in death. We see, from this pure bank, all human things and natural forms impelled in accordance with the true speed of their essence. We are like the dreamer, in whose breast, shapes and thoughts being strangely altered by their flight, things and their transformations intermingle and are blent. Here everything is negligible, yet everything counts.

Crimes engender immense benefits, and the greatest virtues develop fatal consequences: our judgment settles on nothing, idea becomes sensation before our very eyes, and every man drags after him a chain of monsters inextricably wrought of his acts and the successive forms of his body. I think of the presence and of the habits of mortals in this so fluid stream, and reflect that I was one among them, striving to see all things just as I see them at this very moment. I then placed Wisdom in the eternal station which now is ours. But from here all is unrecognizable. Truth is before us, and we no longer understand anything at all.[24]

Phaedrus remains in doubt. He remembers, and tells Socrates, how he had once found in Eupalinos, the architect and engineer, a certain "power of Orpheus."[25] The nauseating situation in which they both find themselves (a situation "like that of a dreamer," in which "everything is negligible, yet everything counts") can clear up through this power—and he begins to speak about it as the power of the architect. The architect is to be capable of finding a discernment within such a confused presence of truth, he considers. It involves a peculiar manner of abstracting from all details, such as to keep the memory of a vivid experience effective and alive in what Valéry calls "a mathematical image";[26] the power of Orpheus is to ideate mathematically. What is postulated thereby is the old idea that between soul and mathematics, there is a correspondence—all liveliness may be washed away by the river of time, but if the souls are washed to the shore and can contemplate "the true flow of beings," this is to be precisely what mathematical ideation is capable of. Socrates is incredulous, even though he knows well another power quite similar in kind. He knows the power of words—and it resides precisely in attending to even the finest details in order to keep the essence of a thing present. What Phaedrus talks to him about, on this peculiar power of the architect to draw up and realize a mathematical image, sounds bewildering to him: "What enthusiasm of a shade for a phantom!"[27] he exclaims amused. "This is because you always wish to draw everything out of yourself,"[28] Phaedrus replies. The architect's power to link up analysis with ecstasy by mathematical thinking never aims at fully elucidating and exposing the essence of things—but it does maintain a relation to truth.[29] The architect seeks to provide a residence for a truth, such as to help it to a certain duration of being effectively present. His relation to the essence of things is always mediate. But despite the immateriality of mathematical ideation, for the architect, this mediacy is crucially constituted by the body. The idea Valéry develops here thinks inversely about the body: the body, usually praised in philosophy for granting a certain immediacy to experience, is precious here for the architect *because* it grants a mediacy. This mediacy relies upon a *via negativa* to one's own body; indeed, the body itself becomes an "admirable instrument"[30]—and through that, a site of ecstasy. "What a marvelous substance we are made of," Phaedrus recounts the words of Eupalinos.[31] And furthermore, we learn that it is through this substance that we participate in what we see and what we touch: we are stones; we are trees; we "exchange contacts and breaths with the matter that englobes" us.[32] Bodies are a site of ecstasy to the architect because in our bodies, soul and nature interpenetrate—this interpenetration is what is capable of hosting a speculative site to stand besides oneself. Bodies "touch, they are touched; they have and lift weight; they move, and carry their virtues and vices about; and when they fall into a reverie or into indefinite sleep, they reproduce the nature of waters, they turn into sand and clouds . . . [O]n other occasions they store up thunderbolts and hurl them abroad."[33] Such standing besides oneself is not a question of either or. Rather there is a graduality to it—this is crucial. Training to connect with the capacity of the body to facilitate such gradual ecstasy, "it is necessary to abstract oneself from the spells of life and from immediate enjoyment, even if for this purpose we must make a stern effort against ourselves."[34] To make a stern effort against oneself means apportioning ones' attentions. It means arranging problems in a variety of speculative orders for "there is a commerce between your acts and your latest observations."[35] This commerce allows endowing experiences with a lasting presence in architectonic form that originates in ultimate impotence, in death.[36] The architect's act of conception involves the body in this way—the body, if it conspires with the (immortal) soul, can recall the soul back to reality "as the anchor calls back the ship."[37] Let us cite in full this passage, which elaborates on this mystic instrumentality of the body:

> But I . . . say in the full light, I repeat to myself with every dawn: "O body of mine, that recallest to me at every moment this tempering of my tendencies, this equilibrium of thy organs, these true proportions of thy pard, which make thee to be and to stablish thyself ever anew in the very heart of

moving things; keep watch over my work; teach me secretly
the demand of nature, and impart to me that great art, with
which though art endowed even as by it thou art made, of
surviving the seasons, and of saving thee from the incidents
of change. Grant me to find in thy alliance the feeling of
what is true; temper, strengthen, and confirm my thoughts.
Perishable as though are, though art far less so than my dreams.
Though endurest a little longer than a fancy; though payest
for my acts, and dost expiate my errors. Instrument though,
of life, though art for each one of us the sole being which
can be compared with the universe. The entire sphere always
has thee for a centre. O mutual object of the attention of
all the starry heavens! Thou art indeed the measure of the
world, of which my soul presents me with the shell alone.
She knows it to be without depths, and knows it to so little
purpose that she sometimes would class it among her dreams;
she doubts the sun. . . . Doting on her ephemeral fabrications,
she thinks herself capable of an infinity of fabrications, she
thinks herself capable of an infinity of different realities; she
imagines that other worlds exist, but thou recallest her to
thyself, as the anchor calls back the ship."[38]

Soul and body form an alliance in architectonic conception. When
asked if this power involves conception, Eupalinos responds, "Yes and
no. Yes as a dream. No, as a science. . . . It is not in my power to link
up, as I ought, an analysis with an ecstasy."[39] Conception here is, quite
bodily, an act where the powers of abstraction and imagination are being
summoned "from the great desire" and "naively formed of the extreme
expectation of my soul"—only to then "interrupt the very birth of Ideas,"
through apportioning attention, arranging a problem in another order,
and again, another order. Yet despite this violent effort to go against
one's immediate inclination (namely, to dwell or realize an idea right
away), the act of conception cannot be willed. It is an erotic act. Even
though entirely within one's head, it is of bodily intensity, experience,
gesture. Valéry describes it thus:

When it makes its presence known, dear Phaedrus, I am already
as different form myself as a tightened string differs from itself

when loose and sinuous. I am quite other than what I am. All is clear and seems easy. Then my schemes follow their own course and are preserved in a light that is mine. I feel my need of beauty, proportionate to my unknown resources, engendering of itself alone forms that give it satisfaction. I desire with my whole being . . . the powers assemble. The powers of the soul, as you know, come strangely up out of the nights. . . . By force of illusion they advance to the very borders of the real. I summon them, I adjure them by my silence. . . . Here they come, charged with clarity and with error. The true, the false shine equally in their eyes, on their diadems. They crush me with their gifts, they besiege me with their wings. . . . Phaedrus, here lies the peril. It is the most difficult thing in the world.[40]

We can see now how mathematical images are thought by Valéry to be composed—by a kind of natural, physical communication: These "mysterious and overbountiful favors," he says, "I must arrest them, O Phaedrus, and they must await my signal."[41] Having obtained them by a sort of interruption of his life, he still forces himself "to divide the indivisible and to temper and interrupt the very birth of Ideas."[42] What this yields is freedom, he says, freedom to do *Entwurf*.[43] Body and mind, this "finite and this infinite which we bring with us, each in accordance with his nature, must now unite in a well-ordered structure."[44] And if they work in concert, if they "interchange fitness and grace, beauty and lastingness, if they barter movements for lines and numbers for thoughts, they will then have discovered their true relationship, their act. . . . Stones and forces, outlines and masses, lights and shadows, artificial groupings, the illusions of perspective and the realities of gravity, all these are the object of their commerce."[45] *Entwurf* is about drawing up "the profile of this commerce" such that it captures in its externalization of such interiority—the interiority built up by linking analysis with ecstasy, without being able to say how—the richness of the architectonic act of contemplation as "incorruptible wealth," as the edification of a mathematical image.

With this, we have a context now to turn to René Descartes, in order to approach his text *Discourse on Method* from the angle of *Entwurf*. Descartes too was essentially concerned with a method that could establish a mediate relation between knowledge and the world.

René Descartes's *Entwurf* of the Method

It was not until 2013 that Descartes's text on method was published for the first time in its original context, which Descartes had written it for, in a German edition, translated, edited, and introduced by Christian Wohlers under the title *Entwurf der Methode*.[46] In it, this founding text of modern rationalism is presented with its complements by three so-called probes (*Essais*) that were to demonstrate what this proposed universal method is capable of accomplishing (how it can guide reason in the pursuit of scientific truth). The three *probes* (essays) were on dioptra, meteora, and geometry. The field of dioptra concerns sight *rendered* relative to optical instruments. That of meteora involves singular and unsteady weather phenomena like lightening or rainbows, earthquakes or meteorites. And geometry—well, geometry was usually—*more geometrico*—how methods are thought to work deductively, by proceeding from Euclidean axioms. Not so in Descartes; here geometry is treated algebraically. It acts as both—a field of science wherein "there are truths to be found" and the source of provision for deductive methods. It has often been highlighted that Descartes introduced an analytic employment of geometry, but its algebraic constitution (codification) has seldom been accentuated. Yet it is crucially important to see how in all three domains here, which are to act as exemplary probes to illustrate the workings of his universal method, his method follows and directs the codification of statements. In all three fields that Descartes chose, we are confronted with what could be called "edifices of codification" with respect to the natural laws at work within those fields. What is more: all three fields articulate and organize, explicitly so, the treatment of light. This would perhaps not appear so significant, if Descartes had not called the book, of which this was to be a miniature version in disguise, *The World*, by the subtitle of *A Treatise on Light*.

The Ethics of Its Discourse
(an Impredicative Method that Has "Nothing" to Teach)

What I will try to demonstrate is a reading of Descartes that understands the proposed method as a method for self-instruction in the service of intellectual craftsmanship.[47] It is a method that takes no object exterior to itself. Rather, the path it takes leads circularly back to the agency that makes use of it. It is a method that would not do its job if it were not used in a self-referential and self-informing manner. This expresses Descartes's concern with academic approaches to pedagogy that rely on a faculty psychology[48] and that "understand the imagination as an empty vessel to be filled."[49] Cartesian imagination is not an empty vessel; it is a plenum from which the right conduct of one's reason knows how to subtract what must be omitted—not by taboo, but by submission to the law at work in nature as a political withholding power. The fact that both texts, the *Discourse on Method* and *The World*, are written in the tone and form of an autobiographical fable, then, wants less to emphasize the subjective bias inherent to all methodical reason than to facilitate a methodical manner of setting free the capacity to imagine—so that it can move and quicken thought not by fancy, but objectively and reasonably so. In his recent book *Fable, Method, and Imagination in Descartes*, James Griffith elaborates: "The imagination necessarily remains, to some degree, distinct from the mind, which is why fables, histoires, dialogs, and so on can have the effect of deforming and reforming the mind at all."[50] An analytical method is preferable to Descartes over synthetical methods, Griffith rightly argues, because the latter requires that those who practice synthetic forms of reasoning can only come to a true conclusion if "they are already in possession of the substance of the conclusion."[51] It is important for Descartes to maintain that there be a universal architectonics, to set the imagination free from, first, its heavy-footed and immobile clumsiness (that comes from thought being naturally flooded by imagination, with no training in distinguishing between clarity and obscurity, and hence in keeping flashes of imagination at bay, while submitting to—concentrating, partitioning attention to—others), and, second, from any one particular notion of psychology that were to be legitimated in applying its dogma indisputably.[52] The power or the force of the imagination is to imagine the limits of the imagination, Griffith argues. For Descartes, the imagination imagines the imaginable in imagining the unimaginable.[53]

Is this not a reasoning that proceeds *subtractively*, by means of a *via negativa* quite similar to the one associated with the gesture of *Entwurf* that we saw with Massimo Cacciari? How would Cartesian rationalism present itself if we thought about his architectonics as universal and committed to just such a gesture of *Entwurf*—as feeling the pull of its (project's) throw? The pursuit of its method in the sciences would manifest in great variety of manners, and in multifarious ways—it would be capable of *rendering* demonstrations of the world in disjunctive regularities that nevertheless are to be respected as being of one (universal) kind. The imagination is the driving force for both fable and light, that which allows for experience and comprehension at all, Griffith elaborates. "The experience of light, the motion that generates and maintains motion in the world, is interpretable, and so the world itself is interpretable"—this is because the imagination can suppose the order of the world, of the body, to operate with a machine-like regularity. It is a regularity that the imagination "perceives"—via fabulation—through the sensory organs: "The fable is the inaugurating, regulated and regulating, motion of the mind that would imagine the world to have regularity,"[54] and fabulation depends upon architectonic ideation capable of imagining what Valéry calls "mathematical pictures." Descartes's book *The World* takes the form of a fable, but it needs to be regarded as a fable of objective and natural imagination because the way it is scripted and contemplated is mediated by the algebraic renderings of analytical geometry. There is method to such fabulation, and yet the fable is a rhetorical form. It has morals; it is biased and inclined in one direction or another. What Descartes develops, hence, is a strange thing: it is an impredicative method of a kind of quantitative contemplation. To our ears today this sounds like a contradiction in terms, but this is—if we read Descartes as living up to what the architectonic gesture of *Entwurf* entails—precisely what makes him such an architectonic thinker. The nature at stake with such a method for quantitative contemplation is its capacity to transcribe or convert *light into imagination and imagination into light*—without ever hoping to terminally settle the methodic equation for good. Doing the algebra in such a convertive equation (between light and imagination) articulates the terms in a codified manner. In Descartes's case, it is the cohabitation of the differently fashioned truth, each instance of universality but also inevitably subject to dogma in science. What the universal method facilitates is a practical dogmatics whose conflicting aspiration depends upon being sustained by an intellectual kind of craftsmanship. Could it be that Descartes's rationalism was in the service of how moral grounds can be respected and treated with the greatest possible adequacy, rather than establishing a program of normative clarification? Could it be that his rationalism can show us a way of respecting, in science too, the inevitably moral grounds—whereby a *practical* (not a theoretical) dogmatics can help to proceed with the greatest possible adequacy for the making of cases out of singular events?

At the risk of overstretching this point perhaps: Descartes seems to have been thinking of his method in terms of algebra, as a kind of physico-mathematical "communication." His *mathesis* involved an explicit awareness of the role of code in both language and mathematics. His "rationalism" seems to have not yet had broken with the ancient tradition that relates mathematics to learning, from the Greek *mathēma*, literally "that which is learnt."[55] What he "finds" in the sources from antiquity that he names for his own *universal method* (specifically Pappos and Diophant) requires acts of deciphering—it "cannot simply be read in the works of the mathematicians of antiquity."[56] It appears to have been through the *codification* of meaning, by placing meaning as the algebraic X in the place of the unknown variable, that we have to think of the mechanistic and instrumental manner of reasoning that his method began to propagate. Instruments then are not to replace the role of perception; they are to augment perception and to establish a publicness for knowledge so edified.[57] Descartes himself thought that the mathematicians in the past "must have made a kind of pact" to keep their true methods from their readers and from the world posterior to them.[58] Mathematics, for Descartes, involved an intellectual inwardness or relation to meaning, like dialectics does. His critique against the said "pact" of the mathematicians prior to his own time targets perhaps the occultist or hermetic gesture of building secret societies based on politically motivated and instituted "rites" of initiation.

Descartes, then, would appear like the propagator of an "open" science. This is the line this chapter wants to incite. For if this were so, how would Descartes have conceived of this "openness"? As a political terrain, I will argue.

Omitting "the True Nature of Light" from Scientific Description: Fabulating the *Plenum Spatium* for an Open World

The argument I wish to purse in the following is that Descartes was committed to a notion of openness. My proposal is that he was thinking of the encrypted content, which his universal method is to range over, through the framing of a codified exegesis, as a form of juridical dogmatics with respect to the natural laws at work in physics. What is spelled out within the reservations kept by brackets, in his algebraic method, is meaning fashioned by dogma; meaning accommodated in "settled opinion, a principle held as being firmly established."[59] What I wish to consider is both that and how Descartes's proposal is that of an architectonics of the world in the light of laws of nature—laws that are to contract the pursuit of science as a geophilosophical practice; science set apart (separated) from the culturally specific enactment of theological, religious, or political codes.

In the sixth chapter of *The Treatise on Light*, Descartes asks his readers to imagine a new world, "very easy to know, but nevertheless similar to ours," consisting of an indefinite space filled everywhere with "real, perfectly solid" matter, divisible "into as many parts and shapes as we can imagine."[60] Of this world, he postulates that "from the first instant of creation," God "causes some [parts] to start moving in one direction and others in another, some faster and others slower," and that, subsequently, "he causes them to continue moving thereafter in accordance with the ordinary laws of nature."[61] This imaginary world is Descartes's model for a physics that is common to all things and all beings for which there exists divine law (universal nature) and ordinary laws of nature (locally diverse, geographic conditions of natural law). Descartes is very conscious about the model character of his approach: he wants to begin with a description of light, he says, but he also tells us that he will omit something from this description, namely, the "true nature [*vray quelle est sa nature*] of light."[62] The omission of saying anything about the true nature of light is why Descartes speaks of a natural geometry, in distinction to reasoning helped by mechanical instruments. The "nature" that geometry measures is the "nature of light," which can never be described entirely adequately. Descriptions achieved by means of geometry always tell us about the order of the world—and not a supposed order of universal nature itself.

The new world Descartes is inviting his readers to imagine is a plenum, a notion Descartes takes from Aristotle for whom it meant a *plenum spatium*—a space exhaustingly filled with things. For Aristotle, it contrasted the notion of a vacuum, an empty and centrally coordinated space, in which all things are thought to find a place. In the tradition of philosophy, this pair of notions stands for the problem of action, of the origin of movement. It is, arguably, this problem that Descartes wants to treat physically, with his mechanistic rationalism that was to be independent of any one particular psychology (theory of the principle seat of animation, namely, the soul). Descartes wins such independence by liberating imagination from the accounts of it in faculty psychology. He treats the imagination like he treats the "true nature of light": he does not seek to explain them; he treats them cryptically and simply starts with their objective givenness. The abstract model of his plenum-vacuum distinction is considered as an algebraic model, a model which aims to consolidate the polarizing role of the vacuum (when admitted to play a role in science). For theological sensibilities, admitting the vacuum is scandalous because it admits to the possibility of God's rule being absent. But, in conflict with this, algebra—the work in modern metrical methods—introduced the symbolization of the zero as a placeholder for precisely this (the possibility of God's rule being absent, or "overruled," or otherwise relativized). The employment of the symbol zero in modern mathematics raised, almost inevitably, associations to the theological problem of the vacuum. Descartes admitted to the algebraic employment of the zero, but only virtually so: by saying that "God caused some [parts] to start moving in one direction and others in another, some faster and others slower," he introduced "cracks" into the indefinite space of the plenum. We should think of this imaginary world (the plenum) such that light, in its material *Stofflichkeit* (physics of light), keeps filling up ceaselessly these cracks, he tells us, such that there never is *actual* empty space. Such cyclical dynamics are well known from mechanical instruments, for the construction of which the location for an algebraic point zero—a virtual fulcrum—is decisive as well. With his mechanistic worldview, Descartes invented an architectonics of the world that can maintain that the true nature of the world is rule based (light, God's causation), but also rule generating (imagination objectively empowered and hence in moderate, proportionable, ways, through being constrained by optical devices, generating local geographies of "ordinary" laws).

The world Descartes is describing begins with light being there. It does not need any explanations as to where it came from or how it got there, but it also does not prevent theological speculations with respect to its origins. It abstains from wanting to say anything about creation. Descartes's natural philosophy breaks with the assumption that it should or could give comprehensive and exhaustive accounts of what is. It contents itself with its accounts being based on regularity and relative precision—and hence to reasonable and mechanically reproducible accounts. This world still finds comfort within a cosmos of universal law and nature, where the presence of God's rule is not put into question, but knowledge that belongs to the world (can be sought through science) must by necessity be knowledge dwelling in an element of doubt. *Method*, then, becomes something that allows one *to keep with doubt*, a state of mind that bears with being of split mind.

Method, then, does not *lead* us anywhere that could already be located on a map. And yet it delivers the one who follows it somewhere—into exposure of a self to openness.

Coda: Diachronicity, Politics, and Architectonic Constitutions

Descartes's universal method has nothing in particular to teach, I argued. Now we can better see why: because it allows to build the self of such self-instructive and autobiographical fabulation, in building the self that proceeds by it *subtractively* and *discretely*, on the grounds of architectonic ideation.

Walter Gropius, in what came to be the founding document of Bauhaus, writes: "The idea of today's world is already clearly in sight, yet its *Gestalt* is still unclear and confused."[63] The "old and dualist world picture, the self—counter to the All (universe)—is fading," he continues. In its stead, the idea of today's world bears "the thought of a novel world unity within itself," in which "all oppositional tension is in absolute balance." What Gropius spoke about was "a dawning understanding of unity of all things and appearances." It was this unity that, he thought, could lend "a common and profound *worth* to work (*Arbeit*)"—work that would manifest our universal innermost being. Bauhaus was inspired to think that the meaning of this work becomes self-referential thereby, as self and All (universe) no longer form a dualism; both are supposed to crystallize in "work" and manifest in what "work" is capable of producing. One hundred years later, this Bauhaus vision is painfully present in the now current discussion on the "postpolitical" condition.[64]

The notion of public space has always sought to address what is indispensable, indisposable, and at the same time, from an economic standpoint, unsalvageable. Indeed, it is the room for the stranger that turns a village into a city. It is also through such hospitality that the notion of the public can never rid itself from its ties to the sacred. Today, this latter aspect is not properly named and presents itself hidden in the themes of safety and pollution.[65] The current lines of interest in spatial culture discourses consume themselves in asking how public space could be thought of relationally, and this without it dissolving into urban space or lived space—that is, space conditioned by economy and particularist interest; space as itself but a product, one commodity to be socially produced along with all other commodities. The Bauhaus vision, viewed in today's light, confronts us with a connection to vanity inherent in its aspired universalism. If a project is underway today to found a New European Bauhaus, we must ask ourselves with this in mind—what does it mean to be European? Is the New European Bauhaus speaking about a "citizenship of the universe" as an aterritorial kind of citizenship? If so, how to prevent the complete depoliticization implicit in this formulation?

Cartesian rationalism is European in the sense that it is coined by a cultural setup that affirms its own struggle to keep with differences—a culture that lives from giving authority to inventive but reasonable systematics over any one particular and local tradition and custom.

European culture in this sense is a culture that admits to the necessity of change, without trivializing the metaphysical implications of this issue. The initiative of building a New European Bauhaus is timely today because, like in Descartes's own time, we are challenged with a similar setup that needs to affirm its own struggle to keep with difference in order to cultivate diversity. Here lies the crux: it cannot be about a universal citizenship; it is about a universal culture. How and what kind of "culture" can "grow" from the pursuit of rationalism along an impredicative universal method? It is here that we can truly see the importance of such a rationalism: because the explication of the *Entwurf* of method *contracts* responsibility without legitimizing its own validity. It makes subjects properly *nameable* (proper names, "proper" relative to contracted objectivity), and it makes objects *addressable* (somewhere within the spectrum between global and local, singularly relative to the contracted, named, subjectivity). In that sense, the rationalism of a universal method *constitutes* a publicness of space that is aterritorial, but geophilosophical. Common sense may well be what is given to start from,[66] but it is not per se in any proportion to a particular nature of the human or psychology of faculties. For Descartes, common sense is *therefore* given in the terms of a *physics*—a physics of light wherewith a plentiful imagination, that dwells in an element of doubt, is capable of learning-imagining the edification of reasonable intellection. This is what the world is all about, for the geophilosophy of a Cartesian rationalism. The subtractive education at stake in Descartes's universal method, is self-instructive education that serves the rendering of all the diverse dogmas of "common sense" back to a comprehensive dogmatics of universal culture—a dogmatics that lives in *practice*, not in theory. The equality at stake with Cartesian discourse-as-*Entwurf* needs to be actively sought for each situation where ordinariness gets into trouble. The equality at stake can never be settled; a sense of equality can never deem itself assured of itself; it needs to be actively and delicately maintained. We can see now how the importance of natural laws for Cartesian philosophy is perhaps precisely to *unsettle* any notion of justice or equality that would claim for itself to dwell in an element of righteousness. It is in this role that natural law can be an analytical "foundation" for civic law.

But where, then, does the generic cogito of such a rationalism "dwell"? To imagine this, in a way that was adequate—proportionate, in the sense of coefficient with—the effective abstractions at work in our science and technology today, as did Plato with the *Timeaus*, as did Descartes with his imaginary world as a plenum with cracks. Our time too needs to fabulate architectonic tales in metaphysical gesture. Mathematics thereby is not our enemy; it is our unobtrusive guide. Elias Zafiris, a mathematician and theoretical physicist, has recently written on the importance of what he calls "an involution for architects"—a turning outside-in, an inverse movement to that of evolution. What he has in mind thereby is a regaining of self-consciousness that leads out of the currently submissive and self-destructive relation architecture maintains with technology. This relation is arguably due to a separation between the liberal arts and the polytechnical disciplines (and their respective mentalities), which had been instituted throughout the eighteenth century. Contrary to what this division suggested, mathematical thinking is at work in both. Zafiris tells us how we can think of this. "The two most predominant characteristics of mathematical thinking [are] abstraction and diachronic validity," he emphasizes. He goes on to say: "By the former we understand a process of percolation, which allows the filtering out of all irrelevant details pertaining to a particular problem, so that the invariants are eventually revealed. It is precisely the latter that enunciate the diachronic validity of mathematical thinking."[67]

With this peculiar relation to time that only mathematics is capable of maintaining, the New European Bauhaus can act counter to the direction its former version ended up taking, namely, to fill up the world with goods and commodities drawn from inside (the self) out, delivered into the world. The New European Bauhaus would be about interiorization of All into the selves—to the effect of bringing about and caring again for something indisposable, unsalvageable but also indispensable, and thereby reinventing architectonic constitutions for a politics of universal culture.

Notes

1. Cf. https://europa.eu/new-european-bauhaus/index_en.

2. Michel Foucault's book on method, *The Archaeology of Knowledge and the Discourse on Language*, is one of the rare attempts to engage with Cartesian architectonics in its own right—that is, by neither subjecting him to a transcendentalist approach via Kantianism or phenomenology, nor by stripping his mathematical proposals from their metaphysical context by regarding him through the lens formalist epistemologies.

3. Valéry, *Introduction to the Method of Leonardo da Vinci*, 31.

4. Valéry, 31.

5. Valéry, 31.

6. Greek *dēmiourgos*, literally "public or skilled worker, worker for the people," from *dēmos* "common people" and *ergon* "work." See https://www.etymonline.com/search?q=demiurg.

7. McDonough, "Descartes' 'Optics.' "

8. This is why I call it "mechanical"; as a water mill must be informed by—but ultimately leaves aside—the question of the true nature of water, Descartes brackets out the question of the true nature of light for the descriptions that his rationalism is to facilitate.

9. Plato, *Timeaus*, 35b.

10. Plato, 35b.

11. Plato, 35b.

12. Valéry, *Introduction to the Method of Leonardo da Vinci*, 31.

13. Valéry, 31.

14. Valéry, 32.

15. Valéry, 32.

16. Valéry, 32.

17. Valéry, 32.

18. Cacciari, "The Project."

19. Cacciari, 123.

20. Valéry, *Introduction to the Method of Leonardo da Vinci*, 31.

21. Valéry, "Eupalinos or the Architect," 66–67.

22. Valéry, 66–67.

23. As Phaedrus recounts the words of Eupalinos. Valéry, 86–87.

24. Valéry, 67.

25. Valéry, 70.

26. Valéry, 82.

27. Valéry, 70.

28. Valéry, 79.

29. The architect's relation to truth appears in the first part of Valéry's text to be quite different from that of words, of which the philosopher is in command; yet this contrast transforms later on in the text. For reasons of length, I do not elaborate further here.

30. Valéry, 90.

31. Valéry, 90.

32. Valéry, 90.

33. Valéry, 90.

34. Valéry, 85–86.

35. Valéry, 86.

36. Valéry, 89.

37. Valéry, 91.

38. Valéry, 91–92.

39. Valéry, 87.

40. Valéry, 88.

41. Valéry, 88.

42. Valéry, 88.

43. Valéry, 88.

44. Valéry, 86.

45. Valéry, 91.

46. Descartes, *Entwurf der Methode*.

47. Griffith, *Fable, Method, and Imagination in Descartes*.

48. *The Great French Encyclopedia*, by d'Alembert and Diderot, famously organized all its entries according to such three faculties of the human mind, namely *memoire* (memory), *raison* (reason), and *imagination* (imagination).

49. Griffith, *Fable, Method, and Imagination in Descartes*, 137.

50. Griffith, 147.

51. Griffith, 129.

52. This very conflict with respect to a perfect regularity that would set a soul in motion, hence a notion of measurable beauty, is being elaborated in Paul Valéry, "Dance and the Soul," although no reference is made by Valéry to Descartes.

53. Griffith, 145.

54. Griffith, 145.

55. From *manthanein*, "to learn."

56. Wohler, "Einleitung."

57. This resonates also with the reading that Simone Weil gives of Descartes in her thesis "Science and Perception in Descartes."

58. Wohler, "Einleitung," xi.

59. From Latin *dogma*, "philosophical tenet," from Greek *dogma* for "opinion, tenet," literally "that which one thinks is true."

60. McDonough.

61. McDonough.

62. Griffith, 138.

63. Gropius, *Idee und Aufbau des Staatlichen Bauhauses*, here my own translation.

64. E.g., Mouffe, *On the Political*.

65. Douglas, *Purity and Danger*.

66. As Descartes begins his "Discourse on Method"; some translations work with "good sense" others with "common sense"; the French original is "*bon sense*," the German translation is usually "*gesunder Menschenverstand*."

67. Zafiris, *Mathematical Thinking*.

Bibliography

Cacciari, Massimo. "The Project." In *The Unpolitical, On the Radical Critique of Political Reason*, translated by Massimo Verdicchio, 122–45. New York: Fordham University Press, 2009.

Douglas, Mary. *Purity and Danger. An Analysis of Concepts of Pollution and Taboo.* New York: Routledge, 1966.

Foucault, Michel. *The Archaeology of Knowledge and the Discourse on Language.* Translated by A. M. Sheridan Smith. New York: Pantheon Books, 1972.

Griffith, James. *Fable, Method, and Imagination in Descartes.* London: Palgrave Macmillan, 2018.

Gropius, Walter. *Idee und Aufbau des Staatlichen Bauhauses.* München: Bauhausverlag, 1923.

McDonough, Geoffrey. "Descartes' 'Optics.'" In *The Cambridge Descartes Lexicon*, edited by Larry Nola. Cambridge: Cambridge University Press, 2015. https://scholar.harvard.edu/files/mcdonough/files/30_descartes_optics_the_cambridge_descartes_lexicon.pdf.

Mouffe, Chantal. *On the Political.* Abingdon: Routledge, 2005.

Plato, *Timeaus.* Translated by Benjamin Howett. Project Gutenberg Ebook, 2008.

Serres, Michel. *Musique.* Paris: Editions le Pommier, 2011.

Valéry, Paul. "Dance and the Soul." In *Dialogues*, translated by William McCausland Stewart. Princeton, 27–64. New Jersey: Princeton University Press, 1989.

Valéry, Paul. "Eupalinos or the Architect." In *Dialogues*, translated by William McCausland Stewart, 65–152. Princeton, New Jersey: Princeton University Press, 1989.

Valéry, Paul. *Introduction to the Method of Leonardo da Vinci*. Translated by Thomas McGreevy. London: John Rodker, 1929.

Weil, Simone. "Science and Perception in Descartes." In *Formative Writings 1929–1941*, edited and translated by Dorothy Tuck McFarland and Wilhelmina Van Ness, 21–88. London: Routledge, 2009.

Wohler, Christian. "Einleitung." In *Entwurf der Methode: Mit der Dioptrik, den Meteoren und der Geometrie*, by René Descartes, translated by Ch. Wohler. Leipzig: Felix Meiner Verlag, 2013.

Zafiris, Elias. *Mathematical Thinking: An Involution for Architects*. Vienna: TU Academic Press, 2022.

3

Europe as the Crisis of Play

Frank Chouraqui

In this chapter, I try to introduce one hypothesis about the essence of European modernity, namely, that it should be defined as the cultural invention of seriousness. I begin by examining one of the things that we take to be raising questions about the very essence of Modern Europe, namely, the current refugee crisis and its effects on European societies and institutions. I suggest that what this crisis indicates, as it were negatively, is that Europe is to be defined as a social, historical, and existential compound informed by a tension between care and action. I continue by examining the relations between Europe so defined and the more traditional Nietzschean idea of Europe as nihilism. This allows me to make the initial suggestion more palatable as well as to analyze the implications of the tension between care and action in ontological terms. Finally, I suggest that the resulting notion of Europe is most consonant with one offhand remark from Johan Huizinga's *Homo Ludens* (1938), where he seems to define European modernity as the dismantlement of play. I conclude that the examination of the refugee crisis and nihilism, on the one hand, and of play, on the other, reflect fruitfully on each other. All of this, it goes without saying, is highly speculative and programmatic.

Crises indicate essences: in any crisis worthy of the name, what is at stake for the entity facing the crisis is nothing short of itself. To say that something is in crisis is to say that its essence is at stake. If its essence isn't already known, as is the case for Europe, the crisis has the potential to reveal it to itself and to us. Conversely, the "What is?" questions that are so dear to philosophers always carry within them the critical question: What would it take to make X lose their essence? "What is X?" is therefore also always "What would count as a crisis for X"? It seems widely agreed that Europe is currently facing one such crisis. Talk of "the crisis of Europe" is recurring and pervasive in public discourse. Let us assume that there is some truth to this anxious refrain. If so, such a moment of crisis is bound to offer an opportunity to uncover something essential about Europe, and I shall follow this clue.

The Refugee Crisis as a Clue to the Essence of Europe

Let me begin with a quick account of what we might call the "crisis of Europe." My purpose here is to set up this account in a way that is intuitive and that can be easily related to the less intuitive thesis according to which the European culture is a culture of seriousness. Although it is difficult to generalize on such global events and their complex implications (including the role of other factors, such as the distrust of the elites, guilt for environment devastation, and the rise of new media), it seems acceptable to understand the phrase "crisis of Europe" as referring (among others) to two problematic responses to one current event, which is the refugee crisis.[1] Europeans and their institutions are facing a reckoning with their collective guilt of the past (associated with colonialism, racism, and sexism) and their current guilt before the human tragedy unfolding in the Mediterranean and elsewhere. Conversely, but relatedly, Europe is confronting a nativist, populist, and illiberal countermovement. The renewal of the traditional trope of "fortress Europe" for example seems to cover both these responses in one expression, and it brings out that they are in fact two sides of the same coin: a walled-up (populistic) entity confronted to a tide of external interference, and responding to it with the indifference of the stones.[2]

It seems quite well accepted therefore that the refugee crisis represents a double challenge for Europe. The first is an existential challenge that generates a reserve of political energy currently tapped by populist movements. The second challenge is moral: the refugee crisis confronts Europe and the Europeans with their own sense of guilt, and responsibility, both current and past. Under our watch, sometimes as a result of active efforts on the part of entities that Europe cannot disown without losing its own sense of self (specific states, border police units, legal systems etc.), innocent people suffer and die tragically, on an industrial scale. If this sense of guilt and outrage is to count as a crisis of Europe, however, we must suppose that Europe's essence is bound up with a moral project. In short, it seems we feel like there is a significant sense in which it is Europe that refuses to let refugees drown in the sea *and* that it is Europe still that allows them to drown. There is also a strong sense in which Europe cannot do this morally bankrupt entity and still be Europe. As a source of crisis for Europe, the refugee tragedy means: Is Europe still Europe when it drowns children under red tape and politicking?

It seems to me that at the intuitive level, the experience of this crisis of Europe is to be understood as an existential situation that affects European people, peoples, nations, and institutions. The question is not so much what populism and the refugee crisis *are* (something best left to sociologists and political scientists), but what is the kind of sensibility that is informed by our experience of this double crisis and that informs them in return (for example, what kind of ambient sensibility needs to be presupposed in order to explain how migration triggers populism). So, we need to ask ourselves why the refugee crisis and the populist wave are experienced in Europe as a crisis *of* Europe.

If we are to regard the refugee situation in the Mediterranean as well as the populist wave as converging into a crisis of Europe, we also have to regard them as aspects of one unique crisis. After all, it is only if we believe that populism is problematic that we regard the refugee crisis as a source of guilt: it is, after all, populism that keeps us from rescuing our brethren. Those who regard the moral crisis of Europe as a crisis of the European identity do so because it threatens the values of brotherhood without which Europe is not itself. Conversely, from the perspective of a supporter of the populist wave, the crisis is a crisis of an identity that is threatened: for the nativist, the expression "refugee crisis" refers not to a humanitarian disaster, but to the perceived threat represented by the newcomers. Let us therefore think of the crisis of Europe as neither the refugee nor the populist crisis, nor of them as two different crises. But rather, let us consider that the crisis that has Europe as its stake is unified and possesses two expressions. Both these expressions are to do with the relation that Europe entertains with non-Europe. In its relation with non-Europe, its "other" if you will, Europe is caught within the impossible alternative between indifference and guilt. If, as I suggested at the beginning, crises indicate essences, and assuming that we are indeed before a crisis of Europe, then the clue that the crisis provides is this: Europe is this that at once essentially collapses into the alternative of indifference (populism) and guilt (for our treatment of refugees) *and* becomes impossible once this alternative becomes institutionalized. Here is the question that needs addressing therefore: What sort of thing is Europe so that it is rendered impossible by the irreconcilability of guilt and indifference?

Posed in this way, the question remains too abstract. Let me try to spell out more concretely what this alternative of guilt and indifference entails and whether it can be reduced to one single factor. I will consider indifference as the excess of our ability to act over our ability to care, and guilt, conversely, as the excess of our ability to care over our ability to act. After all, indifference is the refusal to respond when you are able to respond, and similarly, guilt is the feeling that one doesn't do what one knows themselves to have the duty to do.

This is not as strange as it looks; indeed, this is an intuition that has been expressed at the level of mass culture by Angela Merkel's famous "wir schaffen das" as well as by the many in Europe who took Merkel's framing of the issue as successfully capturing the stakes of the moment in the context of public discourse. Merkel's expression seems to address directly the question of the mismatch of care and action, and the context of this famous remark was saturated with a pragmatic discussion of potential and ability for action. On August 31, 2015, she declared that "the motive with which we approach these matters must be: we have already managed so much, we'll manage this." Her message was this: We have the means to act in accordance with what we care about, if only we could find the will to. "I put it simply, Germany is a strong country."[3] It was, in Merkel's characteristic fashion, a precise and sharp appeal to matching care with action.[4] The effect of her intervention was to point out that more action was possible toward achieving a fit between our care to save those drowning in the sea (an urge for solidarity that she unquestioningly attributed to the German people) and our capacity to act.

So, it seems that characterizing the refugee crisis as this that poses the question of Europe's inability to match care and action is not so far-fetched after all. When expressed by one of the most distinctively European leaders, it seems to hit the nail on the head. Europe is this that is essentially embroiled in the mismatch of care and action, and the job of a leader in Europe, like Merkel, is to restore this match. But where does this mismatch come from and why should we see it as specific to Europe? I will have to stay content to address the latter question by merely pointing out that this is a view very close to a number of traditionally accepted notions of Europe, in particular, the Nietzschean idea that there is something specifically European about (a certain kind of) nihilism. This question will establish the focus of the rest of the chapter. I will argue with reference to Johan Huizinga that the fundamental "thing" that leads Europe to the tension between care and action is a certain preexisting historical process of dismantlement of the experience of play that is specifically European.

European Nihilism

Let me begin by explaining what I mean by the mismatch of care and action in the context of the affinity of Europe with nihilism. It will allow me to support my claim that the mismatch is a phenomenon unified enough to be used to define European modernity. The key here is to establish that nihilism is at heart a fetishistic theory of care. For the nihilist, to care for X (say, human rights) is to believe that there is an object (a "fetish") that mandates and justifies our caring for X. I call this a "fetishistic" view because it shares two key features with the fetishism described by anthropologists and psychoanalysts.[5] The first is the metaethical view that values (which determine care worthiness) are derived from objects, and the second is the metaphysical view that some objects (i.e., fetishes) carry within them their own value, that they are self-justifying. Pietz calls these fetishes "value-objects."[6] This is why fetishes are contradictory objects. They are both independent from the world within which care takes place (our world), and yet they place demands upon it, and therefore depend on what takes place in this world for their satisfaction. Like a fetish, this "thing" (Nietzsche sometimes calls it "god") is both in-itself and for-us. This fetishistic view of care worthiness, which subjects care worthiness to the objective realm, is opposed to the immanent notion of care, according to which care worthiness is constituted not by a reference to an object and its existence, but by the caring itself (You will note that in the latter case, we have a constitutive match between caring and the reasons to care). As I shall discuss below, this immanent view is best exemplified by the paradigm case of play.

The fetishistic view of care implies a web of justification that obeys a certain logic of truth: to care for X (say, human rights again) implies that we believe that Y (the fetish, say, "nature as reason") exists, that it mandates our caring for X, and that the function of thinking is to retrieve the truths about Y. I call this a logic of truth because it is a logic in which care about human rights (which belongs broadly to the realm of the "ought") is justified by the truth about nature as reason (in the realm of the "is"). I should care about human rights because it is true that nature is reason. To care for human rights in this context means to believe that there is a fact about nature to the effect that human rights are to be cared for. In short, it is to regard the *meaning* and *value* of human rights as dependent on the *fact* of nature. This leads us to an important metaphysical decision, a decision about what meaning is. In this nihilistic view, meaning is this that is *retrieved* by interpretation. Because it is retrieved, it is expected that the meaning of the object of care is independent from its retrieval that succeeds it, and whose standard of success are to be found in the presumed correspondence with the meaning intrinsically contained in the thing. In other words, nihilism is premised on the idea that there is such a thing as meaning-in-itself. The meaning of X is the truth maker of an interpretation, not its *result*. Interpretation *reveals* a certain characteristic of X but—God forbid—it doesn't perform any meaning-*attribution*. Nihilism outlaws meaning attribution and replaces it with blind objectivism. For Nietzsche indeed, nihilism is defined by the thesis that meaning is *found* rather than *made*.[7] We can see why Nietzsche calls nihilism an excess of seriousness. It sees seriousness not as a characteristic of one's subjective attitude, but as something about the object taken seriously. To take X (say human rights) seriously is to *believe it to be the case* that X is objectively serious, and beliefs are about facts and truths.

All of this suggests that nihilism relies on the thesis that the hermeneutic realm should be subjected to the epistemic realm. Let me explain. The hermeneutic realm deals with interpretations and meanings. The core aim of hermeneutics is understanding. The epistemic realm deals with knowledge and truth. Its core aim is knowledge. As Nietzsche indicates often,[8] these are profoundly divergent concerns that carry with them entirely different worldviews. The hermeneutic view presupposes that there is meaning, whereas the epistemic view places this presupposition in abeyance. There is meaning only if there is something objectively real that undergirds meaning. This epistemic approach involves a displacement of the notion of meaning. It cannot be doubted however, that there is meaning in a weak sense: that some things mean something to us sometimes. This is the starting point of the hermeneutic approach: in interpretation, institution (or meaning-attribution), and recognition (or meaning discovery) are one thing. There is some minimal experience of meaning, therefore. And the epistemic approach cannot deny this sort of meaning. If it is to question whether there is meaning at all, it must change the notion of meaning altogether, to subject it to truth requirements. It must assume that there is no meaning if there is no objective source for this meaning and disqualify even this minimal notion of meaning, by cashing it out as "the false belief that so-and-so meant something." It only exposes itself to the easy objection to the effect that having a belief, even a false belief, about something, is already grasping this thing as meaning. Under the epistemic approach, therefore, the question becomes: Is the meaning we experience true? You will note that this involves a commitment to an objectivist notion of meaning that is momentous. Namely, it takes for granted that (1) one can be wrong about meaning, (2) that there are objective standards for the correctness of meaning, (3) that the sort of correctness appropriate to meaning is identical to the sort of correctness appropriate to truth, and in particular (4) that the binary logic whereby everything that is not true is false can be applied to the realm of meaning: that things are either meaningful or meaningless. It is easy to see how this leads to nihilism in several of the senses used by Nietzsche[9] and the tradition that follows him. In particular, the epistemic view seems to underpin nihilism as

- the view that nothing has meaning (for indeed, nothing is meaningful enough to resist the charge of meaninglessness),

- the view that there is no meaning in life or that life is not worth living (after the death of God that is, since God stands for all fetishes),

- the view that all meaning should be abandoned as illegitimate,

- the view, which Nietzsche mischievously draws from the traditional third-man argument, that there is no meaning at all, unless we commit to fetishism. For only the fetishistic view that some objects are both value and value justifying can escape the objection to the effect that the objectivism of nihilism involves an infinite regress: if meaning can only be grounded by an external entity that is its source, but by the same token, this very entity cannot ground its own meaning, resulting in an infinite regress.

In order to measure the stake of this hostile takeover of the hermeneutic logic by the epistemic logic (Nietzsche calls this moment the "slave revolt in morality"), one could point to very concrete examples of everyday life. In our engagement with fiction for example, meaning (and one of its varieties, care) is experienced without any reference to truth. This is famously dramatized in some strands of contemporary philosophy as the so-called "paradox of the emotional response to fiction."[10] The existence of this paradox, where it is asked how we can feel real emotions about fictional characters that we know to be unreal, is directly related to the epistemic assumption that meaning cannot exist without a truth to support it. Without this premise, there would be no paradox. But this premise stands or falls with fetishism. And this is not just a matter of the phenomenon of fiction either. We find a similar structure at the heart of the phenomenon of play as a realm in which commitment, the attribution of importance, and the investment of care are entirely unrelated to any objective source of meaning, yet, unquestionable.[11] One could make the same argument about myth and love and several other important phenomena of everyday life. What the epistemic logic of truth does with the hermeneutic logic of meaning is that it replaces its immanent self-referentiality with the transcendent referentiality to an object. As a result, the standard for care has moved from self-grounding to objective grounding. Denouncing this shift is, broadly speaking, the project of the hermeneutic critique of modernity.

Thus, considering nihilism in the context of care allows me to tie my suggestion that Europe is defined by a mismatch of care and action to a more commonly accepted notion of Europe as nihilistic. In the canonical case of Nietzsche's analysis of European nihilism, for example, we see nihilism as resulting from the combination of the epistemic thesis (whereby caring is only made legitimate by objectivity) and the thesis of the death of God (who stands for all possible such legitimizing objects or fetishes) (Chouraqui, 2022). One of the consequences of this combination, Nietzsche asserts, is a certain state of existential funk: The nihilistic subject is stuck before the necessity to care (imposed by the mere fact of being alive, for the will to power is Nietzsche says, care or "interest") and the impossibility to act, for acting is no longer objectively warranted. Indeed, in the context of nihilism, indifference as well as action are prescribed at once.[12] This double bind results in either blind action or blind indifference.[13] Nietzsche therefore moves on to observing that nihilism produces two attitudes: "active nihilism," which acts without care, and "passive nihilism," which cares without acting.

Let's sum up. So far, we have zeroed in on the idea of Europe as a mismatch between care and action. I tried to flesh out this idea with reference to European nihilism as the subjection of the hermeneutic to the epistemic. This leaves us with four questions.

1. A metaphysical question: How can we draw a unified essence of Europe from a phenomenon here described as a mismatch between two things (care and action) and there described as the subjection of one (the hermeneutic) to the other (the epistemic)? If Europe is a certain relation (of mismatch or of subjection), how can it be one thing?

2. The second is genealogical: How did this situation come about?

3. The third is axiological: What is wrong with such a mismatch?

4. Finally, we have an empirical question: Why call this mismatch Europe?

As one might expect, those four questions have one single answer. For it is to be expected in answer to 1 that the situation we now call Europe, which is best defined as a relation and not a thing, came about as the distortion of a single and unified ground; in answer to 2 that this ground itself contained the dynamic potential required for its own dismemberment; in answer to 3 that this dismemberment, although an authentic potentiality of the basic ground, constitutes a misrepresentation of it (if by "misrepresentation" we simply mean an unworkable interpretation) and therefore, in answer to 4 that there are two answers. First, that this dismemberment, because it was possible but not necessary, came about for a set of contingent reasons one may justifiably associate with the sociohistorical entity we call Europe. Second, that this dismemberment, as we shall see, is identical with the dismemberment of care and action. In short, we are looking for a certain unified ground that, in the contingent circumstances called Europe, would engage in its own self-dismemberment in such a way that this dismemberment might correspond to the mismatch of care and action. I will argue that this basic ground is called "play."

Europe as the Graveyard of Play

This set of questions delineates a context in which one intriguing thought from Johan Huizinga seems to find its place. Talking about the civilization of modern Europe, Huizinga writes: "In the development [of civilization] we must not think of seriousness degenerating into play or of play rising to the level of seriousness. It is rather that civilization gradually brings about a certain division between two modes of mental life which we distinguish as playfulness and seriousness respectively, but which originally formed a continuous mental medium wherein that civilization arose."[14] We, with our interest in distilling the essence of Europe, have reason to be intrigued by this thought. After all, Huizinga, a specialist of medieval Europe, who was writing in 1938, is also concerned about a certain crisis of Europe (one that bears many similarities to our own). His concern was with a crisis constituted by "a society rapidly goose-stepping into helotry."[15] Additionally, Huizinga, as a historian, seemed to be led to such abstract conclusions not because he was carried away by the bad habits of his trade (something that would be a reasonable suspicion, had he been a philosopher), but *in spite* of his discipline's mistrust of grand conceptual constructions. Something seems to have imposed itself on him. After the cue provided by the quick analysis of the refugee crisis, let us take Huizinga's thought as an additional clue to the definition of Europe, or at least of the very Europe that is now, once again, in crisis.

So, it looks like "the play-element" in Huizinga's sense is a good candidate for the basic unitarian phenomenon we are seeking and therefore that the events covered by this epoch called modernity can be interpreted in terms of the internal dynamics that take place in play. But this leaves us with the question of the relations between play and the dynamic of care and action that has occupied us so far. I will try to clarify this relation by looking more closely at Huizinga's sketch of a phenomenology of play.

What would this clue suggest? First, we note that what Huizinga calls "the play-element" is precisely that unitary and primary "mental continuum" which we are seeking. Second, that the civilizing process should be regarded as a process in which this unitary phenomenon was broken up, and its components became extricated from each other and neatly distributed around a binary opposition. Third, that these two components should be called "puerilism"[16] and seriousness. Fourth, that European history is not only the process by which Europe as we know it came about, but it is at the same time and for the same reasons the process by which the separation of puerility and seriousness became stabilized and institutionalized. Huizinga gives examples of this institutionalization in war, in the arts, and in politics among other domains of culture. For these fields and others, the civilizing process cum-dismemberment of play made them less and less structured by rules (which accommodate playfulness alongside seriousness) and more and more by references to objective truth and goodness (which demands that seriousness dominate playfulness).

Why Is Play Primary?

We must begin by asking what allows Huizinga to speak of play as a unity of opposites in the first place. Huizinga's hypothesis relies on the distinction between the "play-element" and "playfulness"[17] (he also says "puerilism").[18]

> According to our definition of play, puerilism [*puerilisme*] is to be distinguished from playfulness. A child playing is not puerile in the pejorative sense we mean here. And if our modern puerilism were genuine play we ought to see civilization returning to the great archaic forms of recreation where ritual, style and dignity are in perfect unison. The spectacle of a society rapidly goose-stepping into helotry is, for some, the dawn of the millennium. We believe them to be in error.[19]

The play-element cannot be reduced to "puerilism" because play cannot take place in the spirit of puerilism alone. This is illustrated by Huizinga's analysis of the spoilsport. The spoilsport is a player who is too aware that the game is *only* a game. They, for this reason, cease to play and undermine the game for others and themselves. Too much playfulness, Huizinga concludes, prevents play from taking place. Proper play therefore *matches* puerilism with seriousness: a certain commitment to the game, which limits and organizes puerilism (sometimes this is figured by rules, but more generally, we should think of any behavior that allows the game to go on). Of course, the element of seriousness (*Ernst*) alone is insufficient too, because if not supplemented by the spirit of playfulness, it will—just like its opposite, the spoilsport—refuse to engage in play at all until a good justification for it is proposed. Play can die two deaths: from too much playfulness or too much seriousness equally.

This suggests three things. First, play proper is best understood without reference to any dichotomy between seriousness and frivolity. Second, in play, we experience restricted seriousness and restricted playfulness (they are restricted by each other). Third, Huizinga makes an extra move: Seriousness and playfulness as they appear in play, that is, as restricted by each other, are not *a certain kind* of seriousness and playfulness or *a certain kind* of experience of play or of seriousness. They are *the paradigm* and genealogical archetype for all subsequent forms of playfulness and seriousness. Play is a basic element, and it cannot be reduced to any other element. This genealogical precedence of seriousness as we encounter it in play over seriousness as we encounter it in our modern, nihilistic times, is made explicit by Huizinga: "You can deny seriousness but not play."[20] There are expressions in Huizinga that make the same point about puerility, although he takes the latter point to be more self-evident. A final point therefore is that seriousness unrestricted by puerilism is a distortion of its own source, which is the kind of seriousness that we find in play. There lies Huizinga's basic analysis of modern fetishism, one that is strikingly parallel to Nietzsche's. The spirit of seriousness involves a category mistake because it seeks to ground seriousness into an objective fact whereas seriousness can only ever come from a decision to play which eschews the question of justification. Playing is neither justified nor unjustified, it precedes the question of justification.

Why Is Play Self-Dismantling?

If play is a unitary and primary "ground," we must assume that it grounds something. When we experience play, we experience this unity of puerility and seriousness, but we also experience seriousness and puerility as potentially distinguishable. There is, according to Huizinga, a spontaneous dynamic at work within the element of play, and this dynamic can be considered as the initial intimation of their potential separation. Indeed, despite its primary unity, any instance of play involves a certain preconceptual awareness of the distribution of seriousness and playfulness. Play studies are divided between those who hold that the notion of rules is essential to that of play and those who reserve rules for a certain kind of games. If you are among the first, it will be easy to see how this distribution arises from within the experience of play. If play always has rules, these rules are precisely rules of division. They always at least serve to distinguish between the play world and the "real" world, and it is visible in this context that what is serious in play (for example "winning") is frivolous when considered from outside the game. The rules are to be taken seriously from the point of view of the game, playfully form the point of view of the nongame. This is the function of Huizinga's famous analysis of the magic circle, which is "magical" because it provides a unity of opposites, because it separates and maintains the continuity between the frivolous and the serious. Indeed, this notion of the magic circle (taken in its most minimal sense of the interface between play and nonplay) should accommodate even those play scholars who deny that all play involves rules and suffices to make the point at hand, that play always suggests its own separateness from the real world. In short, the play element that is the unity of frivolity and seriousness includes within itself the potential of leading into what it isn't: namely, the opposition of seriousness and playfulness. This division, in turn, is best understood as a distribution of the puerile and the serious along neat lines.

It is play therefore that is the genealogical source of the experiences of seriousness and playfulness. In the case of seriousness in particular, the insight that seriousness is born in play pushes in favor of the hermeneutic model and against the fetishistic model described above. It suggests that seriousness is a function of engagement, not of belief. It misunderstands itself by taking itself to be referring to a meaningless objective truth (meaningless because objective). The serious person forgets that seriousness is always undermined by its genealogical association with play, and the puerile forgets that nothing is fully puerile since there is no objective standard according to which puerility fails to be serious enough. Both overseriousness and puerility forget that our attitude is not to be indexed on any transcendent ground.

Why Does the Division Lead into Fetishism?

Here is a plausible reconstruction of Huizinga's intuition: Pure seriousness and pure frivolity (as we find them rampant in the streets of Europe today) are only pure because they both refer, in opposite ways, to an objective ground of justification. Certainly, seriousness is an appropriate response if the state of affairs in and of itself demands seriousness (what we called above fetishism). On the same grounds, nihilistic puerilism is an appropriate response when such a ground is lacking. You will note that both attitudes are premised on the same fetishism: the view that what justifies care is something objective. This is for similar reasons, for example, that Nietzsche regards Christianity as a nihilistic religion. Even the faithful are nihilists because they allow the value of the objects of their care to depend on a contingent fact: the existence of an external entity such as God. Their ability to care is therefore dependent on their ability to believe. The fact that Christians are not nihilists in the weaker sense (namely, in the sense that they happen to believe there is no such a guarantee of being) does not exempt them from the charge of deeper nihilism. Nietzsche's complaint is that fetishism makes the meaning of life much more vulnerable to the vagaries of history and knowledge than is necessary. Both puerilism and seriousness, therefore, are premised on fetishism. What is seriousness without play? The belief that seriousness is a feature of things (eventually of the thing that gives other things value). What is frivolity without seriousness? The life of the spoilsport, the collapse of meaning, indifference and a sort of *Clockwork Orange* frivolity.

Modernity as Derived from, Structured by, and Opposing Play

This leads us to the vision of European modernity put forward by Huizinga: modernity is the age in which the false separation of playfulness and seriousness has been consummated institutionally. It is an age where "the play-element in culture" has led to its own undoing; puerility and seriousness have lost their grip on each other, and play is dead by dismemberment. The result is unrestricted frivolity and unrestricted seriousness, both destructive. In addition, Huizinga gives some indications (expanded in his working notes) of the fact that he takes the malfunction of totalitarianism as a logical consequence of this dismemberment. Nazism, he declares, is to be defined as overseriousness (because of its romantic appeal to the race and a world mission) and overfrivolity (as is well known, Arendt will go on to define Nazi evil as "thoughtlessness"[21]), and only robust play can save us from it. What we find instead is frivolity: Munich (recall that Huizinga is writing in 1938). The structural wrongness of totalitarianism is therefore exposed as the result of an ontological fallacy: the belief that seriousness can exist without its opposite, that it can exist purely.

We now have a candidate for a process of dismemberment that we have reason to associate with Europe. But our earlier analysis of the refugee crisis included a further requirement: The dismemberment in question was to be separating care from action. In what sense can we say that the relations of care and action are at stake in the relations of seriousness and frivolity?

Let us return to the earlier point about the unified and primary character of the phenomenon of play. There, two points were made. The first, genealogical one, says that play teaches us what seriousness is. It is the genealogical precondition of the spirit of seriousness (now gone pathological in fetishism). It is also visible by contrast to the attitude of the spoilsport (who doesn't care because they do not believe the game to be serious enough) that what Huizinga regards as seriousness amounts to, or at least includes, what we have called "care" above. Play is the genealogical source of care. The second point, which relates to the analysis of dismemberment, suggests that play is defined as an exact match between care and action. After all, as I mentioned above, play can die one of two deaths: either through overseriousness or through puerility. But what does "dying" mean for play? Simply this, that no playing takes place. Play is identical with the match between care and action, and its dismemberment amounts exactly to the estrangement of care and action that, as I suggested hypothetically, defines Europe. In other words, with the death of play, those of us who remain active lose their ability for restraint and those of us who are passive lose their ability for action.

In terms of the four questions that we were left with at the end of the previous section, this suggests the following answers:

To question 1—If Europe is a certain relation, how can it be one thing?—we can answer that there are things, like play, that although a primary and unified ground, contain within themselves the dynamic of their own division. Call it a dialectic movement.

To question 2 —How did this situation come about? —we can answer that Huizinga's analysis of play suggests that play is the genealogical source of both our sense of seriousness and our sense of frivolity. In other words, if nihilism is precisely, as I argued above, the experience of the alternative between overseriousness and meaninglessness, its basic foundational cognitivist thesis is refuted by the genealogical argument. Seriousness always refers to play, it is the experience of play and nothing else which teaches us what seriousness is.

To question 3 —What is wrong with such a mismatch? —we can consequently answer that it relies on a previous fallacy: the illusion that seriousness can retain any meaning without its embedding in play. Above, I called this view "fetishism." The second fallacy, which involves the separate treatment of care and action, is a function of the previous, which involves the dismemberment of the unitarian ground of play. For if Huizinga is correct in regarding play as the foundational source of meaning, then it is certain that care is to emerge from within the act of play and only from there. In short, to act is to play, and to care is to play, and in play, care and action are always matched. The engagement with play involves by definition the match between care and action. Until the separation comes about and play dies by dismemberment.

To question 4—Why call this mismatch Europe? —I can only gesture at the analysis of the crisis of Europe I present in section 1 as well as the rest of Huizinga's *Homo Ludens* and as his *Waning of the Middle Ages*, which trace the circumstances of Western culture upon which their connection with the dismemberment of play is easy to reconstruct. This, I admit, constitutes only half of an adequate answer to this question, but I would point out that this is the important half. For it is enough to reduce the question to a mere problem of history, and one that we have reason to expect will bear fruit.

Conclusion

This leaves us with not one, but three formulations of the essence of Europe, and I need to put a bit of order into all of this. It is not a matter of reducing the three formulations of Europe to one, but rather to regard them as three different facets that have more or less relevance to different contexts. At the surface level, we have Europe as a mismatch of care and action, and the European soul caught between guilt and indifference. This, however, only tells us of our current condition. It doesn't address the question of whether this mismatch is profound enough to be *essential*. The second formulation, of Europe as nihilistic fetishism, makes a step in this direction mostly because it connects the first formulation to a more generally accepted notion of Europe as nihilism. According to fetishism, care is compelled to justify itself in objective terms. In this context, play can never justify care, and fetishism outlaws play. In other words, fetishism doesn't merely condition the dismantlement of play, but it necessitates it. Yet, this too leaves a question unanswered: Where does such fetishism come from? In order to address this question, we need to suppose the existence of a dynamic principle as a condition for this fetishistic drift. This is the principle Huizinga calls "the play-element": play is the necessary condition of fetishism for two reasons. First, it teaches us about seriousness, and second, it induces from within itself the distinction of seriousness and frivolity. In this context, I argue that Europe should be defined as the impossibility of play and, therefore, the European soul as the soul that oscillates between overseriousness and frivolity. I argue that this is exactly what the current crisis of Europe illustrates, and that consequently, we may take seriously the hypothesis that this crisis is indeed essential, and that therefore, the best definition of Europe is as the graveyard of play.

Notes

1. Bhambra, "The Current Crisis of Europe."
2. Castan Pinos, "Building Fortress Europe?"
3. The relevant parts of the speech make an explicit connection between the refugee crisis and the essence of Europe:

> Let me say this once more: Germany is a strong country. The approach that we must take to these affairs is this: we have already managed so much—We'll manage this! We'll manage this and the obstacles in our way will be overcome and will be worked out. The federal government will do everything in its power, together with the regions and the municipalities, to achieve this. [. . .] There is also the European dimension. And here I think that we must clearly say: Europe as a whole must take action. The states must take responsibility for sharing the refugees seeking asylum. The universal rights of the citizen are indissociably connected to Europe and its history. They are one of the basic impulses of the European Union. If Europe fails on the issue of refugees, then this connection between Europe and universal rights will be broken. It will be destroyed, and Europe will no longer be the Europe we envision, it will no longer live up to the basic myth we are pursuing.

Ich sage ganz einfach: Deutschland ist ein starkes Land. Das Motiv, mit dem wir an diese Dinge herangehen, muss sein: Wir haben so vieles geschafft—wir schaffen das! Wir schaffen das, und dort, wo uns etwas im Wege steht, muss es überwunden werden, muss daran gearbeitet werden. Der Bund wird alles in seiner Macht Stehende tun—zusammen mit den Ländern, zusammen mit den Kommunen -, um genau das durchzusetzen [. . .] Es gibt dann die europäische Dimension, und hier glaube ich, dass wir schon sagen dürfen: Europa als Ganzes muss sich bewegen. Die Staaten müssen die Verantwortung für asylbegehrende Flüchtlinge teilen. Die universellen Bürgerrechte waren bislang eng mit Europa und seiner Geschichte verbunden. Das ist einer der Gründungsimpulse der Europäischen Union. Versagt Europa in der Flüchtlingsfrage, geht diese enge Bindung mit den universellen Bürgerrechten kaputt. Sie wird zerstört, und es wird nicht das Europa sein, das wir uns vorstellen, und nicht das Europa sein, das wir als Gründungsmythos auch heute weiterentwickeln müssen.

For the full transcript of the speech of August 31, 2015, see https://www.bundesregierung.de/breg-de/aktuelles/pressekonferenzen/sommerpressekonferenz-von-bundeskanzlerin-merkel-848300.

4. Holzberg, "Wir schaffen das."

5. Pietz, "The Problem of the Fetish I."

6. Pietz, "The Problem of the Fetish IIIa," 109.

7. Chouraqui, "The Cognitivist Thesis of Nihilism."

8. Chouraqui, "The Cognitivist Thesis of Nihilism."

9. Paul van Tongeren, *Friedrich Nietzsche and European Nihilism*, provides the most expert and comprehensive coverage of the many senses of nihilism in Nietzsche.

10. Radford, "How Can We Be Moved by the Fate of Anna Karenina?"; Levinson, "Emotion in Response to Art."

11. Bogost, *Play Anything*.

12. Chouraqui, "The Duty of Violence."

13. Hegel, *Grundlinien der Rechtsphilosophie*, preface, section 5, and appendix.

14. Huizinga, *Homo Ludens: A Study of the Play-Element in Culture*, 111.

15. Huizinga, 207.

16. Huizinga, 207.

17. Huizinga, 111.

18. Huizinga, 207–10.

19. Huizinga, 207.

20. Huizinga, 3.

21. Arendt, *Eichmann in Jerusalem: Ein Bericht von der Banalität des Bösen*.

Bibliography

Arendt, Hannah. *Eichmann in Jerusalem: Ein Bericht von der Banalität des Bösen.* Translated by Brigitte Ganzow. Munich: Piper, 1989.

Bhambra, G. K. "The Current Crisis of Europe: Refugees, Colonialism, and the Limits of Cosmopolitanism." *European Law Journal* 23 (2017): 395–405.

Bogost, Ian. *Play Anything: The Pleasure of Limits, the Uses of Boredom, and the Secret of Games.* New York: Basic Books, 2016.

Castan Pinos, Jaume. "Building Fortress Europe? Schengen and the Cases of Ceuta and Melilla," Centre for International Border Research (CIBR)-WP18 (2009): 1–29.

Chouraqui, Frank. "The Cognitivist Thesis of Nihilism." *Tijdschrift voor Filosofie* 84, no. 1 (2022): 127–54.

Chouraqui, Frank. "The Duty of Violence." *Human Studies,* online first, November 10, 2021, https://doi.org/10.1007/s10746-021-09611-5.

Hegel, Georg Wilhelm Friedrich. *Grundlinien der Philosophie des Rechts.* Frankfurt am Main: Suhrkamp Verlag, 1986.

Holzberg Billy. " 'Wir schaffen das': Hope and Hospitality beyond the Humanitarian Border." *Journal of Sociology* 57, no. 3 (2021): 743–59.

Huizinga, Johan. *Homo Ludens: A Study of the Play-Element in Culture.* Kettering, OH: Angelico, 2016.

Levinson, Jerrold. "Emotion in Response to Art." In *Contemplating Art.* Oxford: Oxford University Press, 2006.

Merkel, Angela. *Speech of August 31st 2015.* https://www.bundesregierung.de/breg-de/aktuelles/pressekonferenzen/sommerpressekonferenz-von-bundeskanzlerin-merkel-848300, 2015.

Pietz, William. "The Problem of the Fetish I." *Res* 6 (1985): 5–17.

Pietz, William. "The Problem of the Fetish IIIa." *Res* 16 (1988): 105–24.

Radford, Colin. "How Can We Be Moved by the Fate of Anna Karenina?" *Proceedings of the Aristotelian Society, Supplementary Volumes* 49 (1975): 67–93.

van Tongeren, Paul. *Friedrich Nietzsche and European Nihilism.* Newcastle-upon-Tyne: Cambridge Scholars, 2018.

4

Of Ships and Palaces

Inverted Images of Europe in Crisis

RICCARDO M. VILLA

Image and Ocean

"Only on the ocean does the ship become the absolutely inverted image of the house."[1] Among the many icastic formulations on the relationship between "terrestrial" and "maritime existence" to be found in Carl Schmitt's works, this is certainly a lesser known one, but perhaps the most fitting to set the stage for the present essay's guiding question: How does Europe's "image" emerge as an autonomous entity, surpassing historical, analytical, and geopolitical definitions while retaining a connection to them? And how can such an image help us rethink the notion of crisis?

This quote belongs to a commentary that Schmitt writes in response to Ernst Jünger's *Der Gordische Knoten*; in Jünger's book, the antithesis between East and West is interpreted in the light of the "cut" of the mythic Gordian Knot, as something that is cut and, at the same time, continuously reweaves itself.[2] Europe is *at the center* of this antithesis, and not only geographically so. The "image" of Europe has an autonomous statute that goes beyond historical, analytical, or geopolitical definitions, while nevertheless keeping a connection with them. As we will see, this image comes close to the one of *crisis*, understood in all the amplitude of its etymological meaning (*krisis* is both a "cut" and a "judgement," something definitive and defining and, at the same time, something that breaks away from established grounds of evaluation—something that is "resolutive" as much as "absolute"). The image that is here proposed is therefore one of Europe *in crisis*, where crisis is the "state" of Europe, not just as a moment that Europe goes through, but as the architectonic emplacement of Europe itself, one in which history is—as we will see—determined as much as determining. Within the architectonics of crisis, Europe is here reimagined as a reimagining in itself.

Schmitt's formulation is of particular relevance as the notion of inverted image (*Gegenbild*) is assumed by the present essay as a paradigm, as a given model to investigate the overall question of Europe and of its reimagination. In the light of the "cut" and of crisis, Europe itself is a *Gegenbild*, something that, as an "image" (*Bild*) connects while at the same time profiling an inversion, an "against" (*Gegen*). Such a paradigm is nevertheless not an answer to that question and is rather enigmatic in itself. Far from trying to provide "solutions," these two enigmas—the one of the *Gegenbild* and the one of a European *reimagining*—will be pitched against each other, in order to look within this space of double reflection. Several interrogatives start then to flash in this in-between. What does it mean to reimagine Europe through such an inverted image, and how does such an inversion work? If the ship is the inverted image of the house, is then the house the inverted image of the ship? Or does this inversion perhaps go beyond a simple mirroring?

All these interrogatives call for the articulation of an underlying question concerning the possibility of (re)imagination in a time of *Bildverlust*, of image loss. *Only on the ocean* is the inversion fully accomplished, writes Schmitt. The ocean is thus the most absolute affirmation of that "maritime existence" first developed over the sea. In the latter, limited by coasts and harbors, a framing (a *nomos*) is still possible: the "terrestrial order"—one in which "every technical invention naturally falls into precise orders of life and is accepted and framed by them"[3]—eventually prevails even upon the sea. Such a terrestrial order can perhaps be compared to Hans Blumenberg's notion of *world image*, "the epitome of reality in and through which man understands himself, orients his evaluations and goals of action, grasps his possibilities and necessities and develops his essential needs."[4] Yet, Blumenberg argues, the present age is one of a *Weltbildverlust*, of a *loss* of world-images. After Descartes, Blumenberg maintains, the notion of world image has been replaced by the one of "world-model," that is, "the total conception of empirical reality that is dependent on the respective state of the natural sciences and takes into account the totality of their statements."[5] Such a *total* conception is nevertheless never graspable in its entirety; in other words, the world model cannot ever fully be represented in one image, although it can perhaps be accounted through a *picture*, understood as a particular snapshot or a calculated rendering of this general model. The task of philosophy is, according to Blumenberg, to prevent the "stabilization" of the model into an image, or into "specialistic languages" that would pretend to have "fulfilled their own exactness" within themselves. Philosophy must guard off science from saying "more than we can know": such an excess must be protected by being kept out of any image or language, since its "reserve" is what ultimately ensures scientific verification.[6] However, what Blumenberg seems to oversee is that the proximity gained through science and technics to the things of the world after the abrogation of images and of their role of mediation is compensated by another kind of distance, a "gigantic" yet *invisible* one that cannot ever be fully bridged.[7] Schmitt's ocean is itself an image of such an unbridgeable distance, of the loss of images as well as the loss for the possibility of conceiving of a totality. No framing is possible on its surface; its only boundary is the progressive (receding) and unreachable horizon.

Utopia and Project

Blumenberg's argument has the merit of showing how this condition has to be assumed as irrevocable, unless one is ready to refuse the present and to seek shelter in anachronistic worldviews. Yet, if the world has moved towards a "maritime existence," and if Europe, in its "movement" towards the West, largely promoted and contributed to this shift, how can anything be still conceived *as a whole*? How can it be reimagined? Rather than a rhetorical question, what this formulation outlines is a paradox that as such cannot be solved once and for all, but only expressed through further figurations. This paradox must turn into a quest for a limit image, a figure of the impossible, able to operate a reconciliation between terrestrial and maritime existence, a locus in which technical invention is "framed" and "falls naturally in the orders of life" while at the same time "appearing as a progress in the sense of an absolute value in itself."[8] Massimo Cacciari provided an image of such a paradox in his reading of *utopia* as the synthesis of the conflict between "absolute freedom" and the "will of state," a conciliation of the contrast between those two modes of existence described by Schmitt, in the direction of a political philosophy. "Separateness and totality dominate together in Utopia."[9] The *Entortung*, the separation from the land that the image of the ship on the ocean achieved as an inversion to the one of the house is here accustomed and accommodated in the wholeness of an image and of the framing that it provides. In Cacciari's rendition of utopia, Schmitt's maritime existence becomes an *inhabitable* condition, as everything still responds to an overarching order and is sheltered by it. Its insular character ensures its wholeness while at the same time showing how such a totality is produced out of a negative image of the sea.

Cacciari's understanding of utopia could then be considered as a sort of "terrestrialization" of the oceanic features outlined by Schmitt. But does this further inversion resolve itself in a full restoration of all the characters of the terran existence symbolized by the house, or is something left behind? Framed by the waters of the ocean, utopia produces indeed a negative image of it; as a state, it can only be conceived as completely isolated from the rest, whatever that "rest" might be. But—and here is the crux—in order to do so, it is forced to incorporate the character of what it excludes, to accept the "price" of its mediation. To be sacrificed in this transaction is the very notion of *image* as well as of *place*. Utopia does not correspond to a transcendent elsewhere, such as a heavenly city or a promised land, but is literally *nowhere*. As Cacciari remarks, the freedom of utopia fully belongs to "a process of secularization-rationalization."[10] What does step in after such a process has been fulfilled? What does take the place of the image, if not of the notion itself of place? Before attempting to answer the question, we cannot avoid marking the fact that such a "crisis" of image and place echoes the European struggle in reimagining itself, as well as in defining itself as a place with clear boundaries and sharp contours. To that extent, the process that Cacciari outlines is a fully European one.

It is not surprising that, in speaking of Europe, a recurrent term is neither *image* nor *place* but *project*. The project is what fills the "absence" left by the loss of the image and the nowhere of Utopia. "The project," Cacciari writes, "appears constitutively logocentric. Everything that is in the 'meanwhile' between its original word and the realization of its goal (*telos*) carries out a techno-instrumental function, a secondary function, a simple explication of the idea."[11] Imagination is here reduced to a functional process, and the image, to a mere explication. The space of images itself, the symbolic distance they preserve—what Cacciari defines as the *meanwhile*—is to be "liquidated" and operationalized into a linear process: "The ideal, in fact, would be the abolition of 'meanwhile,' the perfect coincidence between the point of the prefiguring-anticipating idea and the line that realizes it."[12]

What the shift to the project foregrounds is an understanding of thinking itself, and hence of reimagining, as a *work* (almost in a physical sense, as the translation of an oriented force into a directed linear displacement) or, in Cacciari's words, of production: "*Producing* and *project* are joint terms representing, in our language, a single family. The project is understood as intrinsically productive: it elaborates models of production."[13] This "elaboration of models" brings the notion of project closer to the side of Blumenberg's *Weltmodell*; however, the relation to a scientific and verifiable conception of empiric reality—thus the promise of a trustworthy, rational ground—starts somehow to be questioned, even if just indirectly. The *poiesis* that the project spells out is less concerned with being a veritable rendering of the absence or of the invisible it materializes and more interested in the *modes* and in the *codes* through which this bringing-into-presence operates: "In the project," Cacciari writes, "one is not limited to 'ideate' this presence; one also has to show with what means and in what ways presence is actually producible."[14] *Dictability*, or the ability of saying—as well as the one of picturing—is not just a boundary to be presided (as in Blumenberg), but acquires relevance and autonomy in itself. Hence the presence, in the project, of what Cacciari defines as a "grammatological perspective" transversal to the project's logocentrism. This perspective "sees in the contents of the project (in the projected) not the signifying of the original *logos*, mere image or figuration of its language, but *programs*, systems of conventional signs (*grammata*) endowed of intrinsic rationality, not external and instrumental films of the true word."[15] Under this light, the constructive (logocentric) power of the project appears to be hindered by its necessity to recur to a deconstructive (grammatological) functioning. "The project is transformed here, precisely, in a text of *programs*, an open system of conventional signs that explain their own reason only in their play of differences."[16] The last image, the one of utopia, is eventually sacrificed in the "sign" of the program.

This transformation is nevertheless not to be mistaken as a "failure" of the project, or as the overcoming of deconstruction over the project's metaphysical system. As a form of imagination on *becoming* this dissolution of project into programs is the *will* of the project, the "fate" of the term itself, as Cacciari calls it. In order to be foreseen and controlled (to be *projected*), becoming must be encrypted into cases by which chance can be objectified. "To define the project of chance entails necessarily a conception of becoming as delinearized pluridimensionality and its languages as systems of sign relative to one another."[17] The project must *necessarily* operate in the form of programs, but this "necessity" is set by the project itself, it is deliberated by its own *logos*. The programmatic determination of the project, its will and necessity to turn into program, is precisely what empowers it. "The project will be the more powerful the more programmatically analyzable and analyzed it is. If the project must have value, it can only have value according to this form."[18] The project *wants* its own deconstruction; in order to really be *pro-ject* it needs to break away from any symbolic understanding of the image, to be *critical* toward it. On this point, the resonance with Blumenberg is quite evident, as well as the overturning of his proposition. Cacciari's *project* fully absorbs the task that Blumenberg hoped to allot to philosophy as a way of preserving its role in the ecology of scientific specialisms.[19] As a form of foreseeing and control over becoming, the project secures the "reserve" of scientific verifiability—but it does so by "stabilizing" it into cases, thus by binding it to a more abstract notion of image. The "cut" becomes here merely operative and procedural, and no representativeness is associated to it. Within the project reimagining—and imagination itself—can only survive as an automatic translation of chance into an economy of cases to be managed and accounted for.[20]

Sign and Resolution

This notion of image is nevertheless a historically determined one, the notion of a "techno-scientific project," as Cacciari calls it. It would be nevertheless naïve to think of such a historical determination as only a face or a moment of an immutable diachronic structure. What the project shows above all is an irreducible mutual *influence* between what is determined and what is determining, as well as their mutual fundamental *estrangement*. The impasse of the project, its aporia, surfaces here under another light. Transcendental forms are not an a priori, but rather something that the project itself actively casts. Its secularizing power is the one of a *mathematics of history* that at the same time belongs to a *history of mathematics*.[21] It is caught in the "paradox of a unilateral synthesis,"[22] of a dictability (a power of saying) and of an expressivity that is always determining *as much* as it is determined. This "as much" is nevertheless not univocally quantifiable. It is not a quantity, but a *quantum.*[23] According to this paradox, quantity is always measured as a contingency, and any sort of necessity cannot be expressed at all, but only indexed *via negativa*, as a noncontingency (a quantum). This paradox excludes the possibility for any general theory of language, as well as for a "fundamental legality" of scientific discourse, as a legality can only be *positionally* constituted and can therefore only be contingent to the specific discourse it supports.[24]

The exclusion of any possibility of the image as representation, even just as a "system" of representations, cannot be more radical. Cacciari's "project" converges here with his work on Benjamin and on his conception of the *Name* as an essence *absolutely other* to language. "The pure symbolic character of the Name represents a statute of separation,"[25] Cacciari writes. Is then the Name another placeholder for what utopia stood for? If so, the name would still "share a border" with the ocean of technics; it would still be comprehended under the project of secularization. But the Name is completely *alien* to this; there is instead something rather "divine" about it. "The symbol is not 'a relation between appearance and essence'—but the very essence of the Name, as the coincidence of idea and thing, as the unity 'of the sensible and the supersensible object' as the unity 'of the sensible object and the supersensible one.' The symbol is a 'theological paradox.'"[26] There is thus a total coincidence (if not almost a transubstantiation) of idea and name; the name is in this sense symbol, a "throwing together" whose identity is not to be looked for outside of it (as in the allegory) but is perfectly *sealed* within, in a tautological manner. In the Name, the idea is not simply given or represented: it *gives* itself, it *represents* itself ("*si* da," "*si* rappresenta"), and it does so in an unintentional way. "The name is, at the same time, maximum closeness to the phenomenal and maximum abstraction: the being of the name is analogous to the pure and simple being of things, yet it is subtracted from any phenomenality. This depends on its immediate *giving itself.*"[27]

But what is then the relationship between Name and language? The absorption in the opacity of the Name of any possibility of nominalism *liberates* the space of language and the one of technics from logocentrism and from any quest for a systematic legitimization. "Having defined the tragic space of the Name as the *absolute* coincidence of idea and thing, extraneous to it, radically *other* than the statute that founds this coincidence, is precisely the space of the *sign*." There is almost an "antivicarious invariance" within the Name that seems to stand as the very condition of possibility for language as a vicarious or "allegoric" space. The Name is what cannot be replaced or substituted and is thus "condemned" to its "destiny." The Name resists any *translation*. Its domain is rather one of *transcription*, and yet it is precisely through the support of transcription that translation—between different languages and different signs—can take place. The "tragedy" of the Name is given not only by its absolute sealing in the symmetry of a tautology[28] but also in the possibility for a *catharsis*. It is only by constantly reacknowledging its opacity that the Name, as symbol, liberates and "purifies" the allegorical space of the sign. The acknowledgment of the absolute difference of the Name, of its tragedy, unchains the reserve from a secularized dominion over becoming; it casts it back into a symbolic domain. "The space of the allegorical is understood only *as alternative and by negation* with respect to the destiny of the symbol. The sign is what appears after this whole affair has been held in the inexpressible. But this *consumption* is therefore *determinant* for the appearance of the sign."[29] This space is, as already discussed in the context of the project, a *technical* space—in the sense of a space of techniques. It is the domain of languages, of different dictabilities, of modes of expression. The space of language, in Cacciari's reading of Benjamin, appears "as alternative and by negation" to the Name. As such, it is a space of the allegory. The identities that it expresses are always vicarious. They can never claim the divine fullness that the Name absorbs in its opaqueness, and they can therefore only *alla-agoreuein*; they can only speak of something else. But their very ability to speak springs precisely from the fact that they are *not* tautological, as this is instead "reserved" to the Name: their statute is the allegorical one of difference, of *crisis*.

Techniques and languages speak and produce in virtue of their "ontological difference." Thus, they are determined by their own crisis, by the unsurmountable difference between what can be spoken—here and now, as a *case*—and what is to be left unsaid.[30] The image of the ocean surfaces again. The space of unbridgeable distances is the domain in which technical invention is affirmed as an absolute value, in which the ship becomes the absolute *Gegenbild* of the house. "Only on the ocean" here means *only upon crisis*. Only upon the loss of a possibility of instituting an order or a balance and thus in the very limit imposed by this *non plus ultra* does the technical domain of the ship arise. In the light of crisis, the ocean represents the exhaustion of every possible analogy; its horizon is the one of entropy. The boundary of crisis is both *(en)tropic* and *mathematical*: no communication can be established beyond that, yet the *mathesis* of its techniques works precisely through a *troping* in the sense of an intransitive "consummation" as a "withholding" (into the unspeakable).[31] It follows that crisis is not just an "event" in the history of techniques but the very principle under which they have to be understood. "Crisis," Cacciari writes, "is not a *moment* that the development of techniques goes through, but their *immanent structure*."[32]

Cacciari's stress on the notion of crisis has to do with the fact that what matters is not an ontological classification between what can and what cannot be expressed (the unspeakable does not 'geometrically' determine what can be spoken of) but rather the very *conflict* (the crisis) between the two: "a conflict to reach the maximum of the *expressible*, to subtract the maximum of the overall idea of the oeuvre from the limits of representation, of language, of its game—to reduce the margin of consumption implicit in each statement, in each voice."[33] What this conflict foregrounds is then a sort of negotiation or of a "pact" that is also a "convention" as it directly deals with the limits (the codes) of its own expression. Techniques are therefore "utopian" in the sense outlined before. Their limit is not the one between territories but is the insular boundary of separation itself—as a conflict that provides the ground for the institution of conventions, of "peace treaties" within "the ocean of the Name-less." The image of Europe that emerges from this ocean is, once again, not one of finite boundaries or clear figures; it is a critical image and, at the same time, an image of crisis.

This conventional character implies that the techniques and the languages that crisis produces are not necessary solutions to the conflict or syntheses but only *resolutions*, contingent manners of bridging such a difference. "Technics," Cacciari writes, "does not mean ideal constitution (*Verfassung*) of signs—but the immanent modalities of those transformations. Technics is the expression of differences, of the *crises* that determine them."[34] The critical definition of techniques implies that their emergence cannot be *impartial*; their transformations cannot represent a single and progressive "universality" but a *partial* position. As Cacciari remarks, such an emergence springs instead "from the affirmation of *one* line, of *one* point of view."[35] In a way, this point was already made via Blumenberg's rejection of world images in favor of a world model, in which the only "picturing" possible would be one of contingent renderings. Yet what is new here is the stress on what could be defined as the *positional value* of the picture (the work). The value of the work—the resolution power that its technique or language has—determines and at the same is determined by its *position* in the conflict—in crisis as the "immanent structure" of its techniques. As Benjamin himself wrote in *The Author as Producer*: "Rather than asking, 'What is the attitude of a work *to* the relations of production of its time?' I would like to ask, 'What is its position *in* them?'"[36]

Through Cacciari's optics, Benjamin's notion of the oeuvre (thus of intellectual work) can be seen as almost analogous with a quantum-physical understanding of observation. The position of the technique determines its resolution power (its "quickness") and vice-versa. Furthermore, the attempt by the oeuvre work "to subtract the maximum of the overall idea of the work from the limits of its technique, to reduce the margin of consumption implicit in each statement"[37] can be compared to the quest for an observation that subtracts the maximum of the overall energy of the work from the limits of the system, to reduce the entropy implicit in each transformation and, conversely, the cost of the observation itself (its informational-energetic expenditure).[38] As intellectual work, philosophy is then not anymore the *other* to science—Blumenberg's guardian of scientific verifiability—nor can it claim an outside "utopian" or "sacred" position to it, but it is brought back *within* science itself, within its very technical nature.

Most importantly though, the cross-movement of liberation of language from the Name (the disappearance of the *aura* from the oeuvre) and the redefinition of technics according not to necessary solutions but to contingent resolutions allows for a freeing of intellectual work (hence of reimagination) from the "imperative" character of the program and a for the opening up, within and through technics—and thus within a historically determined domain of *technischen Reproduzierbarkeit*—of the "deliberative" dimension already implicit in the project (as a "liberation-from"[39]). The question of reimagination is, under this light, one of a "technical reproducibility" subtracted from the secular religion of linear progress.

Norm and Labyrinth

The notion of *image* reached at this point cannot therefore be reduced to a matter of artistic production, of scientific inquiry, or even of philosophical investigation—at least in a traditional sense. Conceiving of such image as an artwork, as an object, or as a theory to be looked at and inspected from the outside is simply out of the question. The mutual link of codetermination that has been established does not allow for such an outside position: any "outside" is always determined by and determining an inside; it is always *within* this relationship, within this "crisis" in the sense just outlined above. It is a matter of techniques and of their *contingent disposition* (of the way they articulate a quantic resolution between position and "quickness"),[40] of techniques as *decided* and *decisive* at the same time: a matter thus of *architecture*, of a "sovereign" and yet "dependent" relation to techniques. Reimagining Europe becomes then not just a philosophical task but also an architectonic one.

At this confluence between architecture and history, Cacciari's work on crisis finds a remarkable "application." Author of this implementation is not Cacciari himself but architecture historian Manfredo Tafuri, who · was concerned about in the deliberative-projectual possibilities of languages and techniques, already before his encounter with Cacciari. His notion of *operative criticism* can in fact be understood just as an inverted image of a technics liberated from the aura. "Operative criticism," writes Tafuri in *Theories and History of Architecture*, "is an analysis of architecture (or of the arts in general) that, instead of an abstract survey, has as its objective the planning of a precise poetical tendency, anticipated in its structures and derived from historical analyses programmatically distorted and finalized."[41] This sort of analysis, conducted mostly by Tafuri's fellow "historians," is therefore a distorted and instrumental use of that liberation, as it submits the deliberative understanding of language and technics (and of the discourses they project) to an ideological patronage. The problem of such a distortion resides in the fact that operative criticism presents itself as a "prescriptive code,"[42] which assumes a *normative* function and does so by exploiting past history as a source of legitimation. "We could say, in fact, that operative criticism *plans* past history by projecting it towards the future."[43] The figure of the project resurfaces here, sided by the one of the *plan*: a programmatic blueprint that "writes in advance" (*prescribes*) the cases of becoming, that *anticipates the past to be*, and does so according exclusively to its own sign (to its own program). There is a whole performative or "athletic" character that makes this attitude perfectly compatible with Blumenberg's world model, and thus with Cacciari's technoscientific project: "Its verifiability," Tafuri writes, "does not require abstractions of principle, it measures itself, each time, against the results obtained."[44] By affirming this measure as its value, the language of operative criticism implicitly lays claim over the *Name*, it is pretending to have a meaning within itself; in other words, it refuses its nature as *allegory*. In this folding of technics and language upon themselves, the code—that is, the contingent convention through which a technique deals with the crisis given by its immanent limits of expression—becomes invisible. It is in the transparency of this particular optics that *operative* becomes synonymous with *normative*.[45]

The transparency of code set by the normative character of criticism (by its *plan*) excludes the possibility of articulating a question over the position *in* the relations of production and their contingency, in the sense advocated by Benjamin. Instead, what this transparency achieves is the promotion of a view that is always preoriented according to the "norm" that its plan establishes—that is thus inevitably "normal" (perpendicular) *to* its invisible geometric plane. Seemingly contradicting positions such as the conservative and the progressive can therefore be understood as just two faces of this same normativity as they both challenge each other under the same currency and within the same theoretical horizon.[46] The concealment of codes engenders an all-encompassing interiority—a sort of gigantic house, to adapt Schmitt's analogy—in which the walls are so diaphanous that one can mistake it for an outside space. This is, according to Tafuri's materialist critique, what not just operative criticism but also the "Plan of the Capital" are able to achieve and what a real criticism must unmask.

But how to pursue the unmasking of what is already invisible? How to conceive of an outside to it or—since an outside would again be an ideological position—a "door" whose frame would allow for these walls to be seen, an intellectual device able to *invert* once again its totalizing image? Schmitt's architectural metaphor of the house becomes in Tafuri a literal one. Architecture, along with the discourses such as criticism and history—the product of certain languages and techniques—is a form of "intellectual work."[47] Conversely, as shown through the paradigm of operative criticism, discourses are always as much analytical as they are *constructive*.

As intellectual oeuvres, both architecture and criticism try to overcome the limits of their own techniques and languages by subtracting the construction of an idea (i.e., the work itself, the oeuvre) from the limits of expression immanent in those languages and techniques. Intellectual work is then a project that implies a planning, a "horizontal" elaboration that weaves together the "vertical" modes of production[48] (and hence of consumption, of "fashions," both in the sense of *mode* as well as of sheaves, *fasci*) immanent to the techniques and the languages that such works make use of. Architecture, institutions, languages, techniques, and historic space are lined up by Tafuri as different "bodies" in which this elaboration takes place. The task of criticism is to avoid adding itself up to this work and to counter the normative character of these constructions by cutting their weavings open, by "revealing" the plan implicit within these projects. To do so, the work of the critic (and of the historian) must look at the subtractions, that is, at the points of resistance—at the *crises*—that the techniques of these projects elaborate upon. This is why Tafuri speaks of history as a *historic space*. It is not the matter of a linear continuity broken by punctual events, but rather of a multiplicity of force-fields, traversed and intersecting in an endless amount of overlapping fault lines. "Historic space," writes Tafuri in *The Sphere and the Labyrinth*, "does not establish improbable links between diverse languages, between techniques that are distant from each other. Rather it explores what such distance expresses: it probes what appears to be a *void*, trying to make the absence that seems to dwell in that void speak."[49] Historic space refuses any dialectic synthesis: "In history 'solutions' do not exist."[50]

There is indeed a *deconstructive* charge in the task assigned by Tafuri to criticism. His notion of historic space is quite akin to an archeological domain of genealogies, to be deconstructed via the different grammatologies. But what appears evident in the double mirror of architecture and history is that the "deconstructive" work of which history and criticism are charged—their *crisis*—must acknowledge in turn its own *constructive* character. According to Tafuri, the analyses of Blanchot, Barthes, and Derrida "can break up works and texts, construct fascinating genealogies, hypnotically illuminate historical knots glossed over by facile readings. But they must necessarily negate the existence of the *historic space*."[51] They must negate their own contingency, the inevitable fact that they are also "spoken" through a series of *crises*: "Textual criticism, semantic criticism, iconological reading, the sociology of art, the genealogy of Foucault, our own criticism: are they not techniques that decipher only by hiding the traces of 'murders' committed more or less consciously?"[52] Any critical language can easily become the instrument of a "sacred rite," according to Tafuri. Ultimately, they still unconsciously claim to speak *in the Name*, to have an outside ("sacred") view on their subjects.

The (re)acknowledgement of historic space is therefore paramount: history, as a critical practice, must *desacralize* any position speaking from an outside and understand itself as always *determining as much as determined*.

In this sense, history must be understood, according to Tafuri, as a *project of crisis*.[53] It must *produce* crisis: separate (*krinein*) the historically determined fashions and conventions (thus show their "plan"), by clashing their different techniques and languages against each other and bringing them to the brink of their limits of expression—it must try to make the "absence" that dwells in what seems to be a "void" between them speak. At the same time, it must understand that this production of crisis is itself historically determined and "positioned," is a *project*, and it must therefore put itself into crisis as well. " 'True history' is not that which cloaks itself in indisputable 'philological proofs,' but that which recognizes its own arbitrariness, which recognizes itself as an 'unsafe building.' "[54]

Analogously to Cacciari's, Tafuri's project becomes here a "movement" (both a dynamism and a mechanics) of liberation (in the sense of a liberation-from, of a subtraction that still "feels the pull of the throw") of history from a linear and logocentric understanding of time, an "optics" (both a seeing and a screening) able to *project* its space out of uncertainty, to *decide* (to "choose" by cutting away from) the connection between position and resolution—and thus put them in communication with each other. It is in these terms that the "historical project" of *The Sphere and the Labyrinth* has to be understood: as a communication between the *absolute position* of the sphere and the *total resolution* of the labyrinth. "Here lies the 'fertile uncertainty' of the analysis itself, its interminableness, its need to return constantly to the material examined, and, at the same time, to itself."[55] In the face of uncertainty, every decision—every project—is a contingent one. In this apparent weakness lies its "fertility." The historic space that Tafuri's project of crisis casts off is one of infinite constructions, of analyses that "incorporate uncertainty," a domain of pure potency, endlessly resourceful and laborious.[56] A domain of reimagination is here recovered within and against the programmatic, operative, and apparently imageless one of the project and within the very "cut" of crisis. Tafuri's project of crisis provides a formidable sharpening of the deliberative power of the project as a form of reimagination. Apparently weakening it by stressing its contingency and arbitrariness, the historic space it opens up is a whole new "ocean" upon the reflection of which a new "ship" can sail and a further *Gegenbild* can be articulated. In this light, Europe is not just a "weak power" but a "weak being"—that *esse debile* that Scholasticism used to characterize images and their power to percolate in between the matter of reality.[57]

Captivity and Congestion

The waters crossed by Tafuri as a historian are traversed, almost in an opposite sense, by Rem Koolhaas as an architect. Presented at the London's Architectural Association along with Madelon Vriesendorp and Zoe and Elia Zenghelis, Koolhaas's graduate thesis was entitled *Exodus, or the Voluntary Prisoners of Architecture*. The utopian paradox of Cacciari's project—the one of a "state" only defined by separation, by its being liberated from—appears here in its inverted image. It is not a state but an *exodus*, a movement, that quits a state; furthermore, such escape is not really a liberation but a *captivity*. What is preserved in this inversion is nevertheless an arbitrariness, the role of decision upon uncertainty incorporated by Tafuri's historic space; the captivity of *Exodus* is a *voluntary* one. Koolhaas's "prisoners of architecture" *want* to be separated, they *want* to live *in crisis*. Their "prison" is a gigantic inhabited wall, which cuts the city of London in two, a "mirror image" of the Berlin Wall, which in those years still stood as the architectural manifestation of the postwar division of the European continent between the United States and the Soviet Union, as the image of a true crisis of Europe. The in-between space of the wall liberates its prisoners from this division—between a "Good Half" and a "Bad Half," as Koolhaas cyphers them. *Exodus* immanently transcends such programmatic divisions from within and lets its prisoners escape in a purely symbolic space: "The life inside," reads the text that accompanies the project, "produces a continuous state of ornamental frenzy and decorative delirium, an overdose of symbols."[58] This is no longer the tragic symbolism of the Name. No "sacred" meaning or truth is to be found in it, only mundane and self-fulfilling desire. Benjamin's *tragedy of the symbol* turns here into a *symbolic satire*: "The most contradictory programs fuse without compromise. . . . Nothing ever happens here, yet the air is heavy with exhilaration."[59]

The image presented by Koolhaas is the one of a house on the ocean: the project of inhabitation *within* the mundane and profane realm of technical invention that nevertheless *escapes* the sovereignty of the latter, its programmatic directionality and "imperative" character. Precisely by affirming its mundanity (its condition of being *within, in the midst of* the world), such an image avoids also its fall into the domain of the Name and of normativity, preserving thus history as a space of indeterminacy—as a domain ruled by an *architectonic* (sovereign yet dependent) *will*.

The paradigm elaborated by Koolhaas in *Exodus* is further developed in his following projects, all of them dealing, one way or another, with the mechanics and optics of this inversion. Koolhaas makes use of the historic "fertility" indicated by Tafuri and exploits the crises immanent to it, in order to build images to dwell upon. *Delirious New York*, arguably his most famous work, is precisely a manifesto of such a sourcing.[60] The novel "retroactively" constructs the history of Manhattan as a blueprint investigated via a Freudian psychoanalysis of the city and its "desires." The diagnosis of "Manhattanism" describes it as a "Capital of perpetual crisis,"[61] in which congestion is not solved but produced and exploited. Crisis, congestion, desires—delirium—all these "irrational" forces are not repressed or mitigated, but augmented, harnessed, and consumed: Koolhaas's Manhattan is perhaps one of the most precise images of the *katechon* that has been given in recent times. What Manhattanism is able to produce is a whole "capital" of profane symbolic values, of images as *goods* in the ambiguous sense of the word; as shareable properties that incorporate a contingent wealth.[62] "I wanted to construct—as a writer—a terrain where I could eventually work as an architect."[63] *Delirious New York* is an *image* of the subtraction—or rather an *abduction*, a form of "voluntary captivity"—of space out of uncertainty through its incorporation, in both senses of the term: a representation of it and, at the same time, a product of its mechanism.

The Palace of Reason

The movement of inversion has perhaps reached its full cycle here. The "house" has been found again. Rather than a domestic space protected from conflicts (or that governs them through a familiar setup), the architecture here outlined is not only exposed to them but built *under* these crises and under the "ocean" of their signs, as their "unstable foundation." It is an architecture that draws from the wealth that techniques bring—the "property" that their purification from the Name brings—and depends on them. At the same time, it does not submit itself to them but preserves the role of will (the "freedom" of the project) as what is able to turn this wealth—this desacralized property—into a *public good*, a palace, rather than a house, in which decision is affirmed in its symbolic value.

The medieval type of the "palace of reason" (*palazzo della ragione*) is perhaps the concluding image of the present discussion, a public palace, a civic tribunal in which the role of decision and of will does not vanish into programmatic transparency. It does not reduce the deliberative character to mere operativity or normativity but assumes visibility within the public space itself. Andrea Palladio designs and builds a famous example of it in Vicenza. His basilica deals with historic contingency as the archways of the exterior walls provide a new image to it by still dealing with the existing gothic building. The *serliana*—a form of opening constituted by an archway sided by two entablatures—is used by the Vicentine architect in order to provide propriety to the façade by finding a language that would speak to the old building without silencing it. The building is covered by a *soffitto a carena di nave rovesciata*, an "inverted ship hull ceiling." The *reason* of this palace is not of a stable and immutable ground, but one that "sails" in the ocean of techniques, of languages, and of their crises without surrendering to the direction of their currents, deciding instead a position in which to find orientation, turning *crisis* back to its duplicitous meaning of "cutting" and "judgment." What this palace of reason as the image of an inverted ship offers is perhaps a fertile enigma—a mechanics and an optics—of the question over Europe and its reimagination.

Notes

1. "Erst auf dem Ozean wird das Schiff zum absoluten Gegenbild des Hauses." Carl Schmitt, "Die Geschichtliche Struktur Des Gegensatzes von Ost Und West. Bemerkungen Zu Ernst Jüngers Schrift: 'Der Gordische Knoten,'" 541. Schmitt developed this theme in *Land and Sea* and most notably and extensively in *The Nomos of the Earth*.

2. "The Gordian knot must be understood as a problem posed by destiny; it continually knots itself together, just as continually the problem itself arises. . . . And, in the same way, we never arrive at a solution nor at a hierarchical order but at fecundity. All this belongs to the constitution, to the structure of the historical world and therefore, in spite of the pains from which it suffers, it cannot be considered a symptom of disease." Ernst Jünger, *Der Gordische Knoten*, 147.

3. Schmitt, 541.

4. Hans Blumenberg, "Weltbilder und Weltmodelle," 69.

5. Blumenberg, 69.

6. Blumenberg says,

Philosophy, in fact, does not transcend science from the outside, but from within. It does not invent the idea of scientific rigor, but brings it to language through the stages of its self-development. In the inaccessible specialized languages of the sciences there is the danger that they seem to have satisfied their exactness already in their formal structure, thus giving the impression of having solved the task of their "scientificity." But the true rigor of a science consists in the congruence of its operational definitions with its results. Do not assert more than we can know—this is infinitely more difficult to achieve with a critical spirit than the amiable observer of science may suspect at first glance. Scientific knowledge is an assertion to be proven with the ever-present reserve of its verification: should it become stabilized in images, this reserve is endangered, weakens, becomes latent and is soon forgotten. 74–75

7. According to Martin Heidegger,

A sign of this event [of the world becoming picture] is the appearance everywhere, and in the most varied forms and disguises, of the gigantic. At the same time, the huge announces itself in the direction of the ever smaller. We have only to think of the numbers of atomic physics. The gigantic presses forward in a form which seems to make it disappear. . . . One thinks too superficially, however, if one takes the gigantic to be merely an endlessly extended emptiness of the purely quantitative. One thinks too briefly if one finds the gigantic, in the form of the continual never-having-been-here-before, to spring merely from a blind impulse to exaggerate and excel . . . The gigantic is, rather, that through which the quantitative acquires its own kind of quality, becoming thereby, a remarkable form of the great. A historical age is not only great in a different way from others; it also has, in every case, its own concept of greatness. As soon, however, as the gigantic, in planning, calculating, establishing, and securing, changes from the quantitative and becomes its own special quality, then the gigantic and the seemingly completely calculable become, through this shift, incalculable. This incalculability becomes the invisible shadow cast over all things when man has become the *subiectum* and world has become picture. Through this shadow the modern world withdraws into a space beyond representation and so lends to the incalculable its own determinateness and historical uniqueness. "The Age of the World Picture." 71–72

8. Carl Schmitt, "Die Geschichtliche Struktur Des Gegensatzes von Ost Und West. Bemerkungen Zu Ernst Jüngers Schrift: 'Der Gordische Knoten.'"

9. Massimo Cacciari, "Project," 137.

10. Cacciari, 141.

11. Cacciari, 125.

12. "Only the liquidation of every traditional organicism, of every symbolic holding between social and political, of every symbolism of the political itself, makes possible the project as calculus, rational will of power, constructive force." Cacciari, 132.

13. Cacciari, 122.

14. Cacciari, 122.

15. Cacciari, 128.

16. Cacciari, 129.

17. Cacciari, 128.

18. Cacciari, 129.

19. Cacciari speaks in fact of "techno-scientific project," indissolubly weaving together technics and science, that Blumenberg assumed as separate. A similar "absorption" to the one operated by the project has been discussed by Heidegger in relation to cybernetics—yet the latter seem to describe the issue from a position in which the "fate" of the project is seen as already fulfilled and in which the project has completely been lost into its "programmatological destiny." See Martin Heidegger, "On the Question concerning the Determination of the Matter for Thinking."

20. "The project appears, thus, finally, as anticipation of chance: the anticipated chance no longer surprises nor irrupts; it is a priori 'accounted for' within the grid of the project, which, in its turn, frees itself from any eschatological characteristic to be transformed in techno-experimental apparatus devoted to the effective pursuit of contingent objectives." Cacciari, "Project," 127.

21. A similar aporia is developed, according to Vera Bühlmann, by Michel Serres in regards to history and science: "We have to think about a *science of history* that is at the same a *history of science*." The only relation between the two is of *equipollence*. See Vera Bühlmann, "Chronopedia I: Counting Time."

22. Pier Vittorio Aureli, *The Possibility of an Absolute Architecture*, ix.

23. "At the extreme moment of the 'fall' into *pure* language, the history that has led to this point also emerges—and this history the artwork *must* represent. And *it can only have to*: because its instruments of representation are now inextricably rooted in the space of signs, of writing. The *quantum* of destiny that appears in *this* work determines its position. The positions are infinite." Massimo Cacciari, "Di Alcuni Motivi in Walter Benjamin.," 236. Under this light we could perhaps see quantum physics as a "physics of (self) determination," as a point of conjunction between information theory and "natural will."

24. This is, according to Cacciari, the point of arrival of Husserl's work: the "*verification* of the *absence* of the transcendental foundation." And again:

"The *Krisis* is implicit as of now: the systematic unity that the philosophical discourse expresses cannot be mediated with the structures of the scientific *operari*." Cacciari, "Project," 216.

25. Cacciari, 224.

26. Cacciari, "Di Alcuni Motivi in Walter Benjamin," 224.

27. Cacciari, 219.

28. "At the root, the symbol is tautology, not synthesis. Here the foundations of the *tragic* interpretation of the symbolic are given." Cacciari, 222.

29. Cacciari, 237.

30. In the same years Cacciari works on Benjamin as well as on what he calls "the genesis of negative thought," namely, the elaboration and the refutation of Hegel by Schopenhauer, Nietzsche, Kierkegaard and Wittgenstein. It is not surprising that Cacciari's interest in Benjamin's work on Name and signs seems to fit well the first and the last theses of the *Tractatus*. See Massimo Cacciari, "Sulla genesi del pensiero negative."

31. A similar "boundary" has been described by Quatremère de Quincy as the "mathematical line." See Quatremère de Quincy, *An Essay on the Nature, the End, and the Means of Imitation in the Fine Arts*, 235. The etymology of trope and of the verb *trepein* (turning) seems closely related to the one of *trephein* (eating, consuming). This "metabolic" understanding of the trope would be supported by its connection with sacrificial rituals as a sort of divine consummation, and further on in the understanding of gods and myth as the "assimilation" of enemies or sacrificial victims. A hint in this direction can be found in George Hersey, "Troping Ornament," 1–10.

32. My italics. "This structure is *critical* towards the representation of its 'idea'; it is critical in relation to any setup *given* (*dato*) by the system." Cacciari, "Di Alcuni Motivi in Walter Benjamin," 239.

33. Cacciari, 236.

34. Cacciari, 238.

35. Cacciari says,

If techniques define *themselves* [*si definiscono*] critically and, as we have seen, determine crises, it means that they are *subjectively* acted upon by *contradictory* social relations—it means that their emergence is the affirmation of *one* line, of *one* point of view, from the conflict expressed in these relations. If the transformations of techniques do not represent 'universalities' that limit themselves to quantitatively shifting the boundaries of the system, to reproducing the system, without affecting or attacking its structure—they depend on, and condition in turn, a working that *interests* that structure. Therefore there cannot be a universal point of view, a paradigm of truth, in the understanding of techniques—the partiality of subjective optics

breaks into their system, as it had already done in the definition of
the new physical universe and its methodologies. 240

36. Walter Benjamin, "The Author as Producer: Address at the Institute
for the Study of Fascism, Paris, April 27, 1934," 770.

37. Cacciari, "Di Alcuni Motivi in Walter Benjamin," 236.

38. Vera Bühlmann, *Mathematics and Information in the Philosophy of Michel
Serres.*

39. "If we analyze, for example, the German term *Entwurf*, then the root of
the project reemerges with force. In the *ent-*, the anticipation, the before (*avanti*)
do not resound; what resounds, rather, is the way-from, the separation-from, the
departing—not so much the constructive-productive in its advance, as much as
the destructive or the overcoming. In *Entwurf* one perceives the 'pull' (*strappo*)
of the 'throw' (*lancio*), not its eventual prefiguring, predictive force." Cacciari,
"Project," 123.

40. "Quickness" is here preferred to more established terms such as "speed"
or "velocity," as it refers to the latter as a "resolution power" and not as a
movement of positively measured distances.

41. Manfredo Tafuri, "Operative Criticism," 141.

42. "In other words, we see already a typical feature of operative criticism:
its almost constant presentation of itself as a prescriptive code. This code may
be dogmatically systematic or methodologically wide open, but the difficulty in
placing this kind of operativity in history comes, doubtless, from its wavering
between the deduction of its values from history itself and the attempt to force
the future by introducing—on a critical level only—brand new values and *a
priori* choices." Tafuri, 144.

43. Tafuri, 141.

44. Tafuri, 141.

45. Tafuri later replaces the term "operative" with "normative criticism."
This invisibility of code is, once again, related to the *gigantic* as outlined by
Heidegger. Tafuri's aim is to unmask such an invisibility.

46. This horizon is, according to Tafuri, the one of "the pragmatist and
instrumentalist tradition." Tafuri, 141. Mannheim's distinction between "conservative" and "progressive thought" is discussed just in relation to what Tafuri
defines as a "mystified version of the functioning and reality of utopia," as it
promotes progressive attitude as the one able to break the order, whereas this
breaking (this *crisis*) is instead perfectly structural to the system. See Manfredo
Tafuri, "Ideology and Utopia," 52. An interesting parallel to this "squaring" can
be found in Schmitt's notion of *complexio oppositorum*. Carl Schmitt, *Roman
Catholicism and Political Form.*

47. It is significant that the original subtitle of Tafuri's book *Progetto
e Utopia, Architecture and Capitalist Development*, takes as model his previous

essay entitled *Intellectual Work and Capitalist Development*, hence suggesting an understanding of architecture as "intellectual work." See Manfredo Tafuri, *Architecture and Utopia: Design and Capitalist Development*; Manfredo Tafuri, "Lavoro Intellettuale e Sviluppo Capitalistico."

48. "Modes of production, isolated in themselves, neither explain nor determine. They themselves are anticipated, delayed, or traversed by ideological currents. Once a system of power is isolated, its genealogy cannot be offered as a universe complete in itself." Manfredo Tafuri, "Introduction: The Historical 'Project,'" 10.

49. Tafuri, 13.

50. Manfredo Tafuri, *Theories and History of Architecture*, 237.

51. Tafuri, *The Sphere and the Labyrinth*, 9.

52. Tafuri, 9.

53. Tafuri says,

> History is viewed as a "production," in all senses of the term: the production of meanings, beginning with the "signifying traces" of events; an analytical construction that is never definite and always provisional; an instrument of deconstruction of ascertainable realities. As such, history is both determined and determining: it is determined by its own traditions, by the objects that it analyzes, by the methods that it adopts; it determines its own transformations and those of the reality that it deconstructs. The language of history therefore implies and assumes the languages and the techniques that act and produce the real: it "contaminates" those languages and those techniques and, in turn, is "contaminated" by them. With the fading away of the dream of knowledge as a means to power, the constant struggle between the analysis and its objects—their irreducible tension—remains. Precisely this tension is "productive": the historical "project" is always the "project of a crisis." 3

For an in-depth investigation of this notion within Tafuri's overall oeuvre, see also Marco Biraghi, *Project of Crisis: Manfredo Tafuri and Contemporary Architecture*.

54. Tafuri, *The Sphere and the Labyrinth*, 12.

55. Tafuri, "Introduction: The Historical 'Project,'" 11.

56. It is an *informational* space (but not one completely without form).

57. Emanuele Coccia, *Sensible Life: A Micro-Ontology of the Image*, 26.

58. OMA, Rem Koolhaas, and Bruce Mau, *S, M, L, XL*, 7.

59. OMA, 19.

60. Rem Koolhaas, *Delirious New York: A Retroactive Manifesto for Manhattan*.

61. Koolhaas, 11.

62. On this relation see Emanuele Coccia, *Goods: Advertising, Urban Space, and the Moral Law of the Image*.

63. Rem Koolhaas, "Why I Wrote Delirious New York and Other Textual Strategies," 42–43.

Bibliography

Benjamin, Walter. "The Author as Producer: Address at the Institute for the Study of Fascism, Paris, April 27, 1934." In *Selected Writings*. Vol. 2, part 2. 1931–1934, 768–82. Cambridge, Massachusetts, and London, England: Belknapp Press of Harvard University Press, 1999.

Biraghi, Marco. *Project of Crisis: Manfredo Tafuri and Contemporary Architecture*. Edited by Alta L. Price. Writing Architecture. Cambridge: MIT Press, 2013.

Blumenberg, Hans. "Weltbilder und Weltmodelle." In *Nachrichten der Giessener Hochschulgesellschaft*, 30:67–75. Gießen: Schmitz, 1961.

Bühlmann, Vera. *Mathematics and Information in the Philosophy of Michel Serres*. London: Bloomsbury, 2020.

Cacciari, Massimo. "Di Alcuni Motivi in Walter Benjamin. (Da «Ursprung Des Deutschen Trauerspiels» a «Der Autor Als Produzent»)." *Nuova Corrente* 67 (1975): 209–43.

Cacciari, Massimo. "Project." In *The Unpolitical: On the Radical Critique of Political Reason*, edited by Alessandro Carrera, 1st ed., 122–45. New York: Fordham University Press, 2009.

Cacciari, Massimo. "Sulla genesi del pensiero negative." *Contropiano* 1 (April 1969): 131–200.

Coccia, Emanuele. *Sensible Life: A Micro-Ontology of the Image*. Translated by Scott Alan Stuart. New York: Fordham University Press, 2016.

Coccia, Emanuele. *Goods: Advertising, Urban Space, and the Moral Law of the Image*. Translated by Marissa Gemma. First edition. Commonalities. New York: Fordham University Press, 2018.

de Quincy, Quatremère. *An Essay on the Nature, the End, and the Means of Imitation in the Fine Arts*. Translated by J. C. Kent. Smith, Elder and Company, 1837.

Heidegger, Martin. "The Age of the World Picture." In *Off the Beaten Track*, edited by Julian Young and Kenneth Haynes. Cambridge: Cambridge University Press, 2002.

Heidegger, Martin. "On the Question Concerning the Determination of the Matter for Thinking." *Epoché* 14, no. 2 (Spring 2010): 213–23.

Hersey, George. "Troping Ornament." In *The Lost Meaning of Classical Architecture. Speculations on Ornament from Vitruvius to Venturi*, 1–10. Cambridge: MIT Press, 1988.

Jünger, Ernst. *Der Gordische Knoten*. Frankfurt am Main: Vittorio Klostermann, 1954.

Koolhaas, Rem. *Delirious New York: A Retroactive Manifesto for Manhattan*. New ed. New York: Monacelli, 1994.

Koolhaas, Rem. "Why I Wrote *Delirious New York* and Other Textual Strategies." *ANY: Architecture New York*, 1993, 42–43.

Office for Metropolitan Architecture, Rem Koolhaas, and Bruce Mau. *S, M, L, XL: Office for Metropolitan Architecture, Rem Koolhaas, and Bruce Mau*. Edited by Jennifer Sigler. New York: Monacelli, 1995.

Schmitt, Carl. "Die Geschichtliche Struktur Des Gegensatzes von Ost Und West. Bemerkungen Zu Ernst Jüngers Schrift: 'Der Gordische Knoten.' " In *Staat, Großraum, Nomos*, 523–51. Berlin: Duncker & Humblot, 1995.

Tafuri, Manfredo. *Architecture and Utopia: Design and Capitalist Development*. Cambridge: MIT Press, 1976.

Tafuri, Manfredo. "Lavoro Intellettuale e Sviluppo Capitalistico." *Contropiano* 2 (1970): 241–81.

Tafuri, Manfredo. *The Sphere and the Labyrinth: Avant-Gardes and Architecture from Piranesi to the 1970s*. Cambridge: MIT Press, 1987.

Tafuri, Manfredo. *Theories and History of Architecture*. First US ed. New York: Harper & Row, 1980.

Part II

Europe's Other(s)

5

Europe and Its Phantoms

Walter Mignolo's Decolonial Critique of Jacques Derrida's Deconstruction

Thomas Clément Mercier

There would be no history in general, and no political history in particular, without at least the possibility of lying, that is, of freedom and of action. And also of imagination and of time, of imagination as time.

—Derrida, *Without Alibi*

I was the girl whose imagination swallowed the house, lagoon, corrals, and woods. My imagination made me pregnant with story. I literally ate my grandmothers' and mother's stories.

—Anzaldúa, *Light in the Dark/ Luz en lo Oscuro*

j'habite une blessure sacrée
j'habite des ancêtres imaginaires
j'habite un vouloir obscur[1]

—Aimé Césaire, "Calendrier lagunaire"

Introduction: Nous lisant imaginant

The *mot d'ordre* that gives this volume its title—*Reimagining Europe*—is a call to action. In its very syntax, first, through the active form of the gerundive but also through the reference to imagination. Imagination always supposes a certain *doing*, a "thinking-doing";[2] and it is so because imagination can only work through a break, a certain translative betrayal of what we call "reality." Whatever its subsequent effects (or absence thereof) on said "reality," imagination, in its very doing, is immediately praxic, active, productive, or transformative because it entertains a differential relation to reality "itself." It maintains an essential link to the production or transformation of said reality, thus implying that the one who imagines is always somewhat a person of action, whatever the consequences might be.[3] Imagination turns to the future; it involves a certain performative opening and inventiveness, a certain fictionality, one that opens reality to its other—here, the reality of what bears the name "Europe."

But what is the other of Europe? If something like "Europe" is to have a future, it will have to imagine or reimagine "itself" so as to become otherwise. Not only because it needs to adapt, to transform its conditions of effectivity and legitimacy, to reassess its mechanisms of *representation*, and produce new schemas of identification and adhesion in a global geopolitics involving a multitude of incompatible interests and an often inscrutable entanglement of alliances and conflicts; but also, quite simply, because imagination is time "itself," as Derrida puts it in our epigraph. On the previous page of the same essay, entitled "History of the Lie," he writes: "Between lying and acting, acting in politics, manifesting one's own freedom through action, transforming facts, anticipating the future, there is something like an essential affinity. The imagination is, according to Arendt, the common root of the 'ability to lie' and the 'capacity to act.' Capacity to produce some image: productive imagination as experience of time, Kant or Hegel would have said."[4]

No future without imagination. Imagination is the condition of movement and time, of the becoming-space of time and the becoming-time of space: "Function of representation, imagination is also the temporalizing function, the excess of the present and the economy of what exceeds presence."[5] Imagination is othering: "It is the other name of differance as auto-affection,"[6] so much so that, when I say that Europe will have to imagine or reimagine "itself," am I not already presupposing the selfness of the subject of enunciation, the relative gathering, solidity, togetherness, and self-presence of something like "Europe," an image or self-image that would already be somewhat homogeneous, stable, or stabilized enough to imagine or reimagine *itself*, or even to be imagined or reimagined under that same name, *Europe*? How can such a *name, word,* or *vocable*, this so-called concept, "Europe," be imagined or reimagined in a way that would indeed be transformative, at least transformative enough to speak to a certain future, the *avenir* or to-come of what enigmatically bears the name *Europe*—the "word" and the "thing," *le mot et la chose*? In order to reimagine "Europe" beyond Europe "itself," one would have to imagine an imagination that would come from Europe's other. But, once again, what is the other of Europe? How does one reimagine something like "Europe"—the "thing" bearing the name "Europe"—from the other and towards the other, but an other that would be otherly enough so as not to be reducible to the other *of* Europe, that is, Europe's own, appropriated, domesticated other?

This question—that of Europe's other—has been central to the postcolonial and decolonial critiques of the European project.[7] How can we reimagine "Europe" after postcolonial and decolonial critiques that pointed to the essentially colonialist dimension of the European project, a project that has advanced itself in the so-called "world" under the name "modernity"?[8] "Reimagining Europe," in these circumstances, would signify breaking away from a certain image or self-image of Europe, one indexed on Eurocentrism and colonialism—the difficulty being that this image is perhaps nothing but Europe "itself" (if this reference to Europe's selfness still means something), an image or self-image that incorporates in itself the colonial project: Europe as imaginal projection and ex-position, forward pro-jection through the imaginal force or power of an uprooting beyond presence, a gathering function of re-presentation also figuring an advance and a heading beyond the self-same of Europe, beyond Europe "as such" and toward its other, an imaginal drive put to the service of a narcissistic will to power and appropriation, one that would therefore be essentially and structurally colonial or colonialist, expansive beyond the self and toward the other—in other words, *conquering*:

> Europe is not only a geographical headland or heading that
> has always given itself the representation or figure of a spiri-
> tual heading, at once as project, task, or infinite—that is to
> say universal—idea, as the memory of itself that gathers and
> accumulates itself, capitalizes upon itself, in and for itself.
> Europe has also confused its image, its face, its figure and its
> very place, its taking-place, with that of an advanced point,
> the point of a phallus if you will, and thus, once again, with

a heading for world civilization or human culture in general. The idea of an advanced point of exemplarity is *the idea of* the European *idea*, its *eidos*, at once as *arché*—the idea of beginning but also of commanding (the *cap* as the head, the place of capitalizing memory and of decision, once again, the captain)—and as *telos*, the idea of the end, of a limit that accomplishes, or that puts an end to the whole point of the achievement, right there at the point of completion. The advanced point is at once beginning and end, it is divided as beginning and end; it is the place from which or in view of which everything takes place.[9]

Europe's image or self-image is thus the idea *itself*, the image or *eidos* of vision, sight, and aim, *theoria*, contemplation, ideation, and imagination "itself," that is, Europe's conquering drive towards the universal through which it grants itself the right and power to exceed its own selfness and self-presence, to transgress its own borders, and to advance itself, project itself into the "world," first and foremost by globalizing the world, by producing the world in its own image, by speculating and reproducing this specular image, through an imaginal force that arms itself and capitalizes itself in the same movement. The "world" is a mirror. And Europe's imagination and image would always-already harbor, at least virtually, a colonial and phallic imaginary. In this sense, the European image or imagination—that is, a certain "representation" of what an image or imagination supposedly *is*: a possibly strictly European or Eurocentric representation of "imagination" (but are there any other "concepts" of imagination?)—would incorporate in itself a drive toward universalism and, thereby, a colonial drive—what I would call a "phallocolonial" drive. The risk, therefore, would be that by obeying the injunction to "reimagine Europe," we might already be subscribing to a certain image or representation of "imagination," of "imagination" understood as the very image or idea—the *eidos*—of "Europe." "Europe" would be essentially linked to this specular image, not only to the image or self-image of Europe, but to *the image of the image*: a *European* image of the image, supposing there can be other (non-European) images or ideas of the image.

Two consequences follow from this: *first*, the recourse to "imagination" might itself be European, too European, and might virtually maintain, willingly or otherwise, an essential relation to European tradition everywhere and every time imagination is brandished as a tool for reinventing Europe, for reshaping or refashioning its image, or as an alternative option to the European project—for example in the form of a "decolonial imaginary"[10] or through the appeal to "a liberatory articulation of a radical imaginary";[11] *second*, there can be a "reimagining of Europe" worthy of the name only on the condition that imagination "itself" be reimagined, transformed, maybe deconstructed, to such an extent that what we call "imagination" and "image" will become, perhaps, unrecognizable as such, *as imagination* and *image*, Europe's image. The other of Europe would thus also be the other of imagination. Beyond imagination as such, it would be, in this very strict sense, *unimaginable*. Imagining the unimaginable, imagination beyond imagination—is that even *possible?*

At this stage, the very idea of image or self-image has become uncanny, troubling, and the mirror itself is becoming blurry, vaguely opaque; having acquired a worrying depth, it now resembles a door or a portal—as if the mirror figured a way in or a way out, an uncertain threshold for invasions or escapades to come. Perhaps here we need a few signposts. This chapter will stage an intervention in a relatively contained debate—but one with virtually limitless implications. The debate concerns more specifically the imperialist tendencies of Europe and European philosophy. In a text published in 1997, American philosopher Robert Bernasconi offered a reading of African American philosopher Lucius Outlaw, in order to interrogate the place reserved to non-European forms of knowledge in the academy.[12] Bernasconi builds on Outlaw's essay "African 'Philosophy': Deconstructive and Reconstructive Challenges," which proposed to analyze the racial and colonial implications of European philosophy's "self-image" and to deconstruct the image of African philosophy imposed by European epistemology, in view of a reconstruction from its margins. While Outlaw draws on Derrida's deconstruction in several key ways, he also argues for the distinctiveness of African philosophy's efforts of deconstruction/reconstruction, embedded as they are in specific historical exigencies conditioning their emergence. In Outlaw's wake, Bernasconi exposed the racist and imperialist character of European philosophy and emphasized the strictly speaking *impossible* position in which European tradition puts non-European forms of "philosophical" thought. While Outlaw's essay was overall sympathetic towards Derrida's project, Bernasconi argues that deconstruction, inasmuch as it presupposes the closure of metaphysics, is similarly guilty of preempting and even preventing any authentic encounter with the colonized other, the other of Europe. Outlaw's and Bernasconi's essays concerned more particularly what we call "continental philosophy" in its relationship with what we call "African philosophy"; but when the Argentinian decolonial thinker Walter Mignolo revisited this debate a few years later, in 2002, he expanded the scope of Bernasconi's critique so as to identify, challenge, and decolonize the global geopolitics of knowledge and colonial difference sustained by Europe in and through the epistemic principles of European philosophy.[13] Here again, Derrida's deconstruction was targeted in a very specific manner; I'll show how and why in the following section. My purpose, of course, is not (not simply) to set the debate straight; rather, I want to untangle some of its chief presuppositions and analyze its broader implications with regards to the colonial imaginary of Europe, in view of examining conditions of possibility and impossibility for an "authentically" decolonial praxis and epistemology, an imagination de-linked from colonial Europe and European thought. Imagine that.

Before we get into the specifics of this debate, I will add one more complication to this tableau—a tableau that I would be careful not to call a "geopolitics of knowledge" (as Walter Mignolo's paradigmatic expression goes), not only because, as we speak of imagination, the matter at hand cannot, perhaps, be reduced to gnoseology or epistemology, to a problem of gnosis or knowledge, especially of knowing as *power*, power-knowledge or power to know; but also because it might even put in question what we call "imagination" or, in other words, it might gesture towards the idea that *we do not know what imagination is*. It might point to something in imagination that cannot in the last instance be made available to an epistemology or to an ontological knowledge of sorts, an exorbitant heterogeneity that would exceed any epistemological or ontological reduction. Here's the complication, the supplementary folding that makes our problem properly abysmal: when I say, "The other of Europe is the other of imagination" and, following this, "The other of Europe is perhaps unimaginable," this can be heard in two different ways—two interpretations that are at once incompatible and inseparable. On *the one hand*, it might signify that the other of Europe cannot be imagined as such, thus suggesting that we are trapped in Europe's colonial imaginary, its circular specularity. Imagination as such—the idea and the thing, imaginal experience "itself"—would maintain an irreducible link to Europe and the European tradition. It would be self-limiting and self-limited, and therefore everything that might be attempted—for example in the form of "decolonial imaginary"—would have to circulate within the closure of imagination (notably by using that word, its lexicon and grammar), forcefully negotiating with this circular limit,[14] letting itself be haunted, translated, contaminated by "Europe," perhaps in view of economic or strategic gains or more or less effective coalitions but never without the *risk* of reproducing the European schemas that imagination keeps in reserve. But, *on the other hand*, this can also suggest that what announces itself as the other of Europe would have to be thought of beyond all imagination. It would exceed the scope of what the European tradition has conceived of as *power* or *faculty* of imagination, be it productive or reproductive imagination,[15] *Einbildung*, *Phantasie*, or *phantasia*[16]—even exceeding, perhaps, the psychoanalytic notion of "phantasm." It would point to a phantasm or phantom beyond phantasmatic imagination, to an overflowing spectrality and fictionality beyond power and beyond knowledge—beyond agential ipseity—beyond presence and, perhaps, beyond life "itself," that is, beyond all ontological and presential reductions of life to an essence, life "as such":

> The question: what is the phantasm? What does phantasm, *phantasma*, revenant, *fantasia*, imagination, fantastic imagination, mean? If everything we've just sketched out concerned above all the phantasmatic nature of what orients our desire and our terror, our experience . . . of the living dead . . . , of the essence or the non-essence, . . . then we're here touching on the simultaneously auto-affective and hetero-affective structure of the phantasm. One cannot think the phantasm without this auto-hetero-affective dimension.
>
> A reflection on the acute specificity of the phantasmatic cannot fail to pass through this experience of living death and of affect, imagination and sensibility (space and time) as auto-hetero-affection.[17]

This phantasmal phantomaticity, as soon as it is thought of as auto-heteronomic force of haunting, must remain, at least in part, inaccessible to any ontological discourse on the truth and essence of being and nonbeing. This always-already complicates the structure of imagination inasmuch as this structure is both the foundation and the *point sensible*, the sensitive point of European ontology, of ontology *tout court*. As such, imagination must be thought of as strictly speaking *impossible*, beyond power and beyond knowledge. There isn't, there has perhaps never been, imagination "as such"—which doesn't entail that it is reduced to nothing or nothingness: "Ghosts always pass quickly, with the infinite speed of a furtive apparition, in an instant without duration, presence without present of a present which, coming back, only *haunts*. The ghost, *le re-venant*, the survivor, appears only by means of figure or fiction, but its appearance is not nothing, nor is it a mere semblance."[18] With these words, Derrida strived to identify a certain "restance" or "remanence" of phantomality in and of imagination, in and of its power of synthesis, which "enables us to recognize in the figure of the phantom the working of what Kant and Heidegger assign to the transcendental imagination and whose temporalizing schemes and power of synthesis are indeed 'fantastic'—are, in Kant's phrase, those of an art hidden in the depths of the soul."[19] Imagination, synthetic and schematic faculty, thus cannot and should not ignore its structural coimplication not only with fictionality but also with phantomality: a heterogeneous, spectral force affecting from within any imaginative or imaginal project, like the auto-hetero-affective movement of its desire. I will return to these questions, which articulate imagination (and writing) with phantasmaticity—supplementary life-death, survival, mourning, haunting—in my conclusion, notably around some of Gloria Anzaldúa's writings on image and imagination. There I will point to a certain queerness of desire, but one that contrasts with the queer-decolonial imaginary usually assigned to Anzaldúa's texts: I want to show that her writings, in their margins at least, suggest something like a phantasmal "logic" of haunting, an uncanny force of (self-)deconstruction which is perhaps more powerful and more irresistible, despite the fallibility to which it infallibly points, than imagination conceived of as sheer power of fictionalization and creation, life-affirming faculty of world-building, or reality-shaping artistry. Can this auto-hetero-affective force of haunting, this undecidable life-death drive or *puissance*, be mobilized by one or the other side within the geopolitical wars we're about to analyze? Can it even be factored into the questions raised in this introduction without wreaking havoc on the presuppositions that put them in motion?

Who/What Is the Other of "Europe"?

In the 1997 essay "African Philosophy's Challenge to Continental Philosophy," Bernasconi interrogated the place reserved to non-European forms of knowledge in the academy: he demonstrated in very convincing terms the strictly speaking *impossible* position in which European philosophy puts non-European forms of "philosophical" thought. Bernasconi—and, after him, Mignolo—describes the way in which European thought has silenced the other. It has made the dialogue with the other impossible. In imposing a certain subject of enunciation and a repertoire of notions, in putting forward a logic of totality and universality as a condition for truth claims, European thought has prevented a meaningful engagement with otherness, an "encounter with the colonized."[20] We are going to see why and how in a moment. Before we get there, I would like to emphasize an aspect of this debate that interests me particularly. As is well known, deconstruction has been very influential on what has been called "postcolonial studies," notably through the work of Gayatri C. Spivak, Homi K. Bhabha, and Dipesh Chakrabarty. However, against the grain of postcolonial theory, Bernasconi and Mignolo argue that the imperialist tendency of European philosophy has been in fact perpetuated and sustained by what they call "postmodernism," "poststructuralism," and "deconstruction"—and their target (among others, but in a very specific manner) is the work of Derrida. This move seems to go against a certain representation of the value and significance of deconstruction for postcolonial and decolonial discourses and struggles, and this is why it is so interesting: both for what it implies in terms of argumentative strategy and for its theoretical and practical bearing regarding the conditions of possibility for decolonizing thought.

Let me first try to expose briefly the general coordinates of the debate. With reference to Robert Bernasconi's analysis of the othering of African philosophy, Walter Mignolo identifies an epistemic violence stemming from "the coloniality of power"—an expression borrowed from Peruvian thinker Aníbal Quijano. The coloniality of power goes hand in hand with a "geopolitics of knowledge." It has epistemological, political, and ontological implications; it is at work in power, knowledge, and being. Bernasconi, and Mignolo after him, describe the *coup de force* of European philosophy—a performative strike that resulted in violently enforcing an epistemic hierarchy in the geopolitics of knowledge and that sustains what Mignolo calls "the colonial difference"—that is, the geopolitical and epistemic subalternization of certain categories of knowledge or "gnosis," as Mignolo puts it, of bodily and psychic world experiences that remain excluded by the imperialist gesture enforced by European philosophy. Therefore, even though the debate I will describe might seem very theoretical, maybe "abstract" in nature, it is important to keep in mind that it has very concrete political, even existential, implications in terms of power-knowledge and epistemic embodiments, notably because it perpetuates ethical prejudices and physical and discursive exclusions not only in the academy but also beyond—and for instance, it may concern what Frantz Fanon and Sylvia Wynter call the "sociogeny" of the colonial subject.[21] We are here at a nexus where the separation between the theoretical and the political is, according to Mignolo, a false dichotomy, an artificial separation that is itself the result of an imperialist gesture and of an epistemic violence perpetrated by Western modernity. The geopolitics of knowledge works by enforcing limits and governing bodies. European philosophy has traced borders, and these borders are as much disciplinary as they are topological and corporeal: the borders are forcefully inscribed in the bodies of subjects and in the cartography of the world. Here I would like to recall that these aspects were also underlined by thinkers such as Foucault and Derrida,[22] but certainly the significance and originality of Mignolo's project (among other decolonial critiques, such as Enrique Dussel's project of transmodernity—an important point of reference for Mignolo all through his corpus) resides in showing how this process is essentially linked to the expansionist politics of European modernity and to the totalizing epistemology attached to universalism, inasmuch as it legitimates imperialism and therefore results in forcefully enacting the colonial difference. Before we get to the more "critical" or "deconstructive" part of this discussion, in which I will raise a few questions concerning such or such aspects of Mignolo's project, I want to emphasize that this type of genealogical critique of the epistemic principles of European modernity remains in my opinion absolutely crucial and necessary, as does the necessity to *still* interrogate, genealogically *and* deconstructively, the epistemic protocols from which said critique draws the condition of validity for its truth claims and empirical findings.

Let's now get into the core of the argument. How does the imperialistic gesture denounced by Mignolo operate? What is the role of European philosophy in legitimating and enacting the colonial difference? Mignolo explains this by quoting and summarizing Bernasconi's argument:

> Simply put, Bernasconi notes that "Western philosophy traps African philosophy in a double bind. Either African philosophy is so similar to Western philosophy that it makes no distinctive contribution and effectively disappears; or it is so

different that its credentials to be genuine philosophy will always be in doubt." This double bind is the colonial difference that creates the conditions for what I have elsewhere called "border thinking." I have defined border thinking as an epistemology from a subaltern perspective.[23]

Here's the double bind: *on the one hand*, if African philosophy is simply considered as "philosophy," and even using that "Greek" name, then it risks being treated as a subcategory of European philosophy, a regional or provincial form of knowledge which will become effectively incorporated within Western thought, assimilated and digested by the appropriative machine of European modernity. But, *on the other hand*, if it is *not* considered as philosophy, it will simply be discarded as nonphilosophical; it will be described as mere "wisdom," mythological thinking, poetry, or even "wizardry" or "magic" and will therefore be systematically disqualified by European models of rational thought as its subalternized other. This epistemological, geopolitical, and ontological gesture of subalternization participates in what Mignolo calls "the colonial matrix of power."[24] In order to sidestep this double bind, Mignolo puts forward what he calls "de-linking," an approximate translation of what Quijano calls *desprendimiento*, that is to say, a breaking away, a rupture from the theoretical and conceptual conditions of truth imposed by the coloniality of power knowledge enforced by European modernity and Western epistemology, represented "in *toto*" through what Mignolo calls "la pensée unique":

> La pensée unique is Western in *toto*, that is, liberal and neo-liberal but also Christian and neo-Christian, as well as Marxist and neo-Marxist. La pensée unique is the totality of the three major macro-narratives of Western civilization with its imperial languages (English, German, French, Italian, French, Spanish, Portuguese) and their Greco and Roman foundations. To de-link from the colonial matrix of power and the logic of coloniality embedded in la pensée unique, it is necessary to engage in border epistemology and in alternatives TO modernity or in the global and diverse project of transmodernity. Why global and diverse?—because there are many "beginnings" beyond Adam and Eve and Greek civilization and many other foundational languages beyond Greek and Latin.[25]

The epistemic and geopolitical effort of de-linking from the colonial imaginary has thus to do with the interrogation of physical and epistemological borders, of a colonial difference violently imposed and sustained through the coloniality of power, and with the topological question of inside/outside, which Mignolo summarizes through the formula "I am where I think"—a phrase with both geohistorical and ontological implications.[26] How does one speak or think "from the exteriority of Western Metaphysics"?[27] According to Mignolo, this radical (epistemic-political) strategy of de-linking would constitute the main distinction of what he calls "decoloniality" as opposed to "postcolonial theory," which remains, according to him, structurally dependent on "postmodern thinkers" such as Foucault, Barthes, Lacan, Lyotard, or Derrida, and which is framed, still according to Mignolo, as a merely *analytic* endeavor from *within* the colonial matrix of power. In order to specify the originality of the decolonial project and of its strategic and geopolitical objectives, Mignolo once again refers to the work of Aníbal Quijano:

> Quijano's project articulated around the notion of "coloniality of power" moves in two simultaneous directions. One is the *analytic*. The concept of coloniality has opened up the re-construction and the restitution of silenced histories, repressed subjectivities, subalternized knowledges and languages performed by the Totality depicted under the names of modernity and rationality. Quijano acknowledges that postmodern thinkers already criticized the modern concept of Totality; but this critique is limited and internal to European history and the history of European ideas. That is why it is of the essence the critique of Totality from the perspective of coloniality and not only from the critique of post-modernity [sic]. Now, and this is important, the critique of the modern notion of Totality doesn't lead necessarily to post-coloniality, but to de-coloniality. Thus, the second direction we can call the *programmatic* that is manifested in Quijano as a project of "desprendimiento," of de-linking. At this junction, the analytic of coloniality and the programmatic of decoloniality moves away and beyond the post-colonial.
>
> Coloniality and de-coloniality introduces a fracture with both the Eurocentered project of post-modernity and a project of post-coloniality heavily dependent on post-structuralism as

far as Michel Foucault, Jacques Lacan and Jacques Derrida have been acknowledged as the grounding of the post-colonial canon: Edward Said, Gayatri Spivak and Homi Bhabha. Decoloniality starts from other sources. From the de-colonial shift already implicit in *Nueva corónica and buen gobierno* by Waman Puma de Ayala; in the de-colonial critique and activism of Mahatma Gandhi; in the fracture of Marxism in its encounter with colonial legacies in the Andes, articulated by José Carlos Mariátegui; in the radical political and epistemological shifts enacted by Amilcar Cabral, Aimé Césaire, Frantz Fanon, Rigoberta Menchú, Gloria Anzaldúa, among others. The de-colonial shift, in other words, is a project of de-linking while post-colonial criticism and theory is a project of scholarly transformation within the academy.[28]

According to Mignolo, postcolonialism remains captive to the coloniality of power and colonial difference imposed by European modernity and continued by "postmodern" European thought and remains therefore entrapped in the geopolitics of knowledge imposed through the colonial matrix of power. By contrast, the decolonial shift purports, in Quijano's terms, "the destruction of the global coloniality of power."[29] It follows that Mignolo's strategy of de-linking and his critique of the geopolitics of knowledge come with a number of ethical and normative claims (which he calls in the above quotation "programmatic"). Mignolo calls "decoloniality" the epistemic and political efforts that consist in de-linking knowledge from hegemonic European categories of thought imposed through modernity and the coloniality of power; in this perspective, decoloniality and de-linking would allow that the colonized have a voice and be respected as such, as otherly, in her own body, epistemology, and world experience. The epistemic embodiment that Mignolo speaks about is an embodied ethics and politics—a "thinking-doing" and "doing-thinking"[30]—claiming to be respectful of the diversity of "horizons of expectation" and of the plurality of "spaces of experience" embedded in "local histories" and identified with specific bodies, localities, and communities.[31] Mignolo's "pluritopic hermeneutics" proposes to reject the universalist and totalizing tendencies of Western thought and instead to put forward "diversality as a universal project,"[32] "a pluri-versal world as a uni-versal project."[33] Through the operation of de-linking, pluriversality would make an authentic opening to the other possible, allowing the other to be themself and to be respected as such, as otherly—and here one can hear echoes of Levinas's ethics as first philosophy and his critique of the totalizing ontology of the One. In several places, Mignolo suggests that Levinas is the only "European" thinker who may contribute to a decolonial account of Europe's totalizing violence and engage in an authentic thinking of otherness "from the exteriority," with and for the other. This singularization of Levinas (among "European" philosophers) is also an important gesture in the work of Robert Bernasconi, Enrique Dussel, and Nelson Maldonado-Torres.[34] "Levinas" would be the name of a certain rupture within European philosophy, breaking away from the principles of universality and totality in view of an ethical and nonviolent thinking of alterity, heterogeneity, exteriority, and plurality. It is also meant to suggest a certain ethics, an ethical difference breaking away from the violent, imperial drive of Western modernity. In Mignolo's words: "Pluriversality became my key argument for calling into question the concept of universality, so dear to Western cosmology. [. . .] Modern ego-centered personalities are driven by competition; decolonial and communal personalities are driven by the search for love, conviviality, and harmony. [. . .] [Decoloniality] withstands alignment with any school or institution that would divert its pluriverse back into a universe, its heterogeneity back into a totality."[35]

After this general overview, let's now focus on Bernasconi and Mignolo's critique of Derrida's deconstruction. The starting point of their argument is a reading of Derrida's 1964 text on Levinas, "Violence and Metaphysics." Bernasconi, and Mignolo after him, argue that, in contrast to Levinas's thought, Derrida's deconstruction remains trapped within the coloniality of power and the matrix of European thought because Derrida maintains that the relationship to the wholly other remains impossible as such. This is where this debate becomes particularly interesting and difficult. Indeed, Bernasconi and Mignolo are not entirely wrong in claiming that Derrida denies the possibility of experiencing otherness *as such*, in a presence. Exteriority, otherness cannot present itself, cannot appear in a presence. And in "Violence and Metaphysics," Derrida indeed explains that Greek European philosophy has always-already preempted the possibility of this "event," of this "encounter with the wholly other," because the philosophical *logos* defines itself from the outset as the thinking of being *and* of its other, of being and of the beyond of being: *epekeina tes ousias*.[36] Philosophy—"Greek," "European," or whatever corpus we approach under these names—will have always already presented itself as a thinking of the one *and its other*, thus denying from the start the possibility of an authentic "event," of what Mignolo calls "exteriority," understood as Europe's exteriority. That is, the Other, finally presenting himself or herself as such: the other of Europe, Europe's other.

Bernasconi and Mignolo thus claim that Derrida (notably through his thinking of "the closure of metaphysics") "maintains the totality": deconstruction is only "from the inside." This is why decoloniality—sometimes described by Mignolo as "deconstruction from the exteriority of Western metaphysics"—must move away from deconstruction; and in Mignolo's work, this critique is also addressed to several postcolonial theorists influenced by deconstruction.[37] But, here, I think there is a misunderstanding on the nature of this totalizing "closure" and on the nature of the so-called "other" who/which is captured in the so-called totality. I must limit myself to a few salient points. What Derrida is telling us is that the experience of otherness cannot present itself *within the limits of philosophy*. Philosophy, inasmuch as it remains dependent on the logic of the proper and of presence, inasmuch as it presents itself as ontological discourse on the truth and essence of being and nonbeing, cannot think something like an encounter with the other (in Levinas's sense) because philosophy has always defined its own logos as principle for thinking the totality of being, thus encompassing the same *and the other* and always-already preempting and appropriating everything that exceeds and resists the philosophical logos. But—and this point is crucial—this resistance already happens *within* philosophy. It supposes a beyond-within, an internal exteriority, enclave, or crypt. It follows that philosophy is nothing but the perpetuation of its own crisis in act as philosophy must negotiate (violently) with the other within and without the limits that it sets for itself (and for the other). It endlessly fights against its "own" heterogeneity: it strives to expel the other (or to appropriate the other, which amounts to the same). In defining itself in opposition to what it is *not*, the philosophical gesture strives to appropriate heterogeneity by defining it and making it its own—a classical dialectical move. This "crisis," this critical or self-critical gesture, according to Derrida, belongs to the very essence of philosophy. It *is* philosophy, in potentiality and in act. And it goes hand in hand, still according to Derrida, with an irreducibly *imperialist* drive of philosophy:

From that moment, the movement of self-critique, if it can be put this way, would belong to what is most proper to the philosophical as such. Philosophy would repeat itself and would reproduce its own tradition as the teaching of its own crisis and as the *paideia* of self-critique in general. This *paideia* always goes hand in hand, and there is nothing fortuitous about this, with a self-confidence [*assurance*] of philosophy, a self-confidence that I will call, without taking it lightly, *imperialist*. Philosophy is an ontology and its *paideia* an encyclopedia. It grants itself the right to define and situate all the *regions* of being or objectivity. It has no particular object proper because it legislates on objectivity in general. It *dominates*, in a precisely *critical* fashion, all the so-called regional sciences, to assign them their limits and legitimacy. Dominating the field of disciplines and so-called regional sciences, cultivating it and marking its property lines or borders, the philosophical onto-encyclopedia is at home everywhere, and its self-critical movement is but the reproduction of its own authority.[38]

This aspect of Derrida's thought—here presented in a conference in Cotonou, in 1978—is not addressed by either Bernasconi or Mignolo. From the outset, Derrida's deconstruction targeted the hegemonic structures of European philosophy and the epistemic principles of Western modernity, challenging its claim to univocal truth, systematic totalization, and universality. Derrida showed that the discourse we call "philosophy" (what reflects itself, presents itself *as* "European"—philosophy) is not a homogeneous system. It supposes a multiplicity of heterogeneous forces and traces that remain to be read, interpreted, and translated: in short, deconstructed. As such, Western knowledge's claim to universality constitutes a forceful gesture of totalization and homogenization, violently erasing differences, denying heterogeneity within and without itself, thereby imposing its epistemic, political, and ontological sovereignty over other, nonphilosophical discourses, local knowledges, regional disciplines, and thoughts categorized as non-European. But this gesture of violent exclusion and/or appropriation is never final. What we call "Europe" or "European thought"—as well as *thought*, or *experience* in general—is structurally heterogeneous. It does not exist *as such*, in self-presence. It has the formless form of a phantasm. The notion that a philosophical corpus, "Greek," "European," or "Western," is homogeneous, unified, one with itself, therefore supposing an inside and outside, an interiority and exteriority separated by a dividing line, an indivisible internal/external border—this notion is itself a phantasm resulting from the efforts of the totalizing, homogenizing drive of philosophy: a phantasm imposing itself through a violence that is nothing less than imperialist, dixit Derrida. The European phantasm supposes the haunting of the other *and* the phantasmatic obfuscation of haunting. The phantasm is also the phantasm of exorcizing the phantom, of discarding the originary and irreducible spectrality that prevents that what we call "Europe" present itself as such, self-gathered and homogenized under that name—a proper name that is therefore very much improper, by way of this force of haunting:

> Haunting is historical, to be sure, but it is not *dated*, it is never docilely given a date in the chain of presents, day after day, according to the instituted order of a calendar. Untimely, it does not come to, it does not happen to, it does not befall, one day, Europe, as if the latter, at a certain moment of its history, had begun to suffer from a certain evil, to let itself be *inhabited* in its inside, that is, haunted by a foreign guest. Not that that guest is any less a stranger for having always occupied the domesticity of Europe. But there was no inside, there was nothing inside before it. The ghostly would displace itself like the movement of this history. Haunting would mark the very existence of Europe. It would open the space and the relation to self of what is called by this name, at least since the Middle Ages.[39]

Originary haunting (haunting before the origin) interrupts the specular image. It interrupts reflexivity while propelling the desire for it. It troubles, excites. It entails a troubling opacity of the mirror, an uncanny imago or imagoes prior to any power of imaging or self-imaging, a split dissemination of the unique before any bifurcation between the one and the other, between reflection and imagination, between truth and fiction, a split that breaks open the space of an auto-hetero-thanato-biographical scene of violence and seduction through which phantasmal ipseity is played and simulated, plays (with) itself and/as the other by telling "oneself" stories—never without a certain perversion or cruelty. In so doing, the unique splits and clones "itself" before and beyond being (itself), invents "oneself" and/as the other, originary simulacrum or simulation without origin, phantasm without homeland, or with *more than one* origin, and therefore *no more one* origin—*plus d'une origine*; there, haunting and/as dissemination interrupts the monogenealogical drive of filiation before the origin, thus giving it its impetus, and resists the gathering, stabilizing force of the name, the naming of any name, thereby prohibiting that something like "Europe" ever reflect itself in its "own" name. It is through this so-called proper name through that Europe imagined itself as origin and end, as the archeo-teleological agent and law of world history, in other words, as the Patriarch, the Father, the phantasm of an inseminating instance, one that is always-already *dead*:

> As he expands, as he claims to extend himself across the world, the Western "father" proceeds to self-destruct, self-dissolve. The marks of Western identity lose themselves as they expand. This is why the familial metaphor is very important here. The father is trapped, he's dying, he *is dead*, he can assert his lineage or filiation or legacy, so to speak, only by losing it, by making it independent from him, to the point when the son no longer needs the father; in a way, paternity succeeds when the father is destroyed, to the extent that he no longer can even claim paternity. This is what I call dissemination. I said somewhere that dissemination is what doesn't return to the father [*ce qui ne revient pas au père*]. Western naivety consists in saying: "I'm going to inseminate the whole world and the whole world will return to me [*me reviendra*] and will recognize my name." But what happens is that it works only by not returning to the father. Not only by not returning to the father, but by showing that it *never came from the father to start with*, that the movement doesn't come from the father.[40]

"The familial metaphor is very important here," as Derrida puts it, not only because it interrogates the genealogical drive for origin and Europe's claim to paternity (which sustains colonialism and colonial differences) but also because it testifies to the inseparability between this genealogical drive and the phallocentric and familialist determination of sexual differences, the attempted stabilization of sexual dissemination.[41] "Europe" speaks the language of the Father. It presupposes; it *is* this paternity claim. It posits itself as origin and end of what it defines as its other, precisely by defining it as *its* other: its "own" other, its progeny. It thereby attempts to *perform* the phantasm of its own homogeneity and genealogy by setting its own limits, striving to appropriate what it excludes, its otherness. Philosophy—and maybe "Europe"—is this very performance, in potentiality and in act. It is nothing but this phantasmatic performance of origin and end. But it is therefore also the irreducible failure to actualize the phantasm: it is its own fallibility. And all the violences associated with "Europe" come from this crisis—this crisis in paternity—from the forceful perpetuation of the crisis that bears the name "Europe," and from the failing performance of this ontological actualization.[42] There isn't, there has never been "Europe" *as such.* "Europe" is but a phantasm, the differantial image of something that never was, never had presence: a violent work of mourning. It is in and through this phantasmal work of mourning, on this foundation without foundation—the bottom without bottom of the phantasm—that all "European constructions," imaginations, or reimaginations become possible, as impossible. The phantasm is both their chance, their sustenance, and their deconstruction at work: a principle of fallibility and ruin at the heart of "Europe" and the phallocolonial drive.

It follows from all this that Mignolo's operation of de-linking must in fact presuppose the *success* of the philosophical performance; it must presuppose the homogeneity of European or Western thought and the neat cut between "Europe" and its "other," while this homogeneity and this cut *are themselves the result of the colonial gesture and of its epistemic violence.* In other words, Mignolo's decolonial critique of the coloniality of power holds a mirror to Europe; it remains captive to what Derrida calls "the onto-encyclopaedic" gesture, that is, the totalizing philosophical gesture of mastery that Mignolo otherwise denounces. Mignolo must posit the homogeneity of Europe (and its other) so as to de-link from its influence. De-linking implies the strict delimitation of Europe, of its colonial imaginary and epistemology, the presupposition of its homogeneity, and the strategic mirroring and reversal of the geopolitics of knowledge. The gesture is necessary—it upholds the system—for there is no de-linking from "something" that would be nonhomogeneous and nonidentical to itself, structurally heterogeneous. The operation of de-linking—its theoretical possibility and strategic effectiveness—presupposes the circumscription of what is thereby located, identified, contained as a geohistorically and epistemologically cohesive and coherent ensemble, and this despite the alleged fictionality of the claims that make up that ensemble, as many "constructions" or "narratives" that Mignolo denounces page after page.

De-linking demands the *solidity* of something like "Europe," the hardness and "gatheredness" of the phallocolonial. To identify the colonial difference *as such*, Mignolo must confirm and reproduce—*ratify* and *sanction*—the violence of its dividing and homogenizing operation. If Mignolo admitted that "Europe" is structurally heterogeneous, phantasmatic, that it never was as solid as it claimed, never present to itself, even as "local history," de-linking would lose all effectiveness and possibility. In its operation, de-linking must deny the structural heterogeneity of "Europe" and the force of haunting; it is an exorcism.[43] Certainly, this could be interpreted as a strategic move on Mignolo's part (although Mignolo does not, and in fact cannot, present it as a *purely* strategic gesture); but strategy, like geopolitics, always involves unpredictable displacements and reversals, so that such or such tactical move always risks playing into the hands of the adversary—this specular or quasi-specular Other to whom or to which I am as if magnetized, *aimanté*; and decoloniality, de-linking, or what Mignolo calls "border-thinking" should also strive to account for the risk of this uncanny or *unheimlich* complicity or captivity, this haunting or colonial *différance* before colonial difference, if only to acknowledge (and perhaps escape) its own ontological presuppositions and conceive the conditions of possibility (and impossibility) of decoloniality as "deconstruction from the outside of Western metaphysics." This recognition is *also* a strategic necessity from the perspective of a "decolonial imaginary" worthy of the name.

Coda: Intersexting Differences
(Colonial, Sexual, Hauntings)

As soon as colonial difference is no longer thought of as dichotomous, as oppositional or dialectical difference, as soon as it is thought from the perspective of haunting and (sexual) dissemination, the exorcizing operation of de-linking remains affected with undecidability.[44] Decoloniality must move, maneuver, and work in the undecidable milieu of *phantasma*, in "the penumbral light of a virtuality that is neither being nor nothingness":

> As we know, *phantasma* also named for the Greeks the apparition of the specter, the vision of the phantom, or the phenomenon of the revenant. The fabulous and the phantasmatic

have a feature in common: *stricto sensu,* in the classical and prevalent sense of these terms, they do not pertain to either the true or the false, the veracious or the mendacious. They are related, rather, to an irreducible species of the simulacrum or even of simulation, in the penumbral light of a virtuality that is neither being nor nothingness, nor even an order of the possible that an ontology or a mimetology could account for or subdue with reason. No more than myth, fable and phantasm are doubtless not truths or true statements as such, but neither are they errors or deceptions, false witnesses or perjuries.[45]

This penumbral milieu—neither light nor darkness—is also that of imagination, of the image, but of an image re-presenting something that was never present as such: image as originary supplement, substitute for life and being "themselves," substitute without origin, imaginal reproduction of something that never *was.*[46] The chance and the risk of decolonial imagination, of a "genuine" decoloniality beyond the traditional European logic of the image, would thus reside in this impossible imagination of image without presence, phantasm, life supplementing "itself" beyond the presence of the present, beyond dualisms and dichotomous thinking. It would have to dwell in the penumbral light, through a sort of survival and a fictionality that would exceed the opposition between being and nonbeing, truth and falsehood, light and darkness. This, which is both a risk and a chance, then, is not foreign, I believe, to what Gloria Anzaldúa calls "mestiza consciousness":

> As a *mestiza* I have no country, my homeland cast me out; yet all countries are mine because I am every woman's sister or potential lover. (As a lesbian I have no race, my own people disclaim me; but I am all races because there is the queer of me in all races.) I am cultureless because, as a feminist, I challenge the collective cultural/religious male-derived beliefs of Indo-Hispanics and Anglos; yet I am cultured because I am participating in the creation of yet another culture, a new story to explain the world and our participation in it, a new value system with images and symbols that connect us to each other and to the planet. *Soy un amasamiento,* I am an act of kneading, of uniting and joining that not only has

produced both a creature of darkness and a creature of light, but also a creature that questions the definitions of light and dark and gives them new meanings.[47]

Against dichotomous thinking that captures life and being from all sides and attempts to reduce their structural multiplicity and heterogeneity into dualistic realities, Anzaldúa's is a call towards a queer-imaginal, quasi-shamanic incantation bridging differences and singularities by producing new symbols and new images, stories exceeding oppositionality through the force of imagination and "acts of imaginative flight." This is the work of writing.[48] It is performed textually, through the intersextual parasitism of tongues, images, symbols. Writing is here envisioned as inseparably spiritual, political, erotic, and embodied[49]—always active and combative: "This intentional interaction [image consciousness] is similar to fiction writing's willed, active fantasy; without any partial control on the dreamer/writer's part, the artist's conscious and unconscious personality unite to create the art produced. The writer records the conversation between these inner images and her ego. You could say that the writer, through her interactive participation, merges herself in the conscious/unconscious processes and gains possession of her characters by allowing them to possess her. Imagination is an active, purposeful creativity."[50]

For Anzaldúa, writing and imagination are life affirming and reality altering, recreative and transformative: "The 'spiritual' part of myself as a writer is also concerned with traveling to other realities, with change, with transformation of consciousness, with exploring reality, with other possibilities and experiences, and with recreating other experiences. You do these tasks through the imagination, through your creative self, creative unconscious."[51] But Anzaldúa also knew very well that as soon as there is writing and imagination—spiritual and bodily travels, border crossings, bridges to otherness, recreations of other experiences, ex-position of the self, encounters with beings "other other other"—the ghosts are already there. As soon as writing and imagination are at work, at play, and as soon as the imaginal involves not only "conscious/unconscious processes" and the exploration of the other, but also a structure of mutual possession, of swallowing and eating others' stories, of incorporating the other, of possessing, of being and letting oneself be possessed, and so on, the ghosts cannot but accumulate.[52] One has to learn to live with the dead, the living dead, to listen to them and let oneself be haunted by them, always with the risk of following them and passing to the other side. This always takes place around some mirror. It involves, if we play a little, a logic of *obsidionality*:

> When my father died, my mother put blankets over the mirrors. Consciously, she had no idea why. Perhaps a part of her knew that a mirror is a door through which the soul may "pass" to the other side and she didn't want us to "accidentally" follow our father to the place where the souls of the dead live.
>
> The mirror is an ambivalent symbol. Not only does it reproduce images (the twins that stand for thesis and antithesis); it contains and absorbs them. In ancient times the Mexican Indians made mirrors of volcanic glass known as obsidian. Seers would gaze into a mirror until they fell into a trance. Within the black, glossy surface, they saw clouds of smoke which would part to reveal a vision concerning the future of the tribe and the will of the gods.[53]

Notes

1. "i inhabit a sacred wound/ i inhabit imaginary ancestors/ i inhabit an obscure will" (653).

2. Mignolo and Walsh, *On Decoloniality*, 9.

3. In *Light in the Dark* (178), Gloria Anzaldúa theorizes *coyolxauhqui's* imaginal power: "The imagination is a powerful generative force, a transformative genius, a genius that transforms the self. In assembling, ordering, and constructing, I myself am assembled, ordered, and constructed. The Latin *ars* is the root of the English 'art' and 'artist.' Contemplation, from the Latin *contemplari*, is the ability to see things as they really are. Imaginary reality. The artist as culture-bearer." See also 34: "This imaging body—or what I call the 'nepantla body'—can be sensed during shamanistic states or whenever you shift attention from the everyday to some feeling, fantasy, or fiction. Everyday reality 'disappears' or is momentarily suspended." And see 41: "Perhaps, as the poet Stanley Plumly suggests, the imagination is the real reality, the ultimate arbiter." I return to this reality-shaping power of imagination and its ambivalent relationship with life-death in the conclusion of this chapter.

4. Derrida, *Without Alibi*, 66.

5. Derrida, *Of Grammatology*, 311.

6. Derrida, 187. For a typically excellent reflection on Derrida's deconstructive reading of imagination, see Johnson, "Touching the Imagination." On the topic, see also Mercier, "We Have Tasted the Powers of the Age to Come."

7. See notably Chakrabarty, *Provincializing Europe* (particularly 90–113), and his deconstruction of the European global history of capital partly indexed on a reading of Derrida's *Specters of Marx* and his notions of trace and supplement.

8. See Mignolo, *The Darker Side of Western Modernity*. On the notion of world—itself far more obscure than it seems—see Mercier, "Uses of 'the Pluriverse'" and "Altérités: pluralité et im-possibilité des mondes."

9. Derrida, *The Other Heading*, 24–25.

10. On the notion of decolonial imaginary, see notably Perez, *The Decolonial Imaginary*; Lugones, "Decolonial"; Mignolo and Walsh, *On Decoloniality*, 34 and 224; Mendieta, "Toward a Decolonial Feminist Imaginary."

11. Mendieta, 245.

12. Outlaw, "African 'Philosophy': Deconstructive and Reconstructive Challenges"; Bernasconi, "African Philosophy's Challenge to Continental Philosophy."

13. Mignolo, "The Geopolitics of Knowledge and the Colonial Difference."

14. On decolonizing philosophy as strategy of negotiation beyond oppositional dialectics, see Kisukidi, "Décoloniser la philosophie," 96–98.

15. Derrida's deconstructive reading of the opposition between productive and reproductive imagination, suggesting their irreducible coimplication and intercontamination, can be found in "Economimesis."

16. As Johnson puts it, nothing prevents us from reading imagination "against its philosophical (metaphysical, humanist) determination." "Touching the Imagination" 71. But Johnson convincingly demonstrates that this cannot be simply decreed: it must be *done*. *Faut le faire*. To be theoretically potent and strategically effective, it requires a patient work of reelaborative deconstruction of imagination's traditional limitations. I also touch on this type of work (theoretical, textual, strategic, and beyond) in Mercier, "Glas Struggles" and "Plastic Events, Spectral Events."

17. Derrida, *The Beast and the Sovereign*, vol. II, 170. On Derrida's phantasm, see also Mercier, "Plastic Events, Spectral Events."

18. Derrida, *Memoires*, 64.

19. Derrida, 64.

20. Bernasconi, 192. Also quoted in Mignolo, "The Geopolitics of Knowledge and the Colonial Difference," 72.

21. On this notion, see Odysseos, "Prolegomena to Any Future Decolonial Ethics."

22. For a critical analysis of Mignolo's significant debt towards Foucault, see Alcoff, "Mignolo's Epistemology of Coloniality."

23. Mignolo, "The Geopolitics of Knowledge and the Colonial Difference," 70–71.

24. Mignolo, "Delinking."

25. Mignolo, 455–56.

26. Mignolo, *Local Histories/ Global Designs*, especially 337–38. The principles of this critical epistemology—indexing thought and being on geohistorical positionality and purporting to interrogate them from the perspective of empirical conditions of enunciation ("lived experiences")—can also be found in Bernasconi. Bernasconi notably accuses "European philosophy" to have ignored "the role of experience in philosophy. The question 'who is speaking?' is one that has been outlawed from philosophy because it seemed to set up an opposition between the authority of the author and universal reason." Bernasconi, "African Philosophy's Challenge," 192. Perhaps, but as soon as one must *also* admit that versions of the question "who is speaking?" were very much central to projects such as Marx's, Nietzsche's, Freud's, or Foucault's, but also Derrida's and many, many others, whatever their merits or demerits from a decolonial perspective, should we then conclude that these projects as well as those they inspired do not belong to the ensemble called "European philosophy"? Or should we rather consider that "European philosophy" and "Europe," if we want to go beyond what Bernasconi admits are "gross caricatures" (184), presuppose cracks and fault lines testifying to their structural heterogeneity?

27. Mignolo, "The Geopolitics of Knowledge and the Colonial Difference," 71. This problem was systematically explored by Enrique Dussel, usually in Levinasian terms, notably in *Philosophy of Liberation*, 48.

28. Mignolo, "Delinking," 451–52.

29. Mignolo, 452.

30. Mignolo and Walsh, *On Decoloniality*, 9.

31. Mignolo, "Delinking," 497. In a recent interview, Spivak lays out a robust critique of some of the chief principles of decoloniality (deemed "liberal-radical fantasy"), starting with Mignolo's position ("somewhat golden-ageist") and his strategy of de-linking: "Delinking is a luxury that can be recommended (though not practised) by the Europeanized elite. To delink is the kind of backward looking nativism which precisely denies that the history of colonialism practices epistemic violence on the subaltern, which continues the violence practised pre-colonially by the hierarchies within the colonized space." Spivak, "Epistemic Daring," 136–37. I thank Sourav Kargupta for pointing me to this interview and for our many conversations on this and other topics.

32. Mignolo, "The Geopolitics of Knowledge and the Colonial Difference," 91.

33. Mignolo, "Delinking," 463. I offered a deconstructive reading of the pluriversal ontologic of several decolonial discourses in Mercier, "Uses of 'the Pluriverse.'" I notably analyzed the disquieting proximity between these discourses on the pluriverse (notably Bruno Latour's and Marisol de la Cadena's) and the epistemic principles governing Carl Schmitt's political anthropology, polemology, and ontology. Mignolo, too, adapts (and adopts) many of Schmitt's concepts

and epistemic categories in his geopolitical analytics and in his description of the decolonial pluriverse as "third nomos" of the earth. See *The Darker Side of Western Modernity*, 52–74.

34. For several decolonial thinkers, Levinas's thought is systematically singled out as enabling a thinking of Europe's otherness and exteriority—not only by Dussel; but also by Escobar, "Worlds and Knowledges Otherwise"; and Maldonado-Torres, "The Topology of Being and the Geopolitics of Knowledge." Mignolo refers twice to Levinas as an "exception" among "male European philosophers" in "Delinking," 491–92. A similar gesture can be found in "The Geopolitics of Knowledge and the Colonial Difference" (75), with reference to Dussel's philosophy of liberation, and in "Introduction: Coloniality of Power and De-colonial Thinking" (165), where Mignolo connects Levinas's thinking of exteriority to "the singularity of the Jewish experience." But this singularization of Levinas is itself ambivalent, as Levinas is also incriminated, quite legitimately, for several blatantly Eurocentric statements (see Bernasconi, 185; Maldonado-Torres). Here is not the place to examine the merits of these various and ambivalent appropriations of Levinas by decolonial thought, but one could interrogate the systematic reontologization of "exteriority" and "the other" operated by those discourses, and a certain immanentization of Levinas's ethics of transcendence and responsibility (often conflated with a communal onto-politics)—two gestures that should be strictly forbidden by Levinas's radical thinking of otherness and responsibility. I thank Felipe Quinteros for his insights on these questions and more.

35. Mignolo, "Foreword: On Pluriversality and Multipolarity," ix–xiv.

36. Derrida, *Writing and Difference*, 191.

37. Mignolo, "The Geopolitics of Knowledge and the Colonial Difference," 71. Like Spivak ("Epistemic Daring," 140), I consider it essential to hold together decolonization and deconstruction and do not think it is possible or even desirable, in both strategic and theoretical terms, to abandon the type of questions opened up by deconstruction—as if one were done with deconstruction and immune to this line of questioning as soon as one is speaking "from the exteriority of Western metaphysics," as Mignolo puts it. Deconstruction, just like decolonization (but why dissociate the two so sharply alongside that dividing line?), works precisely in questioning the colonial inside-outside dichotomy which remains essential to Mignolo's geopolitical architecture. Like Sourav Kargupta, albeit differently, I cannot imagine a deconstruction that would not be as well a "postcolonial deconstruction" (Kargupta, "Can the Subaltern Be Witnessed?"). In previous works (i.e., Mercier, "Resisting Legitimacy"; "Re/pro/ductions: *Ça déborde*"; "Différence sexuelle, difference idéologique," 34–47), I stressed that deconstruction always targets a phallocolonial authority, a seminal figure and power principle, be it logos, the state, or capital, an onto-logic of the proper that performs its own sovereignty by positing itself as origin and truth

of being. This onto-logic always works in neutralizing the effects of différance, contamination, and dissemination, thereby claiming the right and power to define itself and the other: this is ipsocentrism, through which the homo-hegemonic phantasm of sovereignty claims presence and legitimacy by attempting to reduce the irreducible heterogeneity of the disseminal text—and it never goes without violence. In turn, this nonoppositional heterogeneity (sexual, material, textual, and so on) betrays the immanent fallibility of the phallocolonial and propels its transformative deconstruction.

38. Derrida, *Who's Afraid of Philosophy?*, 101, translation modified.

39. Derrida, *Specters of Marx*, 3.

40. Derrida, "La langue de l'autre," 52. This interview, also from 1978, remains unpublished in either French or English. This is my translation.

41. One consequence of Mignolo's paradigmatic privileging of *the* "colonial difference" (singular and dichotomous) is the systematic subalternization of sexual differences. "Gender" and "sexual difference" are presented as subcategories or mere reflections of the colonial difference, itself described as overarching and determination in the last instance because it structures global geopolitics. The topological and ontological (ontopological and communal) geopolitics of knowledge drawn out by Mignolo, as potent as it might be from an analytical and strategic perspective, constantly ignores or deprivileges sexual and gender politics, the differential questions of sex, sexuality, queerness, of imaginal identifications, kin, kinship, filiation, or reproduction, as well as psychoanalytic (or extrapsychoanalytic) motifs such as the phantasm, the unconscious, repression, desire, the economy of the drives, the uncanny, or sexual differences. This move is particularly evident in Mignolo's many references to Anzaldúa's writings, which are systematically reduced to mere expressions of the dichotomous colonial difference ("us versus them") and assimilated as illustrative of his geopolitical analytics of border thinking, without references to Anzaldúa's sexual politics or to the complex poetics of desire and imagination she deploys textually everywhere. A similar critique—though from a different perspective—of Mignolo's dichotomous thinking, of his obfuscation of gender and of his treatment of Anzaldúa, can be found in Negrón-Muntaner, "Bridging Islands," 276–77, and Lugones, "Toward a Decolonial Feminism," 751–56. Spivak, in a particularly daring turn, gives hints of her feminist-Marxist-deconstructive critique of Lugones's decolonial feminism in "Epistemic Daring," 139–40.

42. The phantasm does have "real and *undeniable* consequences" (Derrida, *The Beast and the Sovereign, Vol. II*, 185). For ethico-political analyses of the phantasm's implications for thinking violence, colonialism, power, and legitimacy, see Derrida, *Monolingualism of the Other*, 23–26; 86–88; and Mercier, "Resisting Legitimacy."

43. As Derrida puts it in *Specters of Marx*, 202: "Ontology opposes [hauntology] only in a movement of exorcism." And the difficulty stems from the fact

that the haunting *of* Europe supposes a double genitive. Spectrality—haunting without origin—implies that one cannot know, in all rigor, who/what is haunting whom/what.

44. This suggests, as Derrida puts it, that "like philosophy and the deconstruction of the philosophical, decolonization is interminable." *Who's Afraid of Philosophy?*, 103.

45. Derrida, *Without Alibi*, 28.

46. Derrida:

Imagination is the power that allows life to affect itself with its own re-presentation. The image cannot re-present and add the representer to the represented, except in so far as the presence of the re-presented is already folded back upon itself in the world, in so far as life refers to itself as to its own lack, to its own wish for a supplement. The presence of the represented is constituted with the help of the addition to itself of that nothing which is the image, announcement of its dispossession within its own representer and within its death. The property [*le propre*] of the subject is merely the movement of that representative expropriation. In that sense imagnation, like death, is *representative and supplementary*. *Of Grammatology*, 184

47. Anzaldúa, *Borderlands/ La Frontera*, 80–81.

48. Anzaldúa, *Light in the Dark/ Luz en lo Oscuro*, 7. See also, on the same page: "In rewriting narratives of identity, nationalism, ethnicity, race, class, gender, sexuality, and aesthetics, I attempt to show (and not just tell) how transformation happens. My job is not just to interpret or describe realities but to create them through language and action, symbols and images." Perhaps a question should arise, here, concerning Anzaldúa's apparent dichotomy between "creating" and "interpreting" (or "describing"): Is this distinction tenable? Especially since "creating" is described, in the previous sentence, as a work of "rewriting"? As soon as creation supposes a *re*-writing of narratives, the limit between the creative and the interpretative must become instable, each time repeated anew in and through the split-dissemination mandated by, for example, "symbols and images." The force of iterability (*re*-, that is, writing) always-already splits and divides that limit. Creation, at bottom, designates the spectral revenance of what never took place in a presence—that is, a phantasm.

49. Anzaldúa, *Interviews/ Entrevistas*, 251–2. On "intersextuality" and a certain intersectional-feminist-deconstructive thinking of text and sexual difference beyond humanist-familialist schemas, see Marder, "Insex."

50. Anzaldúa, *Light in the Dark/ Luz en lo Oscuro*, 36.

51. Anzaldúa, *Interviews/ Entrevistas*, 251.

52. See Anzaldúa, *Interviews/ Entrevistas*, 41. Anzaldúa's texts are impossibly haunted; they swarm with spirits, figures, or images. See for example *Light in the Dark/ Luz en lo Oscuro*, 62–63; and see 36:

> The "I" is only one of the many members, imaginal figures, that compose a psyche. Other imaginal figures wander in and out within and without a person, all with lives of their own. "I" am not in charge of "my" images. Images have lives of their own and walk around as they choose, not as "I" choose. Nor do "I" create these images; they emerge from my personal psyche. All images have body and exist in three-dimensional space. Although contemporary theories of identity leave out our innermost spiritual core identity, I'm interested in the connective membrane between the interiority and the exteriority of subjectivity. [. . .] The imaginal's figures and landscapes are experienced as alive and independent of the dreamer. They speak with their own voices; move about at will.

But are they "alive," or "experienced as alive"? Does Anzaldúa allow herself, and us, to choose? Can we? Should we? But what choice do we have when the "life" in question is mobilized by writing and the imaginal—by text, and the genius of replacement: rewriting, recreating, reimagining? Who/what is haunting whom/what? Whose imagination, in whose "psyche"? Whose "I"?

In short: Who's dreaming when there is dream? These "deconstructive" questions do not oppose the decolonial gesture and certainly not in the powerful forms it takes in Anzaldúa's texts. On the contrary, the questions I've raised in this chapter mark the necessity to interrogate the sometimes overly theoretical translation of this gesture by theorists who, when they call on imagination as a tool for decolonization, might forget a little too easily the presuppositions that undergird the language they use, the philosophical grammar and the rhetorical complicities that also give it force and intelligibility. By reading Anzaldúa with Derrida, I want to mark the inseparability between deconstruction and decolonization; this inflection perhaps marks a slight but decisive difference between the phantasmal imaginal I'm sketching out here—marked by auto-hetero-affective contamination, by differantial supplementarity, undecidability, irreducible haunting—and Lugones's decolonial imaginary and coalition of multitude, also drawing on readings of Anzaldúa, but grounded in "communalism" and "lived practices, values, beliefs, ontologies, space-times, and cosmologies." "Toward a Decolonial Feminism," 754. I detect similar desires for ontological presence and the exorcism of haunting and spectrality in Ortega, "Spectral Perception and Ghostly Subjectivity at the Colonial Gender/Race/Sex Nexus"; and in Savransky, "A Decolonial Imagination."

53. Anzaldúa, *Borderlands/ La Frontera*, 42.

Bibliography

Alcoff, Linda Martín. "Mignolo's Epistemology of Coloniality." *CR: The New Centennial Review* 7, no. 3 (2007): 79–101.

Anzaldúa, Gloria E. *Borderlands/ La Frontera: The New Mestiza*. San Francisco: Aunt Lute, 1987.

Anzaldúa, Gloria E. *Interviews/Entrevistas*. Edited by A. Keating. New York and London: Routledge, 2000.

Anzaldúa, Gloria E. *Light in the Dark/ Luz en lo Oscuro: Rewriting Identity, Spirituality, Reality*. Edited by A. Keating. Durham and London: Duke University Press, 2015.

Bernasconi, Robert. "African Philosophy's Challenge to Continental Philosophy." In *Postcolonial African Philosophy: A Critical Reader*. Edited by E. Chukwudi Eze, 183–96. Cambridge and Oxford: Blackwell, 1997.

Césaire, Aimé. "calendrier lagunaire." In *The Complete Poetry of Aimé Césaire*. Translated by A. J. Arnold and C. Eshleman, 652–55. Middletown: Wesleyan University Press, 2017.

Chakrabarty, Dipesh. *Provincializing Europe: Postcolonial Thought and Historical Difference*. Princeton and Oxford: Princeton University Press, 2000.

Derrida, Jacques. "Economimesis." Translated by R. Klein. *Diacritics* 11, no. 2 (1981): 3–25.

Derrida, Jacques. "La langue de l'autre." Unpublished. Fonds Jacques Derrida, 219DRR/256.16. IMEC, Normandy, France, 1978.

Derrida, Jacques. *Memoires—for Paul de Man*. Translated by C. Lindsay, J. Culler, E. Cadava, and P. Kamuf. Rev. ed. New York: Columbia University Press, 1989.

Derrida, Jacques. *Monolingualism of the Other*. Translated by P. Mensah. Stanford: Stanford University Press, 1998.

Derrida, Jacques. *Of Grammatology*. Translated by G. C. Spivak. Corrected ed. Baltimore and London: Johns Hopkins University Press, 1997.

Derrida, Jacques. *Specters of Marx: The State of the Debt, the Work of Mourning and the New International*. Translated by P. Kamuf. New York and London: Routledge, 1994.

Derrida, Jacques. *The Beast and the Sovereign, Vol. II*. Translated by G. Bennington. Chicago and London: University of Chicago Press, 2011.

Derrida, Jacques. *The Other Heading: Reflections on Today's Europe*. Translated by P.-A. Brault and M. Naas. Bloomington: University of Indiana Press, 1992.

Derrida, Jacques. *Who's Afraid of Philosophy? Right to Philosophy 1*. Translated by J. Plug. Stanford: Stanford University Press, 2002.

Derrida, Jacques. *Without Alibi*. Edited and translated by P. Kamuf. Stanford: Stanford University Press, 2002.

Derrida, Jacques. *Writing and Difference*. Translated by A. Bass. London and New York: Routledge, 1978.

Dussel, Enrique. *Philosophy of Liberation.* Translated by A. Martinez and C. Morkovsky. Eugene: Wipf & Stock, 1985.

Escobar, Arturo. "Worlds and Knowledges Otherwise: The Latin American Modernity/ Coloniality Research Program." *Cultural Studies* 21, nos. 2–3 (2007): 179–210.

Johnson, David E. "Touching the Imagination: Aristotle, Derrida, and the Homonymy of Life." *theory@buffalo* 18 (2015): 48–77.

Kargupta, Sourav. "Can the Subaltern Be Witnessed?" *Angelaki* 27, no. 2 (2022): 57–71.

Kisukidi, Nadia Yala. "Décoloniser la philosophie. Ou de la philosophie comme objet anthropologique." *Présence Africaine* 192 (2015): 83–98.

Lugones, María. "Decolonial." In *Keywords for Latina/o Studies.* Edited by D. R. Vargas, N. R. Mirabal, and L. La Fountain-Stokes, 43–47. New York: New York University Press, 2017.

Lugones, María. "Toward a Decolonial Feminism." *Hypatia* 25, no. 4 (2010): 742–59.

Maldonado-Torres, "The Topology of Being and the Geopolitics of Knowledge: Modernity, Empire, Coloniality." *City* 8, no. 1 (2004): 29–56.

Marder, Elissa. "Insex." *Parallax* 25, no. 2 (2019): 228–39.

Mendieta, Eduardo. "Towards a Decolonial Feminist Imaginary: Decolonizing Futurity." *Critical Philosophy of Race* 8, nos. 1–2 (2020): 237–64.

Mercier, Thomas Clément. "Altérités: Pluralité ou im-possibilité des mondes— entre ontologies et déconstructions (Sur un bon mot de Donna Haraway)." *Revue des sciences humaines* 347 (2022): 175–188.

Mercier, Thomas Clément. "Différence sexuelle, différence idéologique: Lectures à contretemps (Derrida lisant Marx et Althusser, dans les années 1970 et au-delà)." *Décalages* 2, no. 3 (2020): 1–51.

Mercier, Thomas Clément. "Glas Struggles." *Oxford Literary Review* 44, no. 1 (2022): 121–38.

Mercier, Thomas Clément. "Plastic Events, Spectral Events: Literature and 'the Real of the Phantasm,' between Malabou and Derrida." In *Literature and Event: Twenty-First Century Reformulations.* Edited by M. Mukim and D. Attridge, 164–79. London and New York: Routledge, 2021.

Mercier, Thomas Clément. "Re/pro/ductions: Ça déborde." *Poetics Today* 42, no. 1 (2021): 23–47.

Mercier, Thomas Clément. "Resisting Legitimacy: Weber, Derrida, and the Fallibility of Sovereign Power." *Global Discourse* 6, no. 3 (2016): 374–91.

Mercier, Thomas Clément. "Uses of 'the Pluriverse': Cosmos, Interrupted—or the Others of Humanities." *Ostium* 15, no. 2 (2019): 1–15.

Mercier, Thomas Clément. "We Have Tasted the Powers of the Age to Come: Thinking the Force of the Event—from *Dynamis* to *Puissance.*" *Oxford Literary Review* 40, no. 1 (2018): 76–94.

Mignolo, Walter D. *The Darker Side of Wester Modernity: Global Futures, Decolonial Options.* Durham and London: Duke University Press, 2011.

Mignolo, Walter D. "Delinking: The Rhetoric of Modernity, the Logic of Coloniality and the Grammar of De-coloniality." *Cultural Studies* 21, nos. 2–3 (2007): 449–514.

Mignolo, Walter D. "Foreword: On Pluriversality and Multipolarity." In *Constructing the Pluriverse: The Geopolitics of Knowledge.* Edited by B. Reiter, ix–xvi. Durham and London: Duke University Press, 2018.

Mignolo, Walter D. "The Geopolitics of Knowledge and the Colonial Difference." *The South Atlantic Quarterly* 101, no. 1 (2002): 57–96.

Mignolo, Walter D. "Introduction: Coloniality of Power and De-colonial Thinking." *Cultural Studies* 21, no. 2–3 (2007): 155–67.

Mignolo, Walter D. *Local Histories/ Global Designs: Coloniality, Subaltern Knowledges, and Border Thinking.* Princeton: Princeton University Press, 2000.

Mignolo, Walter D., and Catherine E. Walsh. *On Decoloniality: Concepts, Analytics, Praxis.* Durham and London: Duke University Press, 2018.

Negrón-Muntaner, Frances. "Bridging Islands: Gloria Anzaldúa and the Caribbean." *PMLA* 121, no. 1 (2006): 272–78.

Odysseos, Louiza. "Prolegomena to Any Future Decolonial Ethics: Coloniality, Poetics and 'Being Human as Praxis.'" *Millennium: Journal of International Studies* 45, no. 3 (2017): 447–72.

Ortega, Mariana. "Spectral Perception and Ghostly Subjectivity at the Colonial Gender/Race/Sex Nexus." *The Journal of Aesthetics and Art Criticism* 77, no. 4 (2019): 401–9.

Outlaw, Lucius. "African 'Philosophy': Deconstructive and Reconstructive Challenges." In *Contemporary Philosophy*, vol. 5, *African Philosophy*. Edited by G. Floistad, 9–44. Dordrecht: Nijhoff, 1987.

Pérez, Emma. *The Decolonial Imaginary: Writing Chicanas into History.* Bloomington: Indiana University Press, 1999.

Savransky, Martin. "A Decolonial Imagination: Sociology, Anthropology and the Politics of Reality." *Sociology* 51, no. 1 (2017): 11–26.

Spivak, Gayatri Chakravorty, Gianmaria Colpani, and Jamila M. H. Mascat. "Epistemic Daring: An Interview with Gayatri Chakravorty Spivak." *Postcolonial Studies* 25, no. 1 (2022): 136–41.

6

Europe without Eurocentrism?

An Essay in Critical-Colonial Studies

CHIARA BOTTICI AND BENOÎT CHALLAND

The Left has been divided on the question of Europe since its very beginning. The European project has often been ignored, if not openly opposed, as a mere technocratic and capitalist project that has nothing to do with a true democratic process of institution building. The criticism is not without basis. The process of political integration has indeed happened as a mere spillover effect of economic integration,[1] so the federalist ideas that accompanied such a process can easily be scorned as sheer ideological cover.[2] And yet, what is often forgotten in this outright opposition to Europe is that the nation-states that compose it were also projects for capital and labor management—a process initiated only a few centuries before that of European "construction." Therefore, we can look at the idealism of nineteenth-century popular nationalist movements and easily dismiss them along with the European federalists. Alternatively, we can consider the two processes of institution building, equally driven by the integration force of capital, and try to investigate which opportunities they may, or may not, disclose. Yet, in doing so, we should not only consider the opportunities that such a process opens (or closes) for those who are full citizens of Europe but also for those who are not. When seen in this double perspective, the technocratic-participatory alternative between Europe and its member states may appear in a different light.

In this chapter we would like to look at the European process of pooling and sharing fragments of sovereignty not only from the inside, as we mainly did in our previous work,[3] but also from the outside, that is, from the liminal zones of a putative European center. Given that the very boundaries of the European project are themselves constantly shifting, we would like to ask: How does the project of "Europe" appear when decentered? How is Europe perceived by those who may be in but are not from Europe,[4] as well as by those who may perceive themselves to be from but will never be allowed to be in Europe—physically or intellectually? Born out of economic imperatives, but also supported by the federalist movement that saw in the project an attempt to go beyond the logic of European nationalism, the project of European integration has from the very beginning implied a process of boundary thinking.

This is one of the reasons why we think it is pivotal to approach the question of Europe from the perspective of a *critical-colonial* approach. With this expression, we mean an approach that unifies the contributions coming from different field of critical colonial studies, including the postcolonial, the decolonial and the settler-colonial critiques. We will be drawing from all of them, and therefore we prefer to use the expression "critical-colonial," to point to the ensemble of critical investigations into the colonial conditions. While the term *postcolonial* may surreptitiously suggest that we are beyond that colonial past, a question that we would like to leave open,[5] the term *decolonial theory* performatively reinstates the speaking subject who is authorized to decide how to undo the colonial past, and thus, when used by theorists of European descent, like ourselves, can equally be interpreted as a gesture imbued with colonial hubris and thus reproduce the same coloniality of power it aims to undo. In sum, we propose a new sensibility that combines both strands of research, the critical-colonial studies produced in the "center" and the anti-imperial type of thinking coming from the "peripheries." In particular, we aim now to explore the claim that Europe was actually made in its peripheries, as has long been emphasized by writers such as Frantz Fanon (1925–1961), Albert Memmi (born 1920), Achille Mbembe (born 1957), and Annibal Quijano (1930–2018). Theory is not only the apanage of Europeans, as some Eurocentric philosophical approaches insisted for way too long; rather a philosophy of Europe can only emerge by attempting a relational and multidirectional gaze between Europe and its colonies, thereby insisting on the zones of contention and the zones of exclusion.[6]

Europe Was Born in the Colonies—
and It Still Thrives There

How can one sustain that Europe, a faltering political project uniting various nation-states in a common political and economic polity, was born in the colonies? Was Europe not born in the 1950s, with a process of "European construction" that began exactly when the former colonial empires collapsed? Is the European Union (EU) not the result of the attempt to make all wars, including imperial ones, impossible, as the advocates of European federalism hoped?[7] This is certainly one of the most powerful founding narratives produced by those who advocated for a process of European integration from the inside. As we emphasized in our *Imagining Europe*, the narrative of "Europe born out of the war" worked as a powerful founding narrative for the project of European integration, a narrative that at times merged with other founding myths, such as that of Europe born out of the classical Greek and Roman civilizations (the classical Europe), Europe as the cradle of a distinct religious identity (the Christian Europe), or Europe as the birthplace of the modern project (the Enlightened Europe).[8] Although one can critically engage with those narratives from the inside, we also need to look at them from the outside.[9]

In his *Wretched of the Earth*, Frantz Fanon made the case that thinking Europe without its global outer layers does not make sense. He went as far as asserting that "Europe is literally the creation of the Third World."[10] Knowing the Martiniquais intellectual's focus in that book on conflictual relations between the colonial realms and Europe, one is tempted to reduce this statement to uniquely material terms: without the riches of the colonies and the plundering of natural and human resources by European imperial powers, Europe and its dominant economic mode of production, capitalism, would not have been possible. And without capitalism, there would not have been any European modernity. Indeed, there is ground to argue that most of the wealth produced by Europeans from the sixteenth century onward was accumulated only marginally from internal surplus production, most of it coming from the raw materials and labor force extracted from its colonies.[11] Only by enlarging the focal point to the whole world can we understand why European wealth and well-being emerged at a given historical moment.

Labels such as the "Third World" work as powerful, unconscious images that establish implicit hierarchies. The material components of a growing division of Europe versus the rest are part of the violence of growing cultural and symbolic differentiations. Fanon captures this schism in his other masterpiece *Black Skins, White Masks*,[12] in which he shows the psychological damage made in the name of an alleged European cultural superiority. Language, accent, and other embodied cultural dispositions are constant reminders of the power asymmetries between metropoles and colonies, power asymmetries that do not need a police force to enact their brutality: they are the internalized police. The trauma of those who consider themselves good but then end up in a pervasive colonial imaginary that stigmatizes "blackness" as "evil" is aptly captured by his description of "the complex of [the] colonized."[13] "There is no forgiveness when one who claims superiority falls below the standard."[14] Cultural superiority, and with it inbuilt racism, runs not on biological grounds but on the performance of whiteness and of a sense of civilization as opposed to the other's primitivism.[15] Psychological alienation reached dramatic and traumatic proportions when the colonial subjects internalized white superiority and the structures of capitalist domination. The consciousness of the white Europeans was naturalized, made invisible, while blackness was bestialized, hypersexualized, and constantly ascribed to the native populations of the colonies, who were thus seduced into trying to pass as "white" by adopting their way of life.[16]

At this point of the argument, one could easily be tempted to argue that this colonial past has been overcome by the formal dissolutions of the European colonial empires and that what we are dealing with today is no longer the past but the present and, possibly, the future of Europe. But has the European project of building a common market (EEC) and, later, a political community (EU) managed to disentangle itself from Europe's role as an imperial and neoimperial power? As we have already mentioned, the founding narrative explaining the initial impetus for European cooperation around coal and steel in the early 1950s is built on postconflict reconciliation between France and Germany and thus on the overcoming of nationalistic wars that was supposed to spill over to other countries and spread peaceful relations. The Schuman Declaration (May 9, 1950) became the symbol of this project. "Europe will not be made all at once, or according to a single plan. It will be built through concrete achievements which first create a de facto solidarity," so stated the French politician Robert Schuman in the eponymous declaration, ritually celebrated as the founding text of the EU. This solidarity was indeed expected to create peace: "The solidarity in production thus established will make it plain that any war between France and Germany becomes not merely unthinkable, but materially impossible." The hope that such a process would lead us beyond the logic of nationalist wars was so strong that it not only led the original six members to create a joint political project, but Schuman himself was later declared the "Father of Europe." Indeed, it does not come as a surprise to learn that, in 2006, the Father of Europe was also declared to be "a servant of god" and candidate for beatification in the Catholic church[17]—a prospected sanctity of which Europeans are reminded every year, since the 1990s, when the EU started to celebrate the day in which the declaration was made (May 9) as Europe Day.

What is often omitted in this (literally) hagiographic narrative is that Schuman was also proposing French-German reconciliation as a way to calm down internal tensions in the French empire, at the time in the form of the French Union (1946–58), the watered-down version of the second French Colonial Empire. In 1950, Algeria was still a full territory of France, and Algerian nationalists were a thorn in the flesh of France. A sentence of the Schuman declaration reveals that the "European construction" (as we call it) was not immune from imperial hubris and the underlying myth of Europe as the agent of civilization. As we read in the text, the hope was also that European integration would lead to a renewal of its imperial role: "With increased resources Europe will be able to pursue the achievement of one of its essential tasks, namely, the development of the African continent."[18]

Schuman foresaw in a nascent "European solidarity" the new and necessary condition for a renewal of the European colonial paternalism. Other statements and projects from the French foreign minister in the early 1950s confirm that hopes were laid in transnational and/ or intergovernmental organizations, either European or Atlantic (*videte* NATO), to preserve the decaying French Empire.[19] Another of the decaying European powers, Great Britain, and its foreign secretary, Ernest Bevin, were also toying with the project of "development" to calm down anticolonial forces, for example, in Egypt, Jordan, and Iraq.[20] The last common European colonial upheaval, and its graveyard, was the Suez crisis of November 1956, but the international context of the Cold War and the tide having swung to an East-West confrontation forced Europeans to acquiesce in their loss of global hegemony. This was also the moment when the divisions between the East and West of Europe rose to prominence, and the former colonial world became the "third" world, in terms of Western Europe's significant other,[21] and was bracketed in the European imaginary. Only for a while, though.

Europe not only was made by the colonies but also still thrives there because European prosperity and stability still depend on these former colonial possessions. Realist accounts of Europe's construction underline that EU regulations are at best a negative form of integration, that is, an integration aimed at generating the best possible conditions for the exchange of goods and services within its borders, and that harsh measures to protect its external borders largely outweigh the pretence of a benevolent empire, willing to export its best norms to its neighbours.[22] Be it with regard to security arrangements during the Barcelona process, or control of migratory flows in the Mediterranean in the last three decades, the EU picks what it needs from its neighbours.

With regard to the former colonies at the southern borders of Europe, the so-called Barcelona process (launched in 1995) was the EU's attempt to generate cooperation with southern Mediterranean countries. However, this turned out to be a vacuous process of "cultural rapprochement" when most agreements were about forcing economic and security collaboration from Northern African states, thereby making sure they would provide cheap early potatoes, bell peppers, and tomatoes when the EU internal market could not produce enough.[23] The overall objective of a free-trade zone managed between the EU and southern Mediterranean states was abandoned and delegated to privatization and neoliberal diktats,[24] which now also have to accommodate the pressures coming from new seats of imperial powers, such as the Arabian Gulf.[25]

It is in this context that we should also interpret the questioning of European borders by migration flows from its former colonies. The EU's inability to deal with the flow of African and Middle Eastern refugees from the 1990s until now is a reminder that the "best norms" of Europe can exist only when the EU's economic performance is at its best, when they exist at all. *Fortress Europe*, a term originally referring to a defence strategy developed by Nazis during World War II, reemerged massively in the 1990 to criticize European discourses aimed at presenting the EU as a benevolent "civil power,"[26] while its policies were de facto aimed at merely preserving certain economic advantages inside of the EU, as well as trade and economic agreements with former colonies that favored capital accumulation. No wonder the project of "European development" is still decried by some as a form of "neocolonialism."[27]

Situating the Coloniality of Power:
Eurocentrism and the Racial View of the World

The process described above, whereby Europe was made by its colonies and vice versa, was accompanied by the rise of a specific worldview in which we are still largely immersed. It is a worldview characterized by a visual organization of political space that established Europe as its center and by a racial organization of bodies across the globe that propped up "whiteness" as the norm. It is important to keep the two categories of racism and Eurocentrism separate because despite the fact that both have their origins in the process described above, they are separate concepts. Also notice that we are here provisionally understanding them in a purely technical way: Eurocentrism being a worldview that literally takes Europe as its center, while racism is the idea that bodies around the globe should be classified according to historically constructed social systems of meanings.

Eurocentrism is a very specific but now pervasive image of the world whereby a globe (the earth) is turned into a bidimensional map, with Europe posed at its very center, a representation that has roots in the time of the so-called great discoveries, with all of the economic and cognitive shifts that these generated.[28] One may think that after a few decades of invitations to provincialize Europe[29] or to unsettle the racist divides generated by the European bourgeois man and "his overrepresentation,"[30] the Eurocentric map of the world has been overcome. But this is far from the case. Consider the image that Google retrieves whenever we type in "political map of the world": it is again one bidimensional map with Europe at its center, a map that we unconsciously reproduce in our everyday language with expressions such as "Middle East" or "Western civilization." From this point of view, one could even argue that Google has become the repository of the global unconscious map of the world.[31] This map is imbued with what Anibal Quijano called "the coloniality of power," an expression he coined to point out that this organization of space presupposes Eurocentrism and thus the racial classification of people that originated with it.[32] Hence the importance of focusing on "coloniality," and not simply "colonialism": whereas the latter may be perceived as an item of the past, coloniality denotes the relations of power that continue to exist even when the formal process of colonization is over.[33]

As Quijano showed in his seminal essay, *Coloniality of Power, Euro-centrism and Latin America*, we cannot understand the range and depth of Eurocentrism as a system of knowledge without keeping in mind how, since the beginning of modernity, the affirmation of a capitalist world system went hand in hand with the emergence of the concept of race, understood as a tool to classify people around the globe and thus for labor control.[34] This does not mean that discrimination did not exist before, but it is only with the emergence of a world capitalist system based on an international division of labor that separated the center from the periphery (and semiperipheries) that the modern concept of race, with its specific biological and hierarchical connotation, became hegemonic worldwide.

The entire history of how we have come to perceive people around the globe as classified according to their racial belonging still needs to be written in detail, with some arguing that it originated in the discussion as to whether the Native "Americans" were humans or not and others pointing to later developments such as the Atlantic slave trade.[35] But in all of the different accounts, it is now clear that Eurocentrism was fully in place when, in the eighteenth and nineteenth centuries, European philosophers and natural historians sitting in their studies systematically elaborated the notion of "race," using information that was by that time largely supplied by travelers involved in missionary activities, colonial enterprises, and the slave trade.[36]

Quijano and others after him carefully focused on the way in which, during the invention of the Americas, racial classification was first mainly understood in terms of the *conquistadores'* Christian identity and then progressively assumed other, and specifically biological, connotations. At the beginning, the main identitarian driving force was the dichotomy Christians versus "Indians," between the civilized versus savages, with its inbuilt allochronisms.[37] The latter, understood as the placing of the other into another time, here specifically a primitive one that can only exist in relation to a supposed superior civilizational stage, worked as a powerful tool for the justification of genocide and elimination: even when the "savages" were recognized with the status of human beings, by being placed at the infancy of humanity in a precivilizational stage, they were also implicitly presented as pre-Christians and thus as immature Christians to be assimilated either through physical elimination or by cultural transformation.

Quijano's influential "coloniality-of-power" thesis connects the critique of Eurocentrism with Karl Marx's concept of world capitalism and Immanuel Wallerstein's world system theory. According to this conceptual synthesis, since 1492—that is, the moment when European colonialism reached the entire globe—the modern capitalist division of labor on a world scale has been and still remains linked to race. The reason for this is easy to understand: as a system predicated on the endless expansion of profit, capitalism needs both the extraction of surplus value from waged labor and the extortion of free labor and resources from unwaged relations of production. Race, and the claims that some human groups are more apt to certain physical activities than others, is what guaranteed that the latter could happen. Without the slaves and Natives, whose labor was extorted for free through colonialism, there could not have been any original accumulation and thus no capitalism.

This explains why Quijano insists on the notion of an intrinsic "coloniality" of modern power. His theoretical move implies distinguishing between colonialism, that is a system of external rule premised on managing differences and which does not, by definition, necessarily imply racism, and the coloniality of the modern system of power, which is unconceivable without taking race and racism into account. It is this centrality of racism to the capitalist world system that explains why Eurocentrism is so pervasive: Eurocentrism, and thus the map of the world described above, is inseparable from a system of knowledge which distinguishes between all different skin colors (black, red, yellow, brown, etc.) from the point of view of an imaginal[38] European skin color identified as "white." There is no black nor red skin without a white gaze, in the same way that there is no "Middle East" without the Eurocentric gaze that assumed Greenwich as the point from which to turn a globe into a bidimensional map.

That white and black are the two colors that serve to classify all others is something built into the racial thinking from its very inception. In his 1777 "Of Different Human Races," Immanuel Kant explicitly states that "negroes and whites are the base races," with all the other colors (olive-yellow, brown, copper red) being the mere result of the combination of them through the influence of climate.[39] This is a crucial text in the history of racial thinking because it is one of the first to recognize that all human beings are part of the same species (that of human beings), but it adds the qualification that they remain divided into different races. Kant defines race here as "deviations that are constantly preserved over many generations and come about as a consequence of migration (dislocation to other regions) or through interbreeding with other deviations of the same line of descent."[40] "Deviations" are, in turn, defined as "hereditary dissimilarities that we find in animals that belong to a single line of descent,"[41] thereby inscribing the concept of race into the realm of hereditary traits and biology. Skin color thus becomes the definitive trait that names the different races, while the level of iron in blood is identified as the main natural cause of the different colors.[42]

Kant does not provide any other explanation for why acids and alkaline content would not be reflected at all in supposedly white-skinned people, and he even admits that his opinions on the question of blood composition are only "preliminary,"[43] but he nevertheless continues to set up whiteness as the norm from which all other colors are derived. In his view, since the part of the earth that has the most fortunate combination of cold and hot regions is that between the northern latitude of 32 and 53 degrees, that is where the "Old World" is located, we should also assume that precisely here we find the human beings "who diverge the least from their original form" and who must therefore have been "well prepared to transplant into every other region of the earth."[44] Thus northern European white and brunette inhabitants are said to be the first lineal root *genus* of the human beings as a *species*, while the "nearest northern deviation to develop from this original form" is said to be "the noble blond."[45] Beginning with this lineal root genus, Kant develops a full classification of four fundamental human races based on skin color and the natural causes that he sees as responsible for their origins, presumably because of their influence on bodily juices: "First race: Noble blond (northern Europe), from humid cold; Second race: Copper red (America) from dry cold; Third race: Black (Senegambia) from humid heat; Fourth race, Olive-yellow (Asian-Indians) from dry heat."[46]

Notice here that Kant, who notoriously never left his native Königsberg, elaborated his classification of human beings into these four races by basing his theory on biology and the accounts of human groups provided by travelers, missionaries and European merchants who were involved in world trade, which obviously included the very profitable slave trades. It is thanks to texts such as this one that skin color and other traits that play with the visual register become crucial ingredients for the modern concept of race, which still now is largely defined in terms of fixed biological differences between human groups.[47] But notice also how the labor capacity, which must have been of crucial interest for the European merchants writing such reports, is explicitly invoked in Kant's argument. For instance, when speaking about the Native Americans, he observes that they reveal a "half extinguished life power," which is probably the effect of the cold weather of that region, and stands in sharp contrast to the humid warm weather where the Negro race developed. Kant further claims this accounts for the "fact that the Negro is well suited to his climate, namely strong, fleshy, and agile" and is only made "lazy, indolent and dawdling" because he is so amply supplied by his motherland.[48] As an indication of this difference in strength, Kant quotes the following example: "To cite just one example, red slaves (native-Americans) are used only for domestic work in Surinam, because they are too weak to work in the fields. Negros are thus needed for fieldwork. The difficulties in this case are not the result of a lack of coercive measures, but the natives in this part of the world lack ability and durability."[49] Kant provides no source for this example, but it is not hard to imagine it must have come from somebody who had been particularly attentive to labor needs.[50] We have insisted on the biological language that Kant uses in his elaboration of the concept of race because, at least in the European political public discourse, we tend to perceive such biologism as outdated. But it is not.

Since the early 1950s (and the UNESCO Declaration on Race and Racial Prejudice), the term *race* has been abandoned in most European public discourses and considered scientifically flawed, precisely because of its problematic biological connotations. And yet, as has been observed, the concept of race survived through other names, such as ethnic origin, civilization, or even culture.[51] The term *race* may have been buried, but, where it was, it was certainly buried alive because constantly reproduced by the institution at the core of the political organization of European modernity: the sovereign state. As Alana Lentin among others noted, the history of racism is intimately linked with that of the modern state.[52]

For example, we tend to forget how the biological understanding of belonging is transmitted and constantly repeated in the legal institution of citizenship, which is at the basis of the very foundation of modern European nation-states. Since the French 1789 Declaration of the Rights of Man and the Citizen, a tension has been established between the universal aspiration of the language of human rights and the particularism of the institution of citizenship, whereby the protection of rights is only accorded to those who belong to a specific state, so that to follow

Arendt's succinct formulation, the crucial question of our time is indeed that of the right to have rights.[53] Race is reproduced daily by the modern European state system because in most European nation-states, citizenship is still defined by a mixture of *jus soli* (the *jus* of the territory) and *jus sanguinis* (the *jus* of blood). That is, the criterion for belonging to a European nation-state is in most cases a mixture of the rights one acquires through presence on a territory (*jus soli*) and that of blood descent (*jus sanguinis*), with some EU countries still basing citizenship on *jus sanguinis* alone.[54] This means that, in some cases, you can automatically acquire European citizenship just because your parents are European citizens, and thus because you have European blood, even if you have never lived in that territory. On the contrary, there are countries where, if you do not have that supposed European "blood," you cannot automatically acquire that citizenship even if you have lived there for most of your life. Notice also that the simple opposition between the two Latin terms may be misleading: even the *jus soli* contains in itself a biological element, in as far as, very often, the criteria for accessing citizenship through *jus soli* is the very fact of being born in a certain country rather than another. Once again, it is not the fact of inhabiting a certain territory, but the biological event of birth inside of that territory that matters, as if a land could ever literally be a motherland or a fatherland.

We tend to think that citizenship is a universal institution and that defining political belonging in terms of the place where one is born (or of the blood of their biological parents) is a normal fact. But this is far from being the case. For centuries, even in Europe, the institution of citizenship did not even exist.[55] This is not to argue that those times were better but rather to emphasize the contingency of the institution of citizenship, and in particular, a contingency that is intimately linked with the history of the modern state and its exclusionary logic that divides territory according to the inside/outside. In the entry "Citizen" that Diderot wrote for the *Encyclopédie* that he coedited with D'Alembert, which remains in European intellectual history a symbol of the spirit of the Enlightenment, Diderot captured this double-sided nature of citizenship very well. "The citizens," he wrote, "in their capacity as citizens, that is to say in their societies, are all equally noble."[56] Although Diderot means here to emphasize how nobility has now been generalized to all citizens belonging to a certain community, this is a double-sided move that enlarges the nobility from one caste to an entire class but thereby only transposes the exclusionary mechanism of nobility from family lineage to political belonging. There is a marriage between the racial understanding of the world and the modern institution of the sovereign state, and that marriage has been sealed and exported to the entire world through the institution of modern citizenship. What may appear as a universalizing institution when looked at from the inside of a nation-state such as Diderot's France suddenly becomes a particularizing one when seen from the outside, and in particular from the colonies. The free French citizens were the "nobility" of Diderot's modern times because they enjoyed privileges that were denied to people of other descent (and, we should not forget, from other genders).

If we now consider that, since the end of World War II, the entire globe is divided into sovereign states, meaning that there is not even a single space on earth that is not subject to state sovereignty, it does not appear as an exaggeration to state, with Fanon, that what divides our world is first and foremost our species, that is, the "race" one belongs to.[57] By elaborating on classical Marxism with his mix of psychology and phenomenology, Fanon, well before Quijano, emphasized that the link between the international division of labor and the racial classification of people across the earth is a twin product of European colonialism.[58] As he goes on to explain, in "the colonies you are rich because you are white, you are white because you are rich, so whereas in the centre of capitalist production it makes sense to distinguish between structure and superstructure, in the colonies we have to emphasize that the super-structure is also the economic infrastructure, and thus the cause is the effect."[59] In contrast to Quijano, we find in Fanon not only an analysis of the intertwinement of racial schemes and world capitalism but also an emphasis, as we have already mentioned, on the reflections of those mechanisms in the social unconscious. Since the capitalist division of labor is global, the unconscious patterns that sustain it must be equally global.

Already in 1961, Frantz Fanon could observe that "the colonized, underdeveloped man is a political creature in the most global sense of the term."[60] We must understand "global" in the dual sense of the depth of oppression but also its range. When we take the perspective of the colonized, and thus of the entire international division of labor that the concept of race came to signify, one cannot but take the entire globe as the framework of analysis. This does not mean that there exists a global racist unconscious that works in the same way and in the same manner all around the globe. Despite the fact that Fanon used the notion of collective unconscious when analyzing the complex of the colonized, he also emphasized how the latter changed considerably from one context to the next. Beginning with Fanon, we can therefore see how, in order to analyze the structures that perpetrate racism, we need both a potentially global framework and also the careful work on the specificity of each context.

From Colonial Politics of the Past to the Necropolitics of the Present

When Frantz Fanon stated that Europe has been "literally the creation of the Third World,"[61] he meant more than the mass plundering of material goods and labor from the colonies. The colonial and decolonization contexts contributed as well to building a certain idea of citizenship, one that has a long history of entrenched Islamophobic and anti-Black racism. In his more recent work, *Arab Sex and France* (2017), Todd Shepard illustrates another legacy of decolonization, the image of a sexually aggressive man, perceived as a danger to French women, and the parallel new paragon of the Arab homosexual, perceived as threatening the heteronormative European cultural order and self-understanding. This stereotyped image of a sexually aggressive Arab man first emerged from social groups who resisted Algerian decolonization, in particular the Organisation de l'Armée Secrète (OAS, a military club of officers refusing de Gaulle's acquiescence to decolonizing Algeria). One publication that distilled racist and homophobic remarks against French Muslims of Algeria was *Europe Action*, a journal frequently associated with "sexual orientalism" and fears of aggressive sexualized others (generally male).[62] The continuity from this right-wing imaginary all the way to the present, with the Front National (FN) of Jean-Marie and Marine Le Pen and other intellectuals from the Nouvelle Droite, such as Alain de Benoist, plays with the fear of France and Europe under threat and is strikingly described by Shepard as part of this long colonial history. The original formulation of the theory of "great replacement," used nowadays by white supremacists to justify their terrorist attacks against Muslims throughout the globe,[63] was first written by Renaud Camus, a journalist and essayist whose ideas crystalized in the context of the 1970s after the Algerian war of the 1970s.[64] According to this conspiracy theory, the very existence of Europe would be threatened by such large and sustained waves of immigration that white people would soon be fully replaced by Muslims and/or people of color.

We can see how the specific colonial context is enmeshed with a larger self-understanding of Europe, and vice versa.[65] Similar arguments would be made about anti-Black feelings in other parts of Europe, such as Winston Churchill considering the slogan "Keep England White" as a possible wining motto for the 1955 elections[66] or Enoch Powell's "River of Blood" speech and hatred-filled discourses against Jamaican immigration in the United Kingdom.[67] The myth of a shared European cultural identity is based on a fantasy of whiteness that runs throughout the European colonial history. Arabs, Turks, or "North Africans" (even when the latter are regular citizens of France, Spain, or Germany) are constantly singled out in xenophobic discourses as outcasts, threats, or lives with less value because they are seen as "nonwhite" and therefore a threat to the fantasized European purity. Those speaking of a "postracial Europe," on the basis that, since World War II, race has largely been banned from European public discourse,[68] should consider the way in which other categories, such as civilisation, ethnicity, or even citizenship, are now doing the same work that biological discourses did in the past. The term *race* may have been buried in the European public sphere, but it is constantly being reenacted at its borders and projected as a threat to citizenship in the various member states.[69]

The current so-called migration crisis, which may indeed only be a crisis from the point of view of this fantasy of pure whiteness (for there have always been large-scale migrations around the globe), must also be read as another episode in this long history of racial discourses. From the early alleged migration crisis of 1991, with the stunning images of the boat *Vlora* full of Albanians who were denied entry to the Italian city of Bari, to the flow of refugees following the war in Yugoslavia, to the endless debates about whether to accept mere dozens or thousands of migrants in the mid-2010s, all the way to the illegal measures by the Italian ministry of Matteo Salvini to criminalize solidarity around the Mediterranean,[70] both European states and Europe have been administering the chances of survival in front of death.

Faced with hundreds of thousands of migrants, the EU has more often than not preferred to let people die on the perilous journey to Europe or turned a blind eye to the paramilitary units making money smuggling refugees towards or in Libya.[71] It is therefore apt to apply the term of *necropolitics* to these instances. Mbembe originally coined the term to depict how modern sovereign power, in general, is much more than Foucault's biopower. For Mbembe, necropolitics is a complement to biopower, as it allows us to understand how weapons create "death-worlds," that is, spaces for the living dead.[72] Later in that article, he explores the specificity of colonial contexts for necropolitics, where the consequences for racialized subjects have been the worst.[73] For him the "most accomplished form of necropolitics is the contemporary colonial occupation of Palestine."[74] Extending his argument, we want to argue that even in the "postcolonial" context (the false belief that we are allegedly *after* colonialism), there continues to be an uneven distribution of violence and inequality in terms of one's chances in front of death. If, during the formal European colonial empires, the European settlers consistently benefitted from high protections and suffered lower rates of mortality than the colonized, similar inequalities are still at play with Fortress Europe in the present. We here use "necropolitics" to denote an uneven "politics of death,"[75] and, in particular, a biopolitical apparatus that distributes different life trajectories according to how close they are to the prospect of premature death.

When seen through the lens of a colonial-critical approach, the language of "crisis" that currently surrounds the European project cannot but appear as misleading. More than a "European crisis" or a "migration crisis," we should speak of a "repoliticization of the battles over borders." Migrants crossing borders and carrying signs such as "We did not cross the border; the border crossed us" remind us that the movement of people and goods between Europe and its colonies has been happening for a long time. Equally, battles over who is in and out of Europe are a stark reminder that human beings have not always lived in political formations characterized by sovereign boundaries demarcating the inside from the outside.

Will there ever be a Europe after Eurocentrism? Only if Europe becomes a space of exchange that encompasses its cultural and political neighbors as well, with liminal zones of crossing, debate, and at times disagreement and struggle, but in which joint emancipatory and solidarity projects can emerge. Europe's history cannot only be the history of its member states: it is also a Europe of its conflicted relations. This means that it is not made up of European voices only, but of intellectuals, thinkers, artists, and migrants, whose very act of crossing the border can have a democratic effect in the etymological sense of an expression of the power of the people. In the current necropolitical configuration, crossing borders illegally ceases to be a mere act of civil disobedience and can indeed become a process of constituent power.[76] Triggered by Europe's colonial past, border crossing can project Europe toward a different future, prefiguring a different form of citizenship outside the exclusionary logic of nation-states, which many Europeans believe is the reason Europe was created in the first place. Maybe the reconfiguration of European citizenship is not the entire story, but it is at least one step closer.

Notes

We are grateful to Simona Forti, Eduardo Mendieta, and Antti Tarvainen for their helpful feedback and criticism and to Muriam Haleh Davis for earlier exchanges on Fanon and new ways to look at North African and European history. An earlier version of this chapter appeared in the online, open-access journal *Crisis and Critique* 6, no. 1 (2020): 57–87.

1. Haas, "International Integration: The European and the Universal Process."

2. Schulz-Forberg and Stråth, *The Political History of European Integration*.

3. Bottici and Challand, *Imagining Europe*.

4. Hall, "In but Not of Europe: Europe and Its Myth."

5. Ann Stoler (*Duress*) is reluctant to use the term *postcolonialism* and prefers to speak of (post)colonialism to show that colonialism is still with us (Stoler, ix) but we think that the expression may still suggest that we are in a "post" condition, which is clearly not the case in settler colonial states (USA, Israel, Australia) and also, as such, does not automatically include the insights from decolonial critique.

6. Elsewhere, we have offered an attempt at a multidirectional critical theory. See Challand and Bottici, "Toward an Interstitial Global Theory." Other authors have proposed to decolonize European sociology, such as Rodríguez, Boatcă, and Costa, *Decolonizing European Sociology*.

7. See below for one of these early statements on European cooperation, namely, the Schuman declaration of May 1950.

8. Bottici and Challand, *Imagining Europe*, 62ff.

9. Anthropological theory has made us aware for a long time now that collective identities are not formed in the center of a polity but in its peripheries. See Barth, *Ethnic Groups and Boundaries*. The recent debates about the meaning of a political Europe after the Russian war against Ukraine are an illustration of this dialectical relation between center and peripheries.

10. Fanon, *The Wretched of the Earth*, 58.

11. For a global narrative of the emergence of "war capitalism" as a necessary condition for the spread of "industrial capitalism," see Beckert, *Empire of Cotton: A Global History*. Among the classical texts, see Luxemburg, *The Accumulation of Capital*.

12. Fanon, *Black Skin, White Masks*.

13. Fanon, 3–5, 61ff.

14. Fanon, 14.

15. Fanon, 62.

16. Fanon, 16–17, 21.

17. http://www.robert-schuman.com/fr/pg-saintete/pourquoi.htm.

18. For the full text, see https://europa.eu/european-union/about-eu/symbols/europe-day/schuman-declaration_en.

19. Hanhimaki, *Understanding the Cold War*.

20. Kingston, *Britain and the Politics of Modernization in the Middle East*, 10–12.

21. Challand, "From Hammer and Sickle to Star and Crescent."

22. One of such accounts of the EU committed to norms and standards is in Manners's "Normative Power Europe."

23. Pepicelli, *Un nuovo ordine mediterraneo?*

24. Cassarino, "Reversing the Hierarchy of Priorities in EU-Mediterranean Relations."

25. Hanieh, *Lineages of Revolt*.

26. Silonen, "Fortress Europe."

27. Rutazibwa, "What's There to Mourn?"

28. See Samir Amin's *Eurocentrism* or Wynter's "Unsettling the Coloniality of Being/Power/Truth/Freedom." The term "discovery" is obviously imbued with Eurocentrism in the technical sense of the term because it presupposes the European gaze as the standard for establishing what is new and what is old.

29. Chakrabarty, *Deprovincializing Europe*.

30. Wynter, "Unsettling the Coloniality of Being/Power/Truth/Freedom," 260.

31. For instance, this Eurocentric image of a bidimensional map with Europe at its center is the image of the world that appears when one searches in Google for "political map of the world" from inside the EU or the United States (https://www.google.com/search?client=firefox-b-1-d&q=political+map+of+the+world. accessed on October 14, 2019).

32. Quijano, "Coloniality of Power, Eurocentrism, and Latin America," 2000.

33. For an argument in favor of this distinction, see Quijano's "Coloniality of Power, Eurocentrism, and Latin America" and Maldonnado-Torres's "Outline of Ten Theses on Coloniality and Decoloniality." Among those who prefer to keep the notion of colonialism, see, for instance, Stoler, *Duress*.

34. A similar point was already made by Williams in 1944, but Quijano has the merit of emphasising the distinction between colonialism and coloniality.

35. Bernasconi and Lott, *The Idea of Race*, viii.

36. Bernasconi and Lott, vii–viii.

37. For the original discussion of allochronism, see: Fabian, *Time and the Other*.

38. By imaginal, we mean here what is made of images, understood as representations that are also presences in themselves because they can be both conscious and unconscious. For a longer discussion of the notion of the imaginal and its political relevance, see Bottici, *Imaginal Politics*.

39. Kant, "On the Different Human Races," 12, 20.

40. Kant, 9.

41. Kant, 9.

42. Kant, 19.

43. Kant, 19.

44. Kant, 19–20.

45. Kant, 20.

46. Kant, 20.

47. Lentin's *Racism* provides this summary definition of race, but later on, she distinguished between racial naturalism and racial historicism, thereby making it clear that even after abandoning the biological connotation of the very first elaborations, the concept of race survived (Lentin, 23). By elaborating on her definition, and the incorporation of racial historicism into it, we would suggest defining race in terms of fixed hereditary differences between groups, thereby suggesting that such hereditary transmission can be considered to happen either through biology or through history or a mix of both.

48. Kant, "On the Different Human Races," 17.

49. Kant, 17.

50. Williams (*Slavery and Capitalism*, chs. 1–2) traces in the making of modern capitalism the origins of such discourses about "suitability" or "natural abilities" of Black enslaved persons to work in hard and hot conditions. When there were not enough indentured servants and Native American slaves, a new justification was needed for the massive exploitation of Black bodies, that of the "natural qualities" to which Kant refers.

51. For a discussion of the 1950 UNESCO declaration and the idea of "racism without race," see Lentin, *Racism*, 92.

52. Lentin, 15–23.

53. No rights without being citizens of any sovereign state, according to Arendt. *The Origins of Totalitarianism*, 267–304.

54. For comparative material on European citizenship and citizenship in Europe, see http://eudo-citizenship.eu/ and http://globalcit.eu.

55. Mendieta, "*Jus Soli* versus *Jus Sanguinis*," 8.

56. Mendieta, 10. Although Mendieta mentions this as an example of the emancipatory potential of modern citizenship, with its "democratization of the spirit of nobility to all citizens," we should also contextualize that effect and looks at it from the point of view of those who are excluded from it.

57. Fanon, *The Wretched of the Earth*, 14.

58. In his oft-forgotten seminal work, Trinidadian historian Eric E. Williams also notes how racism emerged as a justification for the increasing use of slaves in Atlantic commerce. For him, it is capitalism that breeds racism. Williams, *Slavery and Capitalism*, 1944.

59. Fanon, *The Wretched of the Earth*, 14.

60. Fanon, 40.

61. Fanon, 58.

62. Shepard, *Sex, France & Arab Men 1962–1979*, 19–41, 282.

63. For example, the attacks in Christchurch in New Zealand in March 2019, or in El Paso, August 2019, were justified in these terms. For reference to the great replacement in the El Paso shootings, see "Minutes before El Paso Killing, Hate-Filled Manifesto Appears Online," *New York Times*, August 3, 2019.

64. Shepard, 125–29, 282–84.

65. Haleh Davis and Serres, *North Africa and the Making of Europe*.

66. https://www.theguardian.com/news/2021/apr/20/the-invention-of-whiteness-long-history-dangerous-idea.

67. Gilroy, *"There Ain't No Black in the Union Jack."*

68. For a critique of postracial Europe, see Lentin's *Racism*.

69. Boatcă also argues that more work is needed to make Europe's ongoing colonial entanglements theoretically and politically visible, in particular when it comes to Europe's relations with the Caribbean. See Boatcă, "Thinking Europe Otherwise."

70. This was done by denying access to Italian ports for boats rescuing migrants and refugees or by pressing charges against the NGOs staffing these rescue operations. For another example of criminalization on the French-Italian border, see Celikates's "Constituent Power beyond Exceptionalism."

71. For an example of complacency toward Sudanese paramilitary forces and the "migration" question to Europe, see https://www.middleeasteye.net/news/eu-accused-hiding-links-sudan-armed-groups-migration-funding.

72. Mbembe, "Necropolitics," 12, 40.

73. Mbembe, 17, 24.

74. Mbembe, 27.

75. Mbembe, 21.

76. Celikates, "Constituent Power beyond Exceptionalism."

Bibliography

Amin, Samir. *Eurocentrism*. New York: Monthly Press, 1988/2009.
Arendt, Hannah. *The Origins of Totalitarianism*. Boston: Harvest Books, 1973.

Barth, Fredrik. "Introduction." In *Ethnic Groups and Boundaries. The Social Organization of Culture Difference*, edited by F. Barth. London: Allan and Unwin, 1969.

Beckert, Sven. *Empire of Cotton: A Global History*. New York: Knopf, 2014.

Bernasconi, Robert, and Tommy Lott. *The Idea of Race*. Indianapolis, Hackett, 2000.

Boatcă, Manuela. "Thinking Europe Otherwise: Lessons from the Caribbean." *Current Sociology* 69, no. 3 (2021): 389–414.

Bottici, Chiara. *Imaginal Politics: Images beyond the Imagination and beyond the Imaginary*. New York: Columbia University Press, 2014

Bottici, Chiara, and Benoît Challand. *Imagining Europe: Myth, Memory, and Identity*. Cambridge: Cambridge University Press, 2013.

Cassarino, Jean-Pierre. "Reversing the Hierarchy of Priorities in EU-Mediterranean Relations." In *The European Union and the Arab Spring: Promoting Democracy and Human Rights in the Middle East*, edited by Joel Peters, 1–16. Minneapolis: Lexington Books, 2012.

Celikates, Robin. "Constituent Power beyond Exceptionalism: Irregular Migration, Disobedience, and (Re-)Constitution." *Journal of International Political Theory* 15, no. 1 (2018): 67–81.

Chakrabarty, Dipesh. *Deprovincializing Europe: Postcolonial Thought and Historical Difference*. Princeton: Princeton University Press, 2000.

Challand, Benoît. "From Hammer and Sickle to Star and Crescent. The Question of Religion for European Identity and a Political Europe." *Religion, State and Society* 37, no. 1 (2009): 65–80.

Challand, Benoît, and Chiara Bottici. "Toward an Interstitial Global Theory." *Globalizations* 19, no. 2 (forthcoming).

Fabian, Johannes. *Time and the Other. How Anthropology Makes Its Object*. New York: Columbia University Press, 1983.

Fanon, Frantz. *Black Skin, White Masks*. Translated by R. Philcox. New York: Grove, 1952/2008.

Fanon, Frantz. *The Wretched of the Earth*. Translated by R. Philcox. New York: Grove, 1961/2004.

Gilroy, Paul. *"There Ain't No Black in the Union Jack": The Cultural Politics of Race and Nation*. Chicago: University of Chicago Press, 1987.

Haas, Ernst. "International Integration: The European and the Universal Process." *International Organization* 15, no. 3 (1961): 366–92.

Haleh Davis, Muriam, and Thomas Serres. *North Africa and the Making of Europe: Governance, Institutions and Culture*. London: Bloomsbury Academic, 2018.

Hall, Stuart 2003. "In but Not of Europe: Europe and Its Myth." In *Figures d' Europe—Images and Myths of Europe*, edited by L. Passerini, 35–47. Brussels: P. I. E. Peter Lang, 2003.

Hanhimaki, Jussi, and Odd Arne Westad. *Understanding the Cold War: A History with Documents and Eye-Witness Accounts.* Oxford: Oxford University Press, 2003.

Hanieh, Adam. *Lineages of Revolt.* London: Haymarket, 2013.

Kant, Immanuel. "On the Different Human Races." In *The Idea of Race*, edited by R. Bernasconi and T. Lott, 8–22. Indianapolis: Hackett, 2000.

Kingston, Paul W.T. *Britain and the Politics of Modernization in the Middle East, 1945–1958.* Cambridge: Cambridge University Press, 2002.

Lentin, Alana. *Racism. A Beginner's Guide.* Oxford: OneWorld, 2008.

Luxemburg, Rosa. *The Accumulation of Capital.* London: Routledge, 1951.

Maldonado-Torres, Nelson. *Outline of Ten Theses on Coloniality and Decoloniality*, 2016. http://fondation-frantzfanon.com/outline-of-ten-theses-on-coloniality-and-decoloniality/.

Manners, Ian. "Normative Power Europe: A Contradiction in Terms?" *Journal of Common Market Studies* 40, no. 2 (2002): 235–58.

Mbembe, Achille. "Necropolitics." *Public Culture* 15, no. 1 (2003): 11–40.

Memmi, Albert. *The Colonizer and the Colonized.* New York: Orion, 1956/1965.

Mendieta, Eduardo. "*Jus Soli* versus *Jus Sanguinis*: On the Grounds of Justice." In *Latin American Immigration Ethics*, edited by Amy Reed-Sandoval and Luis Rubén Díaz Cepeda. Tucson: University of Arizona Press, 2021.

Pepicelli, Renata. *Un nuovo ordine mediterraneo?* Bari: Mesogea, 2004/2010.

Quijano, Anibal. "Coloniality of Power, Eurocentrism, and Latin America." In *Nepantla: Views from the South* 1, no. 3 (2000): 533–80.

Rodríguez, Encarnacion G., Manuela Boatcă, and Sergio Costa. *Decolonizing European Sociology: Transdisciplinary Approaches.* London: Routledge, 2016.

Rutazibwa, Olivia. "What's There to Mourn? Decolonial Reflections on (the End of) Liberal Humanitarianism." *Journal of Humanitarian Affairs* 1, no. 1 (2019): 65–68.

Schulz-Forberg, Hagen, and Bo Stråth. *The Political History of European Integration: The Hypocrisy of Democracy-Through-Market.* New York: Routledge, 2010.

Shepard, Todd. *Sex, France & Arab Men 1962–1979.* Chicago: University of Chicago Press, 2017.

Silonen, Josi. "Fortress Europe—A Brief History of the European Migration and Asylum Policy," MA thesis, University of Helsinki, 2016.

Stoler, Ann L. *Duress. Imperial Durabilities in Our Times.* Durham & London: Duke University Press, 2017.

Williams, Eric E. *Slavery and Capitalism.* Chapel Hill: University of North Carolina Press, 1944.

Wynter, Sylvia. "Unsettling the Coloniality of Being/Power/Truth/Freedom: Towards the Human, after Man, Its Overrepresentation—an Argument." *The New Centennial Review* 3, no. 3 (2003): 257–337.

7

Reimagining Europe as a Europe of Refugees

A Thought Experiment

AGNES CZAJKA

Recent crises in and of Europe have occasioned, alongside a palpable rise in nationalism and xenophobia, a bout of the kind of soul-searching that "Europe" and self-styled Europeans routinely engage in. What does and what should Europe stand for? What does it mean to be European? To what (histories, ideas, and ideals) and to whom (to which "selves" and to which "others") is Europe responsible or indebted? What is, and what is expected of, a "good European"?

Though at times such soul-searching risks, and indeed comes dangerously close to, the narcissism and navel gazing that typifies Eurocentrism, it is not devoid of critical potential. In the context of a Europe in seemingly interminable crisis,[1] this chapter explores the potential of reimagining Europe by bringing together the work of Jacques Derrida on Europe, Friedrich Nietzsche on the "good European," and Giorgio Agamben on the refugee. Building on the premise that crises bring with them the potential of revitalisation and reimagining, the chapter suggests that the intractable crises of Europe, and more specifically, the successive refugee crises in which Europe is entangled, offer a chance to interrogate the meaning of Europe and reimagine it as a "Europe of refugees"—and in doing so, open up the possibility of an-other future for Europe.

In his gloss on Hannah Arendt's "We Refugees," Agamben explores the possibility of looking to Europe "not as an impossible 'Europe of nations' . . . but as an aterritorial or extraterritorial space in which all the residents of the European states . . . would be in a position of exodus or refuge, and the status of European would mean the citizen's being-in-exodus."[2] Bringing Agamben's work in conversation with that of Derrida and Nietzsche, this chapter explores the potential of figuring Europe as a Europe of refugees. The chapter, and the threading together of the work of Derrida, Nietzsche and Agamben, is a thought experiment. The chapter begins by exploring what Derrida's deconstruction and the *différance* it reveals offer to a reimagining of Europe, arguing that the reimagining of Europe must be grounded, perhaps counterintuitively, in its deconstruction. Second, the chapter turns to Nietzsche, focusing on his conceptualization of the "good European." It suggests that Nietzsche's construction of the "good European" can have relevance for reimagining Europe, and particularly for reimaging it as a Europe of refugees. It asks the questions: Might Nietzsche's conception of the "good European" enable us to imagine the "good European" as the refugee—and conversely, the refugee as the "good European"? Does imagining the refugee as a "good European" help us reimagine Europe? What kind of Europe does it help us imagine? Third, the chapter attends to Agamben, whose musings on the possibilities of Europe and Europeanness as exodus and refuge inspired this chapter. It focuses on Agamben's conceptualization of the figure of the refugee and its critical, political potential. The chapter concludes with the thought experiment itself—juxtaposing Nietzsche's "good European" with Agamben's figure of the refugee and exploring the critical potential of reimagining Europe as a Europe of refugees.

Deconstructing Europe with Derrida

Before turning to Derrida's explicit commentary on Europe, it is useful to briefly consider deconstruction, his ground-breaking "method."[3] Deconstructing Europe—the Europe of nation-states, the supranational Europe of the European Union, and indeed the "idea" of Europe—is fundamental to reimagining it as a Europe of refugees. For Derrida, deconstruction has always comprised such a double, or triple, movement.[4] Deconstruction begins with the articulation a concept or identity—such as Europe. It then immediately takes it apart, undoing or deconstructing it, preparing the "grounds" from which it is possible to reassemble it anew. The movement of deconstruction is thus by turns destructive and constructive, negative and affirmative. Derrida suggests that "deconstruction is always on the side of the yes, on the side of the affirmation of life."[5] The affirmative side of deconstruction is at once an affirmation of its indeterminable and infinite openness to a different future and, I would argue, an invitation to imagine or inherit it.[6] Deconstruction, Derrida argued, should challenge accepted social, political, and cultural truths and denaturalize and revalue accepted values. It should not restrict itself to "an analysis of discourses, of philosophical statements or concepts, of a semantics."[7] Instead, it should "challenge institutions, social and political structures, the most hardened traditions,"[8] and attempt to "intervene responsibly . . . in the cité, the polis and the world."[9] That intervention, I suggest, can, and indeed should, take the form of a reimagining—of the cité, polis, or in this case, Europe.

Important to the deconstruction of any idea or institution, however, is that in disassembling, deconstruction does not aim to "reach the bottom, the original ground, the ultimate foundation" from which to reassemble.[10] Nor does it aim to reconstruct something—an idea, institution, or another Europe—that will then become undeconstructable. The aim is not and cannot be to get at the core of what Europe or Europeanness mean, as deconstruction reveals precisely that there is no bottom, no ultimate foundation, no such thing as a "proper propriety" of Europe.[11] Equally, it cannot be to reconstruct something indestructible as there is no limit or endpoint to deconstruction.[12] What deconstruction discloses, instead, is the originary condition of différance at the heart of all things, including Europe, and in doing so, enables us to reconstruct, or inherit Europe differently—affirming particular strains, interpretations, or trajectories that might have previously been neglected, obfuscated, or ignored.

In the translator's note to The Ear of the Other, Peggy Kamuf situates Derrida's concept of différance at the intersection of the spatial and temporal sense of the verb differer, that is, "to differ" and "to defer."[13] Kamuf notes that since the standard spelling of the noun difference corresponds only to the first sense of the verb (that is, "to differ"), it proved inadequate for Derrida, who wanted to clearly designate both difference and a deferral. The "a" in différance indicates this deferral, "by means of delay, delegation, reprieve, referral, detour, postponement, reserving."[14] Thus, Derrida's différance refers simultaneously to deferral and difference.

The force of différance is thus twofold. It lies, first, in the proposition that there is no ultimate foundation, no "proper propriety" (referring, as it does, to immanent difference). It lies, second, in the proposition that this is always the case (referring, as it does, to perpetual deferral).

A deconstructive approach, then, reveals the inherent heterogeneity and contingency of seemingly homogenous and fixed concepts, structures, and institutions (such as Europe). What a deconstruction of Europe reveals, then, is that what seems determined, recognizable, and fixed, like the meaning and parameters of Europe, is an illusion. As Derrida writes in *Of Grammatology*, deconstruction reveals that "at the heart of something seemingly natural, self-identical, and proper stands something that is unnatural, other, or improper, with the result that the so-called opposition between natural and unnatural, self and other, proper and improper is called into doubt."[15] Or, as he writes in *The Other Heading: Reflections on Today's Europe*, deconstructing Europe reveals that "what is proper to a culture [Europe] is to not be identical to itself. Not to not have any identity, but not to be able to identify itself, to be able to say 'me' or 'we'; to be able to take the form of a subject only in the non-identity to itself."[16]

Deconstruction (and the *différance* it reveals) is thus also key to understanding the potential Derrida sees in Europe, despite its terrifying legacy and history and his own ambivalent relationship with the continent and its political and institutional incarnations. Derrida had a complicated relationship with Europe—or, one could say, Europe had always been a "problem" for Derrida. Born to Jewish parents in colonial Algeria, he epitomized the *nonipseity*, incongruity, and contingency of identity and the inadequacy of the ontology of self and other. Reflecting on his own Europeanness, Derrida said: "I will confide in you a feeling . . . [I]t is the somewhat weary feeling of an old European. More precisely, of someone who, not quite European by birth, since I come from the southern coast of the Mediterranean, considers himself . . . to be a sort of over-acculturated, over-colonized European hybrid."[17] It is perhaps for this reason, though surely among others, that Derrida could not but deconstruct Europe, could not but suggest that there was no such thing as a European culture or identity, but rather that Europe was characterized by inherent and originary difference, a perpetual deferral of meaning, and thus also the potential to be inherited differently and to open into an-other future.

In *The Other Heading*, Derrida thus insists that hope can only be maintained in a deconstructed Europe, from the remnants of which an-other Europe can be inherited and imagined. In fact, for Europe to be worth salvaging, we must deconstruct it. We must disclose the illusion of its *ipseity* and expose its incongruity and contingency or the fact that

Europe and Europeanness never *are* but are always already produced as a process of *becoming* otherwise. This, of course, is in contradistinction to Husserl's bold assertion that "clearly the title Europe designates the unity of a spiritual life and a creative activity—with all its aims, interests, cares and troubles, with its plans, its establishments, its institutions."[18] Derrida's deconstructive approach to Europe, instead, opens up the possibility that there are multiple, heterogeneous Europes, European spirits, and European trajectories gathered under the seemingly self-identical sign—and more fundamentally, that Europe is inherently and originally *nonipseic*, that its nonessential essence is that of nonidentity. Relatedly, a deconstructive approach to Europe reveals the possibility that Europe, or that which it signifies, remains inherently open and perpetually deferred. Its meaning, its (non)identity is never fixed—it is always open to the possibility of becoming otherwise than itself, otherwise than it is or has been. Thus, if we take a deconstructive approach to Europe, we might be able to uncover some of its potential, another trajectory for Europe, a path not *yet* taken for thinking about the identity (or nonidentity) of Europe and its future—perhaps as a Europe of refugees.

Deconstruction, as previously mentioned, is, for Derrida, primarily affirmative—it is always on the side of "yes." It is always on the side of hope—hope as a political responsibility, as Hannah Arendt might have said. For most of its internal and external *others*, Europe has signified colonialism, racism, fascism, nationalism, and war. Yet Europe does not have "one sole memory." It is "bastard, hybrid, grafted, multilinear and polyglot."[19] Determined by *différance*, it is, in essence, self-differentiated and multiple, its meaning indefinitely deferred, never fixed or stabilized. And thus, it can be inherited differently. Derrida's selective inheritance of Europe does not imply a forgetting of Europe's other pasts and spirits—of, for instance, Europe as colonial violence. But it does imply that Europe is not only or solely one thing or another—whether "good" or "bad." As others have argued, including Louis Blond, whom I paraphrase here, to suggest that Europe is only violence misidentifies Europe as univocal rather than a diverse space of multiple practices and historical contingencies. Endorsing Europe's univocality, in turn, confirms Europe's own idealistic account of itself, namely, that it exists as one spiritual image and is formalized as one body of knowledge, one practice, one rational culture.[20]

"Inheritance" (like deconstruction), says Derrida, "is never a given, it is always a task."[21] It is selective; it consists of filtering and sifting—it is work. Thus, while indebted to and dependent on the past, the task of inheritance is also the task of constructing a distinct passage through the past, the present, and into the future. Inheritance is the "reaffirmation of a debt, but a critical, selective and filtering reaffirmation."[22] The sifting, sorting, and selection involved in the task of inheriting and fostering this other Europe necessitates decisions, ones that will determine not only what past(s) will be inherited, but what future(s) will become possible. Such responsibility does (and should) give rise to anxiety—inheritance, as Derrida points out, is "never free of anxiety."[23] Those vested in preserving the *ipseity* of identities and cultures often construct these contestations (and moments of anxiety or crisis) as moments of danger. Yet, as in the case of deconstruction, the threat implied by crisis, and indeed, by an existential crisis of being (a threat stemming from the abandonment of *ipseity*), is simultaneously a chance—a chance to open up to the unforeseeable other, to an-other future, or, as Derrida suggests, to the "to come." Indeed, for Derrida, it is, "the privilege granted to unity, to totality, to organic ensembles, to community as a homogenized whole" that constitutes a danger for politics and ethics, and not deconstruction.[24] Crisis, therefore, is also Europe's chance—to open itself up to the unforeseeable other, to the future within itself, to embrace its promise." One of these futures, I would like to suggest, might be called a Europe of refugees.

Thus, what Derrida's deconstructive approach to Europe reveals is the nonidentity and immanent and perpetual difference at the heart of Europe, obscured in contemporary discourses of European unity and attempts at answering the question of what Europe *is*. It discloses that Europe is riven with *différance*, unable to gather (or be gathered) around a single or definitive meaning, identity, history, or trajectory. It is always already in negotiation, always already becoming (or at least, having the potential to become) otherwise than it presently is. It is this, in turn, that enables Derrida, and enables us, to inherit (and hope for) another Europe. Indeed, it is this hope that confers on us the responsibility of imagining and thus fostering an-other Europe, perhaps, as this chapter suggests, a Europe of refugees. A deconstructive approach to Europe is thus the first step in its reimagining as a Europe of refugees. Deconstructed, Europe reveals itself as differing and diverging from and within itself—not as not having an identity but as possessing a nonidentity, whereby Europe and Europeanness can only be identified through their *différance*, that is, inherent and originary difference and perpetual deferral of identity and meaning.

Reimagining Europe with Nietzsche's "Good Europeans"

Having explored the need to deconstruct Europe and the potential it has for imagining an-other future for Europe, I would now like to turn to Nietzsche's conception of Europe and the "good European." Having deconstructed what Europe *is*, or purports to be, Nietzsche's work can help us to start to inherit Europe differently, and to imagine it as a Europe of refugees.

In his comprehensive treatment of Nietzsche's thought on Europe, Stefan Elbe notes that Nietzsche styled himself as "a thinker who has the future of Europe on his conscience" and saw himself as "definitely a very good European," even if "a bad German."[25] Elbe (2000, 2002, 2003) and Christian Emden (2008) provide exhaustive accounts of Nietzsche's thinking on Europe and Europeanness. From the perspective of this chapter, what is of particular interest is Nietzsche's understanding of Europe as an antidote to the nation-state and, relatedly, his conceptualization of good Europeans as "free spirits."

On Nietzsche's analysis, the Europe of his day was shaken to the core by the "death of God" or the loss of the power of Christianity to render the world meaningful. For Nietzsche, as for Derrida, the existential crisis this generated was not in itself problematic. What was problematic, however, was the response of his contemporaries who, instead of rejoicing at the liberation brought about by the "death of God," were looking instead for another, definitive source of identity and meaning. They found it, according to Nietzsche, in science and nation.

Europe, as Nietzsche theorized it, was an antidote to the latter. "Thanks to the pathological manner in which nationalist nonsense has alienated and continues to alienate the people of Europe from each other," Nietzsche opined, and "to the short-sighted and swift-handed politicians who have risen to the top with the help of this," Europe must "become one."[26] As Elbe suggested nearly twenty years ago, Nietzsche's nineteenth-century passage sounds "strikingly contemporary."[27] It sounds even more so twenty years on. Yet what is more important from the perspective of this chapter is to speculate on what kind of Europe (and Europeans) Nietzsche might have imagined as an antidote to what he saw as the pathology and insanity of nationalism.

Before exploring this Europe and these Europeans, it is useful to pause briefly on Nietzsche's injunction that Europe become "one." It might seem confusing, as Nietzsche was certainly not a theorist of "one"—of self-sameness, *ipseic* identities, unity, or homogeneity. He was, like Derrida, a theorist of the hybrid, the grafted, the multilinear, the polyglot; a thinker of contingency and incongruity. As Elbe points out, Europe becoming "one," and particularly, becoming institutionalized as "one," as in the case of the European Union, would still rest on the same will to truth and thus play the same role that Christianity, science, and nationalism had played in rendering European existence meaningful.[28] Thus, if Europe were indeed to become "one," it would serve as merely another ascetic ideal, another form into which the shadow of God has been recast. As the section on Derrida's deconstruction makes clear, that is certainly not the image of Europe this chapter seeks to advance. What is more, if we are to take Derrida's deconstruction seriously, such a Europe is not only undesirable but also impossible other than as a dangerous illusion that must be promptly deconstructed.

Nietzsche is often inconsistent, perhaps more than most. If we give Nietzsche the benefit of the doubt, the injunction for Europe to become one or for the emergence of a European "identity" can also be understood in the context of his thinking about the violent and divisive nature of nationalism. Yet for the purposes of the argument made in this chapter, we can also leave aside the discussion of Europe becoming "one."[29] Of greater importance for imagining Europe as Europe of refugees is Nietzsche's conceptualization of Europe and Europeanness as not simply antidotes to nationalism but, more fundamentally, as a release from a condition of servitude to the will to truth into a liberating nihilism. It is this Europe, a Europe of "free spirits," that offers the greatest radical potential, and the one we can build on when reconstructing Europe as a Europe of refugees.

What is thus most useful for the purposes of this chapter is Nietzsche's conceptualization of the "good European." Elbe suggests that Nietzsche's idea of the "good European" transcends nationalist perspectives without replacing them with an essentialist idea of Europe.[30] As Elbe notes, Nietzsche's good Europeans should not be confused with good, loyal, and uncritical citizens of Europe or, indeed, the European Union. Instead, good Europeans should remain at a critical distance from the way in which Europe *is* and from the way *it* participates in contemporary politics, in the production of meaning, and in replicating the logics of nationalism.[31] What, then, would characterize good Europeans? For Nietzsche, good Europeans were "free spirits," strangers to the contemporary context. Their identities were *nonipseic*, nonidentical, in the Derridean sense of these terms, "grounded," instead, in the transgression of autochthony. Rather than embodying a European identity, good Europeans engaged in the unsettling of *ipseic* identities and rejoiced in the freedom of indefinite *becoming*.

Nietzsche counted himself among the few good Europeans of his day. While good Europeans were in short supply, Nietzsche could see them coming. In the preface to *Human All Too Human*, which Nietzsche dedicates to these "free spirits," he admits to inventing them for himself—to keep him in "good spirits."[32] Yet he also imagines their future existence: "Free spirits of this kind *could* one day exist . . . [O]ur Europe *will* have such active and audacious fellows among its sons of tomorrow and the next day, physically present and palpable and not, as in my case, merely phantoms and a hermit's phantasmagoria."[33] He conceptualizes these "free spirits" as unfettered from what fetters the fastest. "What fetters the fastest?" asks Nietzsche. "What bonds are all but unbreakable? . . . [T]hat reverence proper to youth, that reserve and delicacy before all that is honoured and revered from of old, that gratitude for the soil out of which they have grown?"[34] These free spirits, these "good Europeans," then, needed to overcome "atavistic fits of fatherlandishness, to unglue themselves from the soil and return to reason," or "good Europeanism."[35] As Daniel Conway noted in his analysis, a good European should affirm and participate in the processes of growth and outgrowth that will deliver Europe to its next self-overcoming, its next incarnation, even if this next incarnation is, at least initially, unrecognizable to most Europeans.[36] This means, as Conway points outs, that good Europeans are not likely to be appreciated as such by their contemporaries; in fact, they are most likely to be viewed as traitors to their nation-states and enemies of progress.[37]

What is also useful for the purposes of this chapter is Nietzsche's attention to the "movement" of his free spirits or of good Europeans. Here is Nietzsche again, in *Human All Too Human*: "Better to die than to go on living *here* . . . and this 'here,' this 'at home' is everything it had hitherto loved! A sudden terror and suspicion of what it loved, a lightning-bolt of contempt for what is called 'duty,' a rebellious, arbitrary, volcanically erupting desire for travel, strange places, estrangements, coldness, soberness, frost, a hatred of love, perhaps a desecrating blow and glance *backwards* to where it formerly loved and worshipped."[38] Of course, Nietzsche is primarily speaking of a metaphorical movement, away from that which has hitherto fettered—history, tradition, duty, and "the fatherland." Yet many have also referenced Nietzsche's own nomadic existence, his lack of citizenship, and his abandonment of "home" as instrumental to his thinking. Some have wondered whether Nietzsche's preference for intellectual homelessness—as well as the image of a "homeless" and "wandering" European—reflected his own situation as legally stateless.[39]

Nietzsche's free spirits and good Europeans would thus be fundamentally different from our existing image of a political being. They would possess a greater tolerance for the ambiguous and enigmatic aspects of existence (as opposed to seeking new ascetic ideals with which to bind themselves). The highest value for good Europeans, argues Elbe, would thus no longer be truth but freedom, and being a good European would consist of freeing European existence from all attempts to determine its meaning and to erect new idols with which to replace the gods that were buried.[40] Nietzsche's good Europeans would explore, and indeed affirm, the possibility of living without true worlds, where inability to articulate Europe and Europeanness would not be concerning but rather liberating because it would coincide with perpetual deferral and overcoming of that which *was*. It is for this reason that Nietzsche, like Derrida after him, repeatedly reminded his readers that "negating and destroying are conditions of saying Yes."[41]

Before moving on to consider the contribution that the work of Agamben might make to reimaging this Europe of the day after tomorrow, it might be useful to briefly reiterate where we have arrived at with Nietzsche and Derrida. By deconstructing Europe, with Derrida, we have arrived at a conceptualization of Europe as *nonipseic*, a nonidentity, a culture of "itself" only if the "self" is always already to be understood as the "other," incongruous with itself and in a perpetual state of becoming something that it is not. From this rather unsteady ground, we have begun to imagine or inherit, with Nietzsche's good Europeans, an-other kind of Europe and Europeanness. This is a Europe of "Europeans" who are strangers to the contemporary context; unfettered from the nation-state and national being; living without its "truths" and embracing instead the inherent openness of existence. If we were to borrow Derrida's words, Nietzsche's good Europeans are those who embody and thus affirm the nonidentity of identity. Related to this, and crucially important, especially as we turn to a discussion of Agamben's figure of the refugee, is Nietzsche's insistence that good Europeans were to be champions of Europe not by virtue of certain racial or geopolitical affinities but as "heirs to Europe's longest and most courageous self-overcoming."[42]

Reimagining Europe with Agamben's Refugee

Much of the recent philosophical interest in the figure of the refugee has been inspired by Giorgio Agamben's interrogation of both the refugee and the space of the (refugee) camp. Agamben's work was, in turn, inspired by the work of Hannah Arendt, so the interest in the refugee has also coincided with a "rediscovery" of some of Arendt's work. It is not necessary to rehearse Arendt or Agamben's arguments as extensive work has been done on the promise and limitations of both. Important from the perspective of this chapter is the direct relationship Arendt draws between the nationalization of the state, its subsequent political entrenchment, and the production of the modern "refugee problem." This relationship, in turn, speaks not only to the unsustainability of the nation-state but also to the potential of the figure of the refugee to expose the fiction on which this global order is founded.[43] Picking up on Arendt's foregrounding of the refugee, Agamben notes that she was the first to point to the potential of the refugee to overturn "the condition of refugee as a person without a country . . . in order to propose this condition as the paradigm of a new historical consciousness."[44]

Recent problematizations of Europe and Europeanness have (at least temporally) coincided with these problematizations of the figure of the refugee. Yet despite their contemporaneous emergence, the question of Europe and the interest in the figure of the refugee have been treated as largely separate concerns. Little attention has thus been paid to Agamben's statement with which I opened this chapter and that seems to point toward a potential connection between them. Most of the debate, instead, has turned on Agamben's treatment of the refugee and, more specifically, on the agency he fails to attribute to refugees. In figuring the refugee as "bare life," Agamben has been seen by critics as dehumanizing refugees, stripping them of subjecthood, political being, and agency. Most of these critiques, however, have overlooked Agamben's treatment of the figure of the refugee as "the only imaginable figure of the people in our day"[45] and "the central figure of our political history."[46]

"The novelty of our era," Agamben argues, "is that growing portions of humanity can no longer be represented within it. For this reason—that is, inasmuch as the refugee unhinges the old trinity of state/nation/territory—this apparently marginal figure deserves rather to be considered the central figure of our political history."[47] Arguing that it is necessary to abandon the concepts through which the subjects of the political have hitherto been represented—man, citizen, sovereign, people, worker—Agamben suggests that the figure of the refugee ought to be retained to ground a new political community.[48] For Agamben, the refugee is the only possible figure as it is the refugee who breaks the identity between human and citizen, and birth and nation.[49] It is, as such, a limit concept that calls into question the categories of the nation-state. The refugee, then, is "the only thinkable figure for the people of our time and the only category in which one may see today . . . the forms and limits of a coming political community."[50]

The figure of the refugee has been marginalized if not erased from within the contemporary political paradigm not by Agamben, but rather by the grounding and delimiting force of the nation-state. Agamben notes, "That there is no autonomous space within the political order of the nation-state for something like the pure man in himself is evident not least in the fact that even in the best of cases, the status of the refugee is always considered a temporary condition that should lead either to naturalisation or to repatriation. A permanent status of man in himself is inconceivable for the law of the nation-state."[51] Yet it is precisely this that Agamben tries to conceive by positioning the refugee at the centre of an-other political imaginary, a "coming political community."[52] And, in positioning Europe as an aterritorial or extraterritorial space in which all the residents would be in a position of exodus or refuge, he also offers a glimpse of "Europe-to-come" as a Europe of refugees.

Agamben's work, then, enables us to think of the figure of the refugee as the political figure par excellence, as the subject position that allows us to conceive of a future political community. As the "other" of the nation-state, it is the figure that allows us to imagine a different kind of political community and, indeed, a different future for Europe. What might this coming political community look like? It might be worth reconsidering, in full, the passage that inspired this chapter. Agamben's proposal for Europe, and indeed, for a new model of international relations, was inspired by Europe's other heading, Jerusalem:

> One of the options considered for the problem of Jerusalem is that it become the capital, contemporaneously and without territorial divisions, of two different states. The paradoxical condition of reciprocal extraterritoriality (or, better, aterritoriality) that this would imply could be generalized as a model of new international relations. Instead of two national states

separated by uncertain and threatening boundaries, one could imagine two political communities dwelling in the same region and in exodus one into the other, divided from each other by a series of reciprocal extraterritorialities, in which the guiding concept would no longer be the *ius* of the citizen, but rather the *refugium* of the individual. In a similar sense, we could look to Europe not as an impossible "Europe of nations," whose catastrophic results can already be perceived in the short term, but as an aterritorial or extraterritorial space in which all the residents of the European states (citizens and noncitizens) would be in a position of exodus or refuge, and the status of European would mean the citizen's being-in-exodus. . . . It is only in a land where the spaces of states will have been perforated and topologically deformed, and the citizen will have learned to acknowledge the refugee that he himself is, that man's political survival today is imaginable.[53]

It is important to take some time to consider this passage and then, given the objective of this chapter, to bring it into conversation not only with Agamben's figuring of the refugee but also with Derrida's work on Europe and Nietzsche's conceptualization of the good European.

Being in Exodus: A Europe of Refugees

Bringing Jerusalem to bear on Europe aligns with Derrida's insistence that it is necessary for Europe to deconstruct itself, to look to another heading, to move past its fiction of cultural self-identity and self-sufficiency, and to experience its culture as a culture of the other. It is not enough, however, for Europe to open itself onto an-other that is, ultimately, like itself. Europe must instead open onto a different kind of other—not just another nation-state or cultural discourse. As Rodolphe Gasché argues, an "opening to an other to come—that is, to an other that is not only unpredictable but also has no assured identity—prevents the passage into the other from becoming a passage into one's own other, or more generally, into any other that is determined or determinable in advance."[54] It prevents the passage, Gasché continues, "from becoming a passage into an identifiable and enduring sameness—in short, into another form of self-identity."[55] This chapter proposes that

Europe might open itself to, or perhaps more appropriately, recognize itself in and reconstruct itself through the figure of the refugee. Thus, if we are to reimagine Europe as something other than itself, if it is to *become* something other than it is, we might do so by reimagining its (non)identity as a Europe of refugees.

It is here that the figure of the refugee, as conceived by Agamben (and Arendt before him) gains importance, and where Nietzsche's conception of the good European can be brought to bear on this imaginary of Europe. The political function and potential of Agamben's figure of the refugee is, after all, not all that distinct from that of Nietzsche's "good European." For Agamben, the refugee is the central figure of contemporary political history who breaks the dyad and reveals the fiction of the nation-state and thus is the only figure that can "ground" an-other political community. Nietzsche's good Europeans, in turn, as strangers to contemporary Europe and ways of being European, likewise reveal the impossibility (and indeed, the undesirability) of conflating political community with the nation-state—or of recasting the shadow of God as the nation. In doing so, they herald the possibility of a different Europe and Europeanness to come.

Like Agamben's refugee, then, Nietzsche's good European enables Europe to experience its nonidentity and to open itself onto "a history for which the changing of the heading, the relation to the other heading or to the other of the heading, is experienced as always possible."[56] Both enable Europe and Europeans to open themselves up to the possibility that Europe could cease to exist as the "impossible Europe of nations" and reemerge as "an aterritorial or extraterritorial space in which all the residents of the European states (citizens and noncitizens) would be in a position of exodus or refuge."[57]

Imagining Europe as a Europe of refugees would, if we use Gasché's words, enable Europe to "recall itself to that which, while not being its opposite . . . is no longer of the order of the head and of a heading, but is the very thing from and thanks to which the binary opposition of heading and the other heading, of self and other, of identity and non-identity, can distinguish their meaning."[58] Helpful here might also be Gasché's "Europe and the Stranger," as the function of the figure of the refugee in relation to Europe might be seen as akin to that of the stranger in Plato's *Sophist*. Gasché argues that the *Sophist*'s stranger represents another beginning of Greek philosophy, and thus another Europe, a Europe to come.[59] As the only stranger in all of Plato's writings who remains anonymous, he is a stranger until the very end.[60] He is not only foreign to Athens, but he is estranged from every home, and thus, much like Nietzsche's good European, he "is no longer native, earthborn, or autochthonous."[61]

Yet what is most important for the purposes of reimagining Europe is that this stranger, while introducing a philosophy of "the other," discloses a different form of otherness, an otherness that is "chopped up and distributed through all the things that are in their relation to one another."[62] Unlike other forms of otherness, which, as Gasché suggests, are actually passages into identifiable and enduring sameness—in short, into another form of self-identity—*this* stranger embodies a form of otherness that is "unlike all the other forms in that it is not only differential (in a passive way), but also actively differentializing."[63] Through his audacious arrival on the scene and his abiding anonymity, he radically unsettles Europe, embodying and revealing the fundamental condition of *différance*—difference, but crucially also, deferral. In the context of Europe, the stranger is thus an injunction to "the radical abandonment and transgression of all autochthony, of all rootedness in oneself, and of all self-identifying retrenchment" and a call "to disown oneself and to become other than oneself."[64] The stranger, in Nietzsche's words, is a good European. In Agamben's political imaginary, it is the refugee.

Conclusion

Inspired by Agamben's musings on the possibility of imagining Europe as the condition of exodus or refuge, this chapter considered the possibility of reimagining Europe as a Europe of refugees. Such reimagining of Europe necessitated, first and foremost, the deconstruction of Europe, which Derrida advocated and in which he engaged during his lifetime. This deconstruction of Europe, which revealed its inherent *différance*, enabled its inheritance and reimagining as something other than "itself." It enabled us to reimagine Europe not as another *ipseic* identity or structure but to think through what Europe might mean if it were to maintain its *différance*, acknowledging both its nonidentity and its perpetual deferral. With the help of Nietzsche's notion of the good European, Agamben's figure of the refugee, and finally, Gasché's interpretation of the stranger, the chapter tried to imagine this Europe to come as one that positions refuge and the refugee at its core—a Europe of refugees.

The staging together of Nietzsche's good European and Agamben's refugee to reimagine Europe from the unsteady grounds of deconstruction is a thought experiment. When Nietzsche imagines the good European, he is not imagining a refugee—neither a person nor a subject position. When Agamben positions the refugee as the central figure of a coming political community, he does not specifically reference Europe or Europeanness. His discussions of Europeanness as the condition of being in exile are not explicitly or substantively linked to his work on the refugee. But what if they were brought together? What if values were revalued, and the refugee became the good European? What if we could reimagine Europeanness as being in exile? Europe as refuge, instead of a fortress? A Europe of (and for) refugees, instead of a Europe of (and for) citizens? The chapter does not purport to offer a blueprint of what Europe and Europeanness, thought of in these terms, would actually "look like." What it does suggest is that thought experiments like this one, in which we imagine ourselves, others, and the spaces we inhabit differently and revalue the values and hierarchies that underpin our sense of ourselves in the world are still important as they are conditions of possibility of an-other future.

Two caveats, with which to conclude. First, while the ongoing "refugee crises" in which Europe is entangled offer a timely occasion for reimagining Europe as a Europe of refugees, we must not conflate the figure or political subjectivity of the refugee, as discussed in this chapter, with the actual, material conditions of refugeehood or the circumstances refugees are made to endure. This chapter sought to explore the political and philosophical potential of situating the subjectivity of the refugee at the center of Europe, not to suggest that imagining Europe as a Europe of refugees offers a material solution to the plight of contemporary refugee populations. While the kind of thought experiment advocated in this chapter can indeed have real-world impact, as do all deconstructions, reimaginings, and revaluations, it is not the objective of this chapter to offer a solution to the current injustices faced by refugee populations in Europe—though just solutions must urgently be sought. It is, rather, to explore the possibility of reimagining Europe in a way that might help us reconstitute it as a different kind of community, which would, in turn, be able to respond differently to crises to come. This can at times seem like a messy and difficult distinction to make, but we must try to maintain it.

Second, it is the "strangeness" of the refugee to the contemporary political landscape—where, as Arendt previously said, "It seems that a man who is nothing but a man has lost the very qualities which make it possible for other people to treat him as a fellow-man"[65]—that enables this figure to serve as a protagonist of a distinct, coming political community and, indeed, a Europe to come. While there are good political and ethical reasons to attempt to point out the similarities between refugee and nonrefugee people, this chapter has a different objective. As in Gasché's discussion of the stranger, the figure or subjectivity of the refugee, as conceived here with the help of Nietzsche and Agamben, prevents the passage into the other, the "coming" Europe, from becoming a passage into the self, one's own, already determined identity. What is called for, then, is the kind of imaginary that constitutes Europe and Europeanness as a permanent condition of refuge and exile from identity into *différance*.

Notes

1. Czajka and Isyar, "Introduction: What Will Become of Europe?," 1.
2. Agamben, "We Refugees," 118.
3. Beardsworth, *Derrida and the Political*, 4–5.
4. Czajka, *Democracy and Justice: Reading Derrida in Istanbul*, 14.
5. Caputo, *Deconstruction in a Nutshell: A Conversation with Jacques Derrida*, 18.
6. For more on the relationship between deconstruction and inheritance, see Haddad, *Derrida and the Inheritance of Democracy*.
7. Derrida, " 'There Is No One Narcissism' (Autobiophotographies)," 214.
8. Derrida, 214.
9. Derrida, "Force of Law: The 'Mystical Foundation of Authority,' " 236.
10. Derrida, "Fifty-two Aphorisms for a Foreword," 125.
11. Derrida, 125.
12. For Derrida on justice as the only limit deconstruction, see Derrida, "Force of Law: The 'Mystical Foundations of Authority,' " 228–97.
13. Derrida, *The Ear of the Other*, xii.
14. Czajka, *Democracy and Justice*, 16.
15. Hill, *The Cambridge Introduction to Jacques Derrida*, 43–44.
16. Derrida, *The Other Heading*, 9–10.

17. Derrida, 6–7.

18. Blond, "Levinas, Europe and Others: The Postcolonial Challenge to Alterity," 260.

19. Derrida, *Ethics, Institutions, and the Right to Philosophy*, 10.

20. Blond, "Levinas, Europe and Others: The Postcolonial Challenge to Alterity," 265.

21. Derrida, *Specters of Marx*, 67.

22. Derrida, 114–15.

23. Derrida, 135.

24. Czajka, 19.

25. Elbe, *Europe: A Nietzschean Perspective*, 12.

26. Nietzsche, *Beyond Good and Evil*, section 256.

27. Elbe, *Europe: A Nietzschean Perspective*, 19.

28. Elbe, 70.

29. For more on the inconsistencies of Nietzsche's thinking on Europe, see Elbe, 68–69.

30. Elbe " 'Labyrinths of the Future': Nietzsche's Genealogy of European Nationalism," 77.

31. Elbe, *Europe: A Nietzschean Perspective*, 70.

32. Nietzsche, *Human, All Too Human*, 6.

33. Nietzsche, 6.

34. Nietzsche, 6–7.

35. Nietzsche, *Beyond Good and Evil*, section 241.

36. Conway, "Wither the 'Good Europeans'? Nietzsche's New World Order," 50.

37. Conway, 50.

38. Nietzsche, *Human, All Too Human*, 6–7.

39. Emden, "The Uneasy European: Nietzsche, Nationalism and the Idea of Europe," 34.

40. Elbe, *Europe: A Nietzschean Perspective*, 90.

41. Elbe, 114.

42. Nietzsche, *The Gay Science*, section 357.

43. Arendt, *The Origins of Totalitarianism*.

44. Agamben, "We Refugees," 114.

45. Agamben, 114.

46. Agamben, 117.

47. Agamben, 117.

48. Agamben, *Means without End: Notes on Politics*, 16.

49. Agamben, 21.

50. Agamben, 16.

51. Agamben, "We Refugees," 116.

52. Agamben, *Means without End*, 16.

53. Agamben, 118–19.
54. Gasché, "This Little Thing That Is Europe," 16.
55. Gasché, 16.
56. Derrida, *The Other Heading*, 17.
57. Agamben, "We Refugees," 118.
58. Gasché, "Feeling the Debt: On Europe," 127–28.
59. Gasché, "Europe and the Stranger," 292–93.
60. Gasché, 293.
61. Gasché, 295.
62. Gasché, 302.
63. Gasché, 11–12.
64. Gasché, 14.
65. Arendt, 300.

Bibliography

Agamben, Giorgio. *Means without End: Notes on Politics*. Minneapolis: University of Minnesota Press, 2000.

Agamben, Giorgio. "We Refugees." *Symposium* 49, no. 2 (1995): 114–19.

Arendt, Hannah. *The Origins of Totalitarianism*. New York: Harcourt Books, 1995.

Beardsworth, Richard. *Derrida and the Political*. New York: Routledge, 1996.

Blond, Louis. "Levinas, Europe and Others: The Postcolonial Challenge to Alterity." *Journal of the British Society for Phenomenology* 47, no. 3 (2016): 260–75.

Caputo, John, ed. *Deconstruction in a Nutshell: A Conversation with Jacques Derrida*. New York: Fordham University Press, 1997.

Conway, Daniel. "Wither the 'Good Europeans'? Nietzsche's New World Order." *South Central Review* 26, no. 3 (2009): 40–60.

Czajka, Agnes. *Democracy and Justice: Reading Derrida in Istanbul*. London: Routledge, 2017.

Czajka, Agnes, and B. Isyar. "Introduction: What Will Become of Europe?" In *Europe After Derrida: Crisis and Potentiality*, edited by A. Czajka and B. Isyar, 1–8. Edinburgh: Edinburgh University Press, 2013.

Derrida, Jacques. *Ethics, Institutions, and the Right to Philosophy*. Translated by Peter Pericles Trifonas. Lanham: Rowman and Littlefield, 2002.

Derrida, Jacques. *The Ear of the Other: Otobiography, Transference, Translation*. Translated by Peggy Kamuf. New York: Shocken, 1985.

Derrida, Jacques. "Fifty-Two Aphorisms for a Foreword." In *Psyche: Inventions of the Other, Volume II*, translated by Andrew Benjamin. Stanford, CA: Stanford University Press, 2008.

Derrida, Jacques. "Force of Law: The 'Mystical Foundation of Authority.'" In *Acts of Religion*, translated by Mary Quaintance. New York: Routledge, 2002, 236.

Derrida, Jacques. *Of Grammatology*. Translated by Gayatri Chakravorty Spivak. Baltimore, MD: Johns Hopkins University Press, 1976.

Derrida, Jacques. *The Other Heading: Reflections on Today's Europe*. Translated by Pascale-Anne Brault and Michael Naas. Bloomington: Indiana University Press, 1992.

Derrida, Jacques. *Specters of Marx: The State of the Debt, the Work of Mourning and the New International*. Translated by Peggy Kamuf. New York: Routledge, 1994.

Derrida, Jacques. " 'There Is No One Narcissism' (Autobiophotographies)." In *Points . . . Interviews, 1974–1994*, translated by Peggy Kamuf et al. Stanford, CA: Stanford University Press, 1992.

Elbe, Stefan. *Europe: A Nietzschean Perspective*. London: Routledge, 2003.

Elbe, Stefan. "European Nihilism and Annihilation in the Twentieth Century." *Totalitarian Movements and Political Religions* 1, no. 3 (2000): 43–72.

Elbe, Stefan. " 'Labyrinths of the Future': Nietzsche's Genealogy of European Nationalism." *Journal of Political Ideologies* 7, no. 1 (2002): 77–96.

Emden, Christian. "The Uneasy European: Nietzsche, Nationalism and the Idea of Europe." *Journal of European Studies* 38, no. 1 (2008): 27–51.

Gasché, Rodolphe. "Europe and the Stranger." *Journal of the British Society for Phenomenology* 47, no. 3 (2016): 292–305.

Gasché, Rodolphe. "Feeling the Debt: On Europe." In *Future Crossings: Literature between Philosophy and Cultural Studies*, edited by K. Ziarek and S. Deane, 125–46. Evanston, IL: Northwestern University Press, 2000.

Gasché, Rodolphe. "This Little Thing That Is Europe." *CR: The New Centennial Review* 7, no. 2 (2007): 1–19.

Haddad, Samir. *Derrida and the Inheritance of Democracy*. Bloomington: Indiana University Press, 2013.

Hill, Leslie. *The Cambridge Introduction to Jacques Derrida*. Cambridge: Cambridge University Press, 2007.

Nietzsche, Friedrich. *Beyond Good and Evil: Prelude to a Philosophy of the Future*. Translated by J. Norman. Cambridge: Cambridge University Press, 2002.

Nietzsche, Friedrich. *The Gay Science*. Translated by J. Nauckhoff. Cambridge: Cambridge University Press, 2001.

Nietzsche, Friedrich. *Human, All Too Human: A Book for Free Spirits*. Translated by R. J. Hollingdale. Cambridge: Cambridge University Press, 1986.

Part III

After the End

8

The End of Europe

Herder and Hegel on Progress and Decline

BART ZANTVOORT

So let no one augur from the greying of Europe the decline and death of our whole species! . . . Why should the western corner of our northern hemisphere alone possess culture? And does it alone possess it?

—Herder, *Letters for the Advancement of Humanity*

When philosophy paints its grey in grey, a shape of life has grown old, and it cannot be rejuvenated, but only recognized, by the grey in grey of philosophy; the owl of Minerva begins its flight only with the onset of dusk.

—Hegel, *Elements of the Philosophy of Right*

What is Europe? Today, beyond all the critiques of European exceptionalism, of its self-conceit regarding its unique place and mission in history, how are we to reimagine the idea of Europe? What are its defining features, its essential characteristics—if it is still possible to ask such a question? Perhaps the idea of Europe has to be thought from the perspective of its end—both the end of *Europe* and the end of the *idea* of Europe, of the possibility of thinking Europe *as* an idea.

In a little volume entitled *The Idea of Europe*, George Steiner distinguishes five features that define Europe. The fifth and final characteristic is that Europe—perhaps uniquely—has a relation toward its own end:

"An eschatological self-awareness which, I believe, may well be unique to European consciousness. . . . It is as if Europe, unlike other civilizations, had intuited that it would one day collapse under the paradoxical weight of its achievements and the unparalleled wealth and complication of its history." From the millenarian phantasies embedded in Christianity to Hegel's philosophy of history to Valéry's diagnosis of the "mortality of civilizations" to Carnot's discovery of the entropic decay of energy, what defines Europe—Steiner suggests—is that it has taken up an active and conscious relation towards the possibility or even inevitability of its own decline and end.[1]

Historically, growing anxieties about Europe's cultural and political decline have been attributed to the experience of totalitarianism and the two World Wars or the loss of geopolitical preeminence to, first, the United States and Russia, and today China. But this topos of decline runs much deeper and emerged much earlier. It is perhaps surprising that it started to reach fever pitch during the time of Europe's greatest industrial, cultural, and geopolitical dominance, during the late eighteenth and nineteenth centuries, when thinkers from Herder to Hegel to Nietzsche developed a philosophical-historical narrative of civilizational decadence and decline.

When thinking about the decline of Europe, Nietzsche's comments on European decadence are likely to come to mind,[2] or Spengler's prediction of the decline of the *Abendland*,[3] or Heidegger's diagnosis of the global dominance of technics that also spells the end of philosophy,[4] or Adorno and Horkheimer's pessimistic analysis of the dialectic of Enlightenment.[5] As I will argue in this chapter, however, the narrative of decline goes back to the philosophies of history of Herder and Hegel, who are still often taken to be relatively straightforward examples of the Enlightenment confidence in reason and progress in history.[6] In both thinkers, however, the notion of progress and historical development is intimately connected with a cyclical theory of civilizational development and decline. For Herder, the advancement and education of humanity under the auspices of providence occurs through an organic process in which cultures grow and decay; none of these cultures has any claim to superiority over any other, and Herder is particularly critical of Europeans' view of themselves as the summit of civilization. Hegel supposedly conceived of European modernity as the "end" of history, and he is usually associated with a progressive view of history, famously claiming in the *Lectures on the Philosophy of World History* that world history is "the progress of the consciousness of freedom."[7] But in Hegel, too, we shall see that historical progress is only possible through a process of cultural development and decline.

The idea of the end of Europe—the end in in the sense of its teleological mission, but also in the sense of Europe's own decline—is thus irrevocably bound up with that other historical narrative about Europe: the Enlightenment notion of an interlocking process of technical, scientific, philosophical, moral, and political progress, expressed most typically in texts such as the Marquis de Condorcet's *Sketch for a Historical Picture of the Progress of the Human Mind*[8] and Kant's *Idea for a Universal History with Cosmopolitan Intent;*[9] a history in which Europe, as the home of philosophical rationality, plays a leading role. According to this view, too, it is Europe's historical self-awareness that sets it apart from other cultures and traditions. But this self-awareness does not express itself primarily in terms of an awareness of the finitude of one's own culture but in terms of the obligation to detach oneself from one's historical foundations and freely determine one's thought and actions on the basis of rational principles. Rather than projecting a sense of decline, it embodies a notion of progress based on *overcoming* one's historical limitations through a process of rational self-criticism.

This is also how Husserl, faced with the double threat of scientific positivism and fascist irrationalism, sought to save both Europe and the idea of Europe by linking the task of Europe to the task of philosophy in *The Crisis of the European Sciences*. As Gasché writes:

> The idea of philosophy . . . is the request that everyone shape his or her life freely—free from all traditionalist conceptions—by not acting or advancing anything that cannot be accounted for in terms transparent to all. . . . This demand, which the Greeks called *logon didonai*, is the demand to be self-responsible and to assume this responsibility by accounting for ones' claims and actions rather than having recourse to inveterate beliefs and ingrained habits of thinking. With this demand emerges a new type of history, the history of a life shaped through ideas and reason, in short, a history of humankind itself.[10]

The defining feature of Europe, according to this line of thought, is that Europe, as the heir of the Greek tradition of philosophy, is the only culture that is truly self-critical: "Europe" has no static, positive content, no fixed identity, but is defined by being permanently open, willing to give up its "inveterate beliefs and ingrained habits of thinking," and reconsider its position under the influence of other points of view. Even when Europe was forced, by the loss of its political preeminence as well as the critique of metaphysical foundationalism and Eurocentrism, to give up its special role in philosophical history, it still held on to its self-regard as the foremost representative of a universalized self-critical humanity: the universal task, rooted in its Greek European origin, "consists in nothing but the critical ability to transcend given identities. Such transcending alone is what constitutes the human." Although Gasché, following Husserl, thus defines the idea of Europe as that which "breaks open Europe's self-immanence towards a transcendence, toward the other, and what is other than Europe," he nevertheless insists that the European-universal task remains "universally valid."[11]

At a surface level, these two "defining features" of Europe—its vision of its decline and fall and its view of itself as the vanguard of human progress—may seem to be opposed. Indeed, they have generally been associated with the fundamentally contrasting attitudes of the Enlightenment and counter-Enlightenment,[12] and they form the foundation for two of the main opposing camps in contemporary politics: on the one hand, universalist liberals who continue to believe in gradual progress through the application of technology and the spread of rational institutions, with Kant, Rawls and Habermas as their intellectual paragons; and on the other hand those politicians who insist on the inestimable value of each particular culture and who exploit the narrative of decline to call for a national renewal. For intellectual inspiration, these movements appeal to a rather confused mix of Hegel, Nietzsche, Spengler, and Heidegger—for example in the Netherlands, with the extreme-right Forum voor Democratie Party,[13] or in the case of "Trumpism," Steve Bannon and the American alt-right, but one can also think of a "Eurasianist" Russian thinker like Aleksandr Dugin, who is mainly inspired by Heidegger.

At a deeper level, however, both the philosophical narrative of progress and the narrative of decline are rooted in a modern, historicized view of the world, which seeks to explain our world in terms of our position in a historical development that has a lawful character and can therefore be, to a greater or lesser degree, rationally comprehended. The European narrative of decline—in Herder, Spengler, and, in a complicated way, also in Hegel—is inscribed in a theory that conceives of history in terms of the rise and decline of cultures. The decline of European culture is thus grasped not in terms of its particularity, its unique historical situation, or contingent characteristics, but in terms of a larger, universal historical theory of development. In this way (despite the antiuniversalist and anti-Eurocentric tendencies in Herder or Spengler), the European experience of decline is transformed into a sort of "negative" universal history: it is precisely by thinking its own end that Europe inscribes itself at the center of the history of the world. But is this sacrificial—or rather, suicidal—gesture more than a last, desperate attempt to cling to this position of privilege?

In his *Lectures on the Philosophy of World History*, Hegel suggests that political stagnation and death are the inevitable fate of nation-states, their natural end: "The natural death of the national spirit may take the form of political stagnation, or what we call habit . . . both individuals and nations die a natural death."[14] Both Herder and Hegel, I will argue in this chapter, conceive of the decline of cultures in terms of a loss of vitality, a process of ossification characterized by a culture falling into habits and becoming inert. This chapter will explore these two great historicist thinkers' ideas on Europe and cultural development and decline in order to shed light on three issues: first, the way in which the narrative of cultural decline and the decline of Europe is interwoven with the notion of historical development and progress in history; second, the organic model of the rise and decline of cultures developed by Herder and Hegel and its relation to the narrative of universal history; and third, the historical law by which, according to Herder and Hegel, cultures decline and the question of what this can tell us about the decline of Europe.

Herder and the "Greying of Europe"

Johann Gottfried von Herder was a profoundly original thinker, whose influence on later European thought is hard to overestimate. He is often considered to be the father of two major intellectual doctrines, historicism and nationalism.[15] He introduced an organicist view of history, arguing that cultures develop, blossom, and decay according to their own internal principles and that each age, each culture, should therefore be understood on its own terms, rather than being subjected to a universalizing pattern of historical development. He criticized Enlightenment rationalism and cosmopolitanism because they disregarded the unique quality and value of different cultures and believed that the large states of his day, such as Prussia and Austria, which bound together different cultures and nationalities under a centralized monarchy, should be replaced with political entities based on a shared language and culture.[16] As such, he has often been considered a forerunner of the rampant nationalism that characterized much of nineteenth- and twentieth-century politics—quite unfairly because he relentlessly criticized those who believed one culture or country ranked above others: "To brag of one's country is the stupidest form of boastfulness. . . . What is a nation? A great wild garden full of bad plants and good."[17] He applied this same principle to Europe, which he censured for its imperialism and its hypocritical self-regard: often, its high-flown notions of civilization and rationality were nothing more than excuses for oppression, conquest, and the extermination of local cultures.[18] "Least of all," Herder writes, "can our *European culture* be the measure of universal human goodness and human value; it is no yardstick or a false one. European culture is an abstracted concept, a name."[19]

Herder is often ranked as a counter-Enlightenment thinker, as the title of Isaiah Berlin's book on Vico, Herder, and Hamann, *Three Critics of the Enlightenment*, suggests. It is true that he shared an appreciation of tradition with the likes of Hamann and Burke, that he was strongly critical of French Enlightenment figures such as Voltaire and the *encyclopédistes*, and that he was a major influence on the German Romantic reaction against the Enlightenment.[20] But his relation to the Enlightenment was ambivalent and complex. Tellingly, Herder was a student at Königsberg under both Hamann and Kant, the first the father of the *Sturm und Drang* movement and a defender of faith and sentiment against the corrosive scepticism of the Enlightenment, the latter the foremost representative of critical rationalism and Enlightenment. Herder maintained close personal relationships with both his teachers during and after his time at Königsberg; although he regularly clashed intellectually with both Hamann as well as Kant, Beiser suggests that Kant's influence, in the end, was the stronger.[21]

There are two tensions in Herder's thought that are central to the present discussion. First, how does he reconcile his historicism, his belief in the unique value and characteristics of particular ages and cultures, with his belief in a shared *Humanität*, universal reason, and natural law, especially with his application of the notion of natural law to historical development? And second, how does he reconcile his belief that there is, at least in some sense, progress in history with both his historicist pluralism and his organicist view of the rise and decline of cultures? In the following, both of these questions will be brought to bear on Herder's idea of Europe.

HERDER'S HISTORICIST PLURALISM

Herder's historicist pluralism has been well documented; according to Isaiah Berlin, it is one of his most original contributions to the history of thought.[22] It is forcefully expressed in early writings such as *On the Change of Taste*, where Herder asks how it is possible for notions of truth, beauty, and morality to claim universal assent, given the large and apparently irreconcilable differences between individuals and between different cultures and ages. "As soon as it is shown that what I on the basis of reasons take to be true, beautiful, good, pleasant can be likewise on the basis of reasons be regarded by another as false, ugly, bad, unpleasant, then truth, beauty, and moral value is a phantom that appears to each person in another way, in another shape."[23] Individuals have a "stubbornly idiosyncratic sense of feeling" that leads them to experience the world in different ways.[24] And history shows us such a spectacle of diversity that we are likely to be led into skepticism: "Time has changed everything so much that often one needs a magic mirror in order to recognize the same creature beneath such different forms. The *form* of the earth, its *surface*, its *condition*, has changed. Changed are the *race*, the manner of *life*, the manner of *thought*, the form of government, the taste of nations—just as families and individual human beings change."[25] Although Herder recognizes that this diversity in values and customs can be a problem insofar as it presents difficulties for any theory of history and a challenge to the Enlightenment precepts of universal rationality, he argues that diversity is something to be valued in its own right.[26] It is precisely on this basis that Herder criticizes Europeans for seeing themselves as the summit and standard of all culture and for rooting out and destroying other cultures under the pretext of bringing them civilization and Christian salvation. In *This Too a Philosophy of History for the Formation of Humanity*, his polemical-ironical takedown of Enlightenment philosophy of history in the tradition of Voltaire's *Essai sur les mœurs et l'esprit des nations*, he applies this criticism both to Europe's colonization of the rest of the world and to "internal" European colonization of the Irish and Scots by the English or the Corsicans by the French. *"Spaniards, Jesuits,* and *Dutchmen*—you human-friendly, unselfish, noble, and virtuous nations!—how much has not the *civilization* [Bildung] *of humanity* to be grateful to you for already in all parts of the world! . . . Shame for *England* that *Ireland* for so long remained savage and barbarous; it is *civilly administered* and *happy.* Shame for England that the *Highland Scots* for so long went without pants; they now bear these, at least with them *on a stake,* and are happy."[27] There could hardly be a more vicious critique of the spirit of European exceptionalism than Herder's:

> If a European collective spirit lived elsewhere than in books, we would have to be ashamed of the *crime of abusing humanity* before almost all peoples of the earth. Let the land be named to which Europeans have come without having sinned against defenseless, trusting humanity, perhaps for all aeons to come, though injurious acts, through unjust wars, greed, deceit, oppression, through diseases and harmful gifts! Our part of the world must be called, not the wise, but the *presumptuous, pushing, tricking* part of the earth; it has not cultivated but has destroyed the shoots of peoples' own cultures wherever and however it could.[28]

Despite his strong and persistent antieurocentrism, however, Herder does not deny Europe's actual global political, technological, and commercial dominance. In his later work *Ideen zur Philosophie der Geschichte der Menschheit,* he gives a careful analysis that accounts for the rise of Europe in terms of the influence of Arabic philosophy and science, institutions such as scholastic philosophy and the legal faculties in medieval universities, independent cities with their civic constitution and guilds, and networks of trading cities such as the Hanseatic league. Ultimately, it was the continent's relative poverty and its geographical location between the wealthier continents of Africa and Asia, along with its internal geography—both intersected and connected by rivers, seas and mountain ranges, allowing for commerce but not for a large centralized state—that impelled its peoples to display the "inventiveness" and "industriousness" which are the roots of its power. "How, therefore, came Europe by its cultivation, and the rank it obtained by it above other countries? . . . The sovereignty of Europe is founded on *activity* and *invention,* on *science* and *united emulative exertions.*"[29] Factors that were central to other thinkers in explaining the rise of Europe, the inheritance of Greece and Rome and Europe's climate, are relegated to a relatively minor role.

In spite of all of his pluralism, history is therefore not, for Herder, "a tale, told by an idiot, full of sound and fury, signifying nothing"—a chaotic development without reason or order. Although he pays much more attention to contingency and concrete historical developments than Kant would do, around the same time, in his *Idea for a Universal History with Cosmopolitan Intent*, there are causes, reasons, and patterns to be discerned in historical development. Moreover, history is not without a final purpose; the aim of history is captured, for Herder, in the word *Humanität*: "The autonomous development of all the physical, sensitive, active and intellectual powers of a human being."[30] There is therefore a sense in which there is progress in history, and as for Kant and for Hegel in their respective philosophies of history, for Herder this progress is underwritten by the Christian notion of Providence.[31]

The Laws of Historical Development

The intellectual career of historicism in philosophy is often traced back from Marx to Hegel to Herder, where it is supposed to have originated. Fredrick Beiser suggests, however, that in an important sense, Herder's historicism must be traced back to Kant, and specifically Kant in his precritical phase. Herder, he argues, was strongly influenced by Kant's 1755 work *Allgemeine Naturgeschichte und Theorie des Himmels*.[32] Kant there argued that the order in the universe can be explained on the basis of the development of a "primal mass" under the influence of the laws of repulsion and attraction, thus obviating the need for a supernatural, divine explanation. In doing so, Beiser argues, Kant historicized Newton's overly static view of nature by showing that "what appears to be given and eternal in nature is in fact the product of time and history."[33] But at the same time, Kant sought to explain human beings and human history in naturalistic, rather than theological, terms; an effort that can still be discerned in *Idea for a Universal History*. By historicizing nature, he also naturalized history; this is the double lesson Herder drew from Kant. The aim of the *Ideen zur Philosophie der Geschichte der Menschheit*, Beiser writes, "is simply to apply Kant's naturalism to the sphere of history itself."[34]

What, then, are the laws that Herder finds in history? There is, on the one hand, an overall tendency for order to emerge out of chaos and for human culture to work its way towards greater *Humanität* under the guidance of Providence.[35] But what is interesting here is rather the specific way in which particular cultures develop, which also presents a law-like pattern. Herder applies an organicist analogy to the workings of human history, which is characterized by the rise, flowering, and decline of cultures or states:

> I am presupposing that cycle to which individually every nation . . . seems to be destined. . . . It is an observation that has inevitably forced itself before the eyes of even the most stupid historian that every people, like every art and science, has its period of growth, bloom, and decline. . . . The first of these usually coincides with the times of virtue and need, the last with those of luxury and rest, between which the middle, highest peak only occupies a short time.[36]

The application of the model of the organism to history was not original; in doing so, Herder followed a tradition from Aristotle to John of Salisbury to Pascal.[37] More immediately, he was influenced by Gibbon's *Decline and Fall of the Roman Empire*: like Gibbon, Herder saw an important role for Christianity in the decline of the Roman Empire, and applied this theory to the state of Europe in modern times.[38] As we will see in the following, Hegel—another admirer of Gibbon—would in turn borrow much from Herder's model of the rise and decline of cultures in his own views on historical development. (And Spengler, too, makes much of the analogy between the decline of Rome and the decline of the West.)

Herder thus conceives of the development of culture in terms of successive phases of childhood, maturity, and old age. Cultures decline by sinking into decadence, "luxury and rest," by losing their vitality; they become stuck in old habits and dogmatic ways of thinking and refuse to change with the times.[39] In his later work the *Letters for the Advancement of Humanity*, Herder describes the situation in Europe around the time of the French Revolution in these terms. The feudal nobility and Catholic Church represent the ossified, outdated order which must make way for progress and move with the "spirit of the times."[40] Europe has its origin in the settlement and conversion to Christianity of Barbarian peoples around the time of the fall of the Roman Empire, that is, in the institutionalization of feudalism and the church, but this "old system of feudalism and conquest" has become obsolete; it "no longer suit[s] our times": "So why do we want to close our eyes to the midday, along with everything that is and happens around us, in the illusion that we really still lived in the times of warring, of the Hun invasions and the crusades?"[41]

Enlightenment rationalism took itself to be a force for progress against the outdated institutions of feudal barbarism and dogmatism. Herder argues, however, that it too has contributed to the death of European culture. In turns of phrase that presage both Nietzsche and Spengler, Herder derides the "mechanistic" character of (French) universalist rationalism that has weakened the forces of life, love, and humanity in Europe:

> Thence it of course now becomes readily intelligible towards *"which center"* this civilization [*Bildung*] strives and ever gets guided: *philosophy!, thought!*—easier *mechanics!, rationalizing* that reaches right down to the *foundation pillars* of society which formerly just *stood* and *carried!* . . . Rationalizing spread too carelessly, too uselessly—*could* it not weaken, and has it not really weakened, *inclination, drive, activity* for living? Nevertheless now, this *exhaustion* may well be comfortable for the spirit of some lands: exhausted limbs have to go on, have no forces except . . . for example, for *counterthought.* Each cog remains in its place from *fear* or *habit* or *luxury.*[42]

The decline of Europe is here conceptualized in terms of the *becoming mechanical* of a culture that used to be active, alive, striving; in terms of exhaustion, decadence, and a sinking into habit. As Nietzsche would later arrange the forces of life against the "pale, Nordic, Königsbergian" spirit of reason,[43] Herder—who spent his formative years in Königsberg and the even "paler" Riga—opposes the vibrancy of "heart, warmth, blood, humanity and life" to the "calculation," "rationalizing," mechanistic "grinding" of European, Enlightened modernity. "Is this, then, the ideal condition toward which we have been formed through everything, which *spreads* abroad further and further in *Europe*, which *sails* to all *parts of the world*, and wants to *civilly administer* everyone *to be what we are* . . . *Human beings?* . . . Perhaps! But . . . each of them in the uniform of his class machines!"[44]

Ultimately, there is an ambiguity in Herder's description of the law of the historical development of cultures and the decline of Europe. There are three main elements to be observed:

On the one hand, it seems as if the decadence, imperialism, and mechanistic rationalism of Europe are the result of a cultural and historical "wrong turn," an excess of a particular branch of rationalism that has allied itself with the political power of the modern "mechanistic" state[45] and imperialist universalism. This wrong turn, Herder suggests, could be remedied, and Europe could still take its place in a peaceful concord of nations;[46] the development of reason and *Humanität* will ultimately lead to an "autumn of sensibleness," where Europe will atone for its crimes: "Europe *must* give compensation for the debts it has incurred, make good the crimes it has committed—not from choice but according to the very nature of things. For reason would be in a bad way if it were not reason everywhere, and the universal good were not also the universally most useful."[47] Decline is therefore not inevitable.

On the other hand, however, decline is described as a natural consequence of the organic constitution of cultures; luxury, decadence, ossification, "mechanism" are inevitable outcomes of the culture reaching the phase of its "old age" and decline. Europe, from this point of view, is already well on the way to death, having turned into nothing more than a machine, and it is trying to drag the rest of the world with it in its old age: "There exist there [i.e., in the rest of the world] peoples in childhood, youth, manhood, and will probably do so for a long time to come before the seafaring old men of Europe succeed in advancing them to old age through brandy, diseases, and slaves' arts . . . the Europeans, with the imposing of their arts, ethics, and doctrines, for the most part played the role of worn-out old men who had completely forgotten what was appropriate to a child."[48]

And third, the process of the rise and decline of cultures is embedded within the broader development of humanity. It is with regard to this broader pattern of development that a culture can become "outdated" or obsolete when compared to the moving "spirit of the times." Different parts of Europe can be said to have fallen behind the "spirit of the times," for example in the sense that Protestant countries have made more progress than Catholic ones.[49] And with regard to non-European cultures, Herder captures the different level of development in terms of the metaphor of childhood and maturity, where a more mature culture is not necessarily "better" than a young one, although it is more advanced; here, too, he does not hesitate to call this progress.[50] Although Herder does not draw this inference clearly, it seems logical to conclude that cultures "fall behind the times" precisely because they become ossified, "mechanistic," "exhausted"; because their ideas become dogmas and their various and lively forms of social and political association are transformed in to the overarching "machine" of the state. As we will see, Hegel will work out this notion in more detail.

What, then, will be the fate of Europe? Despite Herder's occasional hopeful comments about reform and repentance, he ultimately sees a future beyond the "greying of Europe":

> The more their forces and states in Europe age, the more unhappy Europeans some day leave this part of the world in order to make common cause with the oppressed in this place and that. . . . Who has insight into the seed of the future that is perhaps already planted? Cultured states can arise where we hardly believe them possible; cultured states which we considered immortal can wither . . .
>
> *So let no one augur from the greying of Europe the decline and death of our whole species!* What harm would it do to the latter if a degenerated part of it perished?, if a few withered twigs and leaves of the sap-rich tree fell off? Others take the place of the withered ones and bloom up more freshly. Why should the western corner of our northern hemisphere alone possess culture? And does it alone possess it?[51]

Hegel: Death by Habit

That Hegel should have any insights to contribute regarding the future of Europe is perhaps not immediately obvious—doesn't Hegel, after all, proclaim Europe to be the "end of history"? "World history," Hegel claims, "is the progress of the consciousness of freedom"[52] and is characterized by the dialectical progression of a series of cultures, each of which internalizes and builds upon the experiences of the previous ones. This learning process in which, in Hegelian terms, spirit comes to be conscious of itself, culminates in European modernity: "World history travels from east to west; for Europe is the absolute end of history, just as Asia is the beginning."[53]

There is, however, also much in Hegel that speaks against this famous and much-maligned "end of history" thesis.[54] Often cited in this regard are passages in which Hegel cautions against philosophy speaking authoritatively of the future, such as the statement in the *Philosophy of Right* that "each individual is in any case a child of his time" and that thus "philosophy is its own time comprehended in thought,"[55] or instead his own tentative hints about a future beyond Europe, such as the suggestion that "America is the country of the future"[56] or that "the great Slavonic nation" might have a future world-historical role to play.[57]

More significant here, however, if we keep in mind what Herder wrote about the "greying of Europe," is Hegel's famous statement about the owl of Minerva. Philosophy cannot issue instructions as to how the world ought to be, Hegel writes, because it always comes on the scene too late: "It is only when actuality has reached maturity that the ideal appears opposite the real and reconstructs this real world, which it has grasped in its substance, in the shape of an intellectual realm. When philosophy paints its grey in grey, a shape of life has grown old, and it cannot be rejuvenated, but only recognized, by the grey in grey of philosophy; the owl of Minerva begins its flight only with the onset of dusk."[58] This passage, too, is often cited as evidence against the "end-of-history" thesis. If philosophy is only possible once a shape of life has grown old, then Hegel's own philosophical system is the proof that the shape of life of which it is the intellectual expression—European modernity—is in the process of reaching its own end—both in the Aristotelian-teleological sense of actualization in which Hegel uses the term and in the sense of its historical decline and supersession by a new shape of life.[59] From this point of view then, Hegel, like Herder, can be interpreted as theorizing the decline, the "greying" of Europe, rather than its culminating triumph over the forces of dialectical contradiction. But wherein does this decline consist, according to Hegel, and how does it fit with the rest of his philosophy and its apparent emphasis on progress? Here, it will be helpful to bring out the many parallels that exist between Hegel's and Herder's philosophies of history.

HEGEL'S ORGANICIST THEORY OF HISTORY

Though the precise extent of Herder's direct influence on Hegel is difficult to estimate, it is likely to have been significant. He was probably familiar with a number of Herder's works, including the *Ideen zur Philosophie der Geschichte der Menschheit,* and he commented on Herder's philosophy in his text *Glauben and Wissen* from 1802/1803.[60] Although Hegel disagrees with Herder on a methodological level, arguing that the latter's work fails to appreciate the true nature of rational thought and therefore must ultimately remain subjective,[61] Herder's overall influence on Hegel's conception of the historical development of culture is quite clear.

First, Hegel, like Herder, conceives of historical development organically, in terms of the rise and decline of cultures, which he calls "shapes of spirit."[62] In his *Philosophy of History*, Hegel divides history into four stages: the oriental world, comprising China, India, and Persia; the Greek world; the Roman world; and the Germanic world. Again like Herder, Hegel compares these stages with the stages of human development: the oriental world, Greece and Rome represent spirit in its childhood, youth, and manhood, respectively. But when it comes to the final stage, the Germanic world, the analogy no longer applies: "In nature, old age is weakness; but the old age of the Spirit is its complete ripeness, in which Spirit returns to unity with itself."[63] The Germanic world (*die germanische Welt*) here refers not to Germany or the German-speaking parts of Europe but rather to Christian Europe as a whole; like Herder, Hegel believes that the origins of modern Europe lie in the settlement of Germanic tribes in the territory of the declining western Roman Empire and the subsequent fusion of Christian religion, Roman law and institutions, and the Germanic spirit of freedom.[64] Spain, England, and Italy are no less heirs to the realms of the Franks, Lombards, and Visigoths than are Germany and France. The Reformation, however, which for Hegel, as for Herder, plays a crucial role in the development of modern consciousness, will shift the world-historical center of gravity to northwestern Europe.

For Hegel, a culture or "world-historical nation" (*Volk*) is not simply a politically or ethnically defined entity; it is an organic whole that embodies a particular way of looking at the world and living in the world, a form of life with its specific philosophical outlook, religion, legal and political institutions, customs, arts and culture, and form of economic organization. This "way of looking at and living in the world" Hegel calls a nation's "principle," which at first is only implicit and must be developed in the course of history. A nation develops its principle by embedding it in religious and political institutions, laws, and concrete social relations; by giving them objective reality and in this way working out for itself what its principle really is. But this process of realization through objectification also leads to the shortcomings of a nation's organizing principle becoming explicit and eventually leads to its downfall:

The particular history of a world-historical nation contains, on the one hand, the development of its principle from its latent childhood phase until it blossoms out in free ethical self-consciousness and makes its mark in universal history, and, on the other, the period of its decline and fall—for these denote the emergence within it of a higher principle which is simply the negative of its own. This signifies the spirit's transition to the higher principle and hence the transition of world history to *another* nation.[65]

It is therefore this cyclical process of the rise and decline of cultures that gives rise to the overall pattern of progress in history. Progress, for Hegel, is by no means linear since it is always possible for regressions and reversals to occur.[66] Moreover, every transition to a new world-historical period represents both a repudiation *and* an appropriation of the stage that came before. If the French Revolution appeared at first as the radical negation of feudalism and the *ancien régime*, the assertion of absolute subjective freedom and the destruction of all fixed forms and identities, its consolidation under Napoleon and during the restoration necessarily reestablished a continuity with the past.[67] There is a kind of cultural-institutional "muscle memory," a largely unconscious reservoir of internalized attitudes, behaviors, and ideas, which ensures that history progresses through all revolutionary transformations. As Hegel writes at the end of the *Phenomenology of Spirit*, after every transition to a new stage, "Spirit has to start afresh to bring itself to maturity as if, for it, all that preceded were lost and it had learned nothing from the experience of the earlier Spirits. But recollection, the *inwardizing* [*Erinnerung*] of that experience has preserved it. . . . So although this Spirit starts afresh and apparently from its own resources to bring itself to maturity, it is none the less on a higher level that it starts."[68] Although the term *Erinnerung*—memory, recollection, or literally "internalization"—may make it seem as if Hegel is speaking here of a kind of collective memory (or the memory of a mysterious collective agent, "Spirit," as he is easily misunderstood), it is important to keep in mind that this *Erinnerung* is not something purely "mental" and that it is indeed strongly linked to the process through which historical experience is embedded in objective institutions and practices. That is to say, it is connected to the formation of the "social body" as a kind of "second nature" through the internalization of habits, to which we will turn in a moment. Nevertheless, it seems clear that it is this process of internalization that serves as the foundation for continuity in history, thus both allowing us to comprehend history rationally and allowing history to make progress toward the consciousness of freedom.[69]

Although progress for Hegel is therefore not strictly linear, based on passages such as these, it does appear to be *necessary* and necessarily tied to the idea of Europe as the "old age" of mankind that represents the "ripeness of Spirit" and the actualization of freedom.[70] Various attempts have been made to call into question this notion of necessary progress in Hegel; Žižek, for example, argues that necessity in Hegel is always only retrospective or "retroactive" and that therefore Hegel does allow for radical contingency.[71] Although I largely agree with this reading, my emphasis here is different. If, at least on one level, European modernity appears as the culmination and end of the development of freedom—and everything turns here, of course, on how we understand this notion of the "end"—and yet historical development consists of the rise and inevitable decline of cultures, how is this decline to be understood and explained? And does this process of decline also apply to Europe, and if so, how?

MECHANISM AND HABIT

We have seen that Herder characterizes cultural decline in terms of a loss of vitality, a process through which a culture becomes mechanical, habitual, and ossified and which causes it to fail to move with the "spirit of the times." Hegel takes over this notion of decline and gives it a more detailed theoretical elaboration. As I have argued elsewhere, it is the very process of cultural development—the way in which a culture realizes its implicit "principle" by objectifying it in laws, institutions, and other objective social structures—that in the end makes this culture "inert" and unable to develop further.[72] In his early writings, Hegel calls this the problem of "positivity": political or religious institutions are initially formed in accordance with the needs, desires, and character of the culture from which they spring. But it is precisely because they have an objective existence over against the subjects who created them that these institutions can resist change. Over time, they become fixed and rigid and start to live a life of their own; even if changing circumstances, ideas, or norms make change necessary or desirable, inert institutions may persist in being.[73]

Like Herder, Hegel conceives of the decline of culture in terms of the notion of mechanism. Both in the institutions of "positive" religion and, politically, in the state, individuals are reduced to "cogs" in a machine, and are therefore alienated and unfree. Although he sometimes seems to endorse the Romantic notion that the state as such is something "mechanical" and therefore to be overcome, Hegel primarily sees this decline into mechanism as a phase in the development of cultures that will ultimately lead to their overthrow and not as a problem with the state per se. In various early writings and in the *Phenomenology*, he particularly diagnoses the time of the decline of the Roman Empire and his own time, the decline and end of the *ancient régime* in Europe, as such moments characterized by positivity and mechanism. Rather than relating to one another "organically" as free, self-conscious members of a community, or as a community bound together by a shared way of life or religious convictions, individuals in this phase only relate to each other externally through the "mechanism" of the state and the bonds of self-interest.[74]

The problem Hegel associates with positivity and mechanism in his early writings does not disappear in his later work, but it is reinterpreted in terms of the notions of habit and second nature. Whereas in his early writings, mechanism is opposed to political freedom and moral autonomy and, as such, is seen for the most part as something purely negative, Hegel more and more came to see that the social "mechanism"—unreflected habits and customs, objectified institutions, and self-interested economic relations—is a necessary part of political freedom and modern ethical life.[75] We need the external sphere of economic relations—what Hegel in his mature work calls "civil society"—and a shared basis of customs, norms, and institutions that we do not actively legislate or create for ourselves to make free, self-conscious political life possible at all, just as we each individually need to make a great deal of behavior habitual, unconscious, and unreflected in order to make self-reflection, thought, and freedom possible in the first place.

Hegel thus takes the problem of habit, which has a long history in philosophy, and gives it social and political significance. In the "Anthropology" section of his *Philosophy of Spirit*, he claims that, on the one hand, we are freed by habit, yet on the other hand, we are enslaved by it.[76] For Hegel, habit, which he calls the "mechanism of self-feeling," does not refer simply to personal habits like brushing your teeth or going for a walk at a certain time; instead, it is a general principle through which the body and mind form routine patterns of behavior that can serve as "building blocks" for higher or more complex behaviors. Playing music, as one of his examples goes, is only possible if a great deal of complicated mental and bodily machinery—reading notes and translating them into movement of the fingers, adjusting the pressure of the fingers to the pressure of the strings, responding to auditory feedback by slightly changing the way you play—has become fully automated. But this means that what we take to be the highest expressions of spirit (culture and thought; the will, freedom, and self-consciousness) are only possible on the basis of unreflected, unconscious mechanisms—what Nietzsche calls the "underworld of the utility organs"[77]—that are no longer under our active control.[78]

This ambiguous nature of habit also has a political dimension. Institutions, and social life in general, are little more than collective habits: ethical life (Hegel's *Sittlichkeit*) is built up out of customs (*Sitten*). Like habits in individuals, institutions are based on collective routines that have the advantage of being predictable, efficient, shared, and self-replicating but which are also "automated," irresponsive to change, and for the most part not dependent on our conscious assent or active reflection.[79] This is why, to the individual, social reality appears as "second nature," as an objectified totality over which they have little control.

Besides being the organizing principle of both individuals and institutions, habit also forms the bridge between them because it is through habituation, instilled through education, that individuals are integrated into the social body. Hegel writes:

> Education [*Pädagogik*] is the art of making human beings ethical: it considers them as natural beings and shows them how they can be reborn, and how their original nature can be transformed into a second, spiritual nature so that this spirituality becomes habitual to them. In habit, the opposition between the natural and the subjective will disappear, and the resistance of the subject is broken; to this extent, habit is part of ethics. . . . Human beings even die as a result of habit—that is, if they have become totally habituated to life and mentally and physically blunted, and the opposition between subjective consciousness and mental activity has disappeared.[80]

Habit breaks the resistance of the subject: on the one hand, habituation raises the individual to the level of the universal by grinding away their "stubborn ideosyncracies" (this is Herder's term)[81] and turning them into reasonable, politically responsible members of the community. On the other hand, when the individual is fully integrated into the social mechanism the productive difference between it and the community, which is the sole source of vitality and creativity, disappears; the individual no longer has anything to live for, withers away, and dies. The development of spirit is fueled by the lives of individuals, which are used up in the process.[82]

On the one hand, therefore, individuals become free and rational only through habit, but on the other hand, they are enslaved by it and die as a result. But—building on his theory of positivity from his early writings—Hegel also applies this same model to the sociocultural organism that, like the individual, passes through phases of childhood, youth, maturity, and old age. Nations, too, die of habit: a culture declines when its institutions become fully objectified and inert and are divorced from the vital interest that first produced them. In the *Lectures on the Philosophy of History*, Hegel writes:

> The natural death of the national spirit may take the form of political stagnation, or of what we call habit. The clock is wound up and runs on automatically. Habit is an activity with nothing to oppose it; it retains only the formal property of temporal continuity, and the depth and richness of its end need no longer be expressed. It is, so to speak, a superficial and sensuous kind of existence whose profounder significance has been forgotten. Thus both individuals and nations die a natural death. And even if the latter live on, their existence is devoid of life and interest; their institutions have become superfluous, because the needs which created them have been satisfied, and nothing remains but political stagnation and boredom.[83]

This, then, is the core of Hegel's theory of cultural decline. As a nation develops, its institutions become routine, alienating and devoid of life; its citizens become lazy, cynical, detached, and decadent. But the key question is, of course: Does this pattern of development also apply to Europe? Or does Europe, in its "spiritual ripeness," escape decline and death through habit?

Hegel seems to want to say so. Unlike Herder, for whom the "greying of Europe" points, perhaps, to a future beyond Europe, Hegel does seem to believe that this time, it's different; that European modernity, in its cultural self-awareness, has made a qualitative leap beyond the cycle of cultural development and decline. But does this conclusion really follow from his theory?

It is sometimes argued that the modern state, as Hegel envisages it, effectively solves the problem of habit because it has embedded the principle of rational self-reflection in its institutions: modern society is autorejuvenating because it constantly reflects on its bad habits and customs and seeks to correct them, through institutions such as the press and elections for example.[84] However, Hegel himself does recognize that the routinizing-objectifying-mortifying dynamic is not an accidental feature of institutions but is indeed inherent to them. It would be hard, therefore, to maintain that modern Europe would not be subject to institutional decay and cultural decline.[85] To give just one example, Hegel argues that colonization is not just a way to deal with the inevitable poverty and inequality generated by modern civil society and a way to solve the endemic problem of overproduction by opening up new markets[86]; it also provides citizens with an opportunity to escape the "ossified" cultural and economic structures of old Europe to make a life for themselves in the new world.[87] This is why America is the land of the future: "It is a land of desire for all those who weary of the historical arsenal [Rüstkammer] of old Europe. Napoleon is said to have remarked: 'Cette vieille Europe m'ennuie.' It is up to America to abandon the ground on which world history has hitherto been enacted."[88]

Political Postscript: Freedom through Suicide

Quite apart from the question whether Hegel himself believed whether Europe would decline or not—can we really deny that his diagnosis of "political stagnation and boredom" provides quite a striking description of Europe's "posthistorical" condition? The ineffectiveness, indecisiveness, and inertia of European political institutions is much lamented, from all sides of the political spectrum, as is the staleness and self-referentiality of European culture.[89] There is no space to go into the causes and consequences of this sense of cultural exhaustion here. However, I would like to raise two further questions.

First, is the decline of Europe to be a passing away, a final setting of the sun on the Abendland, or a renewal of European identity? Regarding the latter option, on the right-wing side of the political spectrum, the defence of European culture and identity (in the form of the "Judeo-Christian tradition") has strangely become wrapped up in a call for the revival of the nation state and a narrow anti-EU stance. In the center, leaders like Macron and new political movements like the party Volt emphasize the need to cultivate a specifically European cultural identity in which to root political reforms,[90] developing a kind of Euro-nationalism in an attempt to reconquer political ground from the populist and nationalist parties across Europe. If Europe must inevitably decline and the future is to be post-European, however, this too can be imagined in various ways. Will the future be postnational and cosmopolitan, multipolar, or consist of a concord of different cultures bound together by common interests and a shared *Humanität*?[91] Or will the world-historical chalice pass to a different nation, as Hegel suggests, keep traveling West, and come full circle to return to its origin in the Orient?

Second, is the decline of Europe purely a European affair, or is it a universal phenomenon? That is to say, are political inertia and death by habit, which Herder and Hegel diagnose as the cause of cultural decline, restricted to Europe (or the West more generally since the United States seems equally affected), or has global modernity as a whole become a self-sustaining, inert mechanism that is unable to adapt, rejuvenate itself, and respond adequately to global challenges? If what we are facing is only the death by habit of a specific cultural form or tradition, Europe's decline could be the prelude to a different or new beginning—another way of life could institutionalize itself, in Europe or elsewhere, and in turn become subject to inertia and decay. But if it is the institutionalized form of globalized, capitalist modernity (which has its roots in Europe) itself that has become static and ossified—whether it is because of institutional inertia, political stagnation, cultural decadence, the reign of self-interest, and the subjection of politics to the economic sphere, all causes analyzed by Hegel—there is no longer an alternative, and what we are facing is not just the death and decline of Europe but the end of modernity as such.

As was discussed in the introduction, the core characteristics of the European invention of modernity would be the spirit of rational self-criticism, and the historical sense that can both justify the present moment by seeing it as the product of an intelligible historical process and question it by seeing it as the result of contingent historical shifts of power or transformations of discourse.[92] Even after giving up its position as the center or culmination of world history, Europe would still like to claim for itself the privilege of embodying these two principles to the greatest degree. And to the extent that a critique of Europe and Eurocentrism must seemingly inevitably appeal to either or both of these principles, any such critique would only seem to end up reinforcing this self-identity.

What I have tried to show here, however, is that the spirit of critique and the sense of history, and the pathos of progress and freedom that was one of its expressions, are inextricably bound up with the discourse of the decline and the end of Europe. Nations, too, Hegel wrote, die of habit. But if—as he argues—in European modernity, we become aware of the historical process through which nations develop and decline and start to intervene in our own cultural life process, this death can no longer appear as an accident, coming from the outside. Death by habit, by a culture's becoming "mechanical" and falling prey to the dominance of self-interest comes about not accidentally but due to the inescapable dynamic of institutionalization that is the precondition for a culture's development and self-realization in the first place. To the extent that a culture has become self-conscious of this fact and of its own historical situation, its death can therefore only appear as the product of its own actions and interests—as a kind of suicide:

> Since the nation is a universal, a collective, a further deter-minant comes into play. As a collective, the national spirit exists for itself; this also means that the universal aspect of its existence may assume a role of opposition. Its negative side manifests itself; thought rises above the nation's immediate functions. And thus its natural death also appears as a kind of suicide. . . . It is usually associated with some external force which deprives the nation of its sovereignty, so that it ceases to exist as such. But this external force belongs only to the phenomenal world; no destructive force can prevail against the national spirit or within it unless it is already internally lifeless or dead.

This national suicide, however, is nothing less than an expression of freedom. As Hegel explains in the *Philosophy of Right*, suicide is a form of freedom, albeit one-sided, because it is a demonstration that the human spirit, as something that thinks and is universal, is not bound to any particular concrete bodily or historical form of existence: "The human being alone is able to abandon all things, even his own life: he can commit suicide."[93]

Suicide is freedom; freedom is suicide: here, the idea of the end of Europe—in the two senses of its decline and fall and its culmination and highest achievement—comes together. Europe's defining feature has become its historical and critical sense, its constant self-criticism of itself and its own past and its habit of putting itself at the center of all things, but conversely this spirit of self-criticism and self-disavowal has become the mark of Europe's moral and intellectual superiority. Europe has not killed itself. It is perhaps in the process of doing so. But insofar as the spirit of Europe is taken to be constant and continuous self-critique, this is perhaps what Europe is today: in a state of suspended suicide, a constant self-mutilation, constantly with a gun at its own head—but suspended in a state of inertia, stuck in its habits, living in the museum of the past, unwilling to pull the trigger.

Notes

1. Steiner, *The Idea of Europe*, 27–28.
2. Nietzsche, *Beyond Good and Evil*, 89–92, 133–34.
3. Spengler, *The Decline of the West*.
4. Heidegger, "The End of Philosophy and the Task of Thinking."
5. Horkheimer and Adorno, *Dialectic of Enlightenment*.
6. See for example Herman, *The Idea of Decline in Western History*, 31–33.
7. Hegel, *Lectures on the Philosophy of World History*, 54.
8. Lukes and Urbinati, *Condorcet: Political Writings*, 1–147.
9. Kant, *Political Writings*, 41–53.
10. Gasché, *Europe, or the Infinite Task*, 27.
11. Gasché, 26–27. Comay and Ruda write in *The Dash: The Other Side of Absolute Knowing*, 19: "Autocritique can itself, of course become another source of self-aggrandizement, which is why the demand for critique remains interminable, and why this interminability is in turn so easily fetishized: critique itself is always on the verge of becoming an exercise in pious self-humiliation, which is ultimately a form of reattachment."
12. Berlin, "The Counter-Enlightenment."
13. I'm thinking of the speech given by the party leader in March 2019, which started by invoking Hegel's "owl of Minerva" and went on to mix romantic and Spenglerian with neo-fascist themes.
14. Hegel, *Lectures on the Philosophy of World History*, 59.
15. Beiser, *Enlightenment, Revolution, and Romanticism*, 189.

16. Beiser, 211.

17. Herder, *Sämmtliche Werke*. Cited in Berlin, *Three Critics of the Enlightenment*, 224. On Herder and nationalism, see also Berlin, 21; Beiser, *Enlightenment, Revolution, and Romanticism*, 211–12; Ergang, *Herder and the Foundations of German Nationalism*.

18. Herder, *Philosophical Writings*, 325–26.

19. Herder, 396.

20. Beiser, *Enlightenment, Revolution, and Romanticism*, 189.

21. Beiser, 191–97.

22. Berlin, *Three Critics of the Enlightenment*, 20.

23. Herder, *Philosophical Writings*, 247.

24. Herder, 251.

25. Herder, 255–56.

26. Berlin, *Three Critics of the Enlightenment*, 20.

27. Herder, *Philosophical Writings*, 325–26.

28. Herder, 381–82.

29. Herder, *Outlines of a Philosophy of the History of Man*, 631.

30. Beiser, *Enlightenment, Revolution, and Romanticism*, 209.

31. E.g., Herder, *Philosophical Writings*, 221.

32. Beiser, *Enlightenment, Revolution, and Romanticism*, 193–94.

33. Beiser, 194.

34. Beiser, 194.

35. See Beiser, 219.

36. Herder, *Philosophical Writings*, 269.

37. Berlin, *Three Critics of the Enlightenment*, 213.

38. On Gibbon, see Herder, *Outlines of a Philosophy of the History of Man*, 516.

39. Berlin, *Three Critics of the Enlightenment*, 281.

40. Herder, *Philosophical Writings*, 362–63.

41. Herder, 364.

42. Herder, 319–20.

43. Nietzsche, *The Anti-Christ, Ecce Homo, Twilight of the Idols, and Other Writings*, 171.

44. Herder, *Philosophical Writings*, 319–20.

45. Berlin, *Three Critics of the Enlightenment*, 225.

46. Herder, *Philosophical Writings*, 365.

47. Herder, 418. See also Dale, *Hegel, the End of History, and the Future*, 130.

48. Herder, *Philosophical Writings*, 416–17.

49. Herder, 363.

50. Beiser, *Enlightenment, Revolution, and Romanticism*, 208–9.

51. Herder, *Philosophical Writings*, 417–19. See also this wonderful anticolonial statement in *This Too a Philosophy of History*: "The more we Europeans

invent *means* and *tools* to subjugate, to deceive, and to plunder you other parts of the world . . . Perhaps it will one day be precisely your turn to *triumph!* We affix chains with which *you* will pull *us* . . . We are approaching a new act [of the play], even if admittedly only through *decay!*" Herder, 352.

52. Hegel, *Lectures on the Philosophy of World History*, 88. These *Lectures*, or the *Philosophy of History* as the work is also called, have a complicated editorial history. Like most of Hegel's other published works, they were not published during his lifetime and were reconstructed by his editors after his death on the basis of Hegel's manuscripts, lecture notes, and notes made during the lectures by students. The editors of the German edition in the Suhrkamp *Werke* base their text on the version edited by Hegel's son Karl in 1840, which they take to be the most authoritative. The English translations by Sibree (1857, encompassing the whole work) and Rauch (1988, just the long introduction) are based on this text. The translation of the introduction by Nisbet (1975) is based on the 1955 German edition by Hoffmeister, which includes far more material based on students' notes.

53. Hegel, *Lectures on the Philosophy of World History*, 197. The translation "absolute" (for *slechthin*) here is poorly chosen. For a critical discussion of this passage and the end of history thesis more generally, see Dale, *Hegel, the End of History, and the Future*, 177.

54. The well-known criticism by Haym, Popper, and others that history for Hegel culminates in the Prussian state is so clearly a superficial misreading that I will not go into it here. See Haym, *Hegel Und Seine Zeit*, 357, and Popper, *The Open Society and Its Enemies*, 244–73, as well as Stewart, *Hegel Myths and Legends*, part 2, for a detailed discussion and rebuttals. The question whether European modernity in general constitutes the end of history for Hegel is more complex and will be discussed here.

55. Hegel, *Elements of the Philosophy of Right*, 21.

56. Hegel, *Lectures on the Philosophy of World History*, 170.

57. Hegel, *The Philosophy of History*, 366–67. See also Avineri, *Hegel's Theory of the Modern State*, 234–38. For a more general discussion of the notion of futurity in Hegel, see Malabou, *The Future of Hegel: Plasticity, Temporality and Dialectic*.

58. Hegel, *Elements of the Philosophy of Right*, 23.

59. Avineri, *Hegel's Theory of the Modern State*, 129–30; Pippin, *Hegel's Realm of Shadows: Logic as Metaphysics in The Science of Logic*, 312. Comay also reads the owl of Minerva in this way, but she tries to disconnect the Hegelian "birth of a new spirit" from the "logic of inheritance" that transforms the succession of cultures into a necessary process of *Bildung*. See Comay, *Mourning Sickness*, 143.

60. For Herder's influence on Hegel, see Harris, *Hegel's Development: Towards the Sunlight (1770–1801)*, 271; Forster, *Hegel's Idea of a Phenomenology of Spirit*.

61. Hegel, *Faith and Knowledge*, 118–19. See also Englander, "Herder's 'Expressivist' Metaphysics and the Origins of German Idealism."

62. Hegel, *Phenomenology of Spirit*, 492.

63. Hegel, *Introduction to the Philosophy of History*, 95–97.

64. Hegel, *The Philosophy of History*, 364.

65. Hegel, *Elements of the Philosophy of Right*, section 347. See also Hegel, *Introduction to the Philosophy of History*, 75.

66. Hegel, *Lectures on the Philosophy of World History*, 127.

67. Hegel, *Elements of the Philosophy of Right*, section 5.

68. Hegel, *Phenomenology of Spirit*, 492.

69. See Nuzzo, *Memory, History, Justice in Hegel*, for a detailed exploration of the notion of *Erinnerung*, especially on the difference between the *Phenomenology* and the later works.

70. On the necessity of development, see also Hegel, *Phenomenology of Spirit*, 51.

71. Žižek, *Less than Nothing*, 219–26. See also Zantvoort, "Speculating on the Absolute: On Hegel and Meillassoux," on this notion of retroactive causality. Comay, *Mourning Sickness* has a similar reading; see note 61 above.

72. Zantvoort, "Unthinking Inertia: Resistance and Obsolescence in Hegel's Theory of History."

73. The notion of positivity is developed primarily in relation to Christianity in *The Positivity of the Christian Religion* and *The Spirit of Christianity and Its Fate* (in Hegel, *Early Theological Writings*), but Hegel quickly came to see it as a more general problem that also applies to legal and political structures, for example in Hegel, *Natural Law*. I agree with Avineri that the problem of positivity must be considered to be a general "law of historical development." Avineri, *Hegel's Theory of the Modern State*, 28.

74. See especially Hegel, *Frühe Schriften*, 1:234; Hegel, *Early Theological Writings*, 156; Hegel, *Phenomenology of Spirit*, 272. Ross, *On Mechanism in Hegel's Social and Political Philosophy* gives a detailed analysis of the development of the notion of mechanism in Hegel's philosophy.

75. According to Ross, however, even in his early writings, Hegel had a more positive view of mechanism than Herder and his Romantic contemporaries. See Ross, *On Mechanism in Hegel's Social and Political Philosophy*, 4.

76. Hegel, *Hegel's Philosophy of Mind*, section 410Z.

77. Nietzsche, *On the Genealogy of Morals and Ecce Homo*, 57–58.

78. Zantvoort, "Slaves to Habit: The Positivity of Modern Ethical Life."

79. See Hegel, *Elements of the Philosophy of Right*, section 268Z: "[People] trust that the state will continue to exist and that particular interests can be fulfilled within it alone; but habit blinds us to the basis of our entire existence. It does not occur to someone who walks the street in safety at night that this

might be otherwise, for this habit of [living in] safety has become second nature and we scarcely stop to think that it is solely the effect of particular institutions." See also section 296, where Hegel argues that the proper functioning of the state bureaucracy is due to the way civil servants are habituated to focus on universal, rather than particular, interests.

80. Hegel, *Elements of the Philosophy of Right*, section 151Z. See also Hegel, *Hegel's Philosophy of Mind*, section 396Z and section 410.

81. Herder, *Philosophical Writings*, 251.

82. This is Hegel's famous notion of the cunning of reason. See Hegel, *Lectures on the Philosophy of World History*, 89.

83. Hegel, 59. See also Hegel, *Introduction to the Philosophy of History*, 78.

84. See Lumsden, "Habits, Sittlichkeit and Second Nature," 240–41; Zantvoort, "Slaves to Habit: The Positivity of Modern Ethical Life," 45–47.

85. Zantvoort, "Slaves to Habit: The Positivity of Modern Ethical Life"; Zantvoort, "Unthinking Inertia: Resistance and Obsolescence in Hegel's Theory of History."

86. Hegel, *Elements of the Philosophy of Right*, sections 243–46.

87. Hegel, *Vorlesungen Über Die Philosophie Der Geschichte*, 12:109.

88. Hegel, *Lectures on the Philosophy of World History*, 170–71.

89. For example, in a "Manifesto to Save Europe from Itself," Thomas Piketty and a group of other intellectuals argue that saving Europe requires "finally extricating Europe from the eternal inertia of intergovernmental negotiations." On inertia and the sense of being "posthistorical," see also Rosa, *Social Acceleration*, 14–20.

90. Van Middelaar, "Europa Heeft Zich van Zijn Geschiedenis Afgesneden."

91. In "Europe as Borderland," Balibar sketches four ways in which Europe's place in the current geopolitical formation can be conceptualized, which are still quite relevant in terms of a "clash of civilizations," a "global network," a "center-periphery" model, or his own conception of Europe as a borderland. See also Habermas, "Toward a Cosmopolitan Europe."

92. This is why both Hegel and Marx and Nietzsche and Foucault himself form part of the matrix of what Foucault calls "the age of History." See Foucault, *The Order of Things*, 217.

93. Hegel, *Elements of the Philosophy of Right*, section 5Z. According to Todd McGowan, this is the determining feature of subjectivity, a feature that should thus be extended to cultural collectives as well. McGowan, *Emancipation after Hegel*, 67.

Bibliography

Avineri, Shlomo. *Hegel's Theory of the Modern State*. Cambridge: Cambridge University Press, 1972.

Balibar, Etienne. "Europe as Borderland." *Environment and Planning D: Society and Space* 27 (2009): 190–215.

Beiser, Frederick C. *Enlightenment, Revolution, and Romanticism.* Cambridge: Harvard University Press, 2014.

Berlin, Isaiah. "The Counter-Enlightenment." In *Against the Current,* 1–32. Princeton: Princeton University Press, 2013.

Berlin, Isaiah. *Three Critics of the Enlightenment.* Edited by Henry Hardy. Princeton: Princeton University Press, 2013.

Comay, Rebecca. *Mourning Sickness: Hegel and the French Revolution.* Stanford: Stanford University Press, 2011.

Comay, Rebecca, and Frank Ruda. *The Dash: The Other Side of Absolute Knowing.* Cambridge, MA: MIT Press, 2018.

Dale, Eric Michael. *Hegel, the End of History, and the Future.* Cambridge: Cambridge University Press, 2014.

Englander, Alex. "Herder's 'Expressivist' Metaphysics and the Origins of German Idealism." *British Journal for the History of Philosophy* 21, no. 5 (September 2013): 902–24. https://doi.org/10.1080/09608788.2013.805120.

Ergang, Robert Reinhold. *Herder and the Foundations of German Nationalism.* New York: Columbia University Press, 1931.

Forster, Michael N. *Hegel's Idea of a Phenomenology of Spirit.* Chicago: University of Chicago Press, 1998.

Foucault, Michel. *The Order of Things: An Archaeology of the Human Sciences.* New York: Vintage Books, 1994.

Gasché, Rodolphe. *Europe, or the Infinite Task: A Study of a Philosophical Concept.* Meridian, Crossing Aesthetics. Stanford: Stanford University Press, 2009.

Habermas, Jürgen. "Toward a Cosmopolitan Europe." *Journal of Democracy* 14, no. 4 (2003): 86–100.

Harris, H. S. *Hegel's Development: Towards the Sunlight (1770–1801).* Oxford: Oxford University Press, 1972.

Haym, Rudolf. *Hegel Und Seine Zeit.* Hildesheim: Georg Olms Verlagsbuchhandlung, 1962.

Hegel, Georg Wilhelm Friedrich. *Early Theological Writings.* Translated by T. M. Knox and R. Kroner. Philadelphia: University of Pennsylvania Press, 1971.

Hegel, Georg Wilhelm Friedrich. *Elements of the Philosophy of Right.* Edited by A. W. Wood. Translated by H. B. Nisbet. Cambridge: Cambridge University Press, 1991.

Hegel, Georg Wilhelm Friedrich. *Faith and Knowledge.* Albany: State University of New York Press, 1977.

Hegel, Georg Wilhelm Friedrich. *Frühe Schriften.* Vol. 1. Werke. Frankfurt: Suhrkamp, 1986.

Hegel, Georg Wilhelm Friedrich. *Hegel's Philosophy of Mind: Being Part Three of the "Encyclopaedia of the Philosophical Sciences" (1830).* Translated by William Wallace and A. V. Miller. Oxford: Clarendon, 1971.

Hegel, Georg Wilhelm Friedrich. *Introduction to the Philosophy of History.* Translated by Leo Rauch. Indianapolis: Hackett, 1988.

Hegel, Georg Wilhelm Friedrich. *Lectures on the Philosophy of World History.* Translated by H. B. Nisbet. Cambridge: Cambridge University Press, 1975.

Hegel, Georg Wilhelm Friedrich. *Natural Law: The Scientific Ways of Treating Natural Law, Its Place in Moral Philosophy, and Its Relation to the Positive Sciences of Law.* Translated by T. M. Knox. Philadelphia: University of Pennsylvania Press, 1975.

Hegel, Georg Wilhelm Friedrich. *Phenomenology of Spirit.* Edited by J. N. Findlay. Translated by A. V. Miller. Oxford: Oxford University Press, 1977.

Hegel, Georg Wilhelm Friedrich. *The Philosophy of History.* Translated by J. Sibree. Kitchener: Batoche Books, 2001.

Hegel, Georg Wilhelm Friedrich. *Vorlesungen Über Die Philosophie Der Geschichte.* Vol. 12. Werke. Frankfurt: Suhrkamp, 1986.

Heidegger, Martin. "The End of Philosophy and the Task of Thinking." In *Basic Writings.* Edited by David Farrell Krell, 431–49. London: Routledge, 1993.

Herder, J. G. von. *Outlines of a Philosophy of the History of Man.* New York: Bergman, 1966.

Herder, J. G. von. *Philosophical Writings.* Edited by Michael N. Forster. Cambridge: Cambridge University Press, 2002.

Herder, J. G. von. *Sämmtliche Werke.* Edited by Bernard Suphan. Vol. 17. Berlin, 1877.

Herman, Arthur. *The Idea of Decline in Western History.* Riverside: Free Press, 2007.

Horkheimer, Max, and Theodor W. Adorno. *Dialectic of Enlightenment.* Translated by Edmund Jephcott. Stanford: Stanford University Press, 2007.

Kant, Immanuel. *Kant: Political Writings.* Edited by H. S. Reiss. 2nd edition. Cambridge: Cambridge University Press, 1991.

Lukes, Steven, and Nadia Urbinati, eds. *Condorcet: Political Writings.* Cambridge: Cambridge University Press, 2012.

Lumsden, Simon. "Habits, Sittlichkeit and Second Nature." *Critical Horizons* 13, no. 2 (2012): 220–43.

Malabou, Catherine. *The Future of Hegel: Plasticity, Temporality and Dialectic.* London: Routledge, 2005.

McGowan, Todd. *Emancipation after Hegel: Achieving a Contradictory Revolution.* NY: Columbia University Press, 2019.

Middelaar, Luuk van. "Europa Heeft Zich van Zijn Geschiedenis Afgesneden." *NRC Handelsblad*, May 19, 2021. https://www.nrc.nl/nieuws/2021/05/19/europa-heeft-zich-van-zijn-geschiedenis-afgesneden-a4044010.

Nietzsche, Friedrich. *On the Genealogy of Morals and Ecce Homo.* Translated by Walter Kaufmann. London: Vintage Books, 1969.

Nietzsche, Friedrich. *The Anti-Christ, Ecce Homo, Twilight of the Idols, and Other Writings.* Edited by Aaron Ridley and Judith Norman. Cambridge: Cambridge University Press, 2005.

Nietzsche, Friedrich Wilhelm. *Beyond Good and Evil: Prelude to a Philosophy of the Future*. Cambridge: Cambridge University Press, 2002.

Nuzzo, Angelica. *Memory, History, Justice in Hegel*. New York: Palgrave Macmillan, 2012.

Piketty, Thomas. "Our Manifesto to Save Europe from Itself." *The Guardian*, December 9, 2018. https://www.theguardian.com/commentisfree/2018/dec/09/manifesto-divided-europe-inequality-europeans.

Pippin, Robert B. *Hegel's Realm of Shadows: Logic as Metaphysics in The Science of Logic*. Chicago: University Of Chicago Press, 2019.

Popper, Karl R. *The Open Society and Its Enemies*. Princeton: Princeton University Press, 1950.

Rosa, Hartmut. *Social Acceleration: A New Theory of Modernity*. New York: Columbia University Press, 2013.

Ross, Nathan. *On Mechanism in Hegel's Social and Political Philosophy*. 1st edition. New York: Routledge, 2013.

Spengler, Oswald. *The Decline of the West*. New York: A. A. Knopf, 1926.

Steiner, George. *The Idea of Europe*. Tilburg: Nexus Institute, 2004.

Stewart, Jon. *Hegel Myths and Legends*. Evanston, IL: Northwestern University Press, 1996.

Zantvoort, Bart. "Slaves to Habit: The Positivity of Modern Ethical Life." In *An Ethical Modernity? Hegel's Concept of Ethical Life Today*, edited by Jirí Chotaš and Tereza Matejcková, 36–57. Leiden: Brill, 2020.

Zantvoort, Bart. "Speculating on the Absolute: On Hegel and Meillassoux." *Speculations* 6 (2015).

Zantvoort, Bart. "Unthinking Inertia: Resistance and Obsolescence in Hegel's Theory of History." In *Hegel and Resistance*, edited by Bart Zantvoort and Rebecca Comay. London: Bloomsbury, 2018.

Žižek, Slavoj. *Less than Nothing: Hegel and the Shadow of Dialectical Materialism*. London: Verso, 2012.

9

The Ends of Europe

On Patočka's Concept of Post-Europe

OVIDIU STANCIU

One of the major concerns guiding Patočka's last works, the task of compelling urgency he strains to accomplish in the final years of his life, is that of articulating an adequate philosophical diagnosis of the constellation of meaning determining the present. He thus strives to bring out and examine "the distinctive traits of our contemporaneity."[1] This inquiry is motivated by the conviction that illuminating the heights and depths of our present, uncovering the conundrums and predicaments of our actuality constitutes an indispensable means both for acquiring a critical understanding of ourselves and for getting a more lucid grasp of the space of possibilities available for philosophical reflection. Indeed, if the aspiration of overcoming our situatedness, of placing oneself above one's time and achieving an unprejudiced point of view, has proved to be an ill-founded project, then philosophy is bound to engage in a historical self-reflection, to delve deeper into the horizons into which it is embedded, and to take stock of its own situation.

However, the attempt "to get a hold of something like the complete situation of contemporary mankind"[2] does not amount to providing a neutral description of a given landscape, whose shapes and contours are firmly established, and which could be rendered in a matter-of-fact way. A philosophical gaze discloses the present as a tensely woven field, replete with competing forces and discordant tonalities, unresolved tensions, opposing trends struggling to surface, embryonic motifs still awaiting a

fuller realization, and vestigial traces of suppressed possibilities. As Patočka
puts it: "The present harbors in itself countless remnants of the past, just
as age-old geological strata can appear on the surface of the earth's crust."[3]
Moreover, this geological inquiry into the multilayered constitution of
the present must be supplemented by a genealogical perspective: scruti-
nizing the thickness of the living historical present involves formulating
a sweeping narrative capable of accounting not only for the developments
that have engendered such a configuration but also for the projects that
have been aborted, possibilities left unfulfilled, and promises still kept
in reserve. Such a cartography of the present and of its virtualities is
never innocent. It is always formulated from a determinate vantage
point and animated, overtly or tacitly, by a project. Nor is it without
consequences; undertaking it does not leave the landscape intact, for it
necessarily introduces an inflection or a deviation in the texture of the
present. As Patočka states it in the opening pages of *Plato and Europe*:
"The human situation . . . changes once we become self-conscious about
it. A naive and a self-conscious situation are already different. Our reality
is always situational, so that if it is reflected upon, it is already different
by the fact that we have reflected."[4] Therefore, broaching a philosophical
diagnosis necessarily involves taking a stance with regard to the present:
it amounts to situating the present into a broader historical framework,
assessing the possibilities that can be further pursued and intensified and
the dynamics that should be brought to a close.

For Patočka, this way of framing the relation between philosophical
reflection and the historical present entails two important consequences.
First, the recognition of the essential rootedness of philosophical reflection in its present does not imply subscribing to any form of historical
determinism. While the present is, indeed, the inescapable point of
departure of any philosophical undertaking, precisely because it names a
polymorphous and mobile field, it does not predelineate or prescribe the
commitments that must be assumed or the views that must be defended.
Second, examining the present in all its depth leads necessarily to ven-
turing within the broader field of the philosophy of history. As Patočka
straightforwardly puts it, the task of his undertaking is "to examine
and analyze the present time and the previous ones, to put forward a
hypothesis concerning the fundamental framework that determines them,
to verify this conjecture by examining the facts and, from there on, to
risk a glance into the future."[5]

However, Patočka's project of carrying out a philosophical *Zeitdiag-
nose* is motivated not only by the imperative of gaining a clarity about

his own present, of taking hold of the context into which his reflection is inscribed. It is, more fundamentally, prompted by the acute awareness of standing at a critical historical juncture, at a threshold of history, at a moment when the course of an epoch is decided. The sense of immediacy and urgency underwriting Patočka's reflections derives from his characterization of the present as a world-historical turning point and of its attempt to conceptually capture the tectonic movements presiding over this shifting, ambivalent configuration. It is within this context and in view of grasping the most conspicuous features of the contemporary era that he introduces the concept of post-Europe. In a wide array of private lectures and manuscripts from the 1970s and in some published texts belonging to the same systematical context and written in the same period, Patočka devotes decisive analyses to the concept of "post-Europe" (and to related expressions such as *post-European humanity*, *post-European era*, and *post-European world*), a term that comes to function in his thought as a hallmark of our actuality, the emblem of a newly emerging world-epoch.

Post-Europe is a historical category. Through this term, Patočka seeks to characterize a decisive world-historical shift that occurred during the twentieth century and that has profoundly shaped the deep structures of our present. However, the meaning of this historical shift is far from being univocal. Through its very construction, the term *post-Europe* conveys an absence, a departure, a withdrawal: the present is grasped in reference to something that ceased to exist, to a past that lost its force. Considering post-Europe as a proper designation for the historical experiences that define our present is tantamount to suggesting that we find ourselves within an elusive historical configuration, which can be only negatively determined. The only way of making sense of this concept—and of the epoch it denotes—consists in inquiring into the positive term it contains. Indeed, "post-Europe" cannot stand alone as a concept for the meaning it carries depends on the way the question of Europe is broached. It should thus come as no surprise that Patočka considers the conceptual clarification of the term *Europeas* a necessary presupposition for any inquiry into post-Europe. As he puts it a letter from the 1970s "up to now, I haven't written much about post-Europe, because this *post* presupposes the key-term, Europe; and I am struggling with an array of problems that could very well occupy several human lives."[6]

Working out a conceptual analysis of Europe requires, in the first place, the acknowledgment of the polysemy of the term. Patočka identifies three different connotations the concept of Europe carries in itself and, thus, distinguishes between Europe as a principle, as a reality, and as a heritage:

> We will have to distinguish, of course, on the one hand, the European principle (principle of rational reflection, that is, which founds all action and all thought in the evidence proper to the intellectual view), on the other hand, Europe as a unitary political, social and spiritual reality (in what prepares it, in the concrete historical institutions that establish its unity, as well as in the unifying forces that remain even after its dissolution in a plurality of particular sovereign organisms), and finally the heritage of Europe (heritage that consists in what all its heirs adopt from it, what all of them claim as a common good to be taken for granted: science, the rational organization of the economy and society).[7]

However, while the plurality of connotations of the concept "Europe" is uncontested, this polysemy should not be viewed as an ultimate, irreducible fact. On the contrary, grasping the concept of Europe in its full comprehensiveness and rigor requires us to apprehend these different meanings as distinct but not sundered, to show that they are not simply juxtaposed but fundamentally intertwined and, hence, to elaborate a framework broad enough to encompass them all.

Furthermore, the conceptual content of "post-Europe" hinges not only on the determination given to *Europe* but also to the way we understand the particle *post* in *post-Europe*. While the prefix *post* undoubtedly involves the idea of a temporal succession and, thus, points to what comes "after Europe," the shift from one period to another—from Europe to post-Europe—can accommodate a variety of readings. On one hand, the emergence of post-Europe may be understood as resulting from the "collapse of Europe,"[8] its historical demise, whether it is understood as the political and cultural decline of European predominance or as the exhaustion of a set of possibilities pertaining to the European project. On the other hand, post-Europe names the advent of an age characterized not so much by a radical break with Europe but rather by its globalization: "In a certain sense, Europe's shipwreck is at the same time its generalization."[9] On this second reading, post-Europe would involve a shift of emphasis away from Europe that is not synonymous with Europe's downfall but rather with "the expansion of Europe beyond its original bounds,"[10] the abolishment of its shores, its world-wide extension. The end of Europe would thus be equivalent with the "Europeanization" of the world. Moreover, if we take up Patočka's distinction of the three meanings of Europe—as a principle, as a reality, and as a heritage—the apparent opposition of these two interpretations can be superseded, and the "post" in "post-Europe" can be understood to designate the simultaneity of an exhaustion and a generalization, of a proliferation and a crumble. Europe becomes a global "heritage" at the very moment of its breakdown as a dominant political and cultural reality. This means that the post-European world is sharply cut off neither from Europe nor its simple extension or continuation: it is rather the generalization of a heritage disconnected from the principle that produced it and the reality that shaped it.[11]

The picture becomes even more entangled, if we pay heed to the texts where Patočka advances the paradoxical-sounding thesis according to which the end of Europe "has a positive meaning,"[12] so the emergence of post-Europe would be a chance for Europe itself,[13] an opportunity for Europe to engage anew, more thoughtfully and responsibly, with the innermost core of its project. On this third reading, the advent of post-Europe is not simply equivalent with the eclipse of a political reality. Rather, it displays the intrinsic limitations of the dominant version of the European project, of the way in which the European principle has been historically articulated, while at the same time harboring the possibility of a radical transgression, the opportunity for Europe to emancipate itself from the narrowness of its own history and geography. However, if Europe can suspend its past and extricate itself from the history it gave rise to, if at its very core lies a principle robust enough to withstand any collapse or wreckage, does this mean that the European principle is as such untouchable, invulnerable, universally immune, unperishable? Can we say, following de Warren's commentary on Patočka that "although there are endings to Europe, there is no ending that would not leave the residue of its possible renewal?"[14] Or is this renewal predicated by Patočka merely in the "subjunctive mode," as a fragile possibility pointing toward an uncertain future, as a precarious tendency that *might*—but also might *not*—prevail, with nothing, transcendentally or empirically, that could warrant its success?

In what follows, I will explore the various hermeneutical paths Patočka followed in order to properly clarify the concept of post-Europe. I will show that the intricacy of his account derives from his ambition to formulate a unified view, to bring together all the ramifications of this topic, and thus to elucidate the rich semantic field covered by this concept. In the first part, I will examine Patočka's account of the "the shipwreck of Europe" and will bring out the various strands of analysis embedded in this thesis. In particular, I will insist on the intimate link established between the political end of Europe and the intrinsic finitude of the European historical project. Second, I will reconstruct Patočka's philosophical genealogy of Europe and post-Europe and explain that his diagnosis of a "dissolution of Europe"[15] rests on a critical discussion of the teleological narrative of Europe advanced by Husserl in his *Crisis*. Finally, I will try to make sense of Patočka's thesis that the demise of Europe does not foreclose the possibility of a renewal, that even after its historical collapse, there still remains a "specific future for Europe."[16] The overall argument I attempt to develop in what follows is that in his discussion of post-Europe, Patočka does not merely seek to provide a diagnosis of the present. Rather, the question of post-Europe represents a springboard for addressing the more general question of historical meaning and, thus, for articulating an original position within the field of the philosophy of history.

The Ends of Europe

The overarching claim orienting Patočka's approach to the question of post-Europe is that "Europe has come to an end."[17] Or, with an alternative formulation: "today we are standing at the end of the European era as a whole."[18] However, such a bold thesis makes it unavoidable to ask: What is it that actually ends when Europe ends? What are the distinguishing traits of the European era deemed to have been brought to a close? We can indeed distinguish several facets of this "ending of Europe." In a first approximation, this diagnosis can be understood to describe a political situation in which Europe disappeared as the dominant political reality and has lost its political clout on the world stage: "Europe has ceased to play a decisive role both in the field of power and in the cultural sphere."[19] On this interpretation, affirming the end of Europe amounts simply to acknowledging the decline of European predominance, the fact that Europe is no longer the pivot around which world-history revolves: "Europe as a hegemonical power no longer exists."[20] Its function has been overtaken by its "natural" successors, what Patočka calls the "Europeids" or the "post-European giants" (by which he means, writing in the 1970s, the United States and the USSR).[21] But if we follow this line of interpretation, the dramatic undertone conveyed by the affirmation that "Europe has come an end" must be played down. This claim does not refer to a catastrophic event, to a collapse of gigantic proportions, but merely to a shift in the overall geopolitical setting. What has actually come to an end, what was definitively shattered, is simply the geopolitical framework centered around Europe and, with it, the hegemonical position Europe previously held in the world. What has disappeared is Europe's stranglehold over the entirety of the earth. After its end, Europe continues to exist, if only as a parochial entity, a second-string actor on the world-stage—a continent among others. Thus understood, the end of Europe amounts to its displacement from the center of the world-system, its becoming excentric.

Moreover, Patočka claims that Europe did not simply drift into the crisis that brought about its end but in a certain sense actively drove itself into it. The loss of European primacy is not the result of some external circumstances but is rather self-induced: Europe "definitely wrecked itself in the span of thirty years, in two wars, after which nothing remained, nothing of her power that had ruled the world. She destroyed herself, through her own powers."[22] The self-destruction of European in two fratricidal world wars ushers in a new period which Patočka characterizes as a post-European one.

However, Patočka insists that this diagnosis should not be understood only at a geopolitical level. The "end of Europe" means not only that Europe has forfeited its political force, but rather that its spiritual and intellectual authority was debunked, so the post-European world is a "world in which Europe ceases to play a decisive role as a political and a spiritual power."[23] Indeed, far more consequential than the relinquishment of its political supremacy is the loss of its intellectual vitality and appeal: the ideals and models promoted by modern European culture have lost their entitlement and binding force, and the European conceptuality has grown obsolete. Thus, on this reading, the end of Europe is tantamount to a historical delegitimation of the core commitments forming the intellectual underpinnings of European culture. This delegitimation takes two forms: the discrediting of the intellectual authority of objective science, which is deemed no longer adequate to capture what is at stake in the contemporary world; or a dissatisfaction with the European ideals which appear not only as historically outdated but as fundamentally self-delusive.

With regard to the first point, Patočka maintains that the "ideas of the 19th century"[24] represent a paralyzing obstacle for grasping the contemporary world, while "the metaphysics of European history turns out to be utterly inadequate" in order to shed light on the convulsions and catastrophes of the twentieth century. He thus calls for "a new, critical philosophy of history, which avoids the narrowness and particularism of the European philosophy of history."[25] Second, the emergence of post-Europe reflects a disaffection with regard to the hopes and expectations engendered by the European project. In particular, this indictment concerns a certain teleological view of history as a narrative of irresistible progress with its claim that a securely grounded scientific method would bring about the advancement of knowledge, which in turn will allow for a continuously expanding enlightenment and an increased technological mastery of nature and, hence, a complete emancipation of mankind. However, the envisioned and hoped for *regnum hominis* turns out to be a *regimen hominum*:[26] rather than engendering a true "realm of humanity," technoscience gives rise to a historical field of experience characterized by the standardization of life, the systematic regulation of every being and its subjugation to the imperatives of technical organization, the submission of the human being to an impersonal order. Rather than leading to a historical fulfillment of human freedom, this process plunges us into an absolute dependance upon inhuman ordering systems and enhances a predatory stance toward the world. Moreover, this disillusionment also affects the humanistic project that sustained much of the scientific culture of Europe and its promises of providing an "enlightened" foundation of civic and political life. Such a humanistic project appears to be a self-delusion, at best an outworn idea, at worst a metaphysical simulacrum responsible for the calamities and atrocities of the twentieth century.

Furthermore, if the contemporary historical juncture can aptly be characterized as "the end of Europe," it is not sufficient to chart off the various manifestations this ending assumes—the displacement of Europe from its political primacy and the discrediting of its explanatory models—but it is also necessary to construe it as a historical product, to show that it did not appear abruptly on the world scene, for it is rather the result of some internal transformations of a wider historical process. This, in turn, requires reconstructing the epochal dynamic that has given rise to such a situation, exposing its roots and sources, its trajectory and impasses. Following this theoretical impulse, Patočka sets out to articulate a long-range perspective whereby the end of Europe is inscribed as a sequence within a larger historical movement. However, the particularity of the narrative he advances is that the trajectory described is not ascendant and its endpoint is not a culmination or a triumph but rather a dead-end. On this account, affirming the collapse of Europe amounts to saying that the historical arc extending from the Greek inception of philosophy and politics up to modernity has reached a point of dissolution, that the essential possibilities of the European project have been played out. Thus, the end of Europe does not mark the accomplishment of a historical sequence but its exhaustion and failure. It further brings into view the internal limitations and deeper insufficiencies of the European project as such: the end of Europe displays the finitude of Europe. Europe as a historical figure is finite for there are ways of relating to the world that cannot be captured within the framework designed by the European tradition.

However, this way of framing the question of the end of Europe makes it inevitable to inquire into the causes that propelled this downfall. Furthermore, inasmuch this historical collapse is not merely the product of some outward factors, of a series of adversities that blocked the unfolding of the European project, it reflects an intrinsic breakdown. The shipwreck of Europe is the result of a self-undermining process, of a historical movement that went astray. Under the weight of what internal tensions and pressures, difficulties or perplexities has this dynamic spun out of its track and reached a point of disintegration? This is one of the central questions Patočka aims to address in his analysis of post-Europe.

A Philosophical Genealogy of Europe and Post-Europe

As we have seen, the attempt of formulating a diagnosis of our contemporaneity, of lending articulate clarity to the present we inhabit, necessarily involves engaging in a retrospective and a prospective inquiry. The present is never self-enclosed; it is always driven beyond itself toward the antecedent movement responsible for its peculiar physiognomy and toward the horizon opening up in front of it, wherein trajectories already at play in the present could be further pursued. In his project of mapping out the historical itinerary that has brought about the current configuration of meaning, Patočka relies heavily on the genealogical construction advanced by Husserl in his *Crisis*. As he puts it in a private seminar in 1973: "From the time when Husserl wrote his *Crisis*, no philosopher has really reflected upon the problem of Europe and the heritage of Europe."[27] And, in a contemporary text, he writes: "The work written by Husserl to *prevent* the ultimate catastrophe of the European world could perhaps still allow to clarify the situation of humanity *after* the catastrophe, and maybe even to shed light on its first steps in the path leading to the post-European world."[28] Patočka endorses Husserl's view that one of the most blatant symptoms of the European crisis is the reduction of reason to its objective meaning, to the capacity of determining and measuring objective entities, leaving outside of its grasp the whole realm of the subjective, which becomes thus an "enigma"[29] for reason. The historical triumph of this one-sided model of rationality, which comes to identify scientific soundness with technical efficiency, with the capacity of controlling and mastering the world, is responsible for the European dismay: the crisis of knowledge has caused a world-historical wreck and has brought about "an existential catastrophe for the European human being."[30] Patočka further agrees with Husserl that the solution to such a predicament must consist in a "historical-critical" reflection that would bring into view the "originary sources of European *ratio*"[31] and, thus, "deepen the grounds of European rationality."[32] However, the particular way in which Husserl fleshes out this task is deemed unsatisfactory and even a "failure."[33] From this ensues the necessity of engaging a "a debate with the great undertaking the last Husserl attempted in the *Krisis*, a debate of a crucial importance for the problems of a post-European humanity."[34]

Patočka's criticism concerns four aspects of the Husserl's account: (1) the meaning Husserl ascribes to Europe; (2) the way Husserl construes the genealogy of the European crisis; (3) the way Husserl determines the most acute syndrome of Europe's breakdown; and (4) the solution Husserl advances in order to overcome the crisis.

As has been often noted, for Husserl, the term *Europe* does not designate primarily a geographical space, a political entity or a constellation of political entities, or a cultural formation.[35] It names first and foremost a historical project possessing a distinctive "spiritual shape"[36] and defined by "a spirit of free critique and norm-giving aimed at infinite tasks."[37] The organizing center of this historical project is the idea of self-responsibility, the capacity of accounting for one's claims and of actively shaping one's life in accordance with the imperatives of reason. This claim implies that science understood as a specific activity is a secondary or derived instance: its prestige and importance within the European project stems from its capacity to give a concrete form to the idea of self-responsibility, to the project of a life guided by rational insight.[38] Therein lies the ethical core of Husserl's engagement with the crisis of European sciences. When science has forfeited its proper task, that of providing a complete rational determination of everything that is, and has become a mere instrument for the mastery of the world, it has also engendered a crisis in the ambit of self-responsibility: "If science no longer fulfills its ultimate purpose as science, European human being no longer fulfills his ultimate purpose as a European human being."[39] However, the relation between science and self-responsibility is bilateral. While it is indeed self-responsibility that provides sciences with its ultimate legitimation, self-responsibility can accomplish itself only in and through science. Thus, the fate or Europe is inextricably bound up with that of the project of an absolutely grounded rational and universal science. It is this correlation that manifests, on Patočka's view, the fundamental limitations of Husserl's account. By putting forth this radical rationalist thesis, Husserl operates a twofold reduction: the reduction of reason to science and the reduction of Europe to the tradition of scientific reason.[40] Against these restrictions, Patočka points out the insufficiency of "the common view which identifies *ratio* with the understanding (*Verstand*) at work in science and technology"[41] and seeks to rehabilitate, by elaborating on the Hegelian concept of *Vernunft*, an enlarged sense of reason "that expresses itself in ethical life, poetry, art and religion."[42] Restoring a more ample meaning of reason is thus tantamount to showing that the project of a meaningful life—a life that does not avoid the burden of its choices and responsibilities—does not necessarily need the mediation of scientific attitude: it can fully unfold in the registers of ethical life, poetry, art, and religion. Furthermore, Patočka insists that the distinct "spiritual shape" of Europe crystallizes around a constellation of inter-related phenomena: while the emergence of the theoretical attitude is indeed one of the essential elements of such a constellation, so is the institution of a public space where the speech can freely circulate and where new courses of action can be initiated.[43] The theoretical attitude and the "spirit of the *polis*" are equiprimordial, and they contribute in equal measure to defining the characteristic shape of Europe.

This resolute refusal of a univocal determination of Europe also informs the background of Patočka's discussion of Husserl's genealogical narrative of Europe and of its crisis. On Husserl's view, the contemporary crisis of European sciences is attested by the prominence acquired by technical or abstract reason, which in turn manifests a radical impoverishment of the meaning of reason. Such a crisis derives from the fact that science, understood as objective knowledge, has become oblivious of its origin, has cut itself off from the ground upon which it stands. However, as Husserl constantly maintains, the crisis is intrinsic to the very unfolding of the scientific project. In order to achieve its proper goals and offer a complete rational determination of everything that is, science must develop theoretical formulas, abstract instruments, and practical techniques whose functioning does not depend upon a constant reassessment or reenactment of the originary principle. This "automatic" functioning of the techniques is responsible for the staggering achievements of scientific reason. However, such a development can soon give rise to a formalism and a technicism divested of any meaning, but still effective, still capable of producing tremendous practical results. Thus, the drift from responsible scientific inquiry to blind formalism seems to be the quasi-inescapable result of the development of science, the counterpart of its success. While falling prey to this reductive interpretation is by no means a necessary process, the risk as such is unavoidable because it is integral to the scientific enterprise as such. Everything happens as if science would design itself the trap where it could fall. In Patočka's words: "The Husserlian theory of modern science is nothing other than a reflection on the perils of fruitfulness, on the ruses of genius, on the irrationality which rationality itself engenders—not, to be sure, necessarily, yet not wholly accidentally, either. Might not this shadowy side of rationality, this negative aspect of science, lie at the roots of certain specific evils that not only occasioned the catastrophe that Husserl thought to prevent with his reflections?"[44] However, if the European crisis is, in last instance, a crisis of scientific reason, one that is the result of the internal dynamic of the scientific project, then overcoming the crisis amounts to vindicating another, more comprehensive, stance of reason. The deviation of science into a myopic technicism can be avoided if the *Rückfrage* (question in return, reflection back), [45] leading from the efficacious formulae to the forgotten foundation of scientific rationality is constantly enacted, if science strives to constantly incorporate a philosophical questioning.

Patočka challenges both Husserl's monolithic account of the genesis of Europe—what we may call, following Derrida, its "monogenealogy"[46]—and the the solution Husserl puts forth. On Patočka's view,

Husserl's attempt might indeed "point out certain diseases of reason, as when Husserl confronts the most technical of sciences anew with the critical question which Kant addressed to metaphysics. Can it, though, show us a positive way for reason to follow so that it could found not only a new science or a new foundation for science, but a genuine human *praxis?*"[47]

In his alternative reconstruction of the genesis of Europe, Patočka insists not only on the twin emergence and essential entanglement of philosophy and politics but also on a duality present from the outset and lodged at the very heart of the European scientific and philosophic project, namely, the originary duality of the institution of metaphysics—what he calls the "remarkable antagonistic connection of Democritus and Plato."[48] Not one, but two inaugurating motifs have shaped the European project: "One contributed to the building of its ethical ideals and its great universal institutions, while the other put in its hands the forces of nature and, as a result, the means of an ephemeral world domination."[49] Laying out this originary duality and insisting that it has fueled the entire subsequent tradition allows Patočka to account for phenomena that receive an incomplete explanation in Husserl's perspective. If one of the markers of our contemporary conjuncture is that science has become a powerful instrument used for the domination of the world, such a situation cannot be traced back, as Husserl attempted, to the necessary technicism and formalism the scientific project engenders. Husserl's analysis can account for the evolution that led to a purely technical or formal understanding of reason but not for the fact that "rational science has become an unequalled force in human hands."[50] He can account for the emergence of a technical, formal, abstract reason but not for the emergence of an instrumental reason. Furthermore, the intellectual phenomena that, on Husserl's account, epitomize the European crisis—namely, a self-devouring skepticism, and an all-destructive positivism—must be thought of as aspects of a broader picture: "This complete draining of all meaning"[51] is understood by Patočka as having become a dimension of our contemporary historical reality. The insidious senselessness manifested in skepticism and positivism has a far greater reach: it is not located just in the field of meanings but belongs to the sphere of reality itself. It has already transformed our world: the world manifests itself to us as "deprived of all meaning," as "a simple reservoir of forces."[52]

The insufficiencies detected in Husserl's account of our current predicament lead Patočka to adhere to Heidegger's descriptions of "technology" as the contemporary manifestation of the meaning of being. In a decisive passage from a text comparing Husserl's and Heidegger's accounts of science and technology, Patočka writes:

> Heidegger takes the draining of meaning which he decries for an inevitable part of the new meaning of being, characteristic of our time. In Husserl, technicization is something negative, a certain *steresis*, a lack of meaning which can be in principle eliminated by greater attention to the observed continuities of meaning. A broader foundation of a new level, that of the effective transcendental subjectivity, could overcome this state of affairs. For Heidegger, things are otherwise. Precisely the technical procedures of certain and precise calculation belong to the modern way of uncovering being. [. . .] The draining away of meaning, for instance, is here carried over from the sphere of meanings into the realm of reality itself. A process of universal uncovering is set in motion which will pass over nothing: both things and people receive their "meaning," that is, their place within the process. All and every one is set to a certain task, arranged for and placed on order.[53]

Thus, the most radical manifestation of the contemporary crisis, the epochal mutation that has brought about the dissolution of Europe, lies not so much in the fact that, in its historical unfolding, the scientific project has given rise to the formalism of an abstract reason, insensitive to any existential concerns, but rather in the fact that reason appears now as a mere "accumulator of forces."[54] Thus, the end of Europe is synonymous with the emergence of a "neotechnical era":[55] the instauration of a historical era characterized by a calculating, manipulative approach to beings, the unbridled domination of instrumental rationality, the transformation of being in resources.

The Future of Europe

Patočka's extended meditations on the fate of Europe in the wake of its historical demise are, as we have seen, animated by a triple concern: outlining the defining features of our contemporary, post-European, situation; reconstructing the historical dynamic leading to the end of Europe both as both a political force and a cultural and civilizational model; inquiring into the resources of meaning Europe might still possess, in spite of its collapse. The guiding thread of the last line of inquiry is expressed abruptly, when Patočka asks whether "there still is a moment of the European heritage that has not been exhausted,"[56] whether a dimension of the European heritage "was kept alive through catastrophes"[57] or again "whether within . . . the European inheritance, there exists something that could to some extent be believable even for us, that could affect us in a way so that we could again find hope in a specific perspective, in a specific future, without giving in to illusory dreams and without undervaluing the toughness and gravity of our current situation."[58] To these interrogations, Patočka offers a positive answer and maintains that at least a certain dimension of Europe can outlast its defeats and survive its radical collapse, that after its tormented historical trajectory there is something belonging to its very core that remains intact. And when it comes to give precise contours to this unscathed legacy, he offers two different instantiations, which should be understood at the same time as ferments that have nourished the European history, potentialities still worth being realized, and promises inscribed in the present: (1) the care for the soul; (2) the opening of the *one* world.

The care for the soul is, on Patočka's view, the central pivot around which Europe has been built: "Europe as Europe arose from this motif, from the care of the soul, and that it became extinct as a result of that, that it forgot about it."[59] However, the care for the soul is not only the organizing center of historical development of Europe but also what is kept in reserve and, thus, survives Europe's downfall: "What is inexhaustible is the care for the soul understood as a moral axis, a moral discernment."[60] While the concept of the care for the soul carries within itself a host of connotations, it is undoubtful that it primarily designates a form of self-relatedness characterized by the resolute acknowledgment of the problematicity of any received or imposed figure of the self and of any given meaning. Caring for the soul implies adopting an attitude of responsibility for the self and for the truth. The existential stance entailed by the care for the soul amounts "to live in unanchoredness,"[61] "to be exposed,"[62] "to be a quest for oneself."[63]

The other name of the European legacy that has not been played out is the project of "one world" (*die* eine *Welt, un monde* un): "While the European reality has fallen apart, its principle remains effective in and through this dissolution, projecting and holding open the possibility of a *one* humanity and a *one* world that is no longer a simple life-world."[64] The principle embodied in this project is that of a universality disjoined from any form of hegemony, of any tendency of establishing a parochialist monopoly upon the universal. Restoring such a universal-oriented but nonhegemonical Europe is one of the scant, tenuous possibilities that the current post-European configuration harbours. Thus, "Europe has drawn two paths towards the opening of our planet: the exterior path of conquest and of universal hegemony, which has led to its wreck as a historical reality; but also, the interior path of the opening of the world, of becoming-world of the different *Lebenwelten*. The latter path needs to be today rediscovered and followed up to its end."[65]

For all the criticism directed against Husserl's understanding of Europe, in at least one respect, Patočka remained deeply committed to Husserl's project as it is formulated in the Vienna conference from 1935: "The rebirth (*Wiedergeburt*) of Europe from the spirit of philosophy through a heroism of reason."[66] However, for Patočka, it is important to stress that it is a rebirth and not a mere continuation; that a certain Europe has collapsed in the twentieth century; and that post-Europe represents an opportunity for Europe to wrench itself from the strictures of its previous hegemonical figure. Only when the hegemonical Europe collapses, out of its ruins and ashes, a truly universal Europe might, for the first time, emerge.

Notes

The research for this chapter was funded by the ANID Research project Fondecyt Iniciación No. 11220879 developed at the Universidad Diego Portales, Santiago de Chile.

1. Patočka, *Liberté et sacrifice*, 215.
2. Patočka, *Plato and Europe*, 1.
3. Patočka, *Liberté et sacrifice*, 215–16.
4. Patočka, *Plato and Europe*, 1.
5. Patočka, *Liberté et sacrifice*, 216.
6. Patočka, *L'Europe après l'Europe*, 274.
7. Patočka, 42.
8. Patočka and Michalski, "Letters between Krzysztof Michalski and Jan Patočka (1973–1976)," 233.
9. Patočka, *L'Europe après l'Europe*, 212.

10. Patočka, *Heretical Essays in the Philosophy of History*, 83.

11. Patočka formulates this point in reference to Husserl and using a Husserlian terminology. Cf. *Heretical Essays in the Philosophy of History*:

> It is ironic that Husserl wrote the work which contains his phenomenological conception of history on the eve of the second global conflagration that definitively displaced Europe from its leading role in the world. It is true that at the same time it made European science and tech\nology a global link. Yet European civilization became a global link in precisely that form which Husserl's *Crisis of the European Sciences* showed to be decadent, that in it a loss of meaning takes place, the loss of that very meaning-bestowing teleological idea that, for Husserl, makes up the inner, spiritual essence of Europe. 45

12. Patočka, *L'Europe après l'Europe*, 212.

13. Patočka, *Liberté et sacrifice*, 211. See also *L'Europe après l'Europe*, 53.

14. De Warren, "He Who Saw the Deep: The Epic of Gilgamesh in Patočka's Philosophy of History," 137. Cf. in this respect also Rodolphe Gasché, "Patočka on Europe in the Aftermath of Europe," 2, and Marc Crépon, "Histoire, éthique et politique: la question de l'Europe."

15. Patočka, *L'Europe après l'Europe*, 215.

16. Patočka, *Plato and Europe*, 12.

17. Patočka, 9.

18. Patočka, *L'Europe après l'Europe*, 251.

19. Patočka, *Liberté et sacrifice*, 217.

20. Patočka, 211.

21. Patočka, *L'Europe après l'Europe*, 210.

22. Patočka, *Plato and Europe*, 9.

23. Patočka, *L'Europe après l'Europe*, 46.

24. Patočka, *Heretical Essays in the Philosophy of History*, 120.

25. Patočka, *L'Europe après l'Europe*, 253.

26. Patočka, *Liberté et sacrifice*, 199.

27. Patočka, *Plato and Europe*, 152.

28. Patočka, *L'Europe après l'Europe*, 42. For an account of Patočka's discussion of Husserl's *Crisis*, see Ovidiu Stanciu, "Europe and the Oblivion of the World. From Husserl to Patocka," 410–34.

29. Husserl, *The Crisis of European Sciences and Transcendental Phenomenology*, 5.

30. Husserl, *Die Krisis der europäischen Wissenschaften und die transzendentale Phänomenologie: Ergänzungsband*, 108.

234 | Ovidiu Stanciu

31. Patočka, *Liberté et sacrifice*, 181.

32. Patočka, *L'Europe après l'Europe*, 213.

33. Patočka, 213.

34. Patočka, *Liberté et sacrifice*, 181.

35. See, in this regard, Gasché, *Europe, or The Infinite Task*, ch. 1.

36. Husserl, *The Crisis of European Sciences and Transcendental Phenomenology*, 289. Patočka explicitly takes up this Husserlian idea when he evokes the "spiritual foundations" of Europe: "Europe in its political sense is always talked about, but at the same time, the question of what it really is, and what it grows out of, is neglected. You hear about the integration of Europe: but is it possible to integrate something regarding some kind of geographical or purely political concept? This is a concept lying upon *spiritual foundations*." Patočka, *Plato and Europe*, 179.

37. Husserl, *The Crisis of European Sciences and Transcendental Phenomenology*, 289.

38. Patočka clearly acknowledges this aspect of Husserl's thought. See Patočka, *Liberté et sacrifice*, 188.

39. Husserl, *Die Krisis der europäischen Wissenschaften und die transzendentale Phänomenologie: Ergänzungsband*, 108.

40. See, in this regard, Patočka, *Liberté et sacrifice*, 212. For a discussion of this thesis, see O. Stanciu, "Retrouver la *Lebenswelt*, par-delà Husserl. Patocka et Ricœur, lecteurs de la *Krisis*."

41. Patočka, *L'Europe après l'Europe*, 210.

42. Patočka, 210.

43. Cf., in this regard:

> The Western spirit and the world history are bound together in their origins: it is the spirit of free meaning bestowal, it is the shaking of life as simply accepted with all its certainties and at the same time the origin of new possibilities of life in that shaken situation, that is, of philosophy. Since, however, philosophy and the spirit of the polis are closely linked so that the spirit of the polis survives ultimately always in the form of philosophy, this particular event, the emergence of the polis, has a universal significance. Patočka, *Heretical Essays*, 41

44. Patočka, "Edmund Husserl's Philosophy of the Crisis of Sciences and His Conception of a Phenomenology of the Life-World," 142.

45. See, in this regard, Ricoeur, "L'originaire et la question-en-retour dans la *Krisis* de Husserl," 277.

46. Derrida, *L'Autre Cap*, 17.

47. Patočka, "Edmund Husserl's Philosophy of the Crisis of Sciences and His Conception of a Phenomenology of the Life-World," 154.

48. Patočka, *L'Europe après l'Europe*, 41.

49. Patočka, 40.

50. Patočka, "Edmund Husserl's Philosophy of the Crisis of Sciences and His Conception of a Phenomenology of the Life-World," 140.

51. Patočka, 147.

52. Patočka, *Living in Problematicity*, 58.

53. Patočka, "The Dangers of Technicization in Science according to E. Husserl and the Essence of Technology as Danger according to M. Heidegger," 14–15. For a detailed analysis of Patočka's reinterpretation of the question of technology in Heidegger, cf. Stanciu, "La Grande Guerre comme 'événement cosmique': Jan Patočka et l'expérience du front," 507–24.

54. Patočka, *Liberté et sacrifice*, 185.

55. Patočka, *L'Europe après l'Europe*, 48.

56. Patočka, 266.

57. Patočka, *Plato and Europe*, 89.

58. Patočka, 12.

59. Patočka, 70.

60. Patočka, *L'Europe après l'Europe*, 266.

61. Patočka, *Living in Problematicity*, 56.

62. Patočka, 55.

63. Patočka, 54. For a convergent treatment of this topic, cf. Klaus Held, "Heimwelt, Fremdwelt, die eine Welt," 305–37.

64. Patočka, *L'Europe après l'Europe*, 250.

65. Patočka, 43.

66. Husserl, *The Crisis of European Sciences and Transcendental Phenomenology*, 299.

Bibliography

Crépon, Marc. "Histoire, éthique et politique: la question de l'Europe." In *L'Europe après l'Europe*, edited by Jan Patočka, 275–95. Lagrasse: Verdier, 2007.

Derrida, Jacques. *L'Autre Cap*. Paris: Minuit, 1991.

de Warren, Nicholas. "He Who Saw the Dee: The Epic of Gilgamesh in Patočka's Philosophy of History." In *Thinking after Europe: Jan Patočka and Politics*. Edited by D. Meacham and F. Tava, 135–60. London: Rowman & Littlefield, 2016.

Gasché, Rodolphe. *Europe, or The Infinite Task: A Study of a Philosophical Concept*. Stanford: Stanford University Press, 2008.

Gasché, Rodolphe. "Patočka on Europe in the Aftermath of Europe." *European Journal of Social Theory* 21, no. 3 (2018): 391–406.

Held, Klaus. "Heimwelt, Fremdwelt, die eine Welt." *Phänomenologische Forschungen*, nos. 24–25 (1991): 305–37.

Husserl, Edmund. *The Crisis of European Sciences and Transcendental Phenomenology: An Introduction to Phenomenological Philosophy.* Translated by David Carr. Evanston: Northwestern University Press, 1970.

Husserl, Edmund. *Die Krisis der europäischen Wissenschaften und die transzendentale Phänomenologie: Ergänzungsband. Texte aus dem Nachlass 1934–1937.* Husserliana 29. Edited by Reinhold N. Smid. Dordrecht/Boston/London: Nijhoff, 1993.

Patočka, Jan. "The Dangers of Technicization in Science according to E. Husserl and the Essence of Technology as Danger according to M. Heidegger." Translated by Erazim Kohák. In *The New Yearbook for Phenomenology and Phenomenological Philosophy* 14 (2015): 13–22.

Patočka, Jan. "Edmund Husserl's Philosophy of the Crisis of Sciences and His Conception of a Phenomenology of the Life-World." Translated by Erazim Kohák. *Husserl Studies* 2 (1985): 129–55.

Patočka, Jan. *Heretical Essays in the Philosophy of History.* Edited by James Dodd, translated by Erazim Kohák, with a preface by Paul Ricoeur. Chicago: Open Court, 1996.

Patočka, Jan. *L'Europe après l'Europe.* Edited by Erika Abrams, translated by Erika Abrams and Marc de Launay, with a postface by Marc Crépon. Lagrasse: Verdier, 2007.

Patočka, Jan. *Liberté et sacrifice. Écrits politiques.* Edited and translated by Erika Abrams, with a postface by Anne-Marie Roviello. Grenoble: Millon, 1990.

Patočka, Jan. *Living in Problematicity.* Edited by Eric Manton, translated by Eric Manton and Erazim Kohák. Prague: Oikoymenh, 2007.

Patočka, Jan. *Plato and Europe.* Translated by Petr Lom. Stanford: Stanford University Press, 2002.

Patočka, Jan and Krzysztof Michalski. "Letters between Krzysztof Michalski and Jan Patočka (1973–1976)." Edited by Nicolas de Warren, translated by Nicolas de Warren, Patrick Eldridge, and Vera Tylzanowski. *The New Yearbook for Phenomenology and Phenomenological Philosophy* 14 (2015): 223–70.

Ricoeur, Paul. "L'originaire et la question-en-retour dans la *Krisis* de Husserl." In *À l'école de la phénoménologie.* Paris: Vrin, 1986.

Stanciu, Ovidiu. "Europe and the Oblivion of the World. From Husserl to Patocka." In *Thinking after Europe: Jan Patočka and Politics.* Edited by D. Meacham and F. Tava, 410–34. London: Rowman & Littlefield, 2016.

Stanciu, Ovidiu. "La Grande Guerre comme 'événement cosmique' : Jan Patočka et l'expérience du front." *Revue philosophique de la France et de l'étranger* 4 (2018): 507–24.

Stanciu, Ovidiu. "Retrouver la *Lebenswelt*, par-delà Husserl. Patočka et Ricœur, lecteurs de la *Krisis.*" META. *Research in Hermeneutics, Phenomenology and Practical Philosophy,* 9, no. 2 (2017): 437–52.

10

Patočka, the Second World War, and the European Project

LORENZO GIRARDI

According to the Czech philosopher and dissident Jan Patočka, the idea of Europe has reached its end. This chapter examines his thought of the end of Europe in relation to the Second World War. While the war designated the ultimate end of Europe for Patočka, this chapter argues that his work also contains the resources to see this end as a new beginning and that this corresponds, at least in part, to the way the European project developed after the war. This indicates an appropriation of Patočka's work to develop the idea of Europe in a manner that goes beyond Patočka's own writings and inclinations.

Classifications such as the *idea* of Europe and *the* idea of Europe are abstract and do not cover Europe's concrete and inevitably much messier reality. Despite this precaution, they can be helpful in understanding how Europe historically understood itself or what it should be. As far removed as this self-understanding has been from its reality, Europe cannot be understood without it either. Moreover, any end of Europe is the end of a particular idea of Europe. To grasp Patočka's thought of the end of Europe (and what might come after) and to understand some of the moves he makes in doing so, it must be clear what exactly this would be the end of.

The first part of this chapter briefly sketches a general history of the idea of Europe to make sense of Patočka's understanding of Europe in terms of an optimistic rationalism and his suggestion that a cure to the ills of this rationalism might be found in Christianity. This general history overlaps with but is not identical to, at least in emphasis, the history of the idea of Europe that Patočka himself provided. Rather, it provides the historical context of Europe's self-understanding that informed Patočka's account. After this, the end of this modern idea of Europe as discussed in Patočka's work is presented. This is not only done because he experienced and thought through this end of Europe but also in order to turn to his hope and ultimately disappointment in the possibility of a spiritual conversion that would have turned Europe's situation around. Such a conversion would have made this end of Europe a new beginning.

While Patočka did not see this new beginning come about, it is argued that his pessimism on the matter may have been unjustified, at least in part. A form of solidarity such as he related to this conversion arguably did come about after the Second World War and played a role in reshaping Europe, even if no large-scale spiritual conversion took place in the way he had hoped. In Patočka's account, Europe's history is one of repeated reinvention after catastrophe, and the building of political institutions plays an important role in this, even if Patočka himself paid relatively little attention to this aspect. The taking shape of the European Union with explicit reference to the Second World War and the Holocaust in particular can be seen as such a reinvention of Europe after catastrophe, although not without important qualifications.

Given the discrepancy between this latter fact and Patočka's pessimism, it is worth looking into the possible reasons for this discrepancy. These have to do with the specific historical circumstances of both Patočka's pessimism and of the reference to the Holocaust in the European project. This is related to the discussion of the past decades on the role of the Second World War and the Holocaust in European memory and the European project, in particular with reference to the EU's enlargement in eastern Europe. The conclusion reflects on this in relation to current discourse on Europe, paying attention to the lessons Patočka thought we should learn from the catastrophes of the twentieth century.

The Idea of Europe

Historically, the two most prominent ideas of Europe are those of Christendom and the modern idea of Europe and this is reflected in some political views and indeed clashes regarding Europe today.[1] For Patočka, the Greek project of the care of the soul was the singular pillar on which Europe's development rested. But while the influence of antiquity on Europe cannot be denied, in antiquity itself, the latter did not yet exist in any meaningful sense. At best, "Europe" was a vaguely defined geographical notion. Christianity, of course, is not European either. This is the case factually and historically, due to its roots in the Middle East and, essentially, due to its universal aspirations. Before and during the Christianization of the peoples of Europe, the idea of Europe held no special significance. Yet, it is this Christianization to which the idea of Europe owes much of its existence.

Europe becomes more than a geographical notion and starts overlapping with Christianity in a more than contingent sense when Europe is Christianized as much as Christianity is Europeanized. The rise and spread of Islam confined much of Christianity to geographical Europe so that the Christian world, Christendom, becomes virtually synonymous with Europe.[2] This provides a foundation of what will become Europe as we know it today. Yet, if this can be called an idea of Europe, it is not yet a *European* idea of Europe. It still designates a unity, a cultural sense, or community, that is not necessarily or primarily European but Christian.

This overlapping unity and identity that Christianity provided to Europe dissolves in the face of religious strife, notably the reformation and the wars of religion at the onset of modernity. What survives this fragmentation survives not as Christendom but as Europe. This birth of what can be called the "European idea" of Europe is a Christendom detached from its religious substance. Of course, religion continues to play a major role in Europe's reality, but this starts the process whereby the basic framework of Christendom, of Christian civilization against Islamic and pagan "others," becomes secularized.

At the same time, scientific and technological advances start shaping European life in new ways, leading to an optimistic rationalism. Instead of faith, reason becomes the path toward salvation, the key to morality, and that which can bring humankind together. This is how some of the eighteenth-century French *philosophes* saw it, reaching its peak in the nineteenth-century positivistic philosophy of August Comte and represented by Patočka's mentor Edmund Husserl in the twentieth century. Slowly but surely, the role of Christianity in the idea of Europe is taken over by reason. What is seen as distinguishing Europe is not that it is the Christian continent, but that it is the rational continent.

Reason, for the modern European, is what allows for a life not based on one's particular characteristics but on one's essential humanity. In many cases, reason is not seen as merely instrumental, as the tool to figure out the best means to an end, but as capable of determining these ends themselves. As for the ancient Greek philosophers, for many modern Europeans, reason has an existential relevance, allowing for a higher plan for life. European reason's results are seen as valid for everyone and can be—*should be*—spread throughout all of humankind. Rationalization, universalization, globalization, and Europeanization become virtually synonymous in this view, not unlike how Europe was virtually synonymous with Christendom before. Due to the many successes that reason brings and the promises these lead to, this optimistic rationalism could consolidate itself in European consciousness.

Such an understanding of Europe is, of course, a caricature when compared to Europe's reality, and many counterexamples can be mentioned. However, of concern here is not Europe's reality but its self-understanding, and the latter has been shaped by this caricature, at least for many intellectuals during the previous centuries. Moreover, it is important to understand this intertwining of the modern idea of Europe with an optimistic rationalism because it forms the condition to understand the thought of the end of Europe that becomes widespread in the twentieth century. For thinkers such as Husserl and Patočka, the world wars can designate the end of Europe not merely because of their material devastation and geopolitical consequences but because they put in doubt the framework of optimistic rationalism which they saw as characterizing Europe.

The Second World War and the End of Europe

Although Husserl was the last great representative of the modern idea of Europe, he already self-identified as "inappropriate to his time."[3] He held on to the optimistic rationalism at the heart of his thought of Europe, even when the First World War shakes it to its core and even when he becomes surrounded by the irrationalism of the 1930s in Germany. How different it is for Patočka, only a few years later, who seems convinced that Europe has disappeared, "probably forever."[4] He puts it well when he says: "It is true that that irrationalism [of the 1930s] somehow evaporated amid the storms of our time. Yet has the faith in reason as Husserl understood it been restored? Surely it has not."[5] For those who identified Europe with its rationalism, this loss of the faith in reason entails the end of Europe.

The First World War already shook Europe's faith in reason due to the catastrophes it made possible. But for many, this faith was still salvageable. The edifice of reason could be rebuilt on the same foundation. After the Second World War and the Holocaust, the general intellectual sentiment was less hopeful. Reason itself was increasingly seen as complicit in these catastrophes. This famously was the conclusion of the critical theory of the Frankfurter Schule and of many in the phenomenological tradition, including Patočka. If a Husserl in the 1930s was already inappropriate for his time, a Husserl after Auschwitz is virtually unimaginable.

The Holocaust has a special significance for Europe in the sense that it was carried out by Europeans against Europeans and in a context that was intertwined with the modern idea of Europe. As Zygmunt Bauman puts it: *"The Holocaust was born and executed in our modern rational society, at the high stage of our civilization and at the peak of human cultural achievement, and for this reason it is a problem of that society, civilization and culture."*[6] Others, such as the United States, also saw themselves as the embodiment of rational society, but they were not as concretely the place and perpetrator of this catastrophe. Other catastrophes have taken place, and continue to take place, but these were not so intrinsically intertwined with what Europe took itself to be. For European consciousness, the Holocaust was a sign of the destitution of its supposedly higher civilization.

Of course, there are exceptions to this rough classification of the difference in situation after the two World Wars, but as a general classification this distinction has its value.[7] Patočka too conceptualizes such a distinction, although he does not discuss the Holocaust specifically, a matter discussed further below. While he calls the First World War "the decisive event . . . of the twentieth century,"[8] it nonetheless was not universal in character.[9] It could still be approached, even if with difficulty, "in terms of nineteenth-century ideas,"[10] from what he calls "the perspective of peace, day, and life, excluding its dark nocturnal side."[11] That is, it could be seen as an exception to the status quo of Europe's optimistic rationalism rather than as an expression of it. After the Second World War, this older perspective is no longer applicable for what Patočka calls this "epoch of the night, of war, and of death."[12] What came to light with the First World War became universal with the Second. The latter eliminated the distinction between the front-line and the home front due to "aerial warfare that was capable of striking anywhere with equal cruelty."[13] The nuclear threat after the war, and the Cold War in general, made this existential situation the new status quo.

While Patočka sketches a pessimistic image of postwar Europe, he also sees that it is not a complete failure. After the Second World War, European societies as a whole were wealthier than ever and used this wealth to carry out vast social projects. He goes as far as saying that "this civilization *makes possible* more than any previous human constellation: a life without violence and with far-reaching equality of opportunity. Not in the sense that this goal would anywhere be actual, but humans have never before found the means of struggle with external misery, with lack and want, which this civilization offers."[14] Yet, Patočka is pessimistic about the motives behind this social achievement. It was not a great program of achieving a higher form of existence but the result of the fact that "this continent has opted for demobilization because it has no other option."[15] Its social and economic successes hide Europe's spiritual poverty as they make Europe complacent; decadent, as Patočka calls it. He speaks of an addiction to things,[16] skeptical relativism, indifference, and empty intellectualism.[17] Boredom is mentioned in one stroke with the experiences of combat and Hiroshima as decisive for the twentieth century.[18]

This decadence is characteristic of what Patočka calls *moderate overcivilization*.[19] Such a civilization, roughly equivalent to Western liberal democracy, retains some of modern Europe's rationalism insofar as it aims to organize society rationally while also taking freedom as a fundamental value.[20] This prevents it from turning into a totalitarian civilization (*radical overcivilization*) where all of society is organized without remainder, such as was characteristic of Nazi Germany and Stalinist communism. In moderate overcivilization, rationalism does not penetrate everything. The economy in particular is structured according to rational principles, but society retains a space for personal responsibility and autonomy in relation to questions regarding the meaning of life.

While moderate overcivilization retains a space for freedom, it does not provide any spiritual resources to direct this freedom and make it meaningful. It thus cannot function without "the inclusion of something that does not belong to the purely rational system of instrumentality."[21] "*Ratio* cannot live alone," Patočka writes. "Its essence is such that it is not enough for life as a whole, it demands to be completed or replaced by something else."[22] Moderate overcivilization seems to provide but an empty framework. It might not necessarily drag human existence down, but it provides nothing to lift it out of decadence either.[23] Although the postwar socioeconomic successes have their significance (as Ivan Chvatík puts it: "The dead and unable cannot pull themselves into upswing,"[24] that is, lift themselves out of decadence), in the end "exterior successes and failure can never be completely convincing as long as life decisions are concerned, about where is the real, where is the ultimate truth."[25]

For Patočka, Europe was the project of a higher form of life based on truth and freedom rather than material, biological, or economic needs and wants. He sees Europe as originating in ancient Greece because the ancient Greek philosophers first conceived of this project via the use of reason. But throughout modernity, the role of reason was narrowed further and further to a merely instrumental conception, and in the wake of the catastrophes of the twentieth century, what can be called the broader, civilizational concept of reason lost its prior optimistic supports. The omnipresence of reason remains—politics, economics, and even education are seen in terms of "rational," calculable utility. Patočka says we could no longer exist without reason, even though it is no longer the key to a meaningful existence.[26] Nothing has taken its place, while older attempts to shape life have been "swept away—definitely, it now seems."[27] What was an essential part of the idea of Europe can no longer be upheld, and consequently the same goes for this idea of Europe. The latter can be said to have survived, although without its previous vitality, continuing to exist through inertia in a form that no longer suffices.[28]

Given both Europe's role on the global stage in the past centuries as well as the belief that the rationalization of humanity was its Europeanization, this end of Europe ushers in what Patočka refers to as a "post-European age."[29] Somewhat ironically, its fall out of the center of world history after the Second World War coincides with the globalization of its rationalism in the form of the global spread of science and technology. It is clear that Patočka does not consider this a completely positive gift to the world: "European civilization became a global link in precisely that form which Husserl's *Crisis of the European Sciences* showed to be decadent."[30]

While its rationalism may have been catastrophic for Europe, Patočka holds that the situation is not yet so dire for other peoples, cultures, or civilizations because they still have living traditions that can assert themselves against the dominance of modern rationalism.[31] The encounter between these traditions in which a sense for the immaterial is still alive and modern rationalism may lead to unexpected results.

Patočka does not, however, intend for others to find a way to deal meaningfully with the problem so that Europe can then appropriate their solution. Solutions must be found within Europe's own heritage in a similar way that Patočka holds the hope that others can do so in theirs. Crucially, when speaking of the still living traditions in the world, he mentions Christianity in relation to Europe,[32] and in his *Heretical Essays,* he explicitly turns to Christianity as a possible way of addressing Europe's situation.

The Possibility of Spiritual Renewal

While Patočka is pessimistic about the possibility of Europe finding a way out of its decadence, he does speak of the possibility of a "gigantic conversion" or "unheard-of *metanoein.*"[33] For this, he looks to Christianity, which makes sense in light of both Europe's Christian roots and its possibility of providing spiritual guidance. Crucial here is a sense of responsibility that in Christianity arises through a deepening of the self. Responsibility is derived from "an inscrutable relation to the absolute highest being in whose hands we are not externally, but internally."[34] This relation is one to an infinite love, and "humans are individuals because they are guilty, and *always* guilty, with respect to it."[35] It is through this "abysmal deepening of the soul" that "Christianity remains thus far the greatest, unsurpassed but also un-thought human outreach that enabled humans to struggle against decadence."[36]

However, Patočka does not propose anything like a re-Christianization of Europe. While there are many interpretations that emphasize the Christian element in Patočka's thought,[37] there are good reasons to see Patočka's attempt to think Christianity's "unsurpassed but unthought" possibilities as having a nonreligious outcome. Patočka sees Christianity as having played a role in the development that led to Europe's decadence[38] and thinks that "what a person is [. . .] is not really adequately thematized in the Christian perspective."[39] In seminars discussed by Ivan Chvatík,[40] the conversion Patočka seeks seems to lie more in the abandonment of religious faith than in its renewal. Indeed, Patočka speaks of the need for a "fully ripened form of demythologized Christianity,"[41] which he relates to the important topic of sacrifice.

While sacrifice is an important theme within Christianity, this does not lead Patočka to a discussion of religious renewal but to the experience of war. The soldier at the front is taken as the paradigmatic case of sacrifice in relation to the possibility of spiritual conversion. This is highly relevant in light of his comments on the situation after the Second World War as a permanent and universal state of war.

The core of Patočka's account of sacrifice is relatively simple. This is that the very idea of sacrifice presupposes a difference between something higher and lower, something that matters more than something else. In relation to self-sacrifice, such as one can find at the front, this is between one's life and something that matters more than one's life so that one is willing to put it on the line. A sacrifice thus introduces, or rather demonstrates, a difference of order in the world. It is fundamentally at odds with a decadence that does not believe in anything, leveling everything down into materialistic indifference.

In his analysis of the experience at the front, Patočka thematizes the transition from a sacrifice with a relative significance to one that is significant solely in itself. Those sent to the front sacrifice themselves, but initially in a way that makes their lives subservient to a goal set by others. Such a sacrifice is significant only insofar as this goal is significant; it has no meaning in itself. It sees life as insignificant and expendable. However, Patočka notes that the actual experience at the front is different. The relative significance of sacrifice is lost as "it is no longer the cost we pay for a program of development, progress, intensification, and extension of life's possibilities, rather it is significant *solely in itself*."[42] This sacrifice demands endurance in the face of death, and this points towards a higher form of life than mere biological life, even if nothing concrete is encountered as higher. The irreducibility and singularity of one's existence become manifest as life "trips on *nothingness*, on a boundary over which it cannot step, along which everything is transformed."[43]

Here, a positive appropriation of this experience as the possibility of a higher form of existence; in other words, the conversion that Patočka hoped for is indicated. It is precisely in an age devoid of belief in anything higher that a true sacrifice, a sacrifice not in name of anything else but for which one takes complete responsibility, can take place. Moreover, the world turning into a giant state of war where catastrophe can take place at any moment would, paradoxically, be a prime condition for such a conversion to take place on a massive scale.

Yet, Patočka did not think this happened. He explicitly wondered why the arguably universal experience of war of the past century did not bring it about.[44] Patočka's answer is not only that we are distracted by the decadent conveniences of modern life, but also that it is only few who can deal with such a situation and transcend its initial phase of "meaninglessness and unbearable horror, absurdity par excellence."[45] Even for those who can do so, this experience is not a lasting one, but a "summit" from which one "cannot but retreat back into everydayness."[46] It seems difficult to build anything enduring on such a transitory experience. To overcome this, Patočka introduces the idea of a new form of community built on what he calls the "solidarity of the shaken," "the solidarity of those who are capable of understanding what life is about. That history is the conflict of *mere life*, barren and chained by fear, with *life at the peak*, life that does not plan for the ordinary days of a future but sees clearly that the everyday, its life and its 'peace,' have an end. Only one who is able to grasp this, who is capable of conversion, of *metanoia*, is a spiritual person."[47] Continuing his analysis of the experience at the front, Patočka says that it is not only one's own relative significance for the war effort that is transcended. Others, including the enemy, are revealed as fellow participants in this situation. Patočka refers to the phenomena of "prayer for the enemy" and "loving those who hate us,"[48] solidarity in spite of difference and conflict. Unlike the universalism of modern rationalism, this is not a bond that transcends particular differences toward a higher, but inevitably abstract, idea of a human essence. Rather, it comes about in the confrontation with the concrete nullity of humanity's existential situation. It is a coming together in a shared space of meaning, or perhaps it is better seen as a space of meaninglessness.

While the key to the conversion that Patočka hoped for might lie in this community of the shaken, it is unclear not only whether such a community is possible but also what it would provide. He speaks of it as a "spiritual authority" or "spiritual power that could drive the warring world to some restraint, rendering some acts and measures impossible."[49] It seems that it would be a fundamentally dissident community, saying " 'no' to the measures of mobilization which make the state of war permanent," but not offer any positive programs. Insofar as Patočka speaks of this as a possibility, he gives no indication that it has had a transformative effect on Europe.

The Second World War as a New Beginning

According to Patočka, Europe had a spiritual foundation that lay at the basis of both the Christian deepening of the self and the optimistic rationalism of modernity. This is the motivation for his inquiry into the ancient Greek philosophical principle of the care for the soul, which Patočka saw as the earliest development of this foundation. The conversion he hoped for would in some sense be a reestablishment of this principle. Yet, his diagnosis of European life as decadent seems to leave no room for anything like the care for the soul.

However, if we examine Patočka's account closely, strictly speaking Europe was not founded on the care for the soul as such. It was founded as a political project in response to the initial failure of the care for the soul: the death of Socrates. Socrates's care for the soul entailed a care for the soul of the community, holding it to a higher standard. He famously and tragically had to pay for this with his life. According to Patočka, it is this initial catastrophe that led Plato to the idea of the just state as the state where Socrates could have lived.[50] And it is because Plato was "also the founder of the philosophical theory of the state" that Patočka calls him and not Socrates the "founder of European ideals."[51]

This suggestion that for Patočka Europe was not directly founded on the care for the soul in its original form but on a political development of it, while unorthodox, makes sense if we look at his account of the development of this principle throughout Europe's history. While he certainly focusses on the development of the care for the soul as a spiritual principle of individual human existence, the relation to its changing sociopolitical context, in particular the power of the state, is a recurring theme as well. The change of this principle in its spread to the Roman Empire concerned the realization of a more universal state of justice than Athens was, and its transformation from its Roman to its Christian form too rested on the former's inadequate realization of this ideal.[52] Patočka's reflections on moderate overcivilization, specifically the role of the individual's freedom in its economic organization of society, can be viewed as part of this account as well.

This reading not only entails that Europe was also a political project from its very inception but also that this project was formulated as the response to failure, catastrophe even. If this is the case, then the question whether the Second World War and the Holocaust mark the ultimate end of Europe or whether it is also a transformative new beginning, can perhaps be answered in a different way than Patočka himself did.

While Patočka's focus on decadence and the issue of a higher plan for life lead him to draw the conclusion that Europe has come to an end, from a political perspective, specifically the perspective of the theory of the state that he indicated but did not develop, significant changes have taken place since the Second World War. This concerns the Europeanization of various institutions and a new focus on international law and human rights. In the context of his dissidence as part of the Charta 77 movement, Patočka himself refers to the new focus on human rights as indicating a new historical epoch that is not based primarily on fear or profit but on respect for something higher for which one is prepared to face a certain risk.[53] This ties twentieth-century politics of human rights and international law (the aim of Charta 77 was to have the Communist regime uphold international agreements regarding human rights) to the care of the soul.

It is undeniable that the Second World War and the Holocaust had a tremendous influence on Europe, and the project of European integration is clearly more than a mere technical alteration of its political constellation. The spiritual change after the war may not have lifted Europe out of its decadence in the way that Patočka hoped it would, but this should not diminish the changes that *have* come about and that are also relevant to the way Patočka conceived of Europe and its end.

The call *nie wieder*, "never again," functions as a fundamental principle for postwar Europe. Many of its values existed before, but now Europeans hold them with reference to the World Wars and the Holocaust due to the significance these have acquired for Europe. Throughout Europe's diversity and divisions, the European political project after the Second World War has been marked by the aim to never let such a devastation happen again. Can the European political project in the wake of the Second World War not be seen in terms of the solidarity of the shaken? Even if this did not lead to a large-scale spiritual renewal in terms of a higher plan for human existence, is this not akin to Patočka's community of the shaken as rendering some tragedies impossible? Of course, there were and are clear economic and political motives for European integration as well, but the memory of the Holocaust in particular plays a significant and foundational role. This is a common element in today's discourse on the EU. However, the matter is not that simple.

The explicit "Europeanization" of the Holocaust is relatively recent, mainly taking off in the 1990s. Explicit reference to the Holocaust played a remarkably minor role at the beginning of the European project. The war in general and anti-Nazism played a much bigger role but were also used by many to largely put the blame on Germany. Indeed, widespread knowledge of and interest in the Holocaust did not exist until the 1960s, and even from that point on, the Holocaust was not necessarily seen as holding a particular *European* significance. The European memory of the Holocaust consisted of its national memories. It was the EU, the European Parliament in particular, that shaped it as a transnational memory through concrete forms of education, declarations, monuments, and so on.

There is a clear reason for this Europeanization of the Holocaust taking place at the time it did. The sudden emergence of eastern Europe from behind the Iron Curtain and the start of its integration in the western project of European integration necessitated a new focus on European identity. Past attempts at establishing such an identity had proven difficult. They had focused on a shared European heritage that, aside from the elites, did not resonate with many people; or on an orientation toward future integration and prosperity, which did not fare well in times of economic crisis.[54] The memory of the Holocaust proved useful as a foundational, symbolic background for the European project. The Holocaust became "the ultimate evil against which Europe itself was defined," a unique event increasingly seen as incomparable to other tragedies.[55] The latter sentiment had existed before but only now became the standard way of referring to the Holocaust by European political elites.

What is important in the Holocaust's use as a foundational event for the European project is not just the awareness of this catastrophe but a sense of responsibility for it. As mentioned, the Holocaust was seen, at least in part, as a European catastrophe for which some of the blame could be attributed to European civilization. At the very least, this civilization could not prevent it. This aspect of culpability is the foundation of the responsibility not to let something similar happen in the future. In a manner, this combines Patočka's solidarity of the shaken as spurred on by tragedy and his attempt to deepen a sense of responsibility through Christian motifs.

The integration of this sense of responsibility into a civilizational idea was made clear in recent years by German chancellor Angela Merkel's visit to Auschwitz in 2019. She said explicitly that the responsibility for the Holocaust and its remembrance are "an integral part of [German] national identity and defines who we are as an enlightened and liberal society, a democracy and a state based on the rule of law."[56] While Germany, of course, has a special relation the Holocaust, this attitude is by no means unique to Germany and has been expressed by numerous European nations and institutions.

However, this is present much more in western Europe than in eastern Europe. In eastern Europe, a "Holocaust memory" had not developed such as it had in the West. The Communists effectively suppressed it to focus on their own suffering and heroism. The continued presence of anti-Semitic tendencies under communism did not help this matter either. Insofar as a Holocaust memory did develop, this is fairly recent, spurred on by the EU, and many countries are still struggling with this.

The issue lies not just with *what* is to be remembered but also with *how* past events are to be remembered. The sense of culpability, in the West also shared by many who did not feel *directly* responsible for the Holocaust, was absent in many eastern European nations. A sense of victimhood often remains the dominant paradigm that defines eastern European memory of the war and its aftermath. In Poland, for example, the mere suggestion of playing any part in in the Holocaust had become a criminal offence in 2018 before outcry in Europe, the United States, and Israel put an end to this.

These matters problematize the use of the Second World War and the Holocaust as a foundation for Europe's integration and its underlying values. The response to this of European institutions and those in charge of the European project has been mixed. On the one hand, there has been a shift toward the remembrance of both Nazi and Communist crimes. On the other, this has not always been an equal recognition of the trauma of eastern Europe but an expansion or even imposition of western Holocaust-centered memory.[57] One reason for this, aside from an element of Western chauvinism, is the difficulty with which the emphasis on the Holocaust as a unique event can be reconciled with the incorporation of the other tragedies of eastern Europe.

Patočka's Context

The discussed context sheds some light on Patočka's pessimistic attitude toward the Second World War as a potential new beginning for Europe. During most of his life, which tragically ended in 1977, the Holocaust had not yet received much attention; certainly not under the Communist regime in Czechoslovakia but not yet as a touchstone for European integration in the West either.[58] Although it was the topic of a few books and films in Czechoslovakia shortly after the war, the 1948 Communist coup put an end to this. Periods of liberalization allowed for some more freedom, but the works on the Holocaust in those times focused on personal stories, that is, individualization of the war and the Holocaust rather than nationalization, let alone Europeanization.[59]

Moreover, the conditions in the Czech area even in times of liberalization and after the fall of the Communists were resistant to a sense of Czech culpability. Czechoslovakia was one of the first victims of the Nazi's outside of Germany, with the annexation of the Sudetenland in 1938, and in the split of Czechoslovakia during the war, it was the Slovak Republic as a client state of Nazi Germany, not the annexed Czech lands, that was seen as complicit in the Nazi atrocities.[60] The Czechs were on the "right side of history," and it is worth noting that already before many Czechs felt that they were more closely connected to European civilization than others in central Europe. Responsibility lay with the Germans, and the Czech government that had existed under German occupation was largely left out of the postwar narrative.[61] This is by no means meant to attribute any blame to the Czechs, but it helps to understand why there was little to provoke reflection on the Holocaust and the role of the Czechs or of European civilization in it.

None of this directly says anything on Patočka's views on the matter. Yet, this was the general climate in which his postwar thinking developed. His analyses of European reason are clearly linked to the Second World War, and while a sense of responsibility could be deduced from these analyses, this is not yet shaped into a new sense of a responsible European civilization. And while Patočka was disappointed by the Czech failure to live up to many of his ideals, he is not entirely free from the mentioned Czech chauvinism.[62] Moreover, the members of Charta 77, closely related to Patočka, seem to have been aligned with the "standard" Czech narrative presented above as well.[63]

That said, it is impossible to form any proper judgment on the views Patočka would have had on the Holocaust as a new foundation for the European project. He did not find himself in the conditions where such a thought could have developed properly. Not only did the full awareness of the Holocaust come relatively late, including in the West, but its Europeanization is of even later date. Moreover, in the specifically Czech circumstances a sense of culpability could not easily take root. The totalitarianism that still held much of Europe, not the least Czechoslovakia, in its grip and that sharply divided Europe was also a more than legitimate reason to be pessimistic about any new beginning of Europe. However, that does not take away from the fact that Patočka's work forms an interesting resource to help think the Second World War and the Holocaust as both an end and a new beginning for Europe.

Concluding Thoughts

The relatively late use of the Holocaust as a symbolic point of reference for the European project raises the question whether this is not a politicization or instrumentalization for political gain. In terms of Patočka's work, such a utilization of a historical event in light of a certain goal is not necessarily an issue. While it is easy to be led to the thought that the solidarity of the shaken comes about almost spontaneously given certain tragic conditions, he speaks of the community of the shaken as a form that can overcome the transitory and individualizing nature of this experience.[64] It is a *construction* to make this experience a factor in history. The Europeanization of the Holocaust potentially can be seen in this light as well, as a construction to make the Holocaust a lasting factor in history rather than as its instrumentalization.

However, the manner in which reference to the Holocaust in European politics takes place matters a great deal. Those strongly in favor of the EU often attribute the long-lasting peace in Europe after the Second World War to the EU and its predecessors. Combined with the economic prosperity that the postwar period brought, it is all too easy to slip back into a narrative of progress and superior European civilization. The Holocaust often plays a role in this narrative, but its tragic significance is pushed to the back somewhat in an aggrandizing tale about the EU. The focus becomes the success of what Patočka referred to as "the perspective of peace, day, and life," even as Europe's success "contributes to the deepening of the gap between the *blessed haves* and those who are dying of hunger on a planet rich in energy—thus intensifying the *state of war*."[65]

Moreover, it has become clear that little remains of European solidarity or indeed solidarity with those struck by catastrophe as soon as it comes to the matter of, for example, relocating refugees across Europe. Many countries would rather, and indeed have, put up borders again. In this context, there are Eurosceptics that explicitly denounce what they see as the constant, tiring reference to the catastrophes of Europe's past. Perhaps not unrelated to this, these often invoke an older idea of Europe, whether it be that of a Christian Europe or that of modern Europe.

The main, most prominent stances on Europe both forego the significance of the catastrophes on the basis of which postwar Europe started to reinvent itself. They increasingly ignore or dismiss, in Patočka's words, "the *night*," which came "suddenly to be an absolute obstacle on the path of the day to the bad infinity of tomorrows."[66] If a new Europe began to take shape after and on the basis of the Second World War, it is an inherently precarious Europe, in which we should not put too much hope unless we are prepared to take responsibility for it ourselves. Although this new Europe is not developed within Patočka's work, the latter can guide us and help us avoid the pitfalls in attempting to establish it.

Notes

1. The brief history of the idea of Europe presented here mainly draws on the following works: Gerard Delanty, *Inventing Europe: Idea, Identity, Reality*; Heikki Mikkeli, *Europe as an Idea and an Identity*; Anthony Pagden, ed., *The Idea of Europe: From Antiquity to the European Union*.

2. On the matter that Europe came into existence precisely when this universalism was halted, see Delanty, *Inventing Europe*, 26; Guénoun, *About Europe: Philosophical Hypotheses*, 232.

3. Husserl, *The Crisis of the European Sciences and Transcendental Phenomenology: An Introduction to Phenomenological Philosophy*, 289.

4. Patočka, *Plato and Europe*, 89.

5. Patočka, "Edmund Husserl's Philosophy of the Crisis of the Sciences and His Conception of a Phenomenology of the 'Life-World,'" 224.

6. Bauman, *Modernity and the Holocaust*, x.

7. In his overview of the influence of the First World War on philosophy, Nicolas De Warren makes a comparable claim: "A new form of thinking that is fashioned as a response to the First World War becomes internalized into the conceptual vocabulary *after* the Second World War." De Warren, "The First World, Philosophy, and Europe," 732. A similar sentiment was, among others, expressed by Ernst Jünger in his "Across the Line," 95.

8. Patočka, *Heretical Essays in the Philosophy of History*, 124.

9. Patočka, "Ideology and Life in the Idea," 90–91.

10. Patočka, *Heretical Essays*, 119.

11. Patočka, 120.

12. Patočka, 120.

13. Patočka, 132.

14. Patočka, 118.

15. Patočka, 132.

16. Patočka, 113.

17. Patočka, "Zum Begriff der Weltgeschichte," 333.

18. Patočka, *Heretical Essays*, 114.

19. See Patočka, "La surcivilisation et son conflit interne."

20. Patočka, 121.

21. Patočka, 142.

22. Patočka, 155.

23. For a discussion of Patočka's take on this liberalism that balances his criticism with his positive appraisal, see Zvarík, "The Decline of Freedom. Jan Patočka's Phenomenological Critique of Liberalism."

24. Chvatík, "Jan Patočka and the Possibility of Spiritual Politics," 36.

25. Patočka, "Ideology and Life in the Idea," 92.

26. Patočka, "Edmund Husserl's Philosophy," 224.

27. Patočka, *Heretical Essays*, 95.

28. Cf. Tava, "The brave struggle: Jan Patočka on Europe's Past and Future," 243.

29. Patočka, "Europa und Nach-Europa: Die nacheuropaïsche Epoche und ihre geistigen Probleme." Although Patočka's reflections on post-Europe are novel, they are unfinished sketches.

30. Patočka, *Heretical Essays*, 45.

31. Patočka, "Die nacheuropäische Epoche und ihre geistigen Probleme," 68. Patočka speaks of various still living traditions, a list that largely seems defined by the exclusion of European rationalism: "Christianity in its various forms (Western Europe, the United States, Latin America, Africa, and as diaspora in the rest of the world), Judaism, Islam (Arabic world, Asia Minor, Persia, India, Indonesia, parts of the USSR, Africa), Marxism-Leninism (Soviet Union and the people's democracies, China, albeit with a more archaic undercurrent), astrobiology (China, Japan, Hinduist India), Buddhism (parts of India, China, South-east Asia, Japan, etc.), neolithic-precolumbian traditions (Latin America), African traditions which in part are also Neolithic."

32. See previous note.

33. Patočka, *Heretical Essays*, 75.

34. Patočka, 106.

35. Patočka, 107.

36. Patočka, 108.

37. Such as those of Ludger Hagedorn and Martin Koci. E.g., Hagedorn, "Auto-Immunity or Transcendence: A Phenomenological Re-Consideration of Religion with Derrida and Patočka"; Hagedorn, "Beyond Myth and Enlightenment: On Religion in Patočka's Thought"; Hagedorn, " 'Christianity Un-Thought'—A Reconsideration of Myth, Faith, and Historicity"; Koci, "Metaphysical Thinking after Metaphysics: A Theological Reading of Jan Patočka's Negative Platonism"; Koci, "Christianity after Christendom: Rethinking Jan Patočka's Heresy."

38. Patočka, *Heretical Essays*, 69–70.

39. Patočka, 107.
40. Chvatík, "Rethinking Christianity as a Suitable Religion for the Postmodern World."
41. Patočka, "The Dangers of Technicization in Science according to E. Husserl and the Essence of Technology as Danger according to M. Heidegger," 339.
42. Patočka, *Heretical Essays*, 129.
43. Patočka, 131.
44. Patočka, 131.
45. Patočka, 126.
46. Patočka, 134–35.
47. Patočka, 134–35.
48. Patočka, 131.
49. Patočka, 135.
50. Patočka, *Plato and Europe*, 50.
51. Patočka, "Europa und Nach-Europa: Die nacheuropäische Epoche und ihre geistigen Probleme," 210. On the theory of the state in Patočka's work, see Girardi, "From Care for the Soul to the Theory of the State in Jan Patočka."
52. Patočka, *Heretical Essays*, 80–81, 108–9.
53. Patočka, "The Obligation to Resist Injustice," 342. Since this text was written in the context of Charta 77 and intended for a more general audience, its place in Patočka's philosophy and the question whether it should be counted as a proper part of it all is somewhat complicated. Insofar as it is an accurate statement of his views on human rights in the postwar period, however, it suits the present argument.
54. On the matter of the European project's use of various memory frames, see Littoz-Monnet, "The EU Politics of Remembrance: Can Europeans Remember Together?" and Calligaro, "Legitimation through Remembrance? The Changing Regimes of Historicity of European Integration."
55. Littoz-Monnet, "The EU Politics of Remembrance," 1183.
56. Merkel, "Speech by Federal Chancellor Dr Angela Merkel Marking the 10th Anniversary of the Auschwitz-Birkenau Foundation, Auschwitz, 6 December 2019."
57. See Trimçev et al. "Europe's Europes: Mapping the Conflicts of European Memory."
58. On the Holocaust in Czechoslovak culture before 1989, see Sniegon, *Vanished History: The Holocaust in Czech and Slovak Historical Culture*, 56–72.
59. Sniegon, 63.
60. Sniegon, 5.
61. Sniegon, 93.
62. See Tucker, "Shipwrecked: Patočka's Philosophy of Czech History," 196–216.
63. Sniegon, *Vanished History*, 45, 95.

64. Patočka, *Heretical Essays*, 134–35.
65. Patočka, 132.
66. Patočka, 130.

Bibliography

Bauman, Zygmunt. *Modernity and the Holocaust*. Cambridge: Polity, 1989.

Calligaro, Oriane. "Legitimation through Remembrance? The Changing Regimes of Historicity of European Integration." *Journal of Contemporary European Studies* 23, no. 3 (2015): 330–43.

Chvatík, Ivan. "Jan Patočka and the Possibility of Spiritual Politics." In *Thinking after Europe: Jan Patočka and Politics*. Edited by Darian Meacham and Francesco Tava, 29–38. London: Rowman & Littlefield, 2016.

Chvatík, Ivan. "Rethinking Christianity as a Suitable Religion for the Postmodern World." *Phenomenology 2010: Selected Essays from Northern Europe* 4 (2011): 315–25.

Delanty, Gerard. *Inventing Europe: Idea, Identity, Reality*. London: Palgrave Macmillan, 1995.

De Warren, Nicolas. "The First World, Philosophy, and Europe." *Tijdschrift voor Filosofie* 76, no. 2 (2014): 715–37.

Girardi, Lorenzo. "From Care for the Soul to the Theory of the State in Jan Patočka." *International Journal of Philosophy and Theology* 81, no. 3 (2020): 196–210.

Guénoun, Denis. *About Europe: Philosophical Hypotheses*. Translated by Christine Irizarry. Stanford: Stanford University Press, 2013.

Hagedorn Ludger. "Auto-Immunity or Transcendence: A Phenomenological Re-Consideration of Religion with Derrida and Patočka." In *Phenomenology and Religion: New Frontiers*. Edited by Hans Ruin, 131–48. Stockholm: Södertörn University Publishers, 2010.

Hagedorn Ludger. "Beyond Myth and Enlightenment: On Religion in Patočka's Thought." In *Jan Patočka and the Heritage of Phenomenology: Centenary Papers*, edited by Ivan Chvatík and Erika Abrams, 245–61. Dordrecht: Springer, 2011.

Hagedorn Ludger. " 'Christianity Un-Thought'—A Reconsideration of Myth, Faith, and Historicity." *The New Yearbook for Phenomenology and Phenomenological Philosophy* 14 (2015): 31–46.

Husserl, Edmund. *The Crisis of the European Sciences and Transcendental Phenomenology: An Introduction to Phenomenological Philosophy*. Translated by David Carr. Evanston: Northwestern University Press, 1970.

Jünger Ernst, "Across the Line." In *Martin Heidegger, Ernst Jünger: Correspondence 1949–1975*. Translated by Timothy Sean Quinn, 67–102. London: Rowman & Littlefield International, 2016.

Koci, Martin. "Christianity After Christendom: Rethinking Jan Patočka's Heresy." *The Heythrop Journal* (2019): 1–14.

Koci, Martin. "Metaphysical Thinking after Metaphysics: A Theological Reading of Jan Patočka's Negative Platonism." *International Journal of Philosophy and Theology* 79, nos. 1–2 (2018): 18–35.

Littoz-Monnet, Annabelle. "The EU Politics of Remembrance: Can Europeans Remember Together?" *West European Politics* 35, no. 5 (2012): 1182–1202.

Merkel, Angela. "Speech by Federal Chancellor Dr Angela Merkel marking the 10th Anniversary of the Auschwitz-Birkenau Foundation, Auschwitz, 6 December 2019." Accessed 08/03/2021. https://www.bundeskanzlerin.de.

Mikkeli, Heikki. *Europe as an Idea and an Identity*. New York: St. Martin's, 1998.

Pagden, Anthony ed. *The Idea of Europe: From Antiquity to the European Union*. Washington: Woodrow Wilson Center Press, 2002.

Patočka, Jan. "The Dangers of Technicization in Science according to E. Husserl and the Essence of Technology as Danger according to M. Heidegger." In *Jan Patočka: Philosophy and Selected Writings*, edited and translated by Erazim Kohák, 327–39. Chicago: University of Chicago Press, 1989.

Patočka, Jan. "Die nacheuropäische Epoche und ihre geistigen Probleme." In *Jan Patočka und die Idee von Europa*, edited by Armin Homp and Markus Sedlaczek, 15–34. Berlin: MitOst, 2003.

Patočka, Jan. "Edmund Husserl's Philosophy of the Crisis of the Sciences and His Conception of a Phenomenology of the 'Life-World.'" In *Jan Patočka: Philosophy and Selected Writings*, translated and edited by Erazim Kohák, 223–38. Chicago: University of Chicago Press, 1989.

Patočka, Jan. "Europa und Nach-Europa: Die nacheuropäische Epoche und ihre geistigen Probleme." In *Ketzerische Essais zur Philosophie der Geschichte und ergänzende Schriften*, edited by Klaus Nellen and Jiří Němec, 207–87. Stuttgart: Klett-Cotta, 1988.

Patočka, Jan. *Heretical Essays in the Philosophy of History*. Translated by Erazim Kohák and edited by James Dodd. Chicago: Open Court, 1996.

Patočka, Jan. "Ideology and Life in the Idea." Translated by Eric Manton. *Studia Phaenomenologica* 7 (2007): 89–96.

Patočka, Jan. "La surcivilisation et son conflit interne." In *Liberté et sacrifice: Ecrits politiques*, translated by Erika Abrams, 99–177. Grenoble: Jérôme Millon, 1990.

Patočka, Jan. "The Obligation to Resist Injustice." In *Jan Patočka: Philosophy and Selected Writings*, edited and translated by Erazim Kohák, 340–43. Chicago: University of Chicago Press, 1989.

Patočka, Jan. *Plato and Europe*. Translated by Petr Lom. Stanford: Stanford University Press, 2002.

Patočka, Jan. "Zum Begriff der Weltgeschichte." In *Ketzerisches Essais zur Philosophie der Geschichte und ergänzende Schriften*, edited by Klaus Nellen and Jiří Němec, 331–45. Stuttgart: Klett-Cotta, 1988.

Sniegon, Tomas. *Vanished History. The Holocaust in Czech and Slovak Historical Culture*. New York: Berghahn, 2014.

Tava, Francesco. "The Brave Struggle: Jan Patočka on Europe's Past and Future." *Journal of the British Society for Phenomenology* 47, no. 3 (2016): 242–59.

Trimçev, Rieke et al. "Europe's Europes: Mapping the Conflicts of European Memory." *Journal of Political Ideologies*, 25, no. 1 (2019): 51–77.

Tucker, Aviezer. "Shipwrecked: Patočka's Philosophy of Czech History." *History and Theory* 35, no. 2 (1996): 196–216.

Zvarík, Michal. "The Decline of Freedom. Jan Patočka's Phenomenological Critique of Liberalism." In *The Yearbook on History and Interpretation of Phenomenology*, edited by Jana Trajtelová, 79–99. Frankfurt am Main: Peter Lang, 2016.

11

Solidarity as Freedom

Jürgen Habermas, Jean-Luc Nancy, and the Future(s) of the European Project

THOMAS TELIOS

Whither the EU?

In "European Triarchy," an early treatise on the future of a democratic, participatory, social, and egalitarian Europe published in 1841, Moses Hess writes that "we Europeans are dissatisfied and avid for revolutions."[1] Hess's dissatisfaction was directed toward both the Right Hegelians, who viewed the Prussian state as the ultimate realization of reason, and the Young Hegelians, who—following Heinrich Heine—argued that France should be redesignated the spearhead of progress in order to accomplish the work of the French Revolution. Hess argued for a historical transformation of European nationalist formations toward an inclusive sociopolitical praxis that transcended divisive national(ist) ideologies. Our current predicament is not all that different. The European Union, as a solidified and democratic political form with its own sovereign identity, has never really existed. Rather, the EU is whatever happens to serve national(ist)—primarily German or French—interests that dictate whether the EU will progress, stagnate, or regress.[2]

To identify this state of affairs as a propaedeutic to a promised democratic and perfectible EU-topia that has "Not-Yet-(Come-to-)Being"[3] or must remain "to come"[4] (à venir) is to sugarcoat the fact that—paraphrasing Latour—"we have never been European."[5] The slogan of a "people's

Europe,"[6] which has always accompanied aspirations connected to the political growth of the EU, manifests itself as nothing but a Platonic "noble lie."[7] Nevertheless, the EU has established itself as our sole and unequivocal double bind. As Derrida explains, to be caught in a double bind is "to gesture in opposite directions at the same time: on the one hand to preserve a distance and suspicion with regard to the official political codes governing reality; on the other, to intervene here and now in a practical and engaged manner whenever the necessity arises."[8] Tackling the EU as a/our double bind entails being critical of its alleged limitations and achievements while at the same time acknowledging that we cannot but envisage and strive toward realizing and promoting it.

Building on this notion, I begin in what follows by attributing the failures of European unification thus far to concepts such as Jürgen Habermas's project of juridification (*Verrechtlichung*), which, due to its overt Germanness, is incapable of capturing and manifesting the aspirations and expectations of states that not only do not share but are even diametrically opposed to the political ideals of postwar Germany. After discussing both the genealogical trajectories and the formal/institutional delimitations of juridification with regard to furthering European unification and consolidation, I go on to discuss what Habermas himself considers a viable alternative to his own earlier theory, namely, his concept of "legally constituted civic solidarity."[9] This *social-ontological* (as I view it) understanding of solidarity, which led to a revision not only of Habermas's failed political project of juridification but also of his earlier *moral* theory of solidarity, does seem to correspond to the collective structuring of the EU. However, even this proves theoretically inadequate as a bulwark against the recent reawakening of European neonationalisms, and this for two reasons. The *first* is to be found in what I call Habermas's "political solipsism," which I consider to be the manifestation of Habermas's "linguistic Kantianism"[10] in the political sphere. As Joel Whitebook points out,[11] in following Kantian monism and abandoning Hegelian conflictuality, Habermas forfeited the chance to genuinely conceive of collective entities such as the EU. While Habermas's ethics is pluralist in terms of its discursivity, it is solipsistic in terms of its universalist-pragmatist epistemological assumptions. As such, he misses the chance to extrapolate an equally collective epistemology. The *second* reason for the inadequacy of Habermas's revised theory of solidarity in the face of the fascistization of Europe is the fact that the binary character of the political concepts of a "dual identity"[12] and a "double sovereign,"[13] which Habermas introduces as concrete political manifestations of his "legally constituted civic solidarity," undermines the fundamental social-ontological collectivity that he himself diagnoses as the basis of the EU. As I observe, the split in identity that Habermas postulates has not—at least thus far—managed to overcome well-established nationalisms.

It is a pity that Habermas, who—like no other—has helped us to understand the emergence of national public spheres, is reluctant to advocate the latter in the context of the EU. Nonetheless, the concept of solidarity need not be aborted; on the contrary, it must be upheld and corroborated. In the last part of my chapter, I go on to sketch an understanding of *solidarity as freedom*. I substantiate this interpretation by considering Jean-Luc Nancy's notion of freedom. I argue that Habermas's and Nancy's projects are in fact complementary rather than opposed since they both depart from an acknowledgement that the EU is structured as an originally and fundamentally collective project. As I argue, if we are to "retreat"[14] the European project then we must draft a collective epistemology that obviates solipsism and is therefore able to circumvent power structures, the hegemony of the knowing One, and, last but not least, the totalizations that unravel from such methodological individualisms.

Jürgen Habermas's Concept of Juridification: Balancing German History and European Aspirations

To a certain extent, pointing out its overt Germanness should suffice to establish that Habermas's understanding of juridification is unequipped to elucidate and steer the European project.[15] What was introduced in the *Theory of Communicative Action* (1984/1987) as a critical instrument intended to diagnose a particular mode of capitalistic colonization of the lifeworld was transformed in *Between Facts and Norms* (1992/1998) into a normative value and acquired a pan-European identificatory character to which the whole continent had to adhere despite the various constitutional histories of the EU's member states. Nevertheless, tackling Habermas's concept of juridification is important since it helps us to analyze a series of issues and to understand the origins of a series of failures that revolve, as I argue, around the matter of identity.

As Daniel Loick recently pointed out, Habermas's early understanding of the notion of juridification differs significantly from that of Otto Kirchheimer, who coined the term. Whereas Kirchheimer sees in juridification the formalization and the consequent neutralization of (class) struggles through law, Habermas is suspicious of juridification only when it comes to regulating spheres that are thought to lie outside the scope of the law.[16] Putting to the side the fact that it is only the law that allows itself to exclude certain spheres of the lifeworld from its regulative application, Habermas discerns four "waves of juridification": (1) the bourgeois state, (2) the bourgeois constitutional state, (3) the democratic constitutional state, and ultimately (4) the democratic welfare state.[17] The assumption that not all forms of juridification correspond to forms of the lifeworld leads Habermas to evaluate these waves of juridification differently. Whereas the second and third waves are described as having an "unambiguously freedom-guaranteeing character,"[18] the first and the fourth are described as "dilemmatic" since both the primordial bourgeois state and the later democratic welfare state switched from being means that guaranteed freedom to means that endangered it.[19] In the case of the postwar democratic welfare state within which the EU arose, the processes of constitutionalization and democratization undoubtedly resulted in the broadening of guaranteed social and political rights and of their beneficiaries. Nevertheless, rather than leading through (communicative) consensus to a transformation of the individual's sociocultural forms of life, the processes of constitutionalization and democratization resulted in an equally instrumental (qua legalistic) compromise that left the individual's living conditions once again instrumentalized and colonized—due not to capitalism but to (bourgeois) individualistic law—and ultimately equally unaltered.

Habermas's notion of juridification changes drastically in *Between Facts and Norms* (1992/1998).[20] First, it is no longer dilemmatic, and second, it takes on identificatory traits.

Concerning the former, Habermas calls "for a compensatory legal protection policy that 'strengthens vulnerable clients' legal knowledge, their capacity to perceive and articulate problems, their readiness for conflict and, in general, their ability to assert themselves."[21] Seen this way, Habermas sees in the conference of collective legal protection the regulative power of a juridification that not only relieves "the strain on individuals through competent representation"[22] but, more importantly, has a self-cognitive function that enlightens individuals with regard to "the organized perception, articulation, and assertion of their own interests."[23] By enabling the citizens to "take part in the construction of

countervailing power and the articulation of social interests,"[24] juridification is transformed into "a political process"[25] and becomes the vector
of emancipation.

Concerning the latter, the identificatory trait that juridification
begins to take on in *Facts and Norms*, the fact that juridification is
considered an integrative process leads to a reassessment of its normative
value and functionality. By assuming that juridification is a unique and
solely European trait, Habermas entrusts juridification, and thus also the
law, with an identificatory functionality. Henceforth, juridification is supposed to be able to provide the missing link that can bring (and hold)
the disparate and historically different European states together, thereby
becoming the core element and main vector of European unification.

If, as mentioned above, the four stages of juridification as presented
by Habermas were inspired by—if not plainly taken from—the development of the German (welfare) state then fleeing to law as a means
of self-identification is again a typically neo-German response. In need
of a new state identity "after Auschwitz," the (legal, philosophical, and
political) concept of "constitutional patriotism" was the Germans' last
resort for a national identity after the *Historikerstreit*. Habermas did not
think it inconsistent to project such an overladen concept as a vector
toward a—this time—*European* identity. In this regard, Christian Joerges
is right to locate Habermas's genuine intervention regarding the issue
of European identity in his demand for a dual commitment in which
"Europe's citizens . . . remain citizens of their states, but become citizens
of the Union as well."[26] Even amidst the recent economic crisis and the
rise of the strong secessionist feelings that it brought forward, Habermas
remained loyal to his concept of a dual identity and has always been
a fierce opponent of taking recourse to national statehood.[27] As he
laments in his last book dedicated to the issues of European integration
and solidarity, the *"precise expansion of the We-perspective of national
citizens into one of European citizens,"*[28] so crucial to the generation of
the abovementioned "twofold perspective in the citizens"[29] and thus to
a proper European identity, is not being pursued actively enough but
"is discreetly hidden away in a kind of appendix."[30] More importantly,
though, this doubling affects not only EU citizens but also the holders
of European sovereignty. Just as every citizen is at the same time a
citizen of his/her national state and a citizen of the EU, sovereignty
over the EU is divided among and "shared" by both singular citizens
and the states of Europe.[31]

The Emperor's New Clothes:
The Collective Social Ontology of Solidarity
and the Trap of Individualism

This interdependence, which gives identity a dual character and transforms sovereignty to a shared one, is also reflected in what has always been one of the core values of the EU and a problem-solving mechanism, namely, the notion of solidarity.[32] In the words of the Schuman Declaration, the first political manifesto of the EU: "Europe will not be made all at once, or according to a single plan. It will be built through concrete achievements, which first create a de facto solidarity."[33] What is interesting here is that Robert Schuman did not seem to regard solidarity as a *means* to an end or as a matter to be negotiated.[34] Rather, solidarity is to be considered as a cognitively and consciously outlined, and then decidedly and intentionally materialized, *form of practice*. Habermas is aware of this and goes to great lengths to avoid instrumentalizing solidarity. Not only does he oppose the instrumentalization of solidarity as a means to economic growth as an end.[35] He also stands up to the commodification of solidarity as an exchangeable good that can be bargained and monetarized during the unification process.[36] Yet such an understanding of solidarity seems to demand a different approximation, one that even replaces Habermas's earlier account of solidarity as a moral principle.[37] As Habermas himself admits, he "no longer support[s] the assertion that 'Justice conceived deontologically requires solidarity as its reverse side' "[38] because it depoliticizes solidarity. In contrast, he opts for a concept of solidarity that he calls "*legally constituted civic* solidarity"[39] and that he juxtaposes with forms of solidarity that are derived from prepolitical ethical structures of obligation such as kinship, similarity, or a common identity. Further, this "legally constituted civic solidarity" should not be confused with contractual agreements and their respective obligations. Habermas asserts:

> What differentiates both ethical expectations and appeals to solidarity from law and morality is the peculiar reference to a "joint involvement" in a network of social relations. That involvement grounds both another person's demanding expectations, which may even go beyond what law and morality command, and one's own confidence that the other will behave reciprocally in the future if need be. Whereas "morality" and

"law" refer to the equal freedoms of autonomous individuals, ethical expectations and appeals to solidarity refer to an interest in the integrity of a shared form of life that includes one's own well-being.[40]

What is crucial in this new, nonmoral, noncontractual understanding of solidarity is the notion of "joint involvement" and its conceptual and political ramifications.

What Habermas succeeds in doing when drawing attention to solidarity as joint involvement is to bring to the fore *collectivity* as a constitutive element of the EU. The realization of collectivity does not simply repoliticize the EU. After all, it has always, unambiguously, been a political project, which can only mean a *necessarily collective* project. The EU can and must not continue to be viewed as an individualistic/ nationalistic endeavor. Instead, it must bear witness to its collective structuration through a collectivity of unique contributors. By redesigning the EU from a legalistic compromise to a solidary project, Habermas transforms it from an abstract juridico-political entity to a concrete and experienced, "*shared form of life*."[41]

The philosophical framework of *social ontology* helps us to deepen our understanding of Habermas's conception of solidarity as "joint involvement" precisely because social ontology departs from the assumption that collectivities are the primary actors of social structuration. Apart from underscoring the importance of collectivities for social life, social ontology helps us to enhance and approximate the *nature* and *forms* of solidarity as collective and "joint involvement." For Raimo Tuomela, one of the leading figures of the discipline, social ontology is first and foremost a *hermeneutical* device. He states that "social ontology is not only a study of the basic nature of social reality, but at least in part a study of what the *best-explaining* social scientific theories need to appeal to in their *postulated* ontologies."[42] From this perspective, and if applied to the EU, social ontology invites us to invent a theoretical device that reconceives of the EU as a basically and primordially original collectivity. As such, we no longer need to go through the individual member/national states in order to conceive of the EU. Instead, the social-ontological framework gives us the theoretical means to work on a primary and collective European self-consciousness that does *not* have to be an unavoidable amalgam of national ideologies and identities. Moreover, understanding Habermas's "joint solidarity" from a social-ontological perspective helps us to add two further crucial and interrelated elements to the collective structuration of the EU: *relationality* and *processuality*. Emphasizing both, Brian Epstein argues that "social ontology should not be thought of as the study of 'ontological claims' such as 'social groups exist' or 'there are no social spirits.' Instead, it is the study of *ontological building relations between different kinds of entities*."[43] As I have summarized elsewhere,[44] in lieu of the exhaustive listing of a thing's properties with which we are familiar from classical ontology, social ontology operates on the following twofold basis: First, it sees in its objects not an unchangeable set of qualities and properties but a *dynamic* sum of entities that are fluid and (infinitely) indeterminable because they are the result of the relational interplay of similarly processually constituted objects. Second, it denies the unalterable ahistoricity of ontological entities and views them as *social processes of becoming*. Applied to the EU, both elements have far-reaching consequences. The element of *relationality* means, for instance, that we need to acknowledge that the power that certain national states have both within and without the EU are directly dependent on the fact that those national states are at the same time members of the European construct and thus benefit from not only the prosperity but also the disadvantages of the other member states. The element of *processuality* draws attention to the fact that transformation is on the one hand a necessary outcome of the interactions in which different social agents are engaged and on the other hand the appearance and creation of a new space that is not a mere aggregate of the participating parts.[45]

Despite acknowledging the constitutive role of collectivity in the European edifice, Habermas seems to backpedal, content with the individualist foundations of the legal construction of the EU. As he asserts, "the EU constitution, like all modern legal systems, has a strictly individualistic character, in spite of the fact that one of the two supporting pillars is composed *directly* of collectivities. It rests in the *final analysis* on the subjective rights of the citizens."[46] Habermas is of course aware of this incompatibility, namely, that the fundamentally collectively constituted EU cannot be appropriately represented and captured by an individualistic understanding of democracy and law rooted in the solipsistic epistemology of a metaphysically presupposed sovereign individual. In an attempt to remedy this, he suggests two models:

The first rests on equating the member states with their respective peoples and on replacing the former with the latter. This leads to what Habermas describes as "exercising these two roles [the aforementioned two identities of national and European citizenship] in personal union."[47] By reminding us—evoking Madison—that such debates have always haunted similar complex and multipolar projects, Habermas argues that replacing the member state with its peoples leads to having to grant the European Parliament the same rights as those granted to the European Council. This would ultimately lead to citizens' being able "to form judgements and make political decisions simultaneously and on an equal footing as EU citizens and as members of a particular nation belonging to the EU."[48] In this light, the political actualization of every EU citizen would then take place both in Strasbourg and in Brussels: in Strasbourg through a parliament that represents the citizen in his/her identity as an EU citizen, and in Brussels through his/her heads of government that represent the citizen in his/her particular national identity. Whereas this model (which Habermas has recently called "the doubled sovereign")[49] prevails in Habermas's political thought regarding the EU, a second model seems to be breaking through—one that was precipitated by what Habermas diagnosed as German mismanagement during the last European economic crisis.

This new, second model pertains to the transference of the model of legally constructed civic solidarity not just as a means of solving problems between states but also as a model of communication and therefore as a vector of the integration of national public spheres. As Habermas writes, the citizens of the EU will be able "to participate in a joint process of democratic will-formation reaching across national borders" if—and only if—"the EU citizenry as a whole can share sovereignty effectively with the peoples of the member states."[50] The latter entails that "civic solidarity would have to include the members of each of the other European peoples."[51] Loyal to his model of a public sphere that furthers democracy and realizes emancipation within the national state, Habermas is steadfast in his belief that this model would also prove beneficial with regard to the EU. Taking off from the (optimistic, if not romantic) hypothesis that there are unassailable communicative principles among the EU's state members, Habermas pleads for "European-wide political communication" that, analogously to communication within the limits of the national state, cannot but lead to the creation of a—this time—"European public sphere."[52]

Unfortunately, neither of these models has been able to rectify the fundamental incompatibility, as diagnosed by Habermas, between the factual collective structuration of the EU and the regulative, normative individualism that is inherent to law and that the EU stubbornly insists on upholding as the only vector of integration. And it is a pity that Habermas missed out on this chance to attempt to collectivize the law. Yet, as will be shown right away, the latter is inseparably interwoven within the limits of his own linguistic theory and, more accurately, in his trust in universal pragmatics.

Dead European Man Walking: Habermas's Linguistic Solipsism and the Awakening of European Neonationalisms

Before elaborating on the inherent blind spots of Habermasian linguistics, consider the following two examples, stemming from the time of the last European financial crisis. Take, for instance, German chancellor Angela Merkel's declaration following one of the countless Eurogroup meetings at the beginning of the crisis. In an interview in *Der Spiegel*, Merkel argued, "We [the Germans] can't just show solidarity and say that these countries can just go on as before. . . . Yes, Germany helps, but Germany only helps when the others make an effort. And that must be proven."[53] Put in Habermasian jargon, Merkel's twisted understanding of solidarity as a contractual relationship that generates rights and obligations is not just a contrafactual, idiosyncratic understanding of solidarity furnished with different connotations and historically conditioned individual associations that, out of respect for the dignity of the individual, must be cherished and protected. Rather, it is an ideological manipulation that was callously elaborated to satisfy and promote certain (very concrete) economic and political (national) interests. On a similar note, every time former German finance minister Wolfgang Schäuble rejected a proposition made by his Greek counterpart at the time, Yanis Varoufakis, with the excuse that none of the newly submitted measures was rational, reasonable, sustainable, and/or viable, Schäuble was not simply lacking sincerity, rightness, and truth, to recall some of Habermas's most important validity claims. Schäuble didn't care to persuade his interlocutor, Varoufakis, that he, Schäuble, was "entitled in the given circumstances to claim validity for [his] utterance."[54] Even less did Schäuble intend "to bring about an agreement"[55] that would be " 'binding and bonding' [*bindend*]"[56] for both Germany and Greece. Schäuble was not interested in bringing civic solidarity to fruition, which for Habermas would demand the inclusion of "the members of each of the other European peoples—from the German perspective, for example, the Greeks when they are subjected to internationally imposed and socially unbalanced austerity programmes."[57] Just like his chancellor, Schäuble had in mind the interests of his country and of a certain understanding of the EU, and he was determined to push forward those interests under any cost.[58]

It is at precisely this point that Schäuble forfeits his legitimacy, and Habermas's legal construct of a dual identity reaches its limits. Habermas unmistakably emphasized the constitutive role of collectivity in ethics when he made justice dependent on solidarity in his famous "Justice and Solidarity" (1990). Similarly, he has equally unmistakably recognized and drawn attention to collectivity as a potentially social-ontological mode of the EU's structuration and the European form of life. Yet, by backpedaling regarding the institutionalization of collectivity, by taking refuge in individualistic law, and by Europeanizing the German rendition of legal concepts such as "juridification," Habermas cannot but performatively contradict himself and fall short of his own ambitions. The latter is ironically reminiscent of his critique of Charles S. Peirce. Habermas is of course highly appreciative of Peirce's attempts to foreground "moral norms in communication"[59] in order to supplement the categorical imperative with communication.[60] What Habermas sees in Peirce is the chance to finally put an end to individualist, moral authoritarianism in favor of a rationally and discursively (collectively) achieved consensus.[61] However, Peirce—according to Habermas—remains "monological."[62] And the reason is that Peirce did not realize that communicative action should arise from "symbolic interaction between societal subjects who reciprocally know and recognize each other as *unmistakable* individuals."[63] Unfortunately, Habermas remains equally monological albeit on the political level. His fixation on (solipsistic) linguistic Kantianism prevents him from developing a collective epistemology. Clinging to the individualistic law and putting all his eggs in the basket of power-free consensus are nothing but expressions of such a "political solipsism," as I would like to call it. As Habermas unambiguously puts it, the European public sphere he envisions does not need to be a "new" sphere. On the contrary, the "*existing* national public spheres suffice for this purpose; they only have to open themselves up sufficiently to each other."[64] The performative contradiction, in which Habermas regresses, even when aware of the fundamental role played by solidarity in the European form of life, is herewith complete. "Opening up" national public spheres is not the same and does not result in the restructuring of each European national public sphere so as to *include* every other European people, as the above quote clearly demands.[65] And without a collective epistemology, there is no guarantee that the "Greeks" will not always remain "mistakable" in the eyes and interests of their superior "unmistakables."

This is ultimately my criticism of Habermas's conception of what is to be done concerning the EU. First, Habermasian linguistics does not provide the necessary theoretical tools for a proper critique and debunking of misuses of power within the different European bodies and committees. Second, Habermas's insight into the social-ontological collective structuration of the EU cannot be accommodated by an understanding of law that is not as collective as the structure it seeks to interpret and regulate. And third, confined within the limitations of his (solipsistic) linguistic Kantianism, his political model of a dual identity is helpless when it comes to counteracting the long-established power of the various state nationalisms. Allow me to explain this last point. One might assume that the dual identity model, in which every EU citizen is represented both as a citizen of a national state through his/her head of state in the European Council in Brussels and as an EU citizen through his/her local representative in Parliament in Strasbourg corresponds perfectly with the diagnosed collectivity. Yet this duality is seldom allowed to flourish, for the following two reasons: first, the EU Parliament has no chance of becoming as strong as it needs to be to counter the power of the council. The 2019 European Parliament elections provided bitter proof of the asymmetric power held by the Parliament and the council and was a reminder of the German-French competition that is destroying the EU.[66] Second, the discourse of the national(ist) state continues to prevail over the EU in the following three forms: the first pertains to the current experience of the return of nationalisms that were not dismantled but merely lurking, waiting to spring forth. The second pertains to the particular history of certain European peoples who either never had the chance to have their own national states or, if they did, were soon swallowed up by imperialist politics—such as those of the Soviet Union—and were thus only recently given the opportunity to experiment with their statehood. Third, we are currently witnessing the return of nationalism as an ideologically manipulated and reactionary answer to the failures of the EU.

Even this brief account of the different forms of nationalism currently resurging in the EU suffices to put into doubt Habermas's claim that any further European integration should be done "under the proviso that their nation-states, in their role as future member states, remain *guarantors of the already achieved level of justice and freedom.*"[67] This generalization simply does not apply to all EU member states who viewed joining the EU—even with its democratic deficits—as a chance to overcome their own political pathologies. Admittedly, this resurgence of nationalism is not overlooked by Habermas.[68] As one of the most astute critics of nationalism in his country of origin, Habermas does not hesitate to remind us of the orchestrated effort required to achieve German national unification in the nineteenth century and how "a national consciousness was fostered, indeed produced, by schools, the military, national historiography and the press."[69] Seen in this way, we might ask why Habermas does not also opt for such an apparatus to foster a new and inclusive *European* consciousness. In addition, Habermas seems to take the easy way out when avoiding confronting the question of the reasons for the asymmetry between the Parliament and the council. What Habermas seems to assume is that nationalism is a social phenomenon that can be dealt with both constitutionally, through the strengthening of the law at the level of the European community, and politically/ ideologically, through synthesizing national identity and European identity into a dual identity.[70] In truth, however, the opposite is the case. Nationalism is not a symptom but the very reason why the European Parliament is not—and may never be—granted the same rights as the council.

In this light, it is not solidarity per se that is problematic.[71] Rather, it is Habermas's specific understanding of solidarity, which is inadequate when it comes to freeing the EU and the peoples of Europe from the yoke of state nationalisms. Indeed, we ought to be grateful to Habermas for not abandoning the concept of solidarity as a vector of European integration and for revealing the limits of a certain understanding of solidarity. There is, however, a different form of solidarity that, drawing on the work of the late Jean-Luc Nancy, can be understood as synonymous with freedom and that may prove beneficial to those who seek to relaunch the European project.[72]

Solidarity as Freedom: Jean-Luc Nancy's Concept of Freedom

Bringing together Habermas and Nancy may seem counterintuitive.[73] From their way of writing to the traditions from which they stem, many differences separate the two thinkers. Surprisingly enough, however, Nancy and Habermas have more in common than one might assume. First, Nancy's recent passing deprived the world of one of the last remaining broadly accepted and above-party public intellectuals. Further, both Habermas and Nancy are postmetaphysical thinkers who are trying to amend the pathologies of Western universalist, monadological, and excluding/exclusive thinking by bringing forward collective practices that value inclusion and openness. It is therefore no wonder that communication, community, solidarity, and freedom are concepts that permeate the work of both thinkers. With respect to the process of European unification, Nancy is as categorical as Habermas regarding the nonexistence of a European identity. Moreover, both Habermas and Nancy take the view that the question of a European identity entails (and must tackle) matters of supranationalism. As Nancy states, it is "no accident that Europe cannot locate a political identity: Europe has no sense or Idea of itself. The question of 'global governance' shows clearly that politics gives out (*se dérobe*) wherever everything must pass through the pure management of forces, while at the same time there is nothing to give any meaning to the 'international.' "[74] Finally, and most importantly, both Habermas and Nancy take the collective foundations of European forms of life as a point of departure. Just as Habermas stresses the collective foundations of the EU, Nancy declares that "we come together (in)to the world."[75] In addition, just as Habermas traces back the EU's inability to reconcile collectivity with the individualistic character of the law, Nancy sees in the "constant diversion" of collectivity, as he writes, not just the pathology of individualist understandings of law but "the permanent rule of Western thought (of philosophy)."[76] Ultimately, just as Habermas ventures to detach solidarity from morality, Nancy—following Stella Gaon's reading[77]—revisits solidarity as a *social-ontological* form of being in common that is (*pace* Heidegger) neither purely ontological nor (*pace* Derrida) exclusively ethical.[78]

Turning to what is at stake here, namely the future of the European project, the differences between Habermas and Nancy with respect to the EU have to do with how they understand community. The latter is in turn related to how they substantiate communication. The crucial role that both Habermas and Nancy attach to communication notwithstanding, precisely how they understand that role could not be more different. Whereas for Habermas communication is a matter of expression destined to reach consensual understanding, for Nancy it is a matter of creating something that, while it upholds the communicating parts through what is being communicated, at the same time leads to the creation of something new. In this light, the notions of community, communication, and the subject are not to be thought of as separate from one another or as depicting different instants.[79] Rather, community, communication, and the subject are supposed to be regarded as constructing a co-original collective event. Communication does not merely connect, nor does it simply convey meaning. On the contrary, through this sharing a being is induced that from the very beginning recognizes itself as a being in common because it has been brought forth through sharing. In this light, what is being communicated is technically not something that is already owned and given away. Rather, a new space is opened between the parts that communicate, a space that contains and includes those parts and only apparently gives the impression that this space is the result of the communication of the two parts. As Nancy puts it, "if being is sharing, our sharing, then 'to be' is to share."[80] Thereby, however, Nancy does not just launch yet another sterile and fruitless critique of "any remnant of substantive metaphysics."[81] Rather, Nancy supplements the solipsistic individual of Western metaphysics with an understanding of subjectivity at the core of which lies the subject as a "sharing of singularity."[82] In this light, the subject does not merely become collective to the extent that it becomes aware of itself as possessing a plural core. In addition, the subject realizes that it can exist only in relation to another subject. As Howard Caygill reframes Nancy's core idea, "Freedom . . . is relation and relation is freedom."[83]

This conception of being has repercussions for our understanding of Nancy's—radically different—concept of communication. There is no being prior to communication, and communication does not express a being. Communication neither discloses nor conveys part of a preexisting being by bringing it closer to another equally preexisting being. Rather, communication is a productive process, a mode of subjectivation that brings the being forward. Moreover, and given the fact that communication, as indicated above, is this space that includes the being and its interlocutors, the being that communication brings forward is a being that incorporates its interlocutors. Communication serves, in this regard, as a mode of production of more than one being, where beings are originally collective to the extent that the origination of one being results in the co-origination of another. Seen this way, Nancy's theory of community, against the predominant antisubjectivism of most of the theories of postwar French poststructuralist philosophy, effectively furnishes a type of subjectivity. Unlike his contemporaries, who reject the idea of a subject, Nancy underpins the idea of a subject that is a *"sharing in the guise of assembling."*[84] From this perspective, Nancy offers a middle way between idealist understandings of a monosemantic, one-dimensional, and integral subjectivity and a poststructuralist understanding of a subjectivity that is utterly lacking an identity. Acknowledging the problematic of a subject that—as Butler (1997)[85] has plausibly argued—may not have forfeited its individual agency but has definitely forfeited reasons to act *collectively*, Nancy argues in favor of a subjectivity that is *originally collective*. At the same time, this collectivity is not a metaphysically legitimated ontological derivation. Rather, it is the result of socially embedded historical processes.

Revisiting communication as a sharing that leads to the appearance of the subject as a collective being—or a *compearance*, as Nancy calls it in this neologism—also changes the way in which the subject (re) enacts communication. It no longer suffices to treat communication as the expression of an invidual(ist) subject. Rather, Nancy's linguistic turn departs from Aristotle's notion of *pollakôs legomenon*, which undergoes a radical reappropriation in Nancy's philosophy. This notion becomes the mode of emergence of a subject that has to be (re)told over and over, again and again, just as it has to be seen from more than one perspective and in more than one way in order to be grasped in its entirety. Just like Adorno's understanding of philosophy as a riddle,[86] Nancy's reappropriation of the subject as a being in common allows us to think of a being that "is said in many ways," whose singularity "is its plural" and does not "begin from a presumed, single core of meaning." Rather, "the multiplicity of the said (that is, of the sayings)" results in the subject as a collective being which is the "totality of being [*l'étant en totalité*]"[87] because it includes and encompasses all modes of subjectivity production.

This third, mediating way of regarding subjectivity is related to a different conception of how to realize freedom. Freedom is henceforth not reduced negatively to what one "is able to do or be, without interference by other persons,"[88] nor does it aspire, positively, to find out how one can be one's own master.[89] Furthermore, Nancy's freedom does not designate the normative necessity of a needy (*bedürftig*) subject that must "strive for such forms of being together" if it wants to realize itself in "the complete absence of coercion."[90] Rather, Nancy's understanding of freedom describes the experience of a subject that, through its appearance, brings forth every other subject that has contributed to the creation of the space the subject occupies.[91]

It is in this light that we can better understand why community, for Nancy, does not need to depend on a concrete and determined identity. This also explains why community, like the European Community, is not the contemporary answer to a past event. "Europe" is not a political project that draws its legitimacy from the fact that it materializes, in a pragmatic, postteleological way, the goal of (Kantian) permanent peace as conditioned by the Shoah or the atrocities of the Second World War.[92] Instead, for Nancy, there have always been different, multiple "Europes" that created what we now designate as Europe or European history. For Habermas, and according to his model of communication, the EU cannot but depend on the national states. The latter results—undoubtedly even against Habermas's own intentions—in a European identity as a mere subpart of a national identity since what unravels between two individuals who communicate is to be traced back to the sovereign individuals. From this perspective, while consensus was drafted as a procedure that guarantees that the communicating individuals merge but not dissolve into one another, it ended up being a mechanism that facilitated the perpetuation of power structures. By placing his confidence exclusively in the law, which, as individualistic, does not correspond to the collective structuration of the EU, and by being blind to the nationalisms that remain prevalent within the member states, Habermas undermined the solidarity that he correctly diagnosed as an answer to the structural (and not just conjunctural) problems of the EU. Nancy, on the contrary, sees in communication the creation of a new space that, while framed by the communicating individuals, is a third, distinctive, co-original space that incorporates and sustains its communicating parts without being absorbed or determined exclusively through them. Seen this way, Nancy's freedom results in an excess that permeates the communicating parts only to surpass them. As Stella Gaon puts it, Nancy "opens 'us' (as) (arche-) community to 'our' possible futures."[93]

Herein lies the greatest difference between Habermas's and Nancy's projects regarding the EU. Whereas Habermas is concerned with the member states' pasts, Nancy looks forward to their common and collective future. The translation of Habermas's collective structuration of the EU as resulting in a "dual identity" at the level of individual citizenship and a "doubled sovereign" at the level of political legitimation will always be afflicted by his underestimation of the resurging nationalist tendencies that prevent European identity from achieving the same status as the older and more thoroughly constructed national identities. As long as national identity is not included in European identity, the former will always devour the latter.

As already mentioned, though, there is also a problem of translatability lurking in the models of a "dual identity" and a "double sovereign." The latter has to do with the question whether conceptualizations such as "doubleness," "duality," and "splitness," as Habermas explicates the notions of "dual identity" and "double sovereign" elsewhere,[94] can articulate appropriately at the political level the collectivity that Habermas diagnoses as providing the historical basis of the European project. The quality of doubleness that Habermas views as describing political sovereignty at the European level presupposes that an original is being reproduced such that, in the end, two samples of the same original exist. Yet, as Habermas very well both knows and writes, it is wishful thinking to suppose that the Parliament and the council could ever end up having the same political authority. This discrepancy becomes overt when we talk about sovereignty as split sovereignty. Sovereignty is difficult to split into pieces that can be partially possessed by more than one party. Sovereignty can be shared by more than one party, but it cannot be divided into parts and then distributed. The notion of duality that Habermas uses with regard to identity is definitely more suitable than the other two notions. Yet what gets reinstated through the concept of dual identity is the prevalence of national identity over European identity. Instead of giving birth to a collective identity where the subject is a citizen of both a national state *and* the EU, Habermas's dual identity leads to the subordination of European identity to national identity, which remains primary. In this light, these two identities do not inform each other mutually and retrospectively. They do not become collective since they neither bind nor bond. By assuming that these two identities do not struggle to subjugate each other but are mutually oriented toward consensus achieved through a legal framework, Habermas does not provide a synthetic understanding that can foster both identities. In this light, the concept of a "legally constituted civic solidarity" together with its political expressions, that of a "dual identity" and a "double sovereign," end up functioning as the Trojan horse of the various European nationalisms where European identity is allowed to exist only in order to benefit national identity, and only so long as it does so.

It is from this perspective that we must rethink the notion of free-dom if we want to give rise to a collective identity free from the yoke of nationalism(s) and within which Nancy's understanding of freedom manifests itself as both timely and appropriate. If solidarity is supposed to be the political practice corresponding to the collective structuration of the EU, as Habermas correctly diagnosed and proposed, then solidarity must aim to create a European identity free from national identities. Instead of making European identity a partial identity of the individual and thus rendering it vulnerable and prone to appropriation by the more dominant national identity, the different national identities must be regarded as part of an overarching European identity. Therefore, European identity is not what individuals with different national identities share or a common place where they meet. Rather, European identity is the *genos*, and national identity is the *eidos*. The former is a set—understood mathematically—that includes national identities as subsets and not the intersection of national identities. Last but not least, European identity is a collective identity that contains national identities and functions as a mediator, conduit, and filter through which all communication between national identities must flow. Seen this way, national identities do not forfeit their original singularity. However, seen through the lens of Nancy's understanding of freedom as the creation of an intermediate space, European identity must be recreated as a collec-tive (i.e., a *holistic* and *inclusive*) third that consists of national identities that get triangulating by being forced to relate and be informed from one another. Only in this way can European identity be freed from nationalisms while maintaining the singular, unique histories of the different identities of the peoples of Europe. In this light, European identity is transformed into a solidary project that frees the European identity to such an extent that, while composed of singular national identities, it nonetheless comes to possess a collective character that is genuinely its own. Ultimately, this is the only way to ensure that national states will work in solidarity with one another without allowing the nationalist tendencies within them to take the upper hand.

Notes

1. Hess, *Philosophische und sozialistische Schriften, 1837–1850*, 108.
2. During the 2017 French presidential elections, Jean-Luc Mélenchon boasted that, if he were to find himself in a similar position, he would never

allow himself to be extorted and succumb, like former Greek prime minister Alexis Tsipras, to the demands of his opponents. It is true that he likely would not, but the reason for this is less heroic than Mélenchon claims and is disenchanting in its cynical simplicity: while you can fire the prime minister of Greece (George Papandreou) or, for that matter, the almighty (albeit corrupt) prime minister of Italy (Silvio Berlusconi) and replace them with puppet-like technocrats (Lucas Papademos and Mario Monti, respectively), you cannot fire the president of the French Republic.

3. Bloch, *Zur Ontologie des Noch-Nicht-Seins*.

4. Mallet, *La Démocratie à Venir. Autour de Jacques Derrida*; Derrida, *Rogues*.

5. See Latour, *We Have Never Been Modern*.

6. EC Commission, "A People's Europe: Communication from the Commission to the European Parliament." For a short, informative account of the genealogy of the phrase *the people's Europe* published shortly after its establishment and thus depicting the aspirations that were associated with it, cf. Shore, "Inventing the 'People's Europe.'"

7. I would like to thank Georgios Tsagdis for drawing my attention to Plato's notion of the noble lie. Similarly, I owe the description of the EU as an inescapable double bind to discussions with Rozemund Uljée.

8. Kearney, *Dialogues with Contemporary Continental Thinkers*, 120.

9. Habermas, *The Lure of Technocracy*, 37.

10. See Habermas, *Truth and Justification*, 7.

11. See Whitebook, "The Problem of Nature in Habermas."

12. Joerges, "Europe's Economic Constitution in Crisis and the Emergence of a New Constitutional Constellation."

13. Habermas, *The Lure of Technocracy*, 40.

14. See Lacoue-Labarthe and Nancy, *Retreating the Political*.

15. Bailey, "Democracy as Ideal and Practice: Historicizing the Crisis of the European Union"; Bohman, *Democracy across Borders: From Demos to Demoi*.

16. Loick, "Juridification," 208.

17. Habermas, *The Theory of Communicative Action*, 1: 356–60.

18. Habermas, 361.

19. Habermas, 362. In regard to this point, Habermas remains within Kirchheimer's original understanding of juridification.

20. Except for Loick's "Juridification," see also Blichner and Molander, "What Is Juridification?" and Papendorf, "Juridification, Marginalised Persons and Competence to Mobilise the Law."

21. Papendorf, "Juridification, Marginalised Persons and Competence to Mobilise the Law," 297–98; emphasis added.

22. Habermas, *Between Facts and Norms*, 411.

23. Habermas, 411.

24. Habermas, 411.

25. Habermas, 411.

26. Joerges, "Europe's Economic Constitution in Crisis and the Emergence of a New Constitutional Constellation," 1022.

27. See Habermas, "Remarks on Dieter Grimm's 'Does Europe Need a Constitution?'"; Habermas, "Demokratie oder Kapitalismus? Vom Elend der nationalstaatlichen Fragmentierung in einer kapitalistisch integrierten Weltgesellschaft"; Habermas, "Democracy in Europe: Why the Development of the EU into a Transnational Democracy Is Necessary and How It Is Possible."

28. Habermas, *The Lure of Technocracy*, 10.

29. Habermas, 10.

30. Habermas, 10.

31. Habermas, *The Crisis of the European Union*, 35.

32. See the revised article 2 of the Treaty on EU: "The Union is founded on the values of respect for human dignity, freedom, democracy, equality, the rule of law and respect for human rights, including the rights of persons belonging to minorities. These values are common to the Member States in a society in which pluralism, non-discrimination, tolerance, justice, solidarity and equality between women and men prevail."

33. See Biondi et al., *Solidarity in EU Law*, 2. Additionally, for a thorough discussion of the notion of solidarity as both a philosophical and a legal foundation for the EU, see also Ciornei and Ross, "Solidarity in Europe: From Crisis to Policy?"

34. This is why I cannot adhere to Andrea Sangiovanni's understanding of European solidarity. Sangiovanni argues that European solidarity should be thought of as creating a space where it is "our relation as participants in the maintenance and reproduction of such public goods (rather than our relations as subjects of coercion, bearers of an identity, or democratic citizens) that triggers stronger social justice norms, which are in turn interpreted as demands of reciprocity." Sangiovanni, "Solidarity in the European Union: Problems and Prospects," 410. What is crucial here is that it is not enough to address the public character of certain goods. Rather, the term *European* must be added to—if not replace—the term *public* in order to save public goods from being appropriated by member state nationalisms and then propagated as a national win over Brussels or other member states. Sangiovanni reworked his theory of solidarity so as to connote a joint action. The punchline of the argument is now that solidarity is performative, meaning that solidarity is grounded "in our joint action as authors of *political and social institutions*, rather than in a collective identity grounded in a nation. What matters is what we together *do*, rather than what we happen to *be*, or what we have *experienced*." Sangiovanni, "Solidarity in the European Union: Problems and Prospects," 356. Nevertheless, I find it problematic that Sangiovanni sees a certain teleological necessity in the solidarity involved in sharing and overcoming adversity. Further, I am not

sure what makes the intersubjective reciprocity that Sangiovanni stresses equate to solidarity. The most important element of solidarity as social ontology is its necessity, that is, the fact that solidarity as a collective action is the only thinkable action since it corresponds to the collective structuration of the EU. For a positive recent reading of Sangiovanni that regards solidarity as "the sharing of goals and resources to prevent or redress situations of economic, social, political or environmental adversity," see Ciornei and Ross, "Solidarity in Europe: From Crisis to Policy?," 210.

35. See Enderlein, "Solidarität in der Europäischen Union—Die ökonomische Perspektive."

36. See Schieder, "Zwischen Führungsanspruch und Wirklichkeit: Deutschlands Rolle in der Eurozone"; Offe, *Europe Entrapped*.

37. On Habermas's novel understanding of solidarity, see Carrabregu, "Habermas on Solidarity: An Immanent Critique" and Tava, "Justice, Emotions, and Solidarity." As will be shown, however, I do not think—in contrast to Carrabregu—that the new understanding of solidarity that Habermas brings forward can be accommodated by his earlier, purely moral understanding of solidarity.

38. Habermas, *The Lure of Technocracy*, 157–58, note 23; cf. Habermas, "Justice and Solidarity: On the Discussion Concerning Stage 6."

39. Habermas, *The Lure of Technocracy*, 37.

40. Habermas, 23.

41. Habermas, 23, my emphasis.

42. Tuomela, *Social Ontology*, ix, emphasis added.

43. Epstein, "Framework for Social Ontology," 149.

44. Telios, "Solidarity as Necessity: Subject, Structure, Practices," 36.

45. While I think I am right to argue that Habermas's understanding of the EU's collective structuration is social-ontological in nature, I am not sure whether it can also qualify as a *critical* social ontology. As Reha Kadakal defines the task of a critical social ontology, "Social theory as critical ontology grasps social reality not simply in terms of a positivist notion of 'facts,' but rather in terms of its very processes of becoming, and it attempts to comprehend these processes through questions that are simultaneously theoretical and normative." Kadakal, "Toward a Critical Ontology of the Social," 167. Unfortunately, I cannot delve deeper into this debate here. For primary references, though, see Testa, "Ontology of the False State"; Renault, "Critical Theory and Processual Social Ontology"; Thompson, "Collective Intentionality, Social Domination, and Reification"; and Telios, "Why Still Reification? Towards a Critical Social Ontology."

46. Habermas, *The Crisis of the European Union*, 35.

47. Habermas, 37.

48. Habermas, 37.

49. Habermas, *The Lure of Technocracy*, 40.

50. Habermas, *The Crisis of the European Union*, 45–46.

51. Habermas, 45–46.

52. Habermas, *The Lure of Technocracy*, 39.

53. Gathmann and Medick, "Merkel Blasts Greece over Retirement Age, Vacation."

54. Habermas, *On the Pragmatics of Communication*, 297.

55. Habermas, 298.

56. Fultner, "Formal/Universal Pragmatics," 136.

57. Habermas, *The Crisis of the European Union*, 46. I am confident that Habermas would profit enormously from Sally Scholz's categorization of solidarity in social, civic, and political terms. While both operate with a concept of civic solidarity that in Scholz's account pertains broadly to (1) the relationships between citizens within a state, (2) the obligations of the state towards its citizens, and, last but not least, (3) the obligations of each citizen to his/her co-citizens by virtue of their sharing the same political membership (see Scholz, *Political Solidarity*, 27), I think that Scholz's notion of political solidarity could be the goal toward which Habermas's legally constituted civic solidarity is heading. As Scholz describes her account of political solidarity: "Instead of basing solidarity on varying notions of dependence and group control, the political conception of solidarity highlights individual conscience, commitment, group responsibility, and collective action. Political solidarity arises in response to a situation of injustice or oppression. Individuals make a conscious commitment to join with others in struggle to challenge a perceived injustice. The unity is based on shared commitments to a cause." Scholz, *Political Solidarity*, 33–34. Nationalism and nationalist power structures would then be the situation of injustice or oppression the overthrowing of which is the joint cause to which national states are committed. In his "European Solidarity: Definitions, challenges, and perspectives" (214), Francesco Tava purports a similar reading of Habermas and reminds us of Habermas's concept of an "offensive solidarity" (Habermas, "Democracy, Solidarity, and the European Crisis.") that is oriented towards the future.

58. On the inherently antisolidary character of the European Stability Mechanism (ESM) and how a Habermasian perspective could help rectify it, see Alessandro Volpe and Francesco Tava's recent "Multilevel European Solidarity: From People to Institutions (and Back)" as well as Volpe's "Jürgen Habermas on European Solidarity."

59. Habermas, *Moral Consciousness and Communicative Action*, 195.

60. See Habermas, *Truth and Justification*.

61. See Habermas, *Postmetaphysical Thinking: Philosophical Essays*, 104. It is worth pointing out that, within Habermas's philosophy of discourse, *consensus* has always served as a "touchstone for truth, practical reasoning, political legitimation, and undistorted, ideologically unconstrained communication and understanding." Ingram, "Consensus," 61.

62. Habermas, *Truth and Justification*, 7.

63. Habermas, *Knowledge and Human Interests*, 137, emphasis added.

64. Habermas, *The Lure of Technocracy*, 39, emphasis added. To a certain extent, it could be argued that Habermas is continuing a process that Immanuel Kant initiated in his third Critique. What Kant calls a "broadened way of thinking" (Kant, *Critique of Judgment*, 161) when describing the way in which thinking needs to reorient itself is what I call "collective" since in order to be broadened thinking must leave its original locus, which is the individual, and embrace, engulf, and appropriate the other. This same broadening is transferred by Habermas into the sphere of ethics as well. No matter whether this collectivization is—starting with Kant—political (if not even radical-democratic; see Arendt, *Lectures on Kant's Political Philosophy*), Habermas also collectivizes the sphere of ethics. If my argument that Habermas's monism debilitates his diagnosis of the collective foundations of the EU is correct, then it could be argued that Habermas does not simply fall behind Kant's third Critique, which, as just noted, introduces collectivity into the sphere of aesthetics. Taking into consideration Axel Honneth's older argument that even Kant's first Critique is intersubjective since the subject's knowledge depends for its certainty on being sanctioned and confirmed by the concrete social other (see Honneth, "The other of justice"), it could be argued that Habermas's monism even renders him precritical.

65. See Habermas, *The Crisis of the European Union*, 46.

66. With regard to the 2019 elections, we can all agree that it is a good thing that someone like Manfred Weber was not elected president of the European Commission. However, it was an affront to the peoples of Europe (who for the first time voted according to the—German of course—model of the *Spitzenkandidat*) that, due to the pertinacious resistance of French President Emanuel Macron (an idol of Habermas's), it was not the candidate of the party who won the most seats who was selected as president of the EC but Ursula von der Leyen, an embarrassing compromise between German hegemonic greed and unsatisfied French hysteria.

67. Habermas, *The Lure of Technocracy*, 40.

68. See Habermas, "Moralischer Universalismus in Zeiten politischer Regression."

69. Habermas, *The Lure of Technocracy*, 39.

70. Habermas attributes an equally idyllic role to the media during this process. As he writes, they "must learn also to report on the discussions being conducted in the other countries on the issues of common concern to all citizens of the Union." Habermas, *The Lure of Technocracy*, 39. It would be interesting to see how Habermas intends to educate media outlets like the German FAZ, which took pleasure in cannibalizing the whole of the European South when publishing and defending an interview in which none other than the then

leader of the Eurogroup Jeroen Dijsselbloem stated that "during the crisis of the euro, the countries of the North have shown solidarity with the countries affected by the crisis. As a Social Democrat, I attribute exceptional importance to solidarity. [But] you also have obligations. You cannot spend all the money on drinks and women and then ask for help." Financial Times reprint; see https://www.ft.com/content/2498740e-b911-3dbf-942d-ecce511a351e. The latter does not merely raise, once again, the aforementioned issue of the abuse of the notion of solidarity and its legitimization as contrafactual, nor is it yet another indication of the demise of (European) social democracy. In addition, it raises a further theoretical issue that pertains to the education and steering of the private and/or public media in favor of the EU or the other member states, especially from the perspective of Habermas's previous statements regarding the entanglement of media and politics, for instance, in Italy (see Habermas, "Political Communication in Media Society: Does Democracy Still Enjoy an Epistemic Dimension? The Impact of Normative Theory on Empirical Research," 421–21). Roberto Esposito is adamant concerning the necessity of a Europeanization of media. As he puts it: "As Habermas and others have argued, a constitution can only be the expression of the free choice of a sovereign people. Of course, the fact that there is currently no European people does not prevent it from being gradually "built" by the formation of a conscious public opinion. But this, in turn, presupposes the presence of European media and, before that, a common language—two elements that are currently lacking." Esposito, "Europe and Philosophy," 22.

71. In this regard, namely that solidarity is not dead, see—*contra* Habermas—Christian Lahusen's edited *Citizens' Solidarity in Europe. Civic Engagement and Public Discourse in Times of Crises*, 26.

72. In what follows, I explore Nancy's understanding of freedom in the context of the EU from a political and social-philosophical perspective. For a very helpful legal perspective on Nancy's concept of freedom, cf. Lindroos-Hovinheimo, "There Is No Europe—On Subjectivity and Community in the EU."

73. On Habermas and Nancy, also see James A. Chamberlain's "Motivating Cosmopolitanism: Jürgen Habermas, Jean-Luc Nancy, and the Case for Cosmocommonism" who shares a similar evaluation regarding the commonalities between Habermas and Nancy. On Habermas's concept of civil solidarity and its interesting eclectic affinities with another leading author within the French postwar tradition, namely, Jacques Rancière, see Matthias Flatscher and Sergej Seitz's "Of Citizens and Plebeians. Postnational Political Figures in Jürgen Habermas and Jacques Rancière."

74. Armstrong et al., "Politics and Beyond: An Interview with Jean-Luc Nancy," 99.

75. Nancy, "La Comparution/The Compearance," 373.

76. Nancy, 374.

77. See Gaon, "Communities in Question."

78. There is yet another very important similarity that unfortunately cannot be addressed here. This concerns the fact that both Nancy and Habermas operate in their—distinctive as they may be—philosophies with a concept of co-originality. For Habermas, co-originality is a key concept that designates the structurally simultaneous appearance of, for example, rights and democracy, the public and the private sphere or autonomy, individual rights and public sovereignty, and, last but not least, human dignity. For Nancy, co-originality also designates the structurally simultaneous appearance of the subject with/and/through/as the other. In Nancy's words: "Being is not without Being, which is not another miserable tautology as long as one understands it in the cooriginary mode of being-with-being-itself." Nancy, *Being Singular Plural*, 38.

79. See Nancy, *The Inoperative Community*.

80. Nancy, *The Experience of Freedom*, 72.

81. Caygill, "The Shared World," 26.

82. Nancy, *The Experience of Freedom*, 68.

83. Caygill, "The Shared World," 26.

84. Nancy, *Being Singular Plural*, 30, emphasis added.

85. Butler, *The Psychic Life of Power*.

86. See Adorno, "The Actuality of Philosophy."

87. All references in Nancy, *Being Singular Plural*, 38.

88. Berlin, *Four Essays on Liberty*, 169.

89. Berlin, 178.

90. Honneth, "Three, Not Two, Concepts of Liberty," 192.

91. At this point, Nancy brings together Axel Honneth's theory of social freedom and Karl Marx's understanding of a subject that, even in its "individual existence," is "at the same time a social being" (Marx, *Economic and Philosophic Manuscripts of 1844 and the Communist Manifesto*, 102, in the original German: *in seinem individuellsten Dasein zugleich Gemeinwesen*). For more on this topic, cf. Telios, *Das Subjekt als Gemeinwesen*.

92. The most elaborated concept of solidarity developed as a reaction to the two world wars, and the experience of totalitarianism is likely Jan Patočka's concept of the "solidarity of the shaken" ("solidarité des ébranlés"; cf. Patočka, *Heretical Essays in the Philosophy of History*).

93. Gaon, "Communities in Question," 401.

94. Habermas, *The Lure of Technocracy*, 163, note 14.

Bibliography

Adorno, Theodor W. "The Actuality of Philosophy." *Telos* 31 (1977): 120–33.
Arendt, Hannah. *Lectures on Kant's Political Philosophy*. Edited by Ronald Beiner. Chicago: University of Chicago Press, 1992.

Armstrong, Philip, Jason E. Smith, and Jean-Luc Nancy. "Politics and Beyond: An Interview with Jean-Luc Nancy." *Diacritics* 43, no. 4 (2015): 90–108.

Bailey, Christian. "Democracy as Ideal and Practice: Historicizing the Crisis of the European Union." In *Jürgen Habermas and the European Economic Crisis. Cosmopolitanism Reconsidered*, edited by Gaspare M. Genna, Thomas O. Haakenson, and Ian W. Wilson, 13–37. London and New York: Routledge, 2016.

Berlin, Isaiah. *Four Essays on Liberty.* London: Oxford University Press, 1969.

Biondi, Andrea, Egle Dagilyte and Esin Kucuk, eds. *Solidarity in EU Law. Legal Principle in the Making.* Cheltenham: Edward Elgar, 2018.

Blichner, Lars & Anders Molander. "What Is Juridification?" *ARENA*, ARENA Working Papers, 2005.

Bloch, Ernst. *Philosophische Grundfragen. 1. Zur Ontologie des Noch-Nicht-Seins.* Frankfurt am Main: Suhrkamp, 1961.

Bohman, James. *Democracy across Borders: From Demos to Demoi.* Cambridge: MIT Press, 2008.

Butler Judith. *The Psychic Life of Power: Theories in Subjection.* Stanford: Stanford University Press, 1997.

Carrabregu, Gent. "Habermas on Solidarity: An Immanent Critique." *Constellations* 23, no. 4 (2016): 507–22.

Caygill, Howard. "The Shared World: Philosophy, Violence, Freedom." In *On Jean-Luc Nancy: The Sense of Philosophy*, edited by Darren Sheppard, Simon Sparks, and Colin Thomas, 19–31. New York and London: Routledge, 1997.

Chamberlain, James A. "Motivating Cosmopolitanism: Jürgen Habermas, Jean-Luc Nancy, and the Case for Cosmocommonism." *Contemporary Political Theory* 19 (2020): 105–126.

Ciornei, Irina and Malcolm Ross. "Solidarity in Europe: From Crisis to Policy?" *Acta Politica* 56, no. 3 (2021): 209–19.

Commission of the EC. 1988. A People's Europe: Communication from the Commission to the European Parliament. COM (88) 331/final. Luxembourg: Bulletin of the EC, Supplement No. 2.

Derrida, Jacques. *Rogues: Two Essays on Reason.* Translated by Pascal-Anne Brault and Michael Naas. Stanford: Stanford University Press, 2005.

Enderlein, Henrik. "Solidarität in der Europäischen Union—Die ökonomische Perspektive." In *Europäische Solidarität und nationale Identität*, edited by Christian Callies, 83–98. Tübingen: Mohr Siebeck, 2013.

Epstein, Brian. "Framework for Social Ontology." *Philosophy of the Social Sciences* 46, no. 2 (2016): 147–67.

Esposito, Roberto. "Europe and Philosophy." In *The Routledge Handbook of Philosophy of Europe*, edited by Darian Meacham and Nicolas de Warren, 19–29. London: Routledge 2021.

Flatscher, Matthias and Sergej Seitz. "Of Citizens and Plebeians. Postnational Political Figures in Jürgen Habermas and Jacques Rancière." *European Law Journal* 25, no. 5 (2019): 502–507.

Fultner, Barbara. "Formal/Universal Pragmatics." In *The Cambridge Habermas Lexicon*, edited by Amy Allen and Eduardo Mendieta, 136–41. Cambridge: Cambridge University Press, 2019.

Gaon, Stella. "Communities in Question: Sociality and Solidarity in Nancy and Blanchot." *Journal for Cultural Research* 9, no. 4 (2005): 387–403.

Gathmann Florian, and Veit Medick, "Merkel Blasts Greece over Retirement Age, Vacation,"*Der Spiegel*, May 18, 2011, https://www.spiegel.de/international/europe/german-chancellor-on-the-offensive-merkel-blasts-greece-over-retirement-age-vacation-a-763294.html

Grimm, Dieter. "Does Europe Need a Constitution?" *European Law Journal* 1, no. 1 (1995): 282–302.

Habermas, Jürgen."Moralischer Universalismus in Zeiten politischer Regression. Jürgen Habermas im Gespräch über die Gegenwart und sein Lebenswerk." *Leviathan* 48, no. 1 (2020): 7–28.

Habermas, Jürgen. *The Lure of Technocracy*. Translated by C. Cronin. Cambridge: Polity, 2015.

Habermas, Jürgen. "Democracy in Europe: Why the Development of the EU into a Transnational Democracy Is Necessary and How It Is Possible." *European Law Journal* 21, no. 4 (2015): 546–57.

Habermas, Jürgen. "Democracy, Solidarity, and the European Crisis." Lecture delivered on 26 April 2013 at KU Leuven, Belgium. Text available on KU Leuven Euroforum.

Habermas, Jürgen. *The Crisis of the European Union: A Response*. Translated by C. Cronin. Cambridge: Polity, 2012.

Habermas, Jürgen. "Demokratie oder Kapitalismus? Vom Elend der nationalstaatlichen Fragmentierung in einer kapitalistisch integrierten Weltgesellschaft." *Blätter für deutsche und internationale Politik* 31, no. 5 (2013): 59–70.

Habermas, Jürgen. "Political Communication in Media Society: Does Democracy Still Enjoy an Epistemic Dimension? The Impact of Normative Theory on Empirical Research." *Communication Theory* 16 (2006): 411–26.

Habermas, Jürgen. *Truth and Justification*. Translated by B. Fultner. Cambridge: MIT Press, 2003.

Habermas, Jürgen. *Between Facts and Norms: Contributions to a Discourse Theory of Law and Democracy*. Translated by W. Rehg, Cambridge: MIT Press, 1998.

Habermas, Jürgen. *On the Pragmatics of Communication*, edited by M. Cooke. Cambridge: MIT Press, 1998.

Habermas, Jürgen. "Remarks on Dieter Grimm's 'Does Europe Need a Constitution?'" *European Law Journal* 1, no. 1 (1995): 303–7.

Habermas, Jürgen. *Postmetaphysical Thinking: Philosophical Essays*. Translated by W. Hohengarten. Cambridge: MIT Press, 1992.

Habermas, Jürgen. "Justice and Solidarity: On the Discussion Concerning Stage 6." In *The Moral Domain: Essays in the Ongoing Discussion between Philosophy and the Social Sciences*, edited by Thomas E. Wren, 224–50. Cambridge: MIT Press, 1990.

Habermas, Jürgen. *Moral Consciousness and Communicative Action*. Translated by C. Lenhardt and S. Weber Nicholsen. Cambridge: MIT Press, 1990.

Habermas, Jürgen. *The Theory of Communicative Action*, 2 volumes. Translated by Thomas McCarthy. Boston: Beacon, 1984/1987.

Habermas, Jürgen. *Knowledge and Human Interests*. Translated by James Shapiro. Boston: Beacon. 1971.

Hess, Moses. *Philosophische und sozialistische Schriften, 1837–1850*, edited by Auguste Cornu and Wolfgang Mönke. Berlin: Akademie Verlag, 1961.

Honneth, Axel. "The Other of Justice: Habermas and the Ethical Challenge of Postmodernism." In *The Cambridge Companion to Habermas*, edited by Stephen K. White, 289–324. Cambridge: Cambridge University Press, 1995.

Honneth, Axel. "Three, Not Two, Concepts of Liberty: A Proposal to Enlarge Our Moral Self-Understanding." In *Hegel on Philosophy in History*, edited by Rachel Zuckert and James Kreines, 177–92. Cambridge: Cambridge University Press, 2017.

Ingram, David: "Consensus" In *The Cambridge Habermas Lexicon*, edited by Amy Allen and Eduardo Mendieta, 60–63. Cambridge: Cambridge University Press, 2019.

Joerges, Christian. "Europe's Economic Constitution in Crisis and the Emergence of a New Constitutional Constellation." *German Law Journal* 15, no. 5 (2014): 985–1027.

Kadakal, Reha. "Toward a Critical Ontology of the Social: Hegel, Lukács, and the Challenge of Mediation." *Globalization, Critique and Social Theory: Diagnoses and Challenges* 33 (2015): 165–88.

Kant, Immanuel. *Critique of Judgment*. Translated, with an introduction, by Werner S. Pluhar. Indianapolis and Cambridge: Hackett, 1987.

Kearney, Richard. *Dialogues with Contemporary Continental Thinkers*. Manchester: Manchester University Press, 1984.

Lacoue-Labarthe, Philippe, and Jean-Luc Nancy. *Retreating the Political*. New York: Routledge, 1997.

Lahusen, Christian. *Citizens' Solidarity in Europe. Civic Engagement and Public Discourse in Times of Crises*. Cheltenham: Elgar, 2020.

Latour, Bruno. *We Have Never Been Modern*. Translated by Catherine Porter. Cambridge, MA: Harvard University Press, 1993.

Lindroos-Hovinheimo, Susanna. "There Is No Europe—On Subjectivity and Community in the EU." *German Law Journal* 18, no. 5 (2017): 1229–46.

Loick, Daniel: "Juridification." In *The Cambridge Habermas Lexicon*, edited by Amy Allen and Eduardo Mendieta, 208–11. Cambridge: Cambridge University Press, 2019.

Mallet, Marie-Louise. *La Démocratie à Venir. Autour de Jacques Derrida*. Paris: Galilée, 2004.

Marx, Karl. *Economic and Philosophic Manuscripts of 1844 and the Communist Manifesto*. Translated by Martin Milligan. New York: Prometheus, 1988.

Nancy, Jean-Luc. *Being Singular Plural*. Translated by R. D. Richardson and Anne O'Byrne. Stanford: Stanford University Press, 1996.

Nancy, Jean-Luc. "La Comparution /The Compearance: From the Existence of "Communism" to the Community of "Existence." *Political Theory* 20, no. 3 (1992): 371–98.

Nancy, Jean-Luc. *The Experience of Freedom*. Translated by Bridget McDonald. Stanford: Stanford University Press, 1993.

Nancy, Jean-Luc. *The Inoperative Community*. Minneapolis: University of Minnesota Press, 1991.

Offe, Claus. *Europe Entrapped*. Hoboken, NJ: Wiley, 2015.

Papendorf, Knut. "Juridification, Marginalised Persons and Competence to Mobilise the Law." In *Outsourcing Legal Aid in the Nordic Welfare States*, edited by Ole Halvorsen Rønning & Olaf Hammerslev, 287–310. New York: Palgrave Macmillan, 2018.

Patočka, Jan. *Heretical Essays in the Philosophy of History*. Translated by Erazim Kohák. Chicago: Open Court, 1996.

Renault, Emmanuel. "Critical Theory and Processual Social Ontology." *Journal of Social Ontology* 2, no. 1 (2016): 17–32.

Sangiovanni, Andrea. "Solidarity as Joint Action." *Journal of Applied Philosophy* 32, no. 4 (2015): 340–59.

Sangiovanni, Andrea. "Solidarity in the European Union: Problems and Prospects." In *Philosophical Foundations of European Union Law* Nr. 348, edited by Julie Dickson and Pavlos Eleftheriadis, 384–411. Oxford: Oxford University Press, 2012.

Sartre, Jean-Paul. *Search for a Method*. New York: Alfred A. Knopf, 1963.

Schieder, Siegfried. "Zwischen Führungsanspruch und Wirklichkeit: Deutschlands Rolle in der Eurozone." *Leviathan* 42, no. 3 (2014): 363–97.

Scholz, Sally. *Political Solidarity*. Richmond: Penn State University Press, 2008.

Schuman, Robert. *Robert Schuman Declaration, 9 May 1950*. https://www.robert-schuman.eu/en/declaration-of-9-may-1950. Last checked September 7, 2021.

Shore, Cris. "Inventing the 'People's Europe': Critical Approaches to European Community 'Cultural Policy.'" *Man*, new series 28, no. 4 (1993): 779–800.

Tava, Francesco. "Justice, Emotions, and Solidarity." *Critical Review of International Social and Political Philosophy* (2021): 1–17.

Tava, Francesco. "European solidarity: definitions, challenges, and perspectives." In *The Routledge Handbook of Philosophy of Europe*, edited by Darian Meacham and Nicolas de Warren, 211–221. London: Routledge 2021.

Telios, Thomas. *Das Subjekt als Gemeinwesen*. Baden-Baden: Nomos Verlag, 2021.

Telios, Thomas. "Solidarity as Necessity: Subject, Structure, Practices." In *Unchaining Solidarities: Reflections on Cooperation and Mutual Aid*, edited by Petr Kouba, Catherine Malabou, Dan Swain, and Petr Urban, 31–50. Lanham, MD: Rowman & Littlefield, 2021.

Telios, Thomas. "Why Still Reification? Towards a Critical Social Ontology." In *Georg Lukács and the Possibilities of Critical Social Ontology*, edited by Michael J. Thompson, 223–66. Leiden: Brill, 2019.

Testa, Italo. "Ontology of the False State. On the Relation between Critical Theory, Social Philosophy, and Social Ontology." *Journal of Social Ontology* 1, no. 2 (2015): 271–300.

Thompson, Michael J. "Collective Intentionality, Social Domination, and Reification." *Journal of Social Ontology* 3, no. 2 (2017): 207–29.

Tuomela, Raimo. *Social Ontology: Collective Intentionality and Group Agents.* Oxford: Oxford University Press, 2013.

Volpe, Alessandro and Francesco Tava. "Multilevel European Solidarity: From People to Institutions (and Back)." *Critical Horizons* 25, no. 1 (2024): 63–76.

Volpe, Alessandro. "Jürgen Habermas on European Solidarity." In European Solidarity: Interdisciplinary Perspectives, edited by Francesco Tava and Noëlle Quénivet, 225–41. Colchester: ECPR, 2023.

Whitebook, Joel. "The Problem of Nature in Habermas." *Telos: Critical Theory of the Contemporary* 40, no. 41 (1979): 41–69.

12

The Promise of Europe

Rozemund Uljée

The social and political problems of and in Europe call for a sustained philosophical engagement because the relationship between philosophy and Europe is intricate, profound, and complex. First, unlike other socio-political geographical entities, Europe has always defined itself from the perspective of the constitutive specificity of its philosophical principles: the freedom of the Ancient Greek cities as opposed to the supposedly despotic Asian regimes is a fitting example. In turn, for many philosophers throughout history, the idea of Europe, as philosophical identity, ideal, and project, has at all times touched on the very essence of philoso-phy. For example, in his dissertation, Derrida, commenting on Husserl's account of "spiritual Europe," wrote that Europe is not simply the cradle of philosophy, but "Europe is itself born from the idea of Philosophy."[1]

According to Husserl, philosophy has been viewed as the pursuit of a universal science in the service of a rational and autonomous humanity. Europe had been designated as the particular place where the universal aspirations of philosophy can take place. But it is not only the father of the phenomenological movement who conceives of the relationship between Europe and philosophy in this manner; Hegel, Kant, and Patočka also think Europe in terms of its equivalence with a civilization con-sisting of a rational community. Although very different in inspiration and content, these thinkers share a view of European community as a rational community whose subjects are universal. With their conception of reason, they decide who should be accepted within the borders of their community and who must be rejected as less rational or even irrational.

From this it follows that the borders of Europe not only are conceived in the geographical sense; they function as a philosophical concept in that they delineate the self-assigned domain of universal reason and those who are outside of this domain. In other words, they determine the borders of what is considered, in Husserlian terms, the borders between a "spiritual community" and those who remain different from it.[2]

Philosophically, it has been argued that the conflation of Europe with universal reason has reached its limits. Thinkers such as Agamben, Nancy, Derrida, and Esposito have successfully shown how the traditional way of thinking about universality is particularistic in the sense that this view holds that universality belongs to Europe, which is a particular entity; it has also been condemned as an imperialist, Eurocentric, and colonialist way of thinking.[3] Particularistic ways of thought, on the other hand, are confronted by challenges of their own. They can be accused of a failure to adequately respond to problems that threaten the world in its entirety; the climate crisis is a good example.[4]

The difficult interplay between universalism and particularism opens the question whether Europe as a philosophical idea is exhausted or if there are elements of it that remain worthy of thought in a philosophical sense. In this chapter, I seek to show, with reference to Derrida, that beyond and despite its disqualified version of universalism, Europe still holds a promise for philosophy. As such, the aims of this chapter are twofold. The historical aim is to trace the philosophical self-understanding of Europe as representative of universality throughout its history. Its philosophical aim consists in showing how Derrida's notion of the promise, and the temporal structure that it introduces, guarantees that Europe's traditional self-understanding can no longer be thought in teleological terms. In other words, temporality shows that Europe does not work as a transcendental schema that regulates our historical experience of meaning. Instead, as I seek to make clear, Derrida's account of the promise, and the temporal structure that belongs to it, shows that with each and every decision, we give shape to what Europe is and ought to be, inventing it anew each time.

In order to satisfy these aims, this chapter consists of three steps: the first step of shows how the philosophical self-understanding of Europe throughout history can be conceived as working toward a universal idea of itself that was already present in it from its beginning. I seek to demonstrate how the defining feature of Europe's philosophical self-understanding has always been its *arché-eschatological-teleological* structure.

The second step concerns a discussion of Derrida's understanding of Europe in its relationship to alterity as he presents it in *The Other Heading*. In this work, Derrida conceives of Europe's exemplary position with regard to universality as paradoxical and thus as already revealing its relation to its (self-)difference. I show that Derrida's interpretation of Europe's exemplarity allows for a nonteleological reading of history. In the third and final step, I make the point that due to this nonlinear reading of history, we must view Europe as holding a promise. The temporality that is introduced by the promise reveals that the promise radically differs from the classical telos in the sense that what we consider to be and to belong to Europe is something that must be decided upon each time.

Europe's Traditional Self-Understanding: Universality as Its Telos

Europe, in Emmanuel Levinas's words, is intricately connected to the ideal of a condition of "peace, freedom and well-being" for all humanity "on the basis of a light that a universal knowledge projected onto the world."[5] Here, philosophy is viewed as the pursuit of a universal science in the service of a responsible and autonomous humanity. As Levinas remarks, philosophy consists of nothing but "universal science, science of the world as a whole, of the universal unity of all being."[6] The source of this conception of philosophy, with universality at its heart, is located within Greek thought. The idea of Europe cannot be interpreted without reference to its Greek and Christian paradigm. Or, as Levinas notes, "Europe is the Bible and the Greeks."[7] Both Plato and Aristotle present an account of the human being as capable of liberating itself from the grasp of mythology by questioning. This liberation is interpreted as the movement of reason itself, and the entirety of humanity can be understood as the movement toward self-realisation. Or, in Aristotelian terms, the entelechy of reason contains the actualization of the potentiality of the human being. This actualization simultaneously means becoming rational, and thus free. The intimate relation between freedom and reason is exemplified in Plato, who found that freedom is attained by following the demands of reason, and not those of desire.

The influence of Greek thought within the history of Europe cannot be underestimated; many, if not all eras within European history have remained within it in the sense that they share a vision of humanity as a process towards self-realisation understood in terms of freedom and the universal character of reason itself. The Christian paradigm is not only an inheritance and continuation of its Greek predecessor, but also a transformation of it.[8] Two aspects deserve to be mentioned within the context of this chapter. The first concerns the Christian view of time. As Hannah Arendt points out in *On Revolution*, Christian thought introduces the theme of a "new beginning."[9] Whereas the ancient Greek conception of time is cyclical ("empires would rise and fall"), the Christian conception of time manages to break through it because the birth of Christ was a "new beginning," and a unique, unrepeatable event. Arendt, referring to Augustine, finds that such an event interrupted "the normal course of secular history."[10] Furthermore, and this is the second aspect that deserves to be mentioned, within the Christian paradigm, the human being is defined as a being that is created in the image of God. As Simon Glendinning points out, the origin of man is found in the fall from Eden, and its task is to seek redemption. Both views, Greek and Christian, hold that the human being is grasped as the full actualization of reason. Within the Greek schema, the movement of reason is interpreted as teleological: the necessary development of natural characteristics moves towards a definite end, which is the case for the human being as well as for other parts of nature. Within Christian theology, the promise of redemption for the human being means that an eschatological horizon is added to the Greek telos.

Hegel can be viewed as the ultimate representative of this teleological-eschatological schema since he regards history as the progressive unfolding of truth. For Hegel, truth consists of the movement of reason, which is the history of philosophy itself. This history is progressive, moving into the direction of the universal. He writes in the *Phenomenology of Spirit*: "The true is the whole. But the whole is nothing other than the essence consummating itself through its development."[11] This shows that, for Hegel, the history of humanity consists in the unfolding of the human being as rational, conscious, and free. History, for Hegel, consists of the movement of reason realizing itself. Yet, it is not only Hegel who underlines the link between history and freedom. Husserl also defines the philosophical idea that is present in its history in terms of an "immanent teleology," which manifests "an epoch of humanity that from now on will and can live only in the free fashioning of its being and its historical life out of rational ideas and infinite tasks."[12] Husserl finds that within "European humanity," there is an "innate entelechy that thoroughly controls the changes in the European image," which gives it "the sense of a development in the direction of an ideal image of life and of being, as moving toward an eternal pole."[13] We could say thus, with Glendinning's words, that the European philosophical tradition presents a view of history as the "emancipation and de-alienation of rational subjectivity in time."[14] Within this view, a double movement can be discerned: on the one hand, it is the end that determines the trajectory that humanity must travel; it is a looking back. On the other hand, what is considered the end has already been identified from the beginning, as it lies latently within it, waiting for it to be realized. As Derrida and Glendinning write, we can conceive of the movement of historical thought not only as *teleological-eschatological*, but also as *arché-teleological*.[15]

According to Hegel, and within the broader philosophical tradition, it is true that world history has always been viewed as not merely a European history but also as universal history.[16]

Considered from a Hegelian perspective, the world in its entirety cannot be thought outside the movement of reason. World history as the movement of Spirit manifests itself not only in terms of historical time, but also in terms of space. Therefore, geography belongs to the development of Spirit and constitutes the "infrastructure of [political] history."[17] This point of view allows Hegel to claim that geographical conditions are decisive for the possibility of a people to become properly historical: world history prefers a moderate climate.[18] Consequently, although history as the progressive movement of reason is universal, Europe takes a special place within it because it is only within the European (for Hegel, Germanic) state that freedom can find its most adequate historical form in the sense that the human being can become free as such. Thus, although it is true that the movement of historical thought is conceived in universal terms, Europe is the place that is considered most universal.

Nietzsche, too, remarks on the special position of Europe with regard to the history of humanity. In *Beyond Good and Evil*, he compares Europe with Asia, stating that Europe is that "protruding little peninsula," that "desperately wants (over and against Asia) to stand for the 'progress of humanity.'"[19] The phrase suggests that the geographical shape of Europe shows that it attempts to detach itself from the Asian continent, moving beyond its very own limits, on its way toward the "progress of humanity." Nietzsche's words emphasize that Europe conceives of itself as a historical movement of self-transcendence. Describing Europe in this way is representative for the history of philosophy in the sense that this history has not viewed Europe as a concept but has conceived of it as an idea. What is the difference? Whereas a concept refers to something unified, in which its essence is fully determined, and thus exhausted, an idea cannot be viewed in this way. As Rodolphe Gasché clarifies in his essay "Is Europe an Idea in the Kantian Sense?": "As *eidos*, the idea confronts all things that derive from and participate in it with the form of the thing itself, the *ontos on*, that is, an ideality more perfect than the one that things themselves can accomplish."[20] Gasché adds that, within the context of Europe, its idea of itself means that it opens up its own determinateness and has the possibility of moving beyond it in a self-critical manner. It is no surprise then that Husserl famously called Europe "an idea in the Kantian sense."[21]

However lofty these grand visions of Europe might sound, at present, it is all too clear that Europe's self-understanding as exemplary, rational, and universal is dated. Levinas's words are still most fitting in this context: "[Europe is] a slaughter bench of fratricidal struggles, political or bloody, of imperialism, scorn and exploitation of the human being . . . ; ruthless doctrines and cruelty of fascism and national socialism, right down to the supreme paradox of the defence of Man and his rights being perverted into Stalinism. Hence the challenge to the centrality of Europe and its culture. A worn-out Europe!"[22] It is not a bold claim to state that at this very moment we are witnessing the exhaustion of a determined and linear concept of history as the realization of the European ideal. Or, in other words, the classical discourse of modernity is exhausted; Europe's different crises (it being challenged by nationalism, climate crises, refugees, and so forth) reveal that its traditional self-understanding does not suffice any longer; reality has proven to be far more problematic than Europe's idea of itself has allowed for. Derrida comments on the crisis that Europe finds itself in and remarks that it is possible to speak of crisis "whenever the capital of infinity and universality finds itself in danger, when the *eidos*, limits, ends, confines, the finitude of Europe, emerges."[23] It is in this sense that we can understand the crisis of Europe as one of its spirit.

Derrida: Europe and Its Difference

It has become painfully clear that Europe can no longer be conceived as the place where the idea of universal reason can be properly realized.

In order to understand Derrida's idea of the promise that Europe still holds, let us first take a closer look at his perspective on Europe as he presents it in *The Other Heading*. Here, he offers a reading of Europe and its history that problematizes the aim for universality in the philosophical tradition by appealing to the argument that the constitution of Europe in terms of its exemplarity of universality is always and already in relation to difference. My point with regard to this is that Derrida's interpretation of the exemplarity of Europe allows for a non-teleological reading of history. Here, European history is not understood as reason realizing itself but as always already interrupted, open to the promise that the future holds and that we are responsible for.

The occasion for *The Other Heading* was brought about by the unification of Europe, as well as events in Eastern Europe and the Soviet Union. By commenting on texts by Marx, Husserl, and Valéry, Derrida not only investigates the classical definition of Europe but also shapes the contours of the promise of a new Europe and a corresponding European identity, which simultaneously serves as an invitation to rethink the notion of identity itself:

> Hope, fear and trembling are commensurate with the signs that are coming to us from everywhere in Europe, where, precisely in the name of identity, be it cultural or not, the worst violences, those that we recognize all too well without yet having thought them through, the crimes of xenophobia, racism, anti-Semitism, religious or nationalist fanaticism, are being unleashed, mixed up, mixed up with each other, but also, and there is nothing fortuitous in this, mixed in with the breath, with the respiration, with the very "spirit" of the promise.[24]

The task of redefining Europe, and thus the search for this "spirit of the promise," demands that a nuanced path must be taken, because we are called, as Derrida remarks, to move away from binary language with regards to Europe and its history. Instead, we should attempt to go "beyond the old, tiresome, worn-out and wearisome opposition between Eurocentrism and anti-Eurocentrism."[25] Derrida seeks to do so through an analysis of the exemplarity of Europe. This analysis opens Europe's historical discourse to alterity and thus provides the key to thinking the philosophical heritage of Europe both in terms of its universality and in terms of its relation to difference.

Derrida famously discussed the special position that Europe has assigned to itself within the history of philosophy. In a lecture that he gave to UNESCO in Paris in 1991, he remarks that although the philosophical tradition treats reason as universal, Europe is the place where the universality of reason can unfold itself in its most proper manner.[26] Within world history, what would call itself European humanity belongs to a culture with "this special mission"[27] of being the Enlightened ones, the advance guard of humanity on the way to its proper end. As such, the particularity of Europe is inseparable from its relation to the universal, or its exemplarity *is* its universality. Hence, the discourse of world history "has become the tradition of European modernity."[28] The discourse on the history of Europe presupposes an identifiable heading, a telos, "toward which the movement, the memory, the promise, and the identity, dreams of gathering itself."[29] Like Nietzsche, Derrida also notes that the telos of Europe is exemplified in the geographical shape of the continent. He elaborates on the relation between the physical geography of Europe and its (what Husserl called) spiritual geography, by noting how Europe has always recognized itself as a cape or a headland and thus as the advanced extreme of the Eurasian continent.[30] The geographical extreme of the "cap" is mirrored in Europe's spiritual self-understanding as an advanced point, as being the spiritual heading in the sense of being an infinite (and thus universal) idea, "as the memory of itself that gathers and accumulates itself, capitalizes upon itself, in and for itself."[31] It is in this sense that Europe has viewed itself as the *heading* for world civilization. Derrida writes the following:

> The idea of an advanced point of *exemplarity* is the *idea of the* European *idea*, its *eidos*, at once as *arché*—the idea of beginning but also of commanding (the *cap* as the head, the place of capitalizing memory and of decision, once again, the captain)—and as *telos*, the idea of the end of a limit that accomplishes, or that puts an end to the whole point of the achievement, right there at the point of completion. The advanced point is at once beginning and end, it is divided as beginning and end; it is the place from which or in view of which everything takes place.[32]

Europe has determined and cultivated itself from the finality of the advanced point and remained at home with itself, by identifying itself with itself. It "thus identifies its own cultural identity, in the being-for-itself of what is most proper to it, in its own difference as difference with itself, difference to itself that remains with itself close to itself."[33] In this sense Derrida agrees with the interpretation of Europe as an example or the exemplary. He notes that, correspondingly, European identity presents itself in terms of "the *irreplaceable inscription* of the universal in the singular, the *unique testimony* to the human essence and to what is proper to man."[34]

To think Europe in terms of the "good" or proper example of universality, as has been done by the European philosophical tradition, shows the double function of exemplarity. On the one hand, an example can be thought of in terms of a sample among others, in order to affirm a general series, or multitude, of which it is a particular instance. In this sense, Europe has thought of itself as an example of one, among different, continents that are all within history and stand in relation to it. On the other hand, however, the example raises the question why exactly a particular sample has been destined as an example. Or, in other words, what is it that makes the sample exemplary? The question can be answered by stating that the selected example has a "teleological advantage" in the sense that it is the *proper* example. Europe, in this context, is exemplary because this is the place where universality can properly unfold itself since here universality is manifested as the telos of its history. Consequently, as Hegel already indicated, it is only Europe that can be properly world historical. The empirical types of non-European societies, then, are only more or less historical; at the lower level, they tend toward nonhistoricity.[35]

Thus, Europe functions as the good example because of its claim to universality. Simultaneously, however, the exemplarity of Europe is a necessary sample, without which the discourse of universality would be meaningless. Because what would be left of this discourse of it were not mirrored in real life instantiations? In other words, Europe is not merely an example of one continent among others because the very logic of the example exemplifies Europe itself. According to this logic, the sample cannot be thought as merely being a sample of the whole (universality, in this case) since the whole, or, universality, cannot be what it is without the sample(s) that belong to it. As such, the example is that which interrupts the whole, calling the totality of universality, which has given Europe its exemplarity, into question. The point here is not merely, or only, to question or dismantle Europe's claim to universality but to show that Europe, as the example of universality, must be considered in all its ambiguity. The example is ambiguous because it shows that the relation between the particular and the universal is always already paradoxical: the one thing cannot refer to the other without undermining itself.

With regard to Europe, the ambiguity inherent to exemplarity allows Derrida to show in what sense European identity already deidentifies itself. To clarify this further, he refers to the example from Valéry, who stated that "French are men of universality." In other words, they are special, or singular, because they are universal. But this paradox is not reserved for Valéry only; it was Husserl who said that since the European is committed to universal reason, he is also the "functionary of mankind."[36] Derrida calls this "a paradox of the paradox," which, as such, reveals a deidentification of the capital itself, which has "begun to open up itself unto the other shore of another heading, even if it is an opposed heading . . . , begun to make out, to see coming, to hear or understand as well, the other of the heading in general."[37] In Derrida's words, it reveals that it is only possible to speak of culture, of history, of identity, in terms of its self-difference to itself. Self-difference, that which differs and diverges from itself and of itself, would also be the difference, at once internal and irreducible to the "at home with itself." "This can be said, inversely or reciprocally, of all identity or all identification: there is no self-relation, no relation to oneself, no identification with oneself, without culture, but a culture of oneself *as* a culture *of* the other, a culture of the double genitive and of the *difference to oneself*."[38] This means that a culture never has a single origin and cannot be understood from in itself or as itself, but can only define, and view itself in relation in what and to what it is not. Therefore, the radical implication of Derrida's analysis of exemplarity is the disruption of sameness, and thus the impossibility of a full and complete self-identification.

There are two important implications of this disruption with regard to Europe. The first concerns Europe's discourse regarding its own historical movement. The central insight of *The Other Heading* concerns Derrida's reading of exemplarity. It reveals to and within the historical discourse on Europe is that history in general, and European history in particular, also presuppose that the heading or telos not be *given*, that it not be identifiable in advance. Although Derrida does not offer a comprehensive reading of history in *The Other Heading*, it does become clear that movement of history does not merely follow a previously established trajectory, like the Hegelian spirit. Instead, history must be conceived as openness to what remains different from it. The second implication of this disruption is the opening of an aporetic politics of responsibility. It means, in other words, that Europe's difference in and with itself means that we are caught in a "double bind" for which we are responsible.[39] More precisely, inheriting the history of Europe means inheriting the double bind that consists of the question whether being faithful to the heritage of Europe means a cultivation of the self-difference that is constitutive of identity itself or whether one should limit oneself to an identity and the telos that belongs to it, in which this difference remains gathered. For Derrida, the double bind places us in a paradoxical position: on the one hand, it is necessary to affirm the historical philosophical discourse, and thus the modern idea of Europe as universal and exemplary, and make ourselves the guardians of it. This responsibility is not the result of a choice; "it imposes itself upon us."[40] On the other hand, we must be aware that what is proper to both culture and history is not to be identical to itself, and therefore, an awareness of this means an awareness of Europe as not being a closed identity. Because this is the case, Derrida calls for caution: one must be suspicious of *both* repetitive memory *and* the completely *other* of the absolutely new. One must negotiate between these two standpoints, and this is what responsibility consists in.

Negotiation, as responsibility, amounts to "the experience and experiment of the possibility of the impossible: the testing of the aporia from which one may invent the only possible invention, the impossible invention."[41] The aporia or abyss, the between, does not refer to an absence of rules but points to the necessity of a leap at the moment of ethical or political decision. In this way, "it would seem that European cultural identity, like identity or identification in general, if it must be equal to itself and to the other, up to the measure of its own immeasurable difference 'with itself,' belongs, therefore, must belong, to this experience and experiment of the impossible."[42] This is so because the inheritance of the history and memory of Europe cannot be thought without Europe's relation to what is other than it. The question, for Derrida, then becomes: How can Europe be an identity that is an identity, yet is not closed to what it is not? This is the aporia from which the only responsible politics is possible.

Europe, as Promised

So far, it has become clear that Derrida's reading of exemplarity offers a new perspective on Europe's historical discourse on universality. Thinking the relationship between universality and exemplarity in this manner allows him to present (1) an alternative understanding of history in terms of an openness that is and remains different from the teleological movement of reason; (2) an aporetic politics of responsibility that states that we are responsible for the double bind between the affirmation of Europe's historical philosophical discourse and an awareness of alterity. The alternative understanding of history and the aporetic responsibility show that it is first of all no longer possible to think of Europe in terms of a telos of universality that regulates or structures our historical present. We are called instead to think of Europe in terms of the promise it holds. As I seek to make clear, it is only from the perspective of temporality that a proper distinction between telos and promise appears. The distinct temporal structure of the promise shows that what Europe might become must be invented anew each time with each decision that our responsibility calls for.

Before moving on to a discussion of Derrida's account of the promise, some remarks on Europe's classical discourse on universality are needed. It is important to note that within the discourse on universality, Europe is certainly not conceived as a totality: its trajectory toward its ideal as universal means precisely an opening up and breaking away from any self-enclosed meaning. Or, to phrase it differently, Europe is not a concept in which its aspirations are exhausted. As Nietzsche's words clarify, its historical movement consists in going beyond itself and is thus transcendence, and thereby it is necessarily the breaking up of totality. This is also what Husserl's interpretation of Europe as an "idea in the Kantian sense" confirms. Gasché presents an excellent discussion of the Kantian idea. He offers a nuanced and extensive reading of Kant, after which he concludes that an idea in the Kantian sense is an idea of "unity and maximum of perfection"; it can only be progressively reached, but nevertheless, it plays "a capital, regulative role in the domain of knowledge in spite of its indeterminacy."[43] Thus, even in the case of the ideal not being reached, or the telos not (yet) having realized itself, Europe is still an idea in this manner because its ideal of universality is what regulates our historical present, in the sense that this present is viewed and experienced as a moment of a progressive movement of reason. Thus, even though the Kantian nature of freedom infinitely defers the realization of the telos, the movement of reason is on its way towards it. In this sense, Europe's telos that it has imagined for itself serves as a transcendental condition of history and allows it to be interpreted in terms of its trajectory toward it. Or, phrased differently, Europe's classical discourse can be viewed in terms of a temporal idealism that holds that the interpretation of its historical present is conditioned by its telos.

Let us now turn to Derrida's account of responsibility and the promise it holds for Europe. For Derrida, responsibility within the context of Europe means that we must "respond to the call of European memory, to recall what has been promised under the name of Europe, to re-identify Europe."[44] Although Derrida mentions the promise in *The Other Heading*, he does not elaborate on its temporal structure in this text. In other places, however, he does. In *Memoires for Paul de Man*, Derrida offers an illuminating discussion of the promise in terms of his friendship to Paul de Man. He speaks of the promise here as always excessive and as a commitment beyond expectation or anticipation.[45] Generally speaking, this commitment can be viewed in terms of a response to the other and a response to the future. It is a response to the other in the sense that it consists of a pledge or affirmation of something to someone. The promise is a response to the future because it is not exhausted by its specific content. This is the case, because the promise also carries a performative meaning. A promise promises to be kept; the one who makes a promise makes a commitment to the future. This commitment is a kind of pledge to the future, which, however, carries a radical uncertainty. The person who makes a promise cannot be sure whether she can actually fulfill it, deliberately or not. Moreover, it is impossible to know what it is that one promises or whether someone is still the same person who made the promise that was supposed to be kept. Thus, in the present, the promise responds to the future. In *Rogues*, Derrida speaks of the promise in terms of "the memory of that which carries the future, the to-come, here and now."[46] However, the future that is signified with the promise is not the future that will one day become present. Why is this the case? A promise cannot become present; if a promise is fulfilled, and thus fully realized, it effaces itself and thus ceases to be a promise. A future present is a present that can be foreseen and predicted and thereby no longer possible in an absolute sense. Instead, with the promise, Derrida calls us to think a future that cannot be anticipated or programmed and will never become present but will always remain promised. As such, the promise invites us to reconsider possibility since it moves away from what was already possible, and therefore is no longer possible *as* possible, to a future so distant that it keeps open possibility in a more absolute sense. In this manner, the promise shows that the radically unknowable future is necessarily involved in what we take to be presence and also renders it impossible. As such, the promise carries an aporetic structure and thereby reveals the excessive nature of time, and thus history. More precisely, the promise shows what Derrida, in *Spectres of Marx*, calls the "disjointure" of time itself. ("The time is out of joint" is Hamlet's phrase that Derrida refers to.)[47] The promise reveals that a pure or complete presence of meaning is radically impossible because the present is always already open to what is yet to arrive.

With regard to Europe, the promise and its corresponding temporality thus show that what we render 'universal' is possible because it always already carries its own impossibility. Accordingly, the response to and responsibility for a future that remains promised show that it is impossible to speak of European history in terms of the gradual realization of an idea. Instead, as Derrida shows, the fact that identity itself can only be thought as always already in relation to alterity means that history is always already interrupted, opened to the promise that the future holds. Because is history not precisely the challenging of any given meaning? Thus, the "future of the future" that the promise announces shows that history cannot be saturated because history itself resists it.[48] It means not only that a final eschaton or telos would be impossible, as it would name a situation in which nothing could occur, but also that the temporal structure that the promise introduces, and that we are responsible for, conditions history itself. Levinas's words on Nietzsche are fitting in this context: "The future and the most far-off things [are] the rule for all the present days."[49]

Derrida's gesture of opening the thinking of presence up to its very future through his understanding of responsibility for a promise means that he reinterprets the traditional discourse on Europe. In the traditional discourse, Europe's idea of itself serves as its telos in the sense that it is the ground or condition that gives shape to the historical present and thus serves as its transcendental condition. However, the promise rather operates as a quasi transcendental in the sense that it can no longer be understood as an idea that regulates history. This means, to formulate it in negative terms, that the promise conditions history but does not operate as a transcendental condition.[50] As such, the promise should most surely not be understood in terms of a substitute for the Greek telos. It is not the fulfillment of a promise at the end of the road that shapes the contours of our history and historical present. This is so because the promise reveals a fractured temporality in which transcendental conditioning is no longer an option. There are three interconnected reasons why the temporal structure of the promise forbids it from operating as a transcendental condition for European history. These reasons simultaneously show that what Europe is must be invented time and time again. The first is the impossibility of the realisation of a promise. As noted, to fulfill a promise means to efface its structure in the sense that a fulfilled promise is no longer a promise; a promise can only consist in terms of its appellation to the future that has not arrived yet. But this impossibility of fulfillment does not come from a lack of reason, knowledge, or power of a subject who makes a promise. Instead, the promise is established in relation to an alterity that remains outside the domain of knowledge or power that the promise responds to. Thus, the relationship to alterity that is addressed in the promise cannot be timed, structured, or programmed in advance. The interruption of what might be appear should be awaited and should be anticipated *as* the unforeseeable, the *unanticipatable*, the nonmasterable, nonidentifiable, in short, "as that of which one does not yet have a memory."[51] Europe does not consist in a purpose already determined from the beginning, and there is no telos that can be actualized through the application of a program.

The second reason why the temporal structure of the promise forbids it from operating as a transcendental condition is that the promise is a response and thus a responsibility. As noted, the thinking of alterity means that we are caught in a double bind for which we are responsible in the sense that we must affirm Europe's historical discourse, but that it is also necessary to be aware of the fact that Europe is not a closed entity, and must be viewed in terms of its (self-)difference. For Derrida, Europe can be our future only if we attest to its historical inheritance in terms of its universality and if we take responsibility for its memory, but it also means that we must find a new relation to it. As such, we could say that history must be preserved as a problem.

Responsibility consists in the negotiation between these competing demands of the historical inheritance and Europe in relation to its (self-)difference. Decisions are a negotiation of these demands, and as such, we must calculate. On the one hand, we should make use of all memory, knowledge, and analysis we can muster in order to inform our responsible decisions, but at the same time, knowledge and memory are, in their generality, not sufficient for a decision. Because a decision, for it to be a decision, and not an application, is always singular. Therefore, the structure of a decision is aporetic in the sense that responsible decisions must take

"a leap of faith" and are what Derrida calls, echoing Kierkegaard, "a madness."[52] If this leap were not there, "we could simply unfold knowledge into
a program or course of action. Nothing could make us more irresponsible;
nothing could be more totalitarian."[53] To decide is to be confronted by
the radical impossibility of decision, yet to do the impossible nevertheless.
Because this is so, responsibility is not in the domain of what is possible,
and therefore it is outside the domain where an idea can be realized or
a program can be executed. With regard to Europe, it means that, with
each and every impossible decision that our responsibility calls for each
time, we decide what Europe is and must become.

The third reason is that responsibility means that one must act
with urgency. As noted, Derrida urges us to understand responsibility in
terms of a response to the disjointure of time (and history). Because of
the urgency with which alterity announces itself, because I am called to
respond here and now, responsibility is outside of the domain where a
telos can be articulated or realized. With regard to Europe, the realization
of the idea it has of itself is thus not the application or execution of
previously invented steps formulated in the domain of reason but must
be performed with absolute urgency, at present.

The European historical philosophical discourse has viewed Europe
as on its way to universality. Or, in other words, Europe's conception
of itself has traditionally been arché-teleo-eschatological. The main
feature of this conception of Europe consists in the view that reason is
universal, yet Europe is exemplary in the history of reason in the sense
that it is within Europe that universality can unfold to its proper end.
The movement of unfolding, of which Hegel's thought can be viewed
as representative, holds that the end is always already in view from the
beginning and that the beginning is viewed from its end. It means that,
in Derrida's words, "Europe has a refined taste for finality" because it
views itself "on the horizon, that is to say, from its end." (Derrida refers
to the Greek meaning of horizon here, of which the English translation
is "limit").[54] I have attempted to demonstrate that Derrida's reading of
exemplarity offers an opening to think Europe in and as relation to its
(self-)difference. Thinking Europe in this manner offers an interpretation
of Europe no longer in terms of its telos, but as a promise. Europe as a
promise reveals that it must be invented anew with each decision our
responsibility calls for. I have tried to show that it is, however, only
from the perspective of temporality that the difference between telos and
promise becomes explicit. Whereas a telos operates as a transcendental

condition, the temporal structure of the promise forbids this possibility. It does so because of three interconnected reasons: first, the promise responds to an alterity that, because of its futural character, is outside the domain of knowledge and power; second, responsibility for a promise is not in the domain of the possible and thus outside of the field where a program can be rolled out; third, responsibility for a promise is a disjointure of time, which means that one must act with urgency, at present. This does not mean we should refute old-fashioned universalism but that we should take it over as our heritage, while finding a novel relation to it, continuously testing it against what the present requires of us.

Notes

1. Derrida, *The Problem of Genesis in Husserl's Philosophy*, 155.

2. Husserl, "Vienna Lecture," 275.

3. Allen's *The End of Progress: Decolonizing the Foundations of Critical Theory* is a good example.

4. With regards to the climate crisis, Dipesh Chakrabarty eloquently investigates how this crisis can appeal "to our sense of universals while challenging . . . our capacity for historical understanding." "Climate Change: Four Theses," 201.

5. Levinas, Emmanuel 1999. *Alterity and Transcendence*. Translated by Michael B. Smith. New York: Columbia University Press, p. 132.

6. Husserl, "Vienna Lecture," 276.

7. Levinas, *Alterity and Transcendence*, 132. Husserl as well, refers to the "ancient Greek spirit." See "Vienna Lecture," 3.

8. Glendinning, "European Philosophical History and Faith in God a Posteriori," 66. Glendinning also refers to Derrida's *Of Grammatology* here, in which he writes that a European world began to emerge when the "great epoch covered by the history of metaphysics" made its way into "the narrower epoch of Christian creationism." See *Of Grammatology*, 13.

9. Arendt, *On Revolution*, 29.

10. Arendt, 29.

11. Hegel, *Phenomenology of Spirit*, 11.

12. Husserl, "Vienna Lecture," 274.

13. Husserl, 275.

14. Glendinning, "European Philosophical History," 71.

15. Glendinning, 71. Although the difference with Glendinning here is that he uses the term in a specific sense: to refer to Man's relation to the divine in terms of an a posteriori conception of God, something that is outside the scope

of this chapter. My point in using the terms is that the movement of historical thought consists of the interplay between beginning and end. Derrida also refers to the "archeo-teleological program" of Europe. See *The Other Heading*, 27.

16. Husserl, "Vienna Lecture," 275.

17. Thomas Mertens, "Hegel and the End of Europe," 50.

18. Hegel, *Enzyklopädie der Philosophische Wissenschaften*, par. 393, 58. Husserl, too, presents a "vision of humanity in its totality," and not a view that "remains confined to a specific tribe or region." See "Vienna Lecture," 4.

19. Nietzsche, *Beyond Good and Evil*, 65.

20. Gasché, "Is Europe an Idea in the Kantian Sense?," 33.

21. Husserl, *Ideas*, 397.

22. Levinas, *Alterity and Transcendence*, 132.

23. Derrida, *The Other Heading*, 31.

24. Derrida, 6.

25. Derrida, 6.

26. Derrida, "The Right to Philosophy from the Cosmopolitical Point of View," 8.

27. Derrida, 8.

28. Derrida, 8.

29. Derrida, *The Other Heading*, 25.

30. See also *The Other Heading*, 14. Here, Derrida points out that Cap, from the Latin caput, capitis refers to head. Or "the 'extremity of the extreme' the last, the final moment, the *telos*, (ordered by the man in charge)."

31. Derrida, *The Other Heading*, 24.

32. Derrida, 24–25. Derrida refers to Valéry here, who wrote about Europe in terms of it being the "brain of a vast body" (the body being Asia).

33. Derrida, 25.

34. Derrida, 73.

35. This is Patočka's view for example. See: *Heretical Essays in the Philosophy of History*, xvii (preface).

36. Husserl, *The Crisis of European Sciences and Transcendental Phenomenology*, 17.

37. Derrida, *The Other Heading*, 76.

38. Derrida, 10.

39. Derrida, 29.

40. Derrida, 28.

41. Derrida, 41.

42. Derrida, 45.

43. Gasché, "Is Europe an Idea in the Kantian Sense?," 53.

44. Derrida, *The Other Heading*, 76.

45. Derrida, *Memoires for Paul de Man*, 47, 93.

46. Derrida, *Rogues*, 86.

47. Derrida, *Spectres of Marx*, 61.

48. Rivelaygue's words are helpful here. He points out that in Judaism there is one word for both truth and fidelity. He writes that "truth is the fidelity to the alliance and to the promise; the truth does not designate a uni-totality, but a relation to history as to that what is promised, that which cannot be realized by man alone nor without man." Rivelaygue, *Lecons de métaphysique Allemande*, 288.

49. Levinas, "Meaning and Sense," 93.

50. Derrida, "Force of Law," 257.

51. Derrida, *The Other Heading*, 45.

52. Bennington, "A Moment of Madness: Derrida's Kierkegaard," *Oxford Literary Review*, 103.

53. Derrida, "A Word of Welcome," 21.

54. Derrida, *The Other Heading*, 28.

Bibliography

Allen, Amy. *The End of Progress: Decolonizing the Foundations of Critical Theory.* New York: Columbia University Press, 2016.

Arendt, Hannah. *On Revolution.* London: Penguin Books, 1963.

Bennington, Geoffrey. "A Moment of Madness: Derrida's Kierkegaard." *Oxford Literary Review* 33, no. 1 (2011): 103–27.

Chakrabarty, Dipesh. "The Climate of History: Four Theses." *Critical Inquiry* 35, no. 2 (Winter 2009): 197–222.

Derrida, Jacques. "Faith and Knowledge." In *Acts of Religion*, translated by S. Weber. New York: Routledge, 1998.

Derrida, Jacques. "Force of Law: The Mystical Foundation of Authority." In Acts of Religion, translated by M. Quintance. New York: Routledge, 2002.

Derrida, Jacques. *Mémoires for Paul de Man.* Translated by Cecile Lindsay, Jonathan Culler, and Eduardo Cadava. New York: Columbia University Press, 1986.

Derrida, Jacques. *Of Grammatology.* Translated by Gayatri Chakravorty Spivak. Baltimore, MD: Johns Hopkins University Press, 1976.

Derrida, Jacques. *The Other Heading: Reflections on Today's Europe.* Translated by Anne-Pascale Brault and Michael Naas. Bloomington: Indiana University Press, 1992.

Derrida, Jacques. *The Problem of Genesis in Husserl's Philosophy.* Translated by Marian Hobson. Chicago: Chicago University Press, 2003.

Derrida, Jacques. "The Right to Philosophy from the Cosmopolitical Point of View." In *Ethics, Institutions and the Right to Philosophy*, translated by P. P. Trifonas. Lanham, MD: Rowman & Littlefield, 2002.

Derrida, Jacques. *Rogues: Two Essays on Reason.* Translated by Pascale-Anne Brault and Michael Naas. Stanford: Stanford University Press, 2005.

Derrida, Jacques. *Specters of Marx*. Translated by Peggy Kamuf. New York: Routledge, 2006.

Derrida, Jacques. "A Word of Welcome." In *Adieu to Emmanuel Levinas*, translated by Anne-Pascale Brault and Michael Naas. Stanford: Stanford University Press, 1999.

Gasché, Rodolphe. "Is Europe an Idea in the Kantian Sense?" In *Europe beyond Universalism and Particularism*, edited by Susanna Lindbergh, Mika Ojakangas, and Sergei Prozorov. Edinburgh: Palgrave McMillan, 2014.

Glendinning, Simon. "European Philosophical History and Faith in God a Posteriori." *Aristotelian Society Supplementary* 91, no. 1 (June 2017): 63–82.

Hegel, Georg Wilhelm Friedrich. *Enzyklopädie der Philosophische Wissenschaften*. Werke. Edited by E. Molderhauer and K. M. Michel. Bd. 10. Frankfurt: Suhrkamp, 1968.

Hegel, Georg Wilhelm Friedrich. *Phenomenology of Spirit*. Translated by A. V. Miller. Oxford: Oxford University Press, 1977.

Husserl, Edmund. *The Crisis of European Sciences and Transcendental Phenomenology: An Introduction to Phenomenological Philosophy*. Translated by David Carr. Evanston: Northwestern University Press, 1970.

Husserl, Edmund. *Ideas: General Introduction to Pure Phenomenology*. Translated by W. R. Boyce Gibson. New York: MacMillan, 1931.

Husserl, Edmund. An Introduction to Phenomenological Philosophy. Translated by David Carr. Evanston: Northwestern University Press, 1970.

Husserl, Edmund. "Vienna Lecture." In *The Crisis of the European Sciences and Transcendental Phenomenology*, translated by D. Carr. Evanston: Northwestern University Press, 1970.

Levinas, Emmanuel. *Alterity and Transcendence*. Translated by Michael B. Smith. New York: Columbia University Press, 1999.

Levinas, Emmanuel. "Meaning and Sense." In Collected Philosophical Papers, translated by Alphonso Lingis. Dordrecht: Martinus Nijhoff, 1987.

Mertens, Thomas. "Hegel and the End of Europe." *Archiv für Rechts- und Sozialphilosophie / Archives for Philosophy of Law and Social Philosophy* 89, no. 1 (2003): 38–52.

Nietzsche, Friedrich. *Beyond Good and Evil: Prelude to a Philosophy of the Future*. Translated by Walter Kaufman. New York: Vintage Books, 1989.

Patočka, Jan. *Heretical Essays in the Philosophy of History*. Translated by Erazim Kohak. Chicago: Open Court, 1996.

Contributors

Chiara Bottici is a philosopher and critical theorist, known for her philosophy of political imagination and for her feminist writings. She is director of gender studies and professor of philosophy at the New School, and she is the author, among others, of *Imaginal Politics: Images beyond Imagination and the Imaginary* (2014), *A Philosophy of Political Myth* (2007), *Anarchafemminism* (2021), and *A Feminist Mythology* (2021). With Benoit Challand, she also coauthored *Imagining Europe: Myth, Memory, Identity* (2013) and *The Myth of the Clash of Civilizations* (2010).

Vera Bühlmann studied English language and literature, philosophy, and media studies at the University of Zurich and obtained a PhD in media studies at the University of Basel. Since 2010, she has set up and coheaded the Laboratory for Applied Virtuality at ETH Zurich (with Ludger Hovestadt); since 2016, she has been a full professor and director of the research unit Architecture Theory and Philosophy of Technics at Technical University Wien. Since 2020, she has been acting as a founding codirector of the interinstitutional platform School for Materialist Research (SMR), and in 2023 she was a founding member of Meteora Academy Buti, Italy, an interinstitutional place for research in/on the arts and mathematical thinking. Her special interests include digital architectonics and gnomonics, aesthetics in the optics of new materialisms, and the role of figuration, sculpture, and rhetoric in a tropological humanism of the Anthropocene. She is editor of the Applied Virtuality Book Series at Birkhäuser (with Ludger Hovestadt),. Her publications include *The Digital, a Continent? Nature and Poetics* (2023), *Information and Mathematics in the Philosophy of Michel Serres* (2020), *Die Nachricht, ein Medium: Städtische Architektonik, Generische Medialität* (2014), and several (co)edited volumes, book chapters, and journal articles.

Benoit Challand is an associate professor of sociology at the New School for Social Research, New York. He has held positions as associate professor in sociology at the Scuola Normale Superiore in Florence and professor of contemporary history at the University of Fribourg. He is author of the books *Violence and Representation in the Arab Uprisings* (2023) and *Palestinian Civil Society: Foreign Donors and the Power to Promote and Exclude* (2009). He has numerous coauthored publications such as *Imagining Europe: Myth, Memory and Identity* (2013). He is also interested in democratic theory, Western European Marxism, and settler colonialism.

Frank Chouraqui is an associate professor of philosophy at the University of Leiden (Netherlands). He is the author of *Ambiguity and the Absolute* (2014), *The Body and Embodiment: A Philosophical Guide* (2020), and articles on phenomenological and political ontology and Nietzsche.

Agnes Czajka is a professor of politics and international studies at the Open University, UK. Agnes's research interests include contemporary social and political thought, continental political philosophy, democracy, citizenship, contentious politics, migrant and refugee politics, and European and Mediterranean politics. Agnes's recent books include *Art, Migration and the Production of Radical Democratic Citizenship* (2022), *Democracy and Justice: Reading Derrida in Istanbul* (2017), and *Europe after Derrida: Crisis and Potentiality* (2013).

Lorenzo Girardi received his PhD jointly from the University of Limerick (Mary Immaculate College) and Katholieke Universiteit Leuven. His work focuses on the phenomenological tradition, having published on authors such as Edmund Husserl, Martin Heidegger, and Jan Patočka. In particular, he is interested in the relation between phenomenology, metaphysics, and political philosophy. This is explored in his unpublished monograph, "Europe, Phenomenology and Politics in Husserl and Patočka," which investigates these themes in the context of the idea of Europe. He also contributes to public debate as author and editor of the Dutch political platform Vrij Links.

Thomas Clément Mercier is a postdoctoral researcher at Universidad Adolfo Ibáñez (Santiago, Chile). His work has been published in journals such as *Poetics Today, Global Discourse, Oxford Literary Review, Derrida Today, CR: The New Centennial Review, Aisthesis, Ostium,* and

Philosophiques. He directed and codirected three different issues of *Parallax* and *Síntesis: Revista de Filosofía* on contemporary intersections of matter, body, and desire through deconstructive and materialist approaches. He specializes in twentieth-century and contemporary philosophy, political thought, and international studies, with a particular interest in deconstruction, materialisms (notably Marxist and neomaterialist), queer theory, and decolonial thinking and in their influence in reshaping theories of democracy, violence, and political resistance. He is currently working on a book on Marxist thought and deconstruction informed uniquely by archival research and on the edition and publication of the correspondence between Louis Althusser and Jacques Derrida.

Ovidiu Stanciu is an assistant professor of philosophy at the Universidad Diego Portales, Santiago de Chile, and research associate at the Husserl Archives in Paris. He is a former student of the Ecole Normale Supérieure, Paris. He holds a master's degree in contemporary philosophy (Université Paris I Panthéon-Sorbonne, 2008) and a PhD in philosophy (Université de Bourgogne/Bergische Universität Wuppertal, 2015), with a thesis titled "The Problem of Metaphysics in Heidegger and Patočka." He was a lecturer at the Institut d'Etudes Politiques (Sciences Po), Paris, and at the Institut Catholique de Paris. He is the editor of the volumes *Patočka, lecteur d'Aristote* (2015) and *Finitude and Meaning: Understanding History with Ricoeur and Patočka* (2024).

Thomas Telios is a lecturer of philosophy at the University of St. Gallen, Switzerland. He has studied piano, political theory, and philosophy at the National University of Athens, the Anton-Rubinstein-Akademie Düsseldorf, and the Goethe-Universität in Frankfurt am Main. He received his PhD from the Goethe-Universität Frankfurt and the Centre for Research in Modern European Philosophy at Kingston University London. His research interests include the critical theory of the Frankfurt School, French postwar philosophy, new materialisms, postmodern and queer feminism, theories of subjectivity, theories of individual and collective agency, theories of community, and critical theory of law. He is the author of *Das Subjekt als Gemeinwesen: Zur sozial-ontologischen Konstitution kollektiver Handlungsfähigkeit* (2021). Other publications include *The Russian Revolution as Ideal and Practice: Failures, Legacies and the Future of Revolution* (coedited with Dieter Thomä, Ulrich Schmid, 2019) and articles or chapters in *Symposium: Canadian Journal for Continental*

Philosophy; Transparency, Society and Subjectivity; and *Zeitschrift für Kultur- und Kollektivwissenschaft.*

Georgios Tsagdis is a postdoctoral researcher at Wageningen University and Research Center and lecturer at Leiden University. He is founder of the eco-technical research collective Minor Torus. His essays have appeared in numerous international journals, including *Parallax, Philosophy Today, Studia Phaenomenologica, Metodo, Footprint,* and *Technophany.* Among his recent editorials are "Of Times: Arrested, Resigned, Imagined" (*International Journal of Philosophical Studies,* 2020), *Derrida's Politics of Friendship: Amity and Enmity* (2022), and *Bernard Stiegler: Memories of the Future* (2024).

Rozemund Uljée is an associate professor at the Institute for Philosophy, Leiden University, the Netherlands. She has published different articles on the theme of time and otherness in the domain of phenomenology and is the author of *Thinking Difference with Heidegger and Derrida: On Truth and Justice* (2020) and coeditor of *The Difference between Heidegger, Levinas and Derrida* (2016).

Riccardo M. Villa is a postdoctorate researcher for the Research Unit of Architecture Theory and Philosophy of Technics (ATTP) at the Vienna University of Technology, where he obtained his PhD in 2022. His thesis was published in 2023 by Birkhäuser with the title *Upon Entropy: Architectonics of the Image in the Age of Information.* He holds a master's degree in architecture from the Polytechnic University of Milan and worked for several years as an architect. Riccardo is also a scientific assistant in the Chair of Digital Architectonics (ETH Zürich), working on the legacy of Swiss architect Fritz Haller. He is furthermore a visiting scholar for the SHARE lab (University of Florida), where he focuses on the intersection between architecture, ethics, and artificial intelligence.

Bart Zantvoort is a lecturer in philosophy at Leiden University. His research focuses on the relation between social change and resistance to change in individuals, institutions, and social structures more generally. He has published articles on Hegel, political inertia, critical theory, and Quentin Meillassoux. He is the editor, together with Rebecca Comay, of *Hegel and Resistance* (2018). His recent work includes articles on the political significance of the notions of habit and second nature in Hegel and a Dutch translation of the sections on habit in Hegel's *Philosophy of Spirit.*

Index